D0119152

MUSIC AND THE THEATER

MUSIC
AND THE THEATER

An Introduction to Opera

REINHARD G. PAULY

Lewis and Clark College

PRENTICE-HALL, INC., *Englewood Cliffs, New Jersey*

For illustration credits, see pp. 447–451; for music credits, see the Preface.

Designed by Mark A. Binn

PRENTICE-HALL INTERNATIONAL, INC., London
PRENTICE-HALL OF AUSTRALIA, PTY. LTD., Sydney
PRENTICE-HALL OF CANADA, LTD., Toronto
PRENTICE-HALL OF INDIA PRIVATE LTD., New Delhi
PRENTICE-HALL OF JAPAN, INC., Tokyo

Current printing (last number):

10   9   8   7   6   5   4   3   2   1

13–607002–7   13–607010–8

To the Wienerwald—and to the Oregon National Forest

PREFACE

In *War and Peace* Tolstoy provides an absorbing description of an evening at the opera. We view the proceedings through the eyes of Natasha, who attends the performance as a glamorous social event, knowing little of opera in general or of the work to be performed. Much of her attention is directed toward others in the audience—good-looking officers, elegant baronesses, various acquaintances. Here is Tolstoy on her impression of what she sees and hears:

They all sang something. When they had finished their song the girl in white went up to the prompter's box and a man with tight silk trousers over his stout legs went up to her and began singing, waving his arms about. First the man in the tight trousers sang alone, then she sang, then they both paused while the orchestra played and the man fingered the hand of the girl in white, obviously awaiting the beat to start singing with her.

All this seemed grotesque and amazing to Natasha. "She could not follow the opera nor even listen to the music; she saw only the painted cardboard and the queerly dressed men and women who moved, spoke, and sang so strangely in that brilliant light."[1]

[1] Leo Tolstoy, *War and Peace,* translated by Louise and Aylmer Maude (New York, 1942), p. 622. Copyright 1942 by Simon & Schuster, Inc.

To the person unfamiliar with it, opera today can seem just as strange. And it is chiefly to the newcomer to opera, whatever his knowledge of other kinds of music—that this book addresses itself. It was written out of the conviction that opera can prove exciting and rewarding to the person who approaches it on its own terms and understands some of its ground rules. These have to do with its origins and its social history, with theatrical and musical traditions, and with various conventions of performance. Some of these conventions are changing today; others, so far as traditional opera is concerned, seem to be firmly entrenched. A thoughtful approach, a willingness to understand, and a certain amount of investigation and preparation—these can open up the world of musical drama for us, leading us from a first impression similar to Natasha's to discernment and enjoyment, to rewarding new experiences.

As Grout points out,[2] opera by definition has dramatic continuity, but need not be sung continually from beginning to end. The term "opera," in the present-day sense, did not come into general use until the mid-seventeenth century. Earlier terms, such as *dramma per musica* and *favola* ("fable," "story") *in musica,* also imply that the play was considered the essential thing, to which music had been added. Genuine appreciation and understanding of opera therefore requires that we consider it, in the first place, as drama—drama of a special kind because of the presence of music. Happily this view is gaining ground today, not only in the New World, where opera at first was a foreign, somewhat esoteric, commodity, but also in Europe, where it first flowered. In this book, consequently, I have stressed the dramatic characteristics of opera, especially in the discussion of specific works. I have kept the description and analysis of the music simple, largely for the benefit of the reader who has little technical knowledge of music.

As its title implies, this book is not a history of opera.[3] Its first chapters are intended to serve as an introduction to the medium itself, with emphasis on the differences between spoken drama and musical drama. A historical overview is, however, provided in Chapter 3, to bring the reader up to the point where today's standard repertory begins. Opera first flourished during the Baroque era (ca. 1600–1750). Though few works from that period are widely performed today, many dramatic and musical practices of later opera have their beginnings there. The section on Baroque opera is therefore more historically oriented than the chapters that follow. They are devoted chiefly to discussions of specific works—operas

---

[2] Donald Jay Grout, *A Short History of Opera,* 2nd ed. (New York, 1965), pp. 4–6.

[3] The most serviceable, accessible, and scholarly study available is Grout's *A Short History of Opera,* cited above. Grout provides an extensive bibliography.

that, because they are widely performed, the reader may have opportunities to see.

The book's format (and its purpose, as an introduction to the subject) demanded selectivity. Some readers who already are opera enthusiasts may disagree with my choices and regret the exclusion of some of their favorite works, e.g., some of the operas of Benjamin Britten. Differences of this kind are inevitable. I have tried to choose works that represent different stylistic trends, are mostly from the standard repertory, and, above all, are effective as drama. A chapter on music and the theater in the Orient, so fascinating and so different, was planned but, after much thought, omitted. To treat such a vast subject in an adequate way would have required a good deal more than the amount of space that could be accorded it in a book that serves chiefly as an introduction to opera.

The discussion of specific operas proceeds chronologically. In some cases it includes references to social and intellectual history— to the general and artistic environment in which a particular work was created and first performed. The opera's subject, its literary origin, and its dramatic treatment are then taken up, and the principal characters are considered. An examination of the music follows, for the purpose of clarifying how what happens musically is related to the drama and to the specific words from which the composer drew his inspiration.

Before turning to the discussion of a specific opera, the reader should in each case have read its text (libretto), just as he should have read the entire libretto, not a mere synopsis of the plot, before he attends an opera performance. This preparation is essential to the enjoyment of an opera especially if it is to be sung in a foreign language. To neglect it is to deprive oneself of much of the opera's meaning. Good opera is more than a succession of pretty tunes. Librettos as a rule are short (for reasons to be explained in Chapter 1) and hence quickly read.

Many operas to be discussed were written in Italian, German, or French. In referring to these works I have used the original titles for some, and English translations for others, being guided by present-day custom in English-speaking countries, where, for instance, Rossini's masterpiece is known as *The Barber of Seville,* while Verdi's *La Traviata* is seldom referred to as "The Wayward One." In quoting from the text I have supplied a translation (usually a plain, fairly literal one) where the meaning of the particular passage is essential in the context of the discussion. Otherwise, for mere identification of a passage, I have given only the original words.

Although no general bibliography appears at the end of the book, there are numerous references throughout the text to books, essays, and periodical articles. Many of these will help the reader who wishes to gain further insight into opera. Especially useful are the cited studies by Graf, Grout, Hamm, Kerman, Marek, Martin, and Newman. *Opera News,* published by the Metropolitan Opera Guild, is a most informative magazine, valuable for both its literary and its pictorial content. During the Metropolitan Opera season most issues center around the work to be broadcast on a particular Saturday.

Many persons helped me during the planning and preparation of this study. Officials of the Austrian Government, especially Dr. Ernst Weikert, then of the Ministry of Education, opened many doors for me during a period of research in Vienna. Mr. Herbert Weiskopf, Director of the Portland Opera Association, read substantial portions of the manuscript and made valued suggestions. Their assistance is gratefully acknowledged. Thanks are also due the publisher's editorial staff, especially to Messrs. Alan Lesure and Cecil Yarbrough. Their interest in all aspects of this book made my own task indeed pleasant.

My own "introduction to opera" took place at the tender age of six when I attended a (still unforgettable) performance of Mozart's *Magic Flute* in Berlin. For this I owe a special debt of gratitude to my mother, who not only prepared me for this first acquaintance but helped and encouraged my developing curiosity and enthusiasm in the years that followed.

I am grateful to the following publishers and agents for permission to reprint excerpts from copyrighted works:

The Ballad of Baby Doe: Copyright © 1958 by Douglas S. Moore and Rosalind Rock, as Administratrix of John Latouche, deceased. By permission of Chappell & Co., Inc., and Lucy Kroll Agency.

Pelléas and Mélisande: By permission of Durand et Cie, Paris, France, copyright owners, and Elkan-Vogel, Inc., Philadelphia, Pa., sole agents.

The Rake's Progress: Copyright 1949, 1950, 1951 by Boosey & Hawkes, Inc.

Der Rosenkavalier: Copyright 1910, 1911, 1912 by Adolph Furstner; renewed 1938. Copyright and renewal assigned to Boosey & Hawkes, Inc. By permission of Boosey & Hawkes, Inc.

Salome: Copyright 1905 by Adolph Furstner; renewed 1933. Copyright and renewal assigned to Boosey & Hawkes, Inc. By permission of Boosey & Hawkes, Inc.

Tosca: Copyright 1956 by G. Schirmer, Inc.

Wozzeck: Copyright 1926, renewed 1954, by Universal Edition, A. G., Vienna.

CONTENTS

PART ONE

OPERA AS A SPECIAL KIND OF DRAMA

PART TWO

THE CHANGING STYLES IN MUSICAL DRAMA

CONTENTS

ABBREVIATIONS

HD   Willi Apel, *Harvard Dictionary of Music,* 2nd ed. (Cambridge: Harvard University Press, 1969).

MQ   *The Musical Quarterly*

ON   *Opera News*

SHO   Donald Jay Grout, *A Short History of Opera,* 2nd ed. (New York: Columbia University Press, 1965).

SMH   Oliver Strunk, ed., *Source Readings in Music History* (New York: W. W. Norton & Company, Inc., 1950).

Part One

OPERA AS A SPECIAL

KIND OF DRAMA

A queue for tickets at the Vienna State Opera. Always long, the lines sometimes form the night before the box office opens.

1

THE IMPACT OF MUSIC ON DRAMA

THE VERY SPECIAL KIND OF DRAMA THAT
we call opera has flourished for close to four
hundred years and has at times rivaled the
popularity of spoken drama. It has been the
subject of much criticism, including biting
satire; it has been the preferred entertainment of the aristocracy and the great love of
ordinary people from all walks of life—
students, office workers, pensioners who
would gladly stand in line at the box office
for many hours in order to be able to hear
their favorite singers in their favorite roles.
Other people who genuinely appreciate other
kinds of music find it difficult to grow enthusiastic about opera. Certainly, opera has
its own conventions, and they have changed
greatly during four centuries. Understanding
these special qualities of musical drama[1] may

**MUSICAL DRAMA
AND "REALISM"**

---

[1] The term "music drama" has acquired a more
restricted meaning, referring primarily to the later
works of Richard Wagner (see below, Chapter 7).

remove some obstacles to its enjoyment. Before we examine specific operas it may therefore be helpful to become aware of these qualities, paying special attention to characteristics that often have prevented the newcomer from understanding and enjoying an admittedly complex art form.

Opera is drama—but by its nature, indeed, by definition, it is not realistic drama. By this I simply mean that it is "unrealistic" to have people sing rather than talk to each other. The singing, of course, is intended to heighten the meaning and impact of the words, and what we gain, in the realm of artistic, aesthetic experience, offsets (or at least is intended to offset) any discrepancy with our experience on the nonartistic, everyday level.

Few people, I suspect, are bothered by the singing as such. They do not look for complete realism in other art forms. Indeed, no art of any kind is completely realistic. Hamlet speaking in verse, the very idea of a monologue, the concept of a stage as a room with one wall missing all illustrate the point. One also might recall the many ways in which painting departs from reality, beginning with the confines of a rectangular picture frame. Painting, in many periods, has not aimed at photographic realism. Instead, the artist has selected and emphasized what was important to him, often sacrificing realistic detail to make his point.

More likely it is the amount, nature, and prominence of music that some people find hard to accept in opera. A motion-picture scene with a great deal of vigorous action or with an intensely dramatic dialogue may have music in the background. The average moviegoer may hardly be aware of it. Certainly it will not strike him as unnatural or unrealistic to have the sound track include music. Many a movie or play can be viewed as an episode from real life, carried on in the kind of language that we hear around us every day. Singing, an elevated language, changes the situation. To be sure, we accept a folk song or sentimental popular song as a satisfactory, natural mode of expression, and we may even go along with the arrangement of a modern musical comedy in which the bulk of the action is carried on in spoken dialogue. The difficulty with opera, for some people, is that *too much* of the action unfolds through song, or that the kind of music we hear is inappropriate to the text. A sentence such as "Goodbye, my love, goodbye!" seems to call for music, whereas "Do you have change for a dollar bill?" does not. Yet there are many operas in which every word is set to some kind of music. Some of the reasons for this can be explained historically; we will be examining them in later chapters.

If the inclusion of singing in drama is not realistic, at least in the superficial sense, why has it been so widely practiced? Because on another level opera can be highly realistic: both singing and orchestral music can lend greater force and persuasiveness to the drama. Music can give us insights into the characters and their emotions. A few bars of music can quickly establish the desired mood, making events on the stage more believable. Good opera takes advantage of this by providing dramatic situations in which the special powers of music can be put to work.

Music is eminently suited for the expression of basic affections or emotions, but less so for the expression of complicated reasoning. W. H. Auden has noted that a good libretto "offers as many opportunities as possible for the characters to be swept off their feet by placing them in situations which are too tragic or too fantastic for words."[2] Herbert Graf similarly has defined the nature of opera as "fundamentally unreasonable. It uses facts only as vehicles by which to enter its own dream world. It treats in terms of music not only the story but, more basically, the emotions arising from the story."[3]

That realism in the superficial sense was of little concern to the aristocratic society in which opera saw its early growth is corroborated by many early operatic conventions: the preference for plots based on ancient myths, the use of male sopranos and altos, the preference for certain poetic and musical forms. Operas of the seventeenth and eighteenth centuries contain many unconvincing, contrived dramatic situations. Disguises that could not fool anyone who was not blind or deaf figure prominently among these offenses to reason—offensive to some of us, but less so to audiences of the time. The real drama, for them, was to be found in the basic emotional situations and conflicts expressed through the music, especially through the arias. An understanding of these different premises of Baroque opera is essential if today's listener is not to regard it as little more than a concert in costume.

Disguises of the kind mentioned occur more frequently in opera than in other kinds of drama (though they are not uncommon in Shakespeare), and they continue to be found in nineteenth- and twentieth-century opera as well. Why, in Johann Strauss's *Fledermaus,* does Eisenstein not recognize his wife, with whom he converses and dances, when her only disguise is the customary small black mask worn at a costume ball? And why, in Richard Strauss's *Rosenkavalier,* is the otherwise not so obtuse Ochs merely puzzled, throughout an intimate supper, by "Mariandl's" resemblance to Octavian, without recognizing "her" as the young count with whom he had crossed blades shortly before? The "trouser role"—a male role sung by a woman—is hard for us to accept as credible because not only physical appearance but also voice range

[2] W. H. Auden, "Opera as a Medium," *Opera News,* February 9, 1953. *Opera News* will hereafter be abbreviated *ON.*
[3] *Opera for the People* (Minneapolis, 1951), p. 243.

Beethoven's "Fidelio": the dungeon scene (see below, page 134). Fidelio, here played by Birgit Nilsson, is a "trouser role."

is involved. But the disguise bothers us more than it did audiences of the period. And in *Rosenkavalier* and some other operas the high voices in question might be considered to *symbolize* youth. Perhaps the popularity of trouser roles is related to the fact that, in the eighteenth and nineteenth centuries, women's legs were not normally exposed to public view, in breeches or tights.

Many operas contain scenes that are charged with emotion and therefore call for singing, but at times the singing will seem out of place if we apply standards of superficial realism. Some operatic death scenes have been ridiculed: Valentin (in Gounod's *Faust*) delivers himself of a lengthy aria after having been mortally wounded; weak, consumptive Violetta (in Verdi's *La Traviata*) sings vigorously on her death bed—a scene to which objections were raised even at the first performance. These may be extreme examples, but they show that opera even less than other drama is to be viewed as real life. All art is selective, symbolic, and "artificial"; in the art of opera many scenes will fail to move us if we do not free ourselves of standards that are not applicable to art—if we do not accept song as a symbolic, heightened form of speech.

Most people, excepting perhaps those who already are opera enthusiasts, tend to judge a libretto according to modern standards of language and drama, while they apply no such contemporary standards to the music. This is understandable: in matters of speech we live in the mid-twentieth century; we have kept up to date and we consider ourselves articulate and competent. But the musical idiom, if any, with which theatergoers are familiar is apt to be that of the eighteenth and nineteenth centuries, rather than the music of Stravinsky, Boris Blacher, or Robert Ward. We expect whatever goes on on the stage to make sense because "what happens on the stage is corporeal, what happens in music is free, not bound by pictorial realism. Music need not 'make sense' except in musical terms."[4] We would be wiser not to approach and judge a seventeenth-century libretto by twentieth-century dramatic standards and conventions.

The addition of music to spoken drama has other consequences, some of great practical importance. In a stage play the author exercises control over the words, and though he or the stage director may indicate to some extent the manner of delivery, the actor has considerable control over speed, inflection, phrasing, hesitations, pauses, and the like. In many situations there even is considerable leeway in the timing of entrances and exits and the speed with which the stage business is carried out. It is not hard to see how all this is different in musical drama. Here music—as written by the composer and interpreted, in performance, by the conductor—governs all matters of timing. The musical pulse or beat, as shown by the conductor's baton, constantly determines the pace of the action and inexorably governs everything and everybody from prima donna to electrician. This is generally true in opera, and particularly so in those scores of the nineteenth and twentieth centuries in which the orchestral part is more than an accompaniment—practically all of Wagner's and Strauss's operas, many of Verdi's, and countless others. The composer, through musical notation, has provided something like a stopwatch that regulates not only the speed of singing but also pauses, gestures, movements, and entrances and exits of all.

**MUSIC
AS A
REGULATING FORCE**

Imagine an operatic scene in which singer A soliloquizes for 24 bars about his sorrow that his beloved one, B, is far away. At bar 25 the mood and pace of the orchestral music becomes lively, molto agitato, and on the third beat of bar 28 B rushes in, jubilant. Their expression of delight and surprise, duet style, begins six beats later, the stage directions requiring both of them to have reached the top of a flight of stairs. If B makes her entrance a few seconds later than the score specifies, the following consequences are possible, none of them attractive: (1) "Delight and surprise" begin almost before B has appeared to A and the audience; (2)

[4] George Marek, *Opera as Theater* (New York, 1962), p. vii.

THE IMPACT OF
MUSIC ON DRAMA

The prompter at work.

the intended stage business becomes impossible, since both A and
B stand in the wrong places; (3) singer B, being late, misses her
cue. If this scene took place in a spoken play (where timing can
also be essential), a delay of a few seconds would probably not be
catastrophic. But this is opera, and once the conductor has reached

bar 25 no stopping or slowing down is musically possible. If A has to sing his part of the "delight and surprise" duet before B appears, the effect is ludicrous at best—it simply must not happen.

Since any delay may have catastrophic results, momentary slips of memory must be avoided at all cost. On a first visit to an opera house the spectator may notice a small boxlike protrusion in the center of the stage, near the footlights: the prompter's box. Why does opera require the services of a prompter, and what does he do? The answer to the first question has just been implied: it may be awkward for an actor to forget his lines, but it is infinitely more serious for an opera singer. To prevent this from happening the prompter does more than stand by in case of trouble: rather, on the assumption that a singer *might* forget a cue, he gives *all* cues to *all* singers, from the first to the last line of the opera. His job requires much knowledge of music, acting, and people. From his cramped quarters, partly below the stage floor, he can see the singers well enough, and he can see the conductor and his baton through one or several mirrors. In order to do his job well the prompter must know not only the text, but the score as well. He usually works from a vocal score, and he adjusts his prompting to the requirements of the music, giving a singer his cue at just the right moment, in a fairly loud voice if the volume of the music permits or requires it, or, if necessary, in a whisper. If he does the job well it will go completely unnoticed by the audience, although in a broadcast performance his voice may be picked up by one of the microphones. Aside from giving singers their lines, he may at times double as emergency stage director, motioning to singers who are not standing in the right place, or he may give the pitch for a particularly difficult entrance. In Italy the prompter frequently gives actual cues—hand signals, like a conductor's—while German prompters often give verbal cues. A prompter is essential in the traditional opera house, where a different opera is given every night and where the same singers appear in different roles on successive nights.

The need for a prompter, then, arises from the complete regulation of time in an opera. Matters of timing, it now can readily be seen, affect other aspects of opera than the singing. They make close collaboration between conductor and stage director a necessity. The tempo of an aria, the shape of a musical phrase, the length of a fermata—these musical decisions are closely related to the stage business planned by the director.

Precise timing presents special challenges in complex ensemble and choral scenes. When these involve much movement, major logistic problems have to be solved. The finale of Act II of *Die Meistersinger* is a famous example: here a large crowd has to

9

The Act II finale of Wagner's "Die Meistersinger": a famous crowd scene.

be brought on stage, involved in a vigorous brawl, and again moved off the stage, all the while singing some lively and difficult lines to an equally lively orchestral accompaniment. The stage must again be completely empty at precisely the right moment, and everything must give the impression of just "happening that way." Another example from Wagner (about whose stage requirements more will be said later) occurs in the last act of *Götterdämmerung,* where a funeral pyre must be built, in view of the audience, in exactly the amount of time allotted by the music. If the production is done with realistic sets and properties, the task may be too difficult, and subterfuges (such as having the pyre ready beforehand) may have to be used.

Whether or not a work contains crowd scenes or tricky stage business, opera in general is a more complex art form than other kinds of theater in the sense that it involves more people—onstage and backstage, in the pit, elsewhere. A production like Puccini's *Turandot* at the Met has been estimated to involve 440 persons, all doing different things; yet the coordination, i.e., timing, has to be perfect. One might say, therefore, that in opera more things can go wrong than in any other form of drama.

To say that opera is musical drama does not imply that every good play can be set to music and thereby become good opera. Throughout the history of opera composers have been aware of this and have been plagued by the difficulties of finding good librettos. Mozart said that during one year (1783) he examined 100 librettos or more without finding one that satisfied him. Many plays do not have the qualities that demand or even admit of lyrical treatment, and those stage plays that have appealed to composers almost always have required many changes in order to become opera librettos.

Restrictions apply not only to the literary qualities of a libretto but even to the subject matter. At least a few successful opera composers of our own age have expressed opinions about the kind of subject they consider desirable. Douglas Moore has remarked on the difficulty of finding a good subject—one that lends itself to "the inevitable distortion that comes from singing rather than speaking the lines."[5] A good subject would therefore seem to be one in which the essential inner and outer action involves the kinds of emotional situations that can be well and convincingly expressed through music. A story about complex, introspective people that lacks emotionally straightforward situations is not likely to succeed in an operatic version. Psychological drama certainly is possible in opera; music can do much to clarify and to characterize. But stories with little or no action, consisting of long, cerebral soliloquies[6] and complicated reasoning—these in general have succeeded better through other media. The characters in an opera, therefore, tend to be more simply drawn than those in a stage play.

These reservations aside, we may note that good operas have been written on a great variety of subjects, the degree of success depending more on the *way* in which the text has been fashioned—to say nothing of the musical setting. The "distortion that comes from singing" is in part due to the pace of singing, which is very much slower than that of spoken language. Any operatic aria, especially a serious one, will show this. Even without the repetition of words and phrases, so customary a means for emphasis in singing, an aria by Handel or Mozart in performance will take

THE LIBRETTO

---

[5] "Something about Librettos," *ON*, September 30, 1961, pp. 8 ff.
[6] Soliloquies can, of course, be effective in opera when they are set off, like moments of reflection, from surrounding action. The two monologues by Hans Sachs in *Die Meistersinger* are famous examples.

many times longer than it would take to speak the same lines. The word "libretto," we should remember, means "little book," and the printed textbook of most operas is considerably shorter than a stage play. A good libretto, therefore, presents its story in concentrated form. Later on, when we examine some specific operas and their literary history, it will become apparent how consistently this condensation has been applied to plays that have become librettos. One example may illustrate our point here: the end of Verdi's *La Traviata*. The libretto by Piave was based on Dumas's play. Piave simply has the doctor announce "She has died," whereas Dumas at this point has a rather grandiloquent statement, "Sleep in peace, etc." For the stage play, Piave's few words would hardly have supplied a satisfactory ending, but supported by Verdi's music they are all that is needed, leaving room for the music to express the feelings of those on stage, and of the audience.

Gounod's *Faust* provides a good example of insufficient condensation. Much of the opera follows the plot of Goethe's play: the sequence of scenes, even some of the dialogue—too much so. As a result, the opera today appears lengthy, whereas Goethe's drama has the right pace.

Condensation often means a reduction in the number of characters, and leaving out less essential parts of the plot may result in a libretto that is shorter by several scenes or even acts.[7] Condensation arises from *musical* considerations, and we must not expect it to result in greater literary merit. Some librettos do read well, but this is not the measure of their value, just as the sound track of a motion picture should not be judged by itself, on purely musical grounds. "The opera foe who prefers Shakespeare's *Othello* to Boito's and Verdi's *Otello* has a perfectly valid literary argument, but it does not strike at the core of opera."[8] A libretto's superior literary quality does not guarantee a good opera. The situation is not so different from that in other kinds of vocal music. Some poets, among them Goethe, have been reluctant to have their verses set to music, fearing that the eloquence of music (in Goethe's case the songs of Schubert) might divert attention from, rather than emphasize, the beauty of their poetry. On the other hand, poetry which by itself may seem like doggerel—pedestrian, sober, uninspired, and inelegant—may at times be suitable for music, including opera, if it leaves room for the composer to draw on all possibilities of musical expression.

Since the early days of opera poets and composers have shown a preference for subjects that call for much scenic display,

[7] There are some exceptions. The librettos of Verdi's *Don Carlo* and *Otello* contain scenes not found in the plays on which these operas are based.

[8] John Gutman, "Nothing but Contempt," *ON*, April 11, 1964, p. 11.

stage machinery, crowd scenes, and other spectacular devices and grandiose effects.[9] I am not sure of the reasons for this. Some of them may lie in opera's origin as an intended revival of ancient drama, leading to a natural preference for opera subjects from classical mythology. But aside from these and other historical reasons we may look to the musical forces that were available and were expected to be put to dramatic use. Choral singing, if brought to the stage, naturally could call for massed effects. Ballet, which normally needs music, quite understandably became a part of operatic tradition while continuing to be less usual as an addition to spoken plays. Furthermore, there seems to be an affinity of music, as an affective, emotional language, to the realm of the fantastic, sumptuous, and spectacular.

Most early opera librettos were fashioned directly from a narrow range of subjects drawn from mythology and ancient history (see below, Chapter 3). Such subjects have served for operas up to the present day (Stravinsky, Orff), but the range of subjects has widened greatly, especially since the late eighteenth century, when more and more stage plays and novels were transformed into opera librettos. Beaumarchais's *Le mariage de Figaro* is one of the best known eighteenth-century plays that also became famous as an opera. Other subjects were treated as both novel and stage play before they became operas—e.g., the subject of Verdi's *La Traviata*. Many contemporary operas reveal a similar literary history, though occasionally a stage play is tranformed into an opera with few changes. Berg's *Lulu* (based on two plays of Frank Wedekind) comes to mind,[10] as do Pizzetti's *Murder in the Cathedral* (T. S. Eliot) and Hindemith's *The Long Christmas Dinner* (Thornton Wilder). Douglas Moore, who, like so many composers, has looked far and wide for suitable subjects and librettos, has described how in one instance a stage play (Philip Barry's *White Wings*) became an opera:

It was Barry's idea that it be turned into an opera, and he allowed me to cut and shape the dialogue myself. . . . One thing that Barry and I discovered to our surprise was that so much dialogue could be omitted without harm to the play. Music, although slowing up the pace, can provide many short cuts in characterization and description.[11]

It is interesting, and perhaps not surprising, that composers often received the stimulus for writing an opera from seeing rather than reading a play. Puccini saw *Madame Butterfly, Tosca,* and

[9] Exceptions to this, e.g., opera buffa, will be discussed in a later chapter.

[10] See below, Chapter 12, concerning the relationship of stage play and opera for the same composer's *Wozzeck*.

[11] "Something about Librettos," p. 9.

The Girl of the Golden West as plays, in languages that he could hardly understand. For him the visual, stage impression more than the plays' literary qualities provided the initial inspiration.

By and large the literary value of librettos in our own day has increased—at any rate, it has kept pace with changing concepts in poetry and drama. There is general agreement that a libretto should be dramatically sound and convincing.[12] The unlikely situations, the empty pathos and stilted language found in much nineteenth-century opera and so often ridiculed—these no longer are acceptable. This change is related to the development of drama in general, particularly to the new dramatic media of motion picture and television. The large number of recent librettos of literary substance in turn has increased the prestige, from the poet's point of view, of writing opera texts. Particularly in America, well-known authors today tend to show more interest in collaborating with a composer than they did a generation or two ago.

Should an opera text be poetry or prose? Here again the answer has varied with time, place, and individual. Often, in Baroque and Classic opera, the division into recitative and aria was both textual and musical—prose carried the action forward in recitatives, while poetry served for the more reflective, lyrical, and emotional aria texts (see below, Chapters 3 and 4). Practice among contemporary composers also varies. Some show a preference for prose, possibly because of the rhythmic irregularities of so much twentieth-century music. Other composers, partly because of the nature of a particular subject, have preferred the flavor of poetic language: e.g., Stravinsky in *The Rake's Progress,* an eighteenth-century period piece.

In their desire to achieve complete rapport between libretto and music some composers have turned librettists, supplying all or some of their own texts. Wagner and Menotti are well known for this dual activity, but such talent has been rare, and the search for a good libretto, which plagued Mozart almost two hundred years ago, is likely to remain a concern of opera composers.[13]

MUSICAL REQUIREMENTS: COMPOSING AN OPERA

We have seen that an opera has special dramatic requirements, which through the ages have been met by a variety of textual arrangements. Likewise the drama's musical treatment has assumed different forms according to time and place. Just how a composer and librettist collaborate defies generalization, depending, among other things, on conventions of the time, but also on

[12] Realism in the sense used here does not exclude drama that moves in the spheres of fantasy, surrealism, or symbolism.
[13] Everett Helm's "The Libretto Problem," *Opera 66* (London, 1966), gives a brief historical survey.

the two artists' personalities. At times the collaboration may
amount to a contest of wills, with the stronger one insisting on
changes to suit his demands. The simplest situation, where a
composer finds a libretto that satisfies him completely and sets it to
music, has often existed; in the Baroque era, when a tremendous
appetite for Italian opera resulted in great speed of production, it
was the normal procedure. When composers worked with librettists, however, they often demanded and received numerous
changes in the text—and sometimes singers were able to do the
same thing (see below, p. 71). Later on we also find instances of a
flexible relation between poet and composer, with some give and
take on both sides. Under such circumstances an opera may grow
organically. The composer may explain the dramatic situations he
would like to see, indicating where, for musical reasons, he prefers
a duet or other ensemble, or even requesting specific kinds of
lines—prose or poetry, verses of certain length and rhythm, etc.
The librettist in turn may agree or disagree. He may express dissatisfaction with the way his dramatic intentions have been carried
out by the composer, and thereby bring about musical changes.
Much of the history of opera can be understood in terms of the
changing relative importance of drama and music. Composers of
opera have said a good deal on this subject; so have other musicians, and nonmusicians. The views of Monteverdi, Gluck,
Mozart, and Wagner will be considered later in this book.
Mozart's often-quoted remark that in opera poetry should be the
servant of music needs to be understood in relation to his own
works: they clearly show his concern with dramatic effectiveness,
with the possibilities of the stage.

Considering that the writing of the text usually precedes
musical composition, it is perhaps surprising how often and to
what extent the librettist did serve the composer. Verdi's operas are
prime examples. The self-effacing nature of his librettist Piave
showed itself in constant readiness to make changes, to supply
verses in the exact style, meter, etc., that "the master" demanded.
Such an attitude of complete subservience may seem strange at a
time when Wagner had already formulated completely different
concepts and put them into successful practice. But Piave's attitude
may have been just right to complement Verdi's musical personality, to produce the kind of opera in which this composer excelled.
Verdi's later collaboration with Boito was on a more equal level.
The collaboration of Hugo von Hofmannsthal with Richard
Strauss also showed considerably greater flexibility (see below,
Chapter 11).

Given this flexibility, text–music relationships will vary
greatly from opera to opera. The same subject, even the same

libretto, may inspire different composers differently, and lead to entirely different musical results and different dramatic emphasis. The choice of musical vehicle for a given dramatic situation—spoken dialogue, recitative, or aria; various kinds of ensembles, chorus, or the orchestra alone—depends on the musician's personal interpretation as well as on the conventions of his environment. The same applies to musical form—to the ways in which the composer gives shape, intelligibility, and coherence to his music. Because the formal organization of the text tends to influence musical form, the structural arrangements of the larger forms of abstract music (symphony, concerto) seldom affect the shape of an entire opera. On the other hand, composers (Mozart among them) have sometimes created comparable formal unity through the planned, symmetrical sequence of keys in which larger sections of an opera, such as an act, have been written. Formal devices of symphonic music are also at times suggested by the treatment of important musical themes. Thematic manipulation and development is important in many operas, not only in Wagnerian music drama where the principle of the *Leitmotif* represents a particularly elaborate and methodical approach to thematic work (see below, Chapter 7).

What causes a composer to undertake the writing of an opera? It stands to reason that the subject, its dramatic potential, and its realization (if the libretto already exists) must appeal to him, must somehow excite and inspire him—a reaction which, due to the complexity of the operatic medium, is infinitely more subtle and less predictable than it is with lyrics for a song. Many great composers, especially of the nineteenth and twentieth centuries, have been reluctant to embark on the writing of operas, and many of their opera projects remained incomplete. From a practical point of view, writing an opera is apt to consume more of a composer's time than writing other kinds of music. This alone may be discouraging, but even more so is the virtual impossibility for anyone to predict the success of a new dramatic work—a fact well known to producers of Broadway musicals. Aaron Copland, the writer of a number of operas, has explained his reluctance to tackle once more "la forme fatale": an opera may take two years to write, and its preparation and production will be expensive. "Then in 2½ hours, everybody decides whether it is any good or not. That's an awfully short time to judge the work of two years, and I don't relish being put in that situation. A symphony that was received unfavorably at first may make its way somewhere else, but with an opera, bad reviews in any metropolitan center generally make for insuperable obstacles to the work's future."[14]

[14] Interview in *ON*, January 26, 1963.

Librettos have been set to music in manifold ways. Composers past and present hold differing views and follow different procedures. Yet most of us today would agree that good opera must be more than a concert in costume; that its music must stand in a relation to the text that is readily grasped by the audience—explaining, characterizing, amplifying, and intensifying (but not overstating) the dramatic meaning that the text conveys.[15]

[15] Charles Hamm (*Opera*, Boston, 1966, Chapter 2) gives a good account of the composer's choices and tasks in setting a libretto to music.

Sets for Strauss's "Die Frau ohne Schatten" on the Metropolitan Opera's elevator stage: Upper set is raised out of view as lower set appears. On the rear stage is a third setting.

2

OPERA PRODUCTION

CHOOSING A CAST

BEFORE THE MANAGEMENT OR THE ARTIStic director of an opera company decides that it will perform a certain work, many decisions have to be made. Finding the right singer for each principal and secondary part is, of course, particularly important. The choice will involve dramatic, musical, financial, and other considerations. Aside from ability to sing and act there is the question of "equipment": the singer's figure and general appearance, and the quality (at least partly independent of training and musical ability) of his voice. These requirements may further narrow the choice. While casting for a stage play involves similar decisions, there are at least no such musical considerations. A singer's voice range and tessitura to a great extent determine the roles he can play. Aside from range, voices are classified according to quality—e.g., lyric, dramatic, spinto, coloratura soprano; basso buffo, profondo, etc.[1]

The size of the voice must also be considered. A voice that may sound right in a studio performance or on television (with amplification) may not project in a civic auditorium seating 5,000, just as a very powerful voice may cause difficulties in a television studio. Since the nineteenth century larger opera houses and larger orchestras (especially the augmented brass and percussion sections) have required increasingly powerful voices. Such volume, resonance, and stamina are found, with few exceptions, in a substantial physique only, a dilemma of which those in charge of operatic casting are only too aware. Many tenors with adequate vocal resources for the part of a young Wagnerian hero tax the audience's credulity by their appearance.

The situation is even worse when we search for a Carmen or Salome who looks the part of a young seductress—or for a Brünnhilde, Aida, Isolde, or Violetta; for a Butterfly, supposedly fifteen

Singers from a Wagnerian production of 1896. For a more modern approach to casting, see illustration on page 309.

[1] A good list of operatic voice types is given by George Martin in *The Opera Companion* (New York, 1961), pp. 29 ff. See also Charles Hamm, *Opera* (Boston, 1966), Chapter 1, "The Singers."

years old, or for countless other major roles. Also: a singer may be dramatically right for one part but, for vocal reasons, have to be "satisfied all her life with [a lesser one]. . . . The result is that the operatic stage is packed with psychological misfits."[2]

In our own day the problem has been intensified by our changed ideals of female beauty, especially in America, where beauty without slenderness is inconceivable. Those photos of great operatic singers of the turn of the century which strike us as unconvincing if not ludicrous seemed considerably less so to audiences of a time when reducing diets and sports were of little importance to the fair sex. It has been said, half-jokingly, that only after about 1910 did Wagnerian singers begin to resemble human beings, but this particular problem of casting has continued to vex directors to this day. It is easy to say that operatic acting—to be discussed presently—cannot be realistic anyway, and that therefore the physical appearance of singers is of little concern. But the response of the public contradicts this convenient rationalization: a Carmen who not only sings her part well but also looks it is greeted with enthusiasm by all.

Trouser roles, already mentioned, offer special casting problems. The part of Fidelio, a woman in man's disguise, requires a fairly young-looking soprano who can act the part of a resolute young man but can also sing some dramatic, vocally taxing music. Cherubino in Mozart's *Figaro* calls for a soprano who can act the part of a boy—young, but old enough to fall in love repeatedly. The situation in *Rosenkavalier* is similar but more ingenious. Count Octavian, sung by a soprano, must be convincing as a young man; "he" must also be acceptable in several appearances disguised as a young servant girl. Roles of this nature are hard to cast since they demand rare combinations of physical appearance and vocal equipment, of acting and singing ability.

Secondary parts in opera occasionally are more important than the term implies: they may be secondary only in regard to their function in the drama, but may contain difficult music. It is the mark of an opera company of high caliber to have such parts entrusted to first-rate singers who, on other nights, appear in leading roles.

OPERATIC SINGING

Opera is one of few kinds of music that consistently provide a singer with full orchestral accompaniment. Many singers, as they gather experience, find that such accompaniment offers a more reassuring and substantial foundation for their singing than a mere piano or organ, but it takes time to learn how to sing and act with

---

[2] Ernest Newman, *From the World of Music* (New York, 1957), pp. 46 f. Copyright 1956 by John Calder. Used by permission.

these larger forces. Above all it takes more discipline, for the most experienced conductor and his twenty-five to ninety or more players cannot follow a singer who is unpredictable and takes liberties, even where a skilled pianist might. At any rate, the function of the orchestra rarely is restricted to such following. Even in the kind of opera where the singer reigns, there frequently are situations where, for reasons of precision and ensemble, the singer must follow the conductor. In this matter of following or leading, seventeenth- and eighteenth-century opera offers fewer difficulties. The orchestra is smaller and as a rule is subordinate to the voice. Bel canto singing could develop and flourish under these conditions. Coloratura arias in Mozart and often still in Rossini were (and normally should be today) accompanied by a small group. The orchestra for the first performance of Mozart's *Don Giovanni* numbered twenty-five players, quite normal for the period.

With the changing styles and heavier orchestration found in nineteenth- and twentieth-century operas, the demands on the singer's voice changed. The light, agile voice cherished during the bel canto era no longer sufficed. Today there is an acute shortage the world over of voices that can cope with the demands of Wagner and Strauss. It has been claimed that there are only about fifteen tenors alive who can sing Tristan—this aside from considerations of acting. But aside from volume this repertory makes additional demands on the singer. Much of the musical interest, even the most important musical lines, may be found in the orchestra, so that the singer's task is one of coordinating or subordinating himself, of fitting his melodic line into the complex orchestral texture. This calls for a kind of musicality, especially a sense of pitch and rhythm, that differs from the requirements of most other kinds of vocal music.

Operatic singing often takes place under difficult conditions. An oratorio singer may have to negotiate some taxing coloratura passages, but at least she can do so with both feet on a solid concert platform. In many performances she will be able to use the score, and we can assume that lighting in the hall will permit her to consult it easily and to watch the conductor. We might compare this situation with that of the Queen of the Night in Mozart's *Magic Flute*. According to the stage directions she first appears accompanied by thunder and lightning. In many productions her position is most precarious: she is seated on a throne in the starry sky, many feet above the stage floor (see illustration on page 116). She has just been whisked up to this location on a stage elevator, and with hardly a moment to become accustomed to the dizzying position she must sing her "O zittre nicht," which includes one of opera's famous coloratura passages. Comparable situations can be found in other works, but even under less adverse circumstances the opera singer faces special problems. The easiest way to sing an aria would be to step up to the footlights and face the conductor and orchestra squarely. Though this may happen, it is seldom dramatically desirable or justifiable. Quite often a singer will stand some distance upstage, facing another singer rather than the conductor or audience. Yet his communication with both must be close, and in order to project his voice from such a distance his diction must be impeccable. Toscanini considered diction the most important element in operatic interpretation, and Wagner, well aware of the increased demands of his heavy orchestration, repeatedly admonished his devoted company at Bayreuth to strive for clarity of diction.

With the great demands on his voice the opera singer of today is understandably worried whether and for how long his instrument will stand up under the strain. Here again he is different from the actor on the legitimate stage, who can be reasonably sure of his "equipment" for life. Age may cause an actor to be cast in different roles; age, for a singer, may mean the deterioration of his vocal equipment and the end of his stage career.

OPERATIC ACTING

We have already touched on some of the reasons that opera acting is not completely realistic or naturalistic. The situation can be compared to ballet dancing, where motions also are stylized rather than realistic and are to some extent governed by the music. Moreover, the physiological processes involved in producing and sustaining a beautiful musical tone do not admit of sudden motions, rapid movements of the body, since these might interfere with a steady breath stream. A good portion of the singer's physical energy and mental concentration has to go into tone production. Awkward, twisted positions of the head or body, though perhaps dramatically effective, can interfere with the needed control of the delicate vocal mechanism and may require a greater expenditure of energy than the singer can afford. To be sure, good dramatic coaching will enable a singer who is physically fit to combine singing and other physical activity to some extent. The great Jeritza created a sensation by her interpretation of Tosca, singing her principal aria, "Vissi d'arte," while prostrate on the floor. Other singers, in the role of Butterfly, have negotiated some difficult lines while picking up the child and carrying it across the stage.

Again, we must remember how the flow of the music, regulating all aspects of timing, prevents the singer from introducing spontaneous variations into his acting. Hesitations, a few extra steps or other bits of stage business, if not planned and agreed upon may result in awkwardness and musical inaccuracy. The need for contact with the orchestra, for watching the conductor if only out of the corner of an eye, also restricts the singer in the positions he can assume.

The slow pace of music, as compared to spoken drama, necessarily slows down operatic acting, often requiring larger, more deliberate motions. A musical passage of great intensity—a great swelling of sound—cannot be contradicted by small, inconsequential gestures. Acting must be "in time with the music"; the beginning of a gesture may have to coincide with one chord or

Donna Elvira listens to Leporello in the Catalog Aria from Mozart's "Don Giovanni," Act I.

accent in the music, and its end with another. The varying pace of the music—faster in recitatives, slow, almost static in some arias—also has to be reflected in the acting. Thus the singer is never on his own. Even when he is not singing, his acting cannot be independent of the music. Orchestral introductions to arias, or interludes, present additional challenges: what shall the singer—on stage, but silent—do during such passages? This question looms even larger in duets, or in arias addressed to another character on stage, e.g., for Donna Elvira during Leporello's "Catalog Aria" in *Don Giovanni*. Some interpreters appear to be listening to Leporello, silently registering emotions all the way through. What should Scarpia do during Tosca's "Vissi d'arte"? Figaro, in Mozart's opera, addresses his famous "Non più andrai" to Cherubino, who is silent throughout but should visibly react to Figaro's description of what army life will be like. Situations of this kind demand a stage director's and actor's ingenuity. The temptation may be to have the "silent partner" engage in too much stage business, just because the other singer at such moments is musically preoccupied. But if the business detracts attention unduly from the character who should be the center of it, we have an example of poor directing and acting. Such monologues, incidentally, are far more frequent in opera than on the legitimate stage.

Many subtleties of acting, especially of facial expression, are likely to be ineffective in all but the smallest opera houses. In buildings like the Vienna State Opera a large orchestra pit separates the singer from the holders of the best main-floor seats. Spectators in balcony and gallery, three or four flights up, would be correspondingly less aware of subtle mimic expression. The dilemma, however, is posed not only by distance (which can be partly reduced by using opera glasses) but by the act of singing itself, which, as Ernest Newman has said, is "a full-time job for any human face." He particularly chides Italian singers who may make attempts at facial expression during a recitative, but "the moment they break into an aria . . . become just singing machines, with faces like putty."[3]

At least one composer-director, Menotti, believes that opera singers (especially in Europe) do not attribute sufficient importance to their acting and resent having to spend much rehearsal time on it. The admitted difficulties of operatic acting should not cause us simply to accept its frequently poor quality. Standards seem to be improving, but since newspaper reviewers still consider it worth special mention if a singer acts well, this apparently is the exception rather than the rule.

[3] *From the World of Music*, p. 47.

Rising standards are due to a number of factors. Training institutions today devote considerable time to dramatic coaching and related subjects; more, in many instances, than they did a generation or two ago. In some countries aspiring opera singers must take and pass courses in acting and dancing before they can be accepted into their professional organization. The kind of musical drama written today, frequently performed in the ordinary theater rather than the large opera house, necessitates a different approach. Signs of change can also be seen in recent trends to bring to the Metropolitan and other opera houses stage directors from the legitimate theater and from the movies. If these artists are sufficiently informed about and sensitive to music they may succeed with fresh and unprejudiced approaches to operatic acting.

CHORUS,
ORCHESTRA, BALLET

Before we turn our attention to operatic conducting and directing we should look at the tasks of some of the other participants in opera—others, that is, than the individual singers who usually receive the greatest amount of attention and publicity. Many a famous opera singer had his first opportunity to appear on the stage as a "super," in a nonsinging part, or as a chorus member.

Choral singing occurs in operas of all periods, though the importance and function of the chorus has varied a great deal. Just as an individual singer may vent his thoughts and emotions through music, a chorus may be used by the composer to voice a collective sentiment. It may express the reaction of a group of people, usually in agreement, to the situation at hand. This is its most frequent use, similar in function to the model of Greek tragedy (discussed below, Chapter 3). The moving "Non morir Seneca" from Monteverdi's *L'incoronazione di Poppea* represents this use of the chorus, the emotional intensity being expressed by a rising chromatic line.

But a chorus can function in other ways also: it can be mere window dressing, adding to the visual display and participating musically only by more or less perfunctory exclamations. It can provide pleasant variety for eye and ear: choruses in German and French Romantic operas come to mind, praising the glories of the hunter's or soldier's life. (Smetana's *Bartered Bride* contains a chorus in praise of beer!) Or the chorus can become an integral part of the drama, influencing the course of action, at times even rising to the position of chief protagonist.[4] It need not always represent a unified group of people with a collective opinion and

---

[4] The unusual prominence of the chorus in Moussorgsky's *Boris Godunov* was one of the reasons why the work was not at first accepted for the Imperial Theater in St. Petersburg.

in concerted action. Some of the most effective choral scenes in opera involve masses of people not in agreement with each other. The famous finale of Act II of *Die Meistersinger* serves once more as an example. At times choral singing may take place offstage, lending a sense of space or depth to the action,[5] or serving as the exciting announcement of unforeseen events, such as the return of the two "heroes" in *Così fan tutte*.

The singer in an opera chorus must have special qualifications. He needs a high caliber of musicianship: the ability to hold his own part under trying circumstances; to memorize music reliably and with good diction, often in foreign languages. Since he is an actor as well as a singer, the chorus member must learn the same tricks of discreetly watching the conductor, or at times an assistant conductor in the wings. He must have the courage to come in promptly, on cue, remembering that orchestra players are accustomed to come in *with* the beat, not with the delay so often practiced by choral groups. It is obvious that he must have some acting ability.

Opera orchestras have varied greatly in the number and kinds of instruments included. The nature of the music given to the orchestra, and the manner in which it is related to the drama on the stage, also have differed according to time, place, and type of opera. These matters of style will be dealt with further in Part Two of this book.[6]

Playing in an opera orchestra involves some special tasks and skills. The orchestra pit often is small, with a consequent lack of elbow room especially for the players of string instruments. Crowded conditions aggravate fatigue induced by the length of many operas. Few symphony concerts last as long as most Wagnerian operas, where the intermissions are welcomed by performers on both sides of the footlights.

Aside from possessing the musical and technical skills applicable to other kinds of orchestral playing, the members of an opera orchestra must have the ability to "give"—the flexibility that is needed in accompaniment of any sort. They must be prepared for delays and for notes held by a singer beyond their correct length; they must not confuse the conductor's cues to the singers with their own cues. The music of an opera, more often than that of a symphony or concerto, is apt to move by fits and starts, and the great temptation for an inexperienced player is to jump the gun. Dangers of this kind lurk especially in accompanied recita-

[5] A good example occurs in Act II of Puccini's *Tosca*, discussed in Chapter 9, below.

[6] See also "The Orchestra in Opera," a series of five articles by Robert Lawrence beginning in the issue of *ON* for December 9, 1967.

tives; they demand special skill from both conductor and orchestra. Several bars of rest for the orchestra may be followed by the exposed attack of an awkward passage for the strings, or by a few punctuating chords for the winds. "E Susanna non vien," from Mozart's *Figaro,* is a good example.

A professional player must know the more important places where such pitfalls occur, for in repertory houses, where a different opera is given every night, little rehearsal time is available for standard works.

Some operas call for a stage orchestra, or for several of them, as does *Don Giovanni.* If these are to play simultaneously with the pit orchestra, an assistant conductor standing in the wings or backstage may be needed for synchronization. To have extras on stage simulate playing, while the actual music emanates from the pit, is apt to be unsatisfactory, for the illusion seldom is good. The simulated playing of a single instrument (Don Giovanni's mandolin; Beckmesser's lute) is more easily accomplished.

The inclusion of dancing came naturally to musical drama. Formal ballet is perhaps what we think of first, but opera has included many other kinds of dancing, including the solo dance of which Strauss's *Salome* furnishes the most famous example. Dancing was a part of the forerunners of opera, and from the earliest Florentine operas to those of Stravinsky, Britten, and other contemporaries it has added to the splendor (and expense) of this most complex art form. Like the chorus, the ballet may be related to the drama itself in a variety of ways. It may be part of the drama, even actively advancing the action, but in most operas it remains on the fringes, related to the action but not advancing it. An example occurs in the third act of *Figaro.* A fandango is danced by the Count's loyal subjects while he and the Countess sit and watch; but during the dancing some stage business develops involving the Count, Susanna, and others which is of importance to the further development of the action. In other operas the ballet is incidental—a *divertissement* or added entertainment, not related to the opera itself.[7] And sometimes the spectator may have the feeling that the plot provides only a flimsy reason, not to say excuse, for the ballet: the action is steered in such a direction that an opportunity for a ballet interpolation arises. At that point the action comes to a standstill while the audience, and frequently the protagonists on stage, settle back to enjoy the spectacle. Many operas contain ballet "numbers" of this kind; at times they may have been the main reason for the opera's success. In mid-nineteenth-century Paris the tradition of including an elaborate ballet

[7] At the opening of La Scala in Milan an opera by Salieri was given. Ballets by Legrand and Canziani were performed between the acts.

was firmly entrenched; even Wagner reluctantly had to add substantially to the Venusberg scenes of his *Tannhäuser* for the Paris
production of that work. Many other well-known operas and operettas contain ballet interpolations of this nature, among them
Fledermaus, Traviata, Aida, and *Carmen.*

Librettists and composers, recognizing that dancing (other
than stately minuets and the like) involves physical exertion, as a
rule have not involved singers in dance scenes, *Salome* once more
being a famous exception. Since a separation of duties is possible,
in some opera houses the corps de ballet is not part of the opera
company but, maintaining its own name and direction, is hired by
the opera manager on a casual basis. Most larger opera houses,
however, have not only their own ballet but maintain a school of
dancing as well.

OPERATIC CONDUCTING

With the great number and variety of performers to be
directed and coordinated, the opera conductor faces a complex
assignment. For one thing, the physical setting offers obstacles to
communication not found in the concert hall. In the orchestra pit
of most opera houses (or theaters in which opera might be given)
more players are located to the side of the conductor and fewer are
seated directly in front of him. His baton technique must be
adjusted to this different seating arrangement. It must also allow
for the fact that singers on stage often cannot see him well,
because of their distance from him and the dim lighting in many
scenes. Extremely bright lighting, especially spotlights focused on
a singer, may also interfere. Clearly an opera conductor, mindful
of these conditions, has to employ a technique of conducting
characterized by clear and precise indication of each beat. He
cannot indulge in the "expressive" waving and churning so often
present in the style of choral or symphonic conductors—all the
more so since he often works with guest stars who have not had
time to become accustomed to the maestro's idiosyncrasies. Opera
conducting technique, one might say, is regulated by internationally understood conventions, though this does not mean that all
opera conducting is alike.

Flexibility is a further requirement. There can be no hard
and fast rule that the singer must follow the conductor or vice
versa; this depends on the frequently changing demands of the
score. Even when "following" the singer the conductor must
"lead" the orchestra—a double task that can be accomplished only
with much sensitivity and flexibility. In order to keep singer and
orchestra together in such passages the conductor must have a sixth
sense—he must anticipate what the singer will do, else the orchestra will lag behind. Passages like the one quoted below, in

which the singer's line must be executed freely yet is exactly doubled by the orchestra, demand great conductorial skill; they are precarious at best:

EXAMPLE I   Puccini, *Tosca*, Act III

con grande sentimento
CAVARADOSSI

Oh! dol - ci ba - ci, o lan-gui-de ca - rez - ze, ment-r'io fre -

In passages like this, the conductor will instinctively breathe with the singer to achieve the desired synchronization. (A good accompanist at the piano does the same.) Moreover, the players in a professional orchestra will be particularly alert at such moments, listening to the singer and trying to go along with him.

The stage action makes further demands on the conductor's adaptability. He may have to delay or hasten if a particular note must coincide with some stage business. This may have been well worked out in rehearsal, but if an actor's timing is off the conductor will try to smooth over the inaccuracy. Once the curtain is up he becomes stage director as well, making on-the-spot adjustments where possible. He has to be continually alert to nonmusical matters. Even the falling of the curtain concerns him: he may have to stretch the last few notes so that the music will not end before the curtain is down.

It is helpful for him to know the principal singers as human beings, and especially to know how they feel at the time of the performance. A singer who is nervous, tired, on the verge of a cold, or indisposed for other reasons requires the conductor's special help: more and especially emphatic cues, for example, or faster or slower tempos.

Establishing the proper balance between singers and orchestra is one of the conductor's major concerns. The reader familiar with the seating plan of a symphony orchestra knows that the soft instruments are located closest to the conductor and audience, while brass and percussion are farthest away. In opera all singers are farther away than the orchestra, including the potentially loud and penetrating brass section. This is only partly rectified by the singers' higher elevation.

Another special skill an opera conductor should possess is that of accompanying secco recitative at the harpsichord. (As an important ingredient of seventeenth- and eighteenth-century opera, secco recitative is discussed in Chapters 3 and 4 below.) In modern performances, especially of Mozart's Italian operas, some conductors officiate at the harpsichord, in the manner of the eighteenth-century *maestro al cembalo*. Secco recitatives, arias, ensembles may follow each other without break, so that the harpsichord must be directly in front of the conductor. Having just directed an aria (with orchestra) from a standing position he must be prepared to play immediately the opening chord of the next recitative. Other conductors prefer to have an assistant play the harpsichord.

To take charge of the musicians on stage and in the pit is a formidable assignment, but some operas call for singers and players offstage as well. Act III of *Der Rosenkavalier* provides specially intricate examples. In such instances assistant conductors, stationed in the wings, usually take the beat from the conductor in the pit and communicate it to the hidden performers. To be seen clearly the assistant conductor often stands on a chair or ladder. Closed-circuit television may, in the better equipped houses, help if not eliminate the middleman (the assistant conductor or chorus master) in the actual performance.

In times past the conductor, though nominally in charge, often had to cater to the wishes and whims of primo uomo and prima donna. This is less true today. Even famous singers tend to be more businesslike and to go along with the conductor's interpretation. Traveling from one guest engagement to another the star singer rarely finds that there is time for extensive rehearsal. Under these conditions he will wisely avoid battles and arguments with the maestro, unless very basic points of interpretation are at stake. Furthermore, even well-known and successful singers do not wish to antagonize the local conductor, who may be involved in the hiring of next season's singers.

Opera conducting, then, makes demands of its own: it is an art and skill that requires much special training, observation, and practical know-how. Though many conductors specialize in either symphonic or operatic music, some of the outstanding ones (Furtwängler, Toscanini, Karajan, Leinsdorf) have excelled in both.

The stage director, as a specialist in charge of the visual (as opposed to strictly musical) aspects of the production, did not exist in the early days of opera. Precise information is not plentiful, but we know that the composer-conductor, and the librettist or the impresario, may have had a hand in staging a work. No one person was traditionally in charge, and just who gave directions to the singers and others may have depended on the personalities involved. Lully and Gluck both were autocrats, taking an interest in all aspects of the production of their works and ruling with an iron hand if politeness and diplomacy were of no avail. In the nineteenth century the need for stage direction, as someone's special responsibility, was increasingly recognized, perhaps as the result of the growing complexity of opera in general. The development is similar to the somewhat earlier emergence of another specialist, the conductor. While an orchestra of the size customary in Mozart's time could still be directed by the first violinist, the larger number of players and the increasing difficulty of nineteenth-century music called for the services of someone else whose sole task was to conduct. In our own day few operagoers would doubt that the job of the stage director or régisseur is an important one. From our discussion of operatic acting we already know some of his concerns. The degree to which score and libretto clarify the author's dramatic intentions, which the stage director must bring to reality, varies greatly. Baroque opera librettos at times contain hardly any directions; some do not even indicate whether or not a singer is to exit at the end of an aria. The scene may simply be described as "a road" or "The Elysian Fields," with no further details about sets or props. Later composers (among them Wagner and Strauss) and their librettists supply minute details of staging, costuming, and acting.

Many tasks of the opera stage director correspond to those of his colleague on the legitimate stage, but while the latter deals with people whose principal training has been in the field of acting, the opera régisseur frequently does not. He may at times have to give rather elementary dramatic instruction, which may or may not be appreciated by the singer. Because of the demands of musical time—the inexorable pulse that governs all proceedings on the stage and in the pit—the stage director must be continually aware of the score. He usually plans every gesture, every step to fit in with the pace of the music. Sometimes the musical pace may be too fast, from the stage point of view. Composers have not always been thoughtful of the amount of time needed to bring a large group of people on stage—and the resulting action is unconvincing. People suddenly arrive, all at the same time; they sing, and they all disappear just as suddenly as they came, for no other apparent reason than to clear the stage for the following aria or duet. An imaginative stage director will provide some business to make these comings and goings appear natural.

Frequently the music suggests correlation with some specific action, even if the composer does not expressly call for it in the score. An example from *La Bohème* is Rodolfo's tearing up of his manuscript, each motion coinciding with a chord in the orchestra.

In planning all stage business the director must avoid the incongruities mentioned earlier: late entrances that result in missed cues, or the opposite situation, in which a singer or, worse yet, a whole chorus, reaches its position on stage too early, and then stands, obviously waiting for the cue. But aside from such basic matters of timing the stage director must be familiar with the music for more essentially artistic reasons. The mood of the music must be reflected in the acting. This becomes particularly important in nineteenth-century opera, where so much of the inner action takes place in the orchestra. Often the music, both vocal and orchestral, sheds a light on what goes on in the mind of a character. Graf quotes a good example from Act II of *Der Rosenkavalier*: the flow of the lines which Octavian sings upon his entrance, bearing the silver rose, is hesitating and shy, almost

A rehearsal of the final scene of "Carmen." Note the stage directors at left.

stammering—and his stage deportment must be in accord.[8] Often the music will suggest, more or less definitely, the nature of the acting during orchestral preludes and interludes.

Because of this close interrelation of music and acting the director must have some musical background. He may have been part of the opera world in other capacities, as singer, coach, or conductor. He frequently works from a vocal score interleaved with blank pages on which he plans all details of staging, lighting, acting, etc., in precise relation to the place in the music at which they must occur.

Some of the stage director's importance today can be attributed to the nature of our opera repertory. Far more than before it consists of standard items, of works that have become classics, staged hundreds of times and well known to the public. Operagoers who attend a new production of *Carmen* will expect to hear the same music, but they may hope for something new and different on the stage: sets, costumes, acting. Out of this situation arises a temptation for the stage director to introduce, at times rather forcedly, new devices, gags, or gimmicks into his production of an old standby; bits of staging that may be clever but that detract attention from what is dramatically and musically essential.

STAGE DESIGN   The special demands made by the music also extend to the staging, even to the nature of the sets. To begin with, there are practical considerations: the music may determine the amount of time a singer has to move from one location on the stage to another—from a window to a door, from the top of a grand staircase to the footlights. The dimensions of the set and the location of the props may be affected by this. The space requirements of choral and ballet scenes impose restrictions on set design that do not normally apply to the spoken play; the chorus, for example, needs good lines of sight and sufficient room to move around. A set that rises appreciably toward the back may facilitate communication between chorus and conductor and hence result in greater musical accuracy.

Further practical demands apply to repertory houses like the Vienna State Opera where, on matinee days, two works are given, both of which may have elaborate sets. To accomplish the necessary changes in the short time available, careful planning is needed. Entire sets and major pieces of scenery may be designed with rapid movability in mind. Questions of storage also concern the stage designer: all pieces must fit into the vans that deliver them for the performance and return them to warehouse and work shed, frequently in another part of town. If the company goes on

[8] *Opera for the People* (Minneapolis, 1951), pp. 102 f.

tour, space limitations of the theaters to be visited and of baggage cars or vans cannot be ignored.[9]

Practical considerations of this kind are important, but there are factors of an essentially artistic nature that tend to give a special quality to operatic staging. The "expansiveness of musical emotion" (Graf) which we have already seen to affect the libretto and the style of acting must also be reflected in the staging. Opera, for reasons dealt with earlier, tends to favor the emotional and the imaginative, the poetic and frequently the fantastic and irrational. The mood established and constantly underscored by the music must be furthered and enhanced rather than contradicted and interrupted by the visual aspects of the production. The overall effect of a set, the important first impression as the curtain goes up, must bear this out, as must the other elements of staging, especially the lighting. If the musical mood is disregarded or misinterpreted, the audience may experience a feeling of dissatisfaction without necessarily being conscious of the reason. The tavern scene in Weber's *Freischütz*, for example, must not appear comfortable and gemütlich in the German rustic manner but must communicate something of the ominous, supernatural action, the eerie mood of the dark forest surroundings that speak to the listeners repeatedly through the music.

Because of opera's affinity for large emotions and for the fantastic, opera staging tends to be elaborate and as a rule requires more machinery and technical equipment than does the staging of a straight play. Movable and elevator stages, revolving platforms, cycloramas, and projection facilities are more essential in an opera house than in an ordinary theater.

Since our standard repertory, regrettably conservative, includes a minority of contemporary works, stage directors and designers in opera have felt more tradition-bound than their colleagues in spoken drama, where new and experimental works and staging are apt to have a more cordial reception. But there are signs of change.

How the staging of opera has varied with time and place (the changing emphasis on machinery and the effect of technical innovations, including electricity) will occupy us in several later chapters.

From what has been said in the preceding pages it is easy to see that putting an opera together for performance involves many people and departments. Preparations are correspondingly more

REHEARSING AN OPERA

---

[9] These matters are well discussed by Rose Heylbut and Aimé Gerber: "Setting the Scene," in *Backstage at the Opera* (New York, 1937), pp. 222 ff.

complex than for a stage play.[10] In a sense preparations begin when an individual singer learns a role, perhaps years before he performs it for the first time. But this kind of study usually means learning and memorizing the music; the singer may not benefit from dramatic coaching for the role until its performance has been decided and scheduled. A great many people must confer before rehearsals can get under way: conductor, stage director, and scene designer; before long also those in charge of lighting, costumes, and properties. Once the stage business has been planned, a coach will work with the singer. Though in learning a role singing and acting cannot be completely separated, adding the visual to the musical interpretation is the more customary sequence: the singer becomes accustomed to acting his part while using his voice. Some directors recently have experimented with rehearsals in which singers at first only *speak* their lines, with or without piano accompaniment. The intention here is to get rid of typically "operatic" gestures. Richard Strauss, in the preface to the score of his *Capriccio,* recommended reading rehearsals for the same reason.

The learning of duets and larger ensembles proceeds along similar lines: the singers must know their own parts reliably before they come to be coached, musically and dramatically, as a group. Chorus, orchestra, and ballet likewise must be trained separately before they can take part in stage or full rehearsals. As the time for the first performance approaches, the many separate rehearsals may tax the facilities of the building. In additon to rehearsal stages (where they are available), dressing rooms, foyers, restaurants, and other public rooms may be pressed into service. Preparing a master rehearsal schedule becomes a major logistics problem, especially in repertory theaters where the main stage may be unavailable much of the time because of current performances.

The first stage rehearsals are held with piano accompaniment. It would be uneconomical to use an orchestra when rehearsal time is largely devoted to singing in relation to acting, working out entries and exits, movement on stage—the general continuity of the opera. Later on, as musical balance becomes an important concern, full rehearsals with orchestra are held. These are always complicated and sometimes hectic affairs, with many people giving directions in their particular fields: conductor, assistant conductors, chorus master, stage director, ballet master.[11] Once more we are reminded of the all-important, all-governing role of musical time when we see how many members of the company need to follow a

---

[10] A lively account of what goes into a new production—from the initial planning and casting to all kinds of rehearsals—is given by Martin Mayer in "A High Order of Talent," *ON*, March 21, 1964, pp. 6 ff.

[11] Graf gives a good account of this in *Opera for the People*, pp. 108 ff.

score in order to carry out functions that are not specifically musical: the prompter, the chief electrician (for light cues), and many others.

Normally only a few final rehearsals will involve the orchestra in the pit, though the orchestra too will have had separate rehearsals previously. The instrumentalists by now must know their parts: to rehearse individual orchestra passages while the entire cast and crew stand idly by would indeed be poor budgeting of time and money. During these last full rehearsals balance between singers and orchestra is an important concern—important, but difficult to judge from the conductor's usual position. He may therefore, from time to time, turn over his baton to an assistant and listen from various places in the auditorium.

By the time the dress rehearsal begins, every detail of the new production has been planned, practiced, and understood. The dress rehearsal serves as an important opportunity for the entire cast to go through the opera as a whole. Like any drama, an opera is more than an aggregation of individual dialogues or scenes. For an interpretation that has artistic consistency and the right pace, rehearsals of major portions of the work, without interruption, are necessary. The dress rehearsal, as a performance before the first performance, fulfils this purpose and at the same time is a safety measure for the detection and last-minute correction of any flaws. Opera dress rehearsals, especially in Italy and some other European countries, are public or semi-public.

Even after its first performance an opera may require rehearsals, particularly if changes are made in the cast. In this day of worldwide travel many singers spend only a fraction of the season at the opera house that is their home base and make guest appearances in other cities, countries, and continents. Unless a guest star is given adequate rehearsal time his performance, though vocally excellent, may be marred by lack of rapport with the orchestra, and his dramatic interpretation may not harmonize with what has been planned by the local stage director for the rest of the cast. A guest conductor also will need some rehearsal time to clarify his intentions (tempi, dynamics, and other matters) to singers and orchestra.

OPERA PERFORMANCE CONVENTIONS

Drama of many ages has been connected with ritual, and has accordingly developed its own traditions and conventions. Opera is no exception. Some of its traditions, and especially some practices encountered in performance, are bound to cause surprise, and perhaps displeasure, to the newcomer. That they can be understood in relation to historical developments is not to say that they necessarily are to be condoned today.

To the unprejudiced spectator who looks at opera as a special kind of drama it may seem that too much fuss is being made about the individual singer, especially if his arias are difficult, contain high notes, and are delivered with gusto. This emphasis on song and the singer goes back to seventeenth-century Italian opera (see below, Chapter 3); to varying degrees it has been with us ever since. A large segment of the public today looks at opera primarily as an opportunity to hear beautiful singing. Since practices in the fields of art and entertainment are largely governed by audience tastes, the famous opera singer (the term "prima donna" reminds us of earlier Italian practices) continues to be in the limelight, along with his fellow stars in the worlds of concert, movies, television, and sports. Through the history of opera this rule of the singer has been challenged again and again: by Gluck, Wagner, and other composers, by conductors, directors, and critics. In 1871 Verdi, asked to make recommendations for the organization of musical training in Italy, demanded that an end be put to the reign of the prima donna and that more attention be paid to the dramatic side of opera. But neither Verdi's nor other important voices raised since have brought about a complete realization of this demand. Particularly in Italy and wherever Italian opera is prominent a vociferous segment of the public continues to admire a beautiful voice and a high C more than an interpretation that is dramatically and musically convincing. Capitalizing on this attitude, singers may add high notes, especially at the end of arias, where the composer did not write them. Some of these inauthentic notes have become so established by tradition that singers are afraid *not* to add them, for fear of public criticism. When standards of this kind are applied by some of the public, one can understand the attitude of a famous tenor who recently refused to sing a certain aria in concert because it did not end on a high note. In this star-centered world of opera, clapping after a high final note is almost a conditioned reflex of audiences. More thoughtless is the person who must spoil a beautiful last note or orchestral postlude by premature clapping—insensitive behavior that it would be hard to condone in a circus act, let alone on the musical stage.

Too often applause interrupts the dramatic continuity or illusion and results in ludicrous situations. A singer in a tragic role who graciously acknowledges applause on the open stage at a serious moment in the drama cannot expect the same mood to be sustained thereafter.[12] Aside from being dramatically incongruous, applause other than at the end of acts interrupts and interferes

[12] Graf recalls a performance in which the tenor, supposedly wounded, rose from his stretcher to bow to the audience, then lay down again to be carried out. *Opera for the People*, p. 101.

with the pace of the drama as intended by the author, especially if it forces the conductor to stop where no stop is called for in the score.

The practice of demanding encores is another operatic custom that can be understood only in relation to the singer-oriented view of opera. It is an old custom; even Mozart noted with some pride that audiences demanded to hear certain of his arias again. To this day Italian audiences can be very insistent with their *bis*-shouting. I have attended performances where veritable battles developed between the conductor, who (knowing that the singer was tired) wanted to go on, and the audience, who insisted on hearing its favorite "number" again. Outside of Italy encores today are less frequent, often being forbidden by the management.

Curtain calls at the end of each act, largely abolished on the legitimate stage, are still the rule in opera. In a sense, the curtain call has replaced the epilogue of seventeenth- and eighteenth-century opera in which the entire cast appeared once more, often in front of the curtain, for a final scene or song, and then acknowl-

A curtain call after a performance of Bellini's "I Puritani" in San Francisco.

edged the applause.[13] European audiences tend to be quite outspoken in their expression of approval and disapproval, and outstanding performances may be rewarded with applause that lasts for many minutes. Curtain calls can become an important ritual, with singers and audiences carefully keeping track of the number of both single and group calls.

Perhaps the strangest convention in opera, one which has persisted to this day, is the claque—the hired "hands" that dispense applause for their clients.[14] The person who thinks of opera as an art form in which high achievement can easily be detected and acknowledged by any attentive and impartial audience finds it hard to understand, let alone approve, this practice. Parents and other relatives may clap vigorously at their daughter's performance in a school play—but for a professional singer to buy applause, if only with complimentary tickets for the claqueurs, seems dishonest, mercenary, and inartistic. Since the issue appears clear-cut on moral grounds one might at least try to understand why claques exist to this day in some places. In operas that consist of self-contained musical numbers applause is possible in many places, not only as the curtain comes down. Many members of the audience are not sufficiently familiar with the work to know the "right" places to applaud and may therefore hesitate. Here the members of the claque, who know the work well, may help the audience to express its appreciation at the right moment (this, at least, is the theory), avoiding the premature clapping mentioned above and also stimulating an atmosphere of success and enjoyment by having the applause set in vigorously rather than timidly. Distinctions are possible between the altogether mercenary claqueur whose applause will vary in enthusiasm with the fee he has been paid and the more refined type who will use his own judgment as to the merit of a singer and who may return his fee rather than applaud an inferior performance.

The *raison d'être* of the claque may perhaps be understood by contemporary American audiences who are familiar with the custom of including "canned" (recorded) laughter on television programs, especially comedy acts. Why is such laughter provided, when the programs often are taped in a studio, bit by bit, with no audience present? Producers apparently feel that laughter and

---

[13] The finale of Don Giovanni is a well-known example (though the Don does not reappear). The practice has been revived in Stravinsky's *The Rake's Progress.*

[14] Florence Stevenson, "The Ignoble Romans," *ON,* October 19, 1963, pp. 8 ff., gives a thumbnail sketch of its history from Nero's days to the present time at the Metropolitan, where its existence is abhorred by powerless officials. See also the frequently amusing accounts by Joseph Wechsberg (*Looking for a Bluebird,* Boston, 1945), William L. Crosten (*French Grand Opera . . . ,* New York, 1948), and George Martin (*The Opera Companion,* New York, 1961).

applause, properly timed and in the right places, are essential to success.

Whether the claque will persist depends primarily on the direction in which opera will move. As long as and wherever the view of opera as concert in costume prevails—the term "culinary opera" has sometimes been used for this—the star system with all its paraphernalia including the claque will continue. But an environment in which opera is essentially viewed as musical theater may do away with many of the conventions bred by that system. Such a view appears to be gaining support today.

THE STRENGTHS OF OPERA

Since this chapter and the preceding one have dealt mostly with the "problems" of opera—difficulties, inherent in the medium, brought into focus by rehearsal and performance—a concluding view of its strong points is in order. How does this combination of arts produce results that are especially valid, effective, and exciting? The question should be answered by each reader for himself, especially after he has come to know a substantial number of operas; but in the meantime we may examine the ways in which some of the specific components of opera contribute to its effectiveness.

Song is a natural mode of expression; and when music is added to speech, to the expression of thoughts or sentiments of an individual, the result can be more moving than the mere words themselves. Melody, then, can contribute to the effectiveness of speech, in drama and in other media. But as a single musical line, melody is rarely heard in opera or other kinds of art music of the Western world. In aria, recitative, and other vocal forms the instrumental accompaniment can be dramatically effective, accomplishing things impossible in spoken drama. In its most straightforward application, the orchestral accompaniment merely supplies a harmonic and rhythmic background, reinforcing, in a general way, the mood and meaning conveyed by text and melody. But it can also comment on the text in a pictorial manner: we may hear the jingle of coins when money is mentioned in the dialogue (as in *Falstaff*, Act II).

More subtly, the accompaniment expresses something of the frame of mind, the emotions of the singer, informing us, for instance, of changes in the way he feels. The end of Act II of *Der Rosenkavalier* provides an example: Baron Ochs' excitement and anger, after he has been wounded slightly, gradually give way to a sense of well-being. The wine is taking effect, and Annina has brought good news. This passage owes much of its effectiveness to the orchestra.

Or the accompaniment can create a comical effect by overstating its case. When Count Almaviva threatens Doctor Bartolo with his sword (*The Barber of Seville*), the orchestral accompaniment is extremely serious and intense, with a big tremolo; but because the audience knows that he is faking, the effect is comical.

At times the accompaniment may contradict the singer. In a famous scene from Gluck's *Iphigénie en Tauride,* Orestes sings that "calm is returning to my heart"; but he is given the lie by the orchestra:

EXAMPLE 2   Gluck, *Iphigénie en Tauride,* II/3

At other times the accompaniment may rival the singing in importance and in its bid for our attention. In a scene from Bizet's famous opera (see below, Chapter 8), Carmen and Don José have words; at the same time we hear the bugle call to quarters, reminding them, and us, of the cause of their quarrel.

The accompaniment assumed special significance in the operas of Wagner and other nineteenth-century composers, largely through use of the *Leitmotiv* (see below, Chapter 7).

The orchestra can establish a mood, signal a sudden turn of events, or provide a gradual transition; and it can do all these things with or without singing (for instance, in the introduction to an aria, or in an interlude, where it is not, strictly speaking, an accompaniment). Overtures and other self-contained instrumental pieces may also accomplish this. All these possibilities, though beyond the reach of the spoken play, are used extensively in musical drama of all kinds, including motion pictures and television. Recent works in all these categories have introduced electronic sounds into the accompaniment, thereby enlarging its expressive, coloristic possibilities (Blomdahl, *Aniara,* 1959; Blacher, *Zwischenfälle bei einer Notlandung,* 1966). Electronically produced sounds may alternate with conventional orchestral passages, or the two, and vocal music, may be heard simultaneously.

A special strength of opera lies in the ensemble. To have two or more people express their thoughts audibly at the same time presents a challenge and opportunity to the composer. Such simultaneous speech is hardly possible on the spoken stage, but as part-singing it is a device used by opera composers of all periods. It is, of course, unrealistic in the narrow sense of that term. Furthermore, since two or more different texts being sung simultaneously are not easily understood by the listener, the effectiveness of such ensembles at least in part depends on prior knowledge of the libretto. But to present various and perhaps conflicting views, feelings, and beliefs simultaneously may amount to presenting them all the more effectively. In the hands of Mozart, Strauss, and others, the big ensemble has indeed become "the crowning glory of opera" (Auden).[15]

Choruses offer similar possibilities for simultaneous expression. Impressive crowd scenes abound in opera but, not surprisingly, are rare on the spoken stage. Skilled librettists introduce the chorus where it is dramatically plausible and convincing. Wagner, in *Die Meistersinger,* shows ingenuity in providing situations in which choral singing is natural and well-motivated. Scenes in which soloists and chorus participate offer possibilities of musical contrast, with the group repeating a refrain for emphasis. Gilbert and Sullivan were fond of this device, as were many other writers of operettas. The chorus that is organically related to the action, rather than superimposed upon it for musical reasons, is apt to have great appeal in serious musical drama.

What makes for good opera today? Again I would invite the reader to formulate criteria of his own; the very process of doing so should be stimulating. A few opinions are offered, chiefly as a point of departure, and with the knowledge that there will be disagreement.

To be absorbing for the modern listener, especially the neophyte, an opera must move at a reasonably fast pace—fast enough to insure dramatic continuity and to keep him both intellectually and emotionally involved. I do not mean that every opera should unravel at the pace of Puccini's *Tosca* (which I consider a good opera). The pace of Debussy's *Pelleas and Melisande* is far more deliberate but harmonizes with the kind of action, conflict, and character drawing of that work.

In opera, even more than in other kinds of drama, there should be characters with whom we can identify, particularly on

---

[15] Victor Hugo, eminently successful as a playwright, is said to have remarked of the quartet in the last act of *Rigoletto:* "Unsurpassable! Marvelous! If only in my plays I could have four people speak at the same time and yet have the audience understand the words and different sentiments!"

the emotional level. Convincing character drawing can make an opera effective in spite of inconsistencies and other flaws in the plot. These universally human qualities cause us to be moved by Mozart's *Figaro,* though even after repeated hearings we may find it hard to give a résumé of its plot. Still, to enjoy *Figaro* we need to be familiar with certain eighteenth-century operatic conventions, whereas we can enjoy a stage play of the same period without much special knowledge. Beaumarchais's and Da Ponte's *Figaro* deal, to varying degrees, with burning political and social issues of the time, a fact that added to the audience's close involvement with both play and opera. Success, of course, is not insured by an opera's subject, but might there not be some relation between the small number of successful twentieth-century operas and the fact that subjects of political or otherwise topical significance have been largely avoided?

Many operas that have stood the test of time are in my opinion not good operas today. *Lucia* and *Trovatore,* to mention but two, still are standard repertory, but their success rests on musical grounds alone. Many inveterate fans go to the opera to hear music they love, sung by singers they love. They consider *Trovatore* a good opera because it provides them a satisfactory aesthetic experience. They may not even *want* to understand the text because "all opera texts are silly."

The historical reasons for this attitude can be traced to Baroque opera, and we will examine them in the following chapter. In our own day different standards are being applied by a growing opera audience. Good opera must be good drama. Does this mean that the words are more important than the music? Richard Strauss's *Capriccio* has this question as its central theme; at the end of the opera it is left unanswered—wisely so, for there can be no categorical solution. The following chapters will show that the answer has varied according to time and place—that drama and music have been combined successfully in a great variety of ways.

Part Two

THE CHANGING STYLES

IN MUSICAL DRAMA

Caesar and Cleopatra in a New York City Opera production of Handel's "Julius Caesar."

3

MUSIC AND DRAMA BEFORE 1750

The Sources of Today's Repertory

THROUGHOUT THE HISTORY OF MANKIND, singing has been a natural, spontaneous mode of expression. In primitive and civilized societies alike, it has been common practice to add strength and meaning to spoken words through singing. Likewise the addition of music to drama—from simple dialogue to complex play—has appealed to man from time immemorial. In particular, writers have enlisted the powers of music to heighten the impact on an audience of emotional situations and scenes. Close ties between drama and religion exist in many civilizations, for the powers of music, dancing, and drama have been recognized in most religions. This recognition has produced a variety of attitudes, frequently conflicting, on the part of religious authorities. To the early Christians music was suspect because of associations with pagan rites and dancing; on the other hand, music in some form formed part of their religious activities almost from the beginning. Fear and suspicion of the theater, of its effect on the morals of the viewers, likewise has been characteristic of ecclesiastical authorities. Yet even the medieval church recognized the didactic value of the theater and sponsored dramatic presentations of religious subjects.

A thorough account of the important combinations of music and theater through history would require a book many times the size of this one. Such a study could be extremely interesting; as far as I know it has still to be written. The purpose of the present book, to provide an introduction to musical drama as we are likely to see and hear it today, does not require such completeness. Nevertheless, some knowledge of combinations of music and drama found before the seventeenth century, the so-called forerunners of opera, may be helpful.[1]

ANCIENT GREECE

Uncertainty still exists about the place of music in ancient Greek drama. The subject is especially relevant to us, for the composers of early opera attempted to recreate the manner of singing which they thought to have existed in ancient Greece. Although the preserved examples of Greek music—dramatic and otherwise—consist of a few melodic fragments only, we have enough references in the writings of classic philosophers and historians, as well as pictorial evidence, to know that at least parts of the drama were sung, or chanted, or recited in some musical and rhythmical manner.[2] Musical instruments were also used. Because performances were held outdoors, often in large amphitheaters, musical speech may have been employed partly for practical acoustical reasons: the singing voice carries farther than the speaking voice.[3] Varying emotional content of text passages may have determined the kind of speech used, musical or otherwise.

Both solo and choral singing were employed in Greek tragedy.[4] The chorus, which sometimes was divided, was trained by a leader or leaders who at times sang alternatingly with the group or with one of the actors. All singing, both solo and choral, was in unison. In tragedy as in other kinds of Greek music, instruments may have accompanied by playing along the vocal line, at times

[1] For more detailed information the reader is referred to the opening chapter of Donald Jay Grout's *A Short History of Opera,* 2nd ed. (New York, 1965), hereafter abbreviated *SHO.*

[2] In the late Renaissance, lack of precise information on this subject led to the belief, largely discredited today, that the entire tragedy was sung (see below, p. 51).

[3] Similar considerations may have played a part in the development of chant, in Greek religious ceremonies, as well as in Hebrew and later Christian liturgies.

[4] Grout describes various ways in which the chorus participated (*SHO,* pp. 12 ff.).

varying and ornamenting it. They also may have provided interludes.[5]

There are similarities in all this to opera as we know it. But
the differences, from the areas occupied by performers and audience to the lack of harmony and instrumental accompaniment as
we know it and to the close connection with religious rites, are
considerable. The road from Aeschylus and Euripides to Peri,
Caccini, and Monteverdi is a long one.

Musical drama found its way into the medieval church when
Gospel and other Bible texts of a narrative, dramatic nature were
chanted by several priests rather than one. In a reading of the
resurrection story one priest might chant the words of the angel at
the empty tomb; another would represent the women who had
come to seek the body of Christ. Out of such dialogues in time
grew elaborate dramatic presentations. Many liturgical dramas[6]
about the Christmas, Passion, and Easter stories and about incidents from the Old Testament (e.g., the story of Daniel) have been
preserved. Later manifestations of religious drama, the Mysteries
or (in Italy) *sacre rappresentazione,* were often elaborately produced by the community as a whole. Not a part of the liturgy, they
frequently were given in the vernacular rather than Latin.

Purely secular dramatic activity also existed in the Middle
Ages. Jongleurs, troubadours, wandering musicians of many kinds
would delight audiences in village, town, and castle by dramatizations of familiar stories, legends, and heroic tales. Pantomime may
have been used, with one actor explaining the story in song or
chant, or the actors themselves may have sung.[7] One of these plays
with music, Adam de la Hale's *Play of Robin and Marion* (late
thirteenth century), has at times rather arbitrarily been called the
first opera. It is largely spoken but includes some simple folk-like
songs and dances. Accompaniment was implied but not written
down.

The setting for this play is pastoral, Robin and Marion being
shepherd and shepherdess. In this respect Adam's work points to
the coming Renaissance, especially the sixteenth century, when
pastoral plays enjoyed considerable vogue. As a rule these plays

---

[5] Music also was part of dramatic presentations in ancient Rome. Songs are
believed to have figured so prominently in the ancient Roman *fabula* or *ludus*
that the term "Roman opera" has been considered appropriate by at least one
scholar. (A. Thomas Cole, "Opera in Ancient Rome," *Ventures,* Magazine of the
Yale University Graduate School, Spring, 1967, pp. 35 ff.)

[6] Apel prefers the term "religious drama" to describe these productions, which
were not part of the official liturgy. See the article "Liturgical Drama" in *Harvard Dictionary of Music,* 2nd ed. (Cambridge, 1969), hereafter abbreviated *HD.*

[7] Manuel de Falla's opera *El Retablo de Maese Pedro,* 1919, in which both
puppets and actors appear, recreates this technique.

did not contain strongly dramatic action. They were essentially lyrical in character, and, like the contemporary Italian madrigal, involved pleasant, rustic settings and complications of an amorous nature.

Important for the development of comic opera in particular was the *commedia dell'arte*—the improvised comedy so popular in Italy beginning in the mid-sixteenth century. The larger presentations especially included singing and dancing as part of the comedy itself, not merely as an added entertainment. Since the commedia was improvised, each of the (professional) actors specialized in one of the traditional roles: Pantalone, Truffaldino, Dr. Graziano, and others who can still be recognized in comic operas up to Rossini's *Barber of Seville.* They also populated the madrigal plays, another sixteenth-century forerunner of opera. In these a dramatic and frequently comic text was set to music in madrigal style throughout; i.e., all the text was sung in parts, by the group rather than by individual singers.

Other sixteenth-century plays contained both solo and part singing. Elaborate staging distinguished many of these Renaissance presentations; some of the most distinguished artists and architects designed scenery and invented stage machinery. This preoccupation with stage effects was to characterize Baroque opera as well.

Musical sketches of varying dimensions were given between the acts of many Renaissance plays. Such *intermedi* or *intermezzi*[8] occurred between the acts of classic plays (e.g., the comedies of Plautus revived in Ferrara around 1500) or of newly written works. Composers included Count Bardi, whom we shall encounter again in our discussion of early opera. The vogue for intermedi continued well into the seventeenth century; in some productions these interpolations were more elaborate than the plays themselves.

Other countries besides Italy took part in these developments. In sixteenth-century France and England elaborate ballets were performed at court. They often consisted of many loosely connected scenes with some spoken dialogue and musical accompaniment. In England an entertainment of this kind, the *masque,* preserved its popularity to the end of the seventeenth century. Members of the court frequently participated. Much singing and a good deal of instrumental music were included in English stage plays of the Renaissance—a tradition of which we are reminded by the many occasions for music in Shakespeare's plays.

Extensive cultivation of ballet also characterized the French forerunners of opera. The presentation in 1581 of Beaulieu and

---

[8] In eighteenth-century Italian opera the term "intermezzo" had a somewhat different meaning (see below, p. 72).

Salmon's *Ballet comique de la reine* points toward this later development. The word *comique* here does not denote comedy in our sense but indicates that the work had a certain dramatic continuity. It was given a resplendent production with the participation of the Queen. Both choral and solo singing were included, though they were incidental, as they were in all the "forerunners" discussed so far. Understandably, clear distinctions between some of these and opera proper are not always possible, yet the term "opera" is appropriate only for works in which music came to be employed consistently, as part of the drama rather than as occasional embellishment. This occurred for the first time in early seventeenth-century Italy.

EARLY BAROQUE OPERA

The many combinations of music and drama that we have discussed so far had certain features in common: they were not complete, continuous dramas or, if they were, music did not form an integral part. It was left for the circle of Count Giovanni Bardi in Florence to create the first operas—tangible results of Renaissance interest in Greek civilization. Of the many academies or societies of classically minded Italians, Bardi's group, the so-called Florentine Camerata, was most important for the development of musical drama. Aristocratic scholars and literati, amateurs of music and poetry, but also professional musicians took part in discussions and investigations which led them to believe that the tragedies of ancient Greece had been sung or chanted in their entirety. Out of their studies of Greek literary sources arose the concept of soloistic musical recitation as a way of giving heightened eloquence and power to the word. This concept stood in marked contrast to musical practice around them—the style of late sixteenth-century choral music with its frequently complex part writing in which the text could not be clearly understood. Demands were made that music should express the emotional meaning of a sentence or situation, not merely of individual words; hence all the text should be clearly intelligible. Count Bardi and Vincenzo Galilei, a theorist, writer, and composer who belonged to the Camerata, were among those voicing these demands.[9]

Similar opinions about Greek drama were fairly widespread in the late sixteenth century, and such demands were voiced elsewhere. In the Florentine circle, however, they led to the creation of a style of singing thought to have been practiced in Greek tragedy. Monody was considered the suitable way to set an affective text to music: a soloistic, elevated musical speech or recitation, adhering

[9] Galilei, *Dialogo della musica antica e della moderna* (1581); Bardi, *Discorso sopra la musica antica . . .* (ca. 1580); excerpts from both are included in Strunk, *Source Readings in Music History* (New York, 1950), hereafter abbreviated *SMH*.

PROLOGO
LA TRAGEDIA.

O che d'alti sospir vaga, e di pian ti Spars'or di doglia

hor di minaccie il volto Fei negl'ampi te atri al popol folto Scolorir di pietà volti, e sembian-

ti. Ritornello.

2
Non sangue sparso d'innocenti vette
Non ciglia spente di Tiranno insano
Spettacolo infelice al guardo humano
Canto su meste, e lacrimose scene.

3
Lungi via lungi pur da regij tetti
Simulacri funesti, ombre d'affanni
Ecco i mesti coturni, e i foschi panni
Cangio, e desto ne i cor piu dolci affeti

4
Hor s'auuerrà, che le cangiate forme
Non senza alto stupor la terra ammiri
Tal ch'ogni alma gentil ch'Apollo inspiri
Del mio nouo cammin calpesti l'orme

5
Vostro Regina fia cotanto alloro
Qual forse anco nó colse Atene, ò Roma
Fregio non vil su lonorata chioma
Fronda Febea fra due corone d'oro

6
Tal per voi torno, e con sereno aspetto
Ne Reali Imenei m'adorno anch'io
E su corde più liete il canto mio
Tempro al nobile cor dolce diletto

7
Mentre Senna Real prepara intanto
Alto diadema, onde il bel crin si fregi
E i manti, e seggi de gl'antichi Regi
Del Tracio Orfeo date l'orecchie al câto.

Pastore del Coro.

INFE Ch'i bei crin d'oro Sciogliete lie te allo scherzar de venti E faithfully to the prosody of the text, with a simple harmonic accompaniment.

The first complete dramatic text set to music in this style was Ottavio Rinuccini's *Dafne,* composed by Jacopo Peri (1561–1633) and first performed in 1597 in the palace of a Florentine nobleman. Most of Peri's music is lost. The first preserved operas, therefore, are two settings by Peri and Giulio Caccini (1550?–1618) of the same poet's *Euridice* (both 1600; Caccini's version was not performed in its entirety until 1602).

Rinuccini's text, in the manner of the Renaissance Pastorale, is lyric rather than dramatic. Much of the action in both Peri's and Caccini's versions and in other early operas takes place offstage, in accord with a tradition of Greek tragedy. A messenger, who relates important events to those on stage and to the audience, is one of the important roles.

In both settings *Euridice,* like many later Baroque[10] operas, begins with a prologue. The personification of Tragedy addresses the audience. She alludes to the occasion for the performance: the festivities in honor of the wedding of Henry IV of France and Maria de' Medici.[11] This prologue consists of seven stanzas, each followed by a brief instrumental ritornello (recurring interlude). The prologue, and much of the drama itself, is sung in the monodic style—the *stile rappresentativo* to which Caccini refers in the dedication of his *Euridice.*[12] Close observation of the accentuation of the Italian text is evident, as is the resulting absence of regular, repetitive rhythmic patterns. Yet not all the singing in these two works is purely syllabic recitation. Caccini's score in particular contains vocal flourishes and embellishments for expressive purposes. The accompaniment, consisting of the basso continuo only, tends to move slowly, with cadential chord changes serving as musical punctuation. Such a sustained accompaniment may at first give an impression of harmonic monotony, but because it is static even slight chromaticism and some unexpected chord changes are all the more effective.

Short choruses, including some double choruses, interrupt the flow of the recitative in many places. Again following classic models, the choruses have leaders. Some choruses are simple, homophonic, and dancelike, while others are imitative in the madrigal style of the time. In all, soloistic singing is clearly in the foreground. Though much of the early operatic music, as written down, may seem simple to us, in performance it appeared convinc-

[10] The term "Baroque music" refers to the period from ca. 1600 to ca. 1750. For a definition of Baroque style, in music and other arts, see *HD.*

[11] Such a happy occasion demanded a happy ending, and the ancient myth was modified accordingly.

[12] Translated in *SMH.*

Opposite: Peri's "Euridice": A page from the printed edition of 1600. The Prologue, sung by the personification of Tragedy, for soprano and figured bass.

ing and moving, according to contemporary reports. The early Baroque age already had its famous singers; Caccini himself was one of them, as was Vittoria Archilei, who sang the part of Eurydice in Caccini's work.

No overture was included in Peri's or Caccini's *Euridice,* although it is possible that an instrumental introduction was played anyway. The orchestra was small—understandably so in view of its subordinate function—consisting largely of chord instruments. The musicians were seated behind the scenery.

That composers were aware of the novelty of their style can be seen in the title of the first collection of songs in the *stile recitativo:* Caccini's *Le nuove musiche* (*New Music*), published in 1602. The dedications and prefaces accompanying this and other early publications also show that composers felt called upon to explain and defend what they were doing.

These first operas were followed by others in Florence, Rome, and elsewhere. Perhaps because they represented a conscious effort to establish a new category of music—something most unusual in the arts, where new styles are more likely to evolve than be created—they did not achieve lasting popularity. The first major figure in seventeenth-century opera, one who paid little attention to the Camerata's theories and who created a style in many ways his own, was Claudio Monteverdi (1567–1643).

Imaginative and forward-looking, the young Monteverdi wrote music of many kinds and for many occasions, including madrigals, masses, and other sacred works. His musical language, especially his use of dissonance, seemed startling at the time and soon brought strong objections from composers and theorists. Monteverdi defended his manner of writing, stating his belief that music, above all, should faithfully express the meaning of the text. In retrospect it seems natural that his concern with the musical realization of strongly emotional, affective texts should have led Monteverdi to dramatic music.

Claudio Monteverdi, *Orfeo* (Mantua, 1607)

Orfeo is Monteverdi's first preserved opera. The libretto by Alessandro Striggio, a musician and poet of that northern Italian city, was published the same year; the score, dedicated to the ruling prince, appeared two years later. First performed privately at an academy, *Orfeo* was successful enough to be given several performances in court theaters during the next few years. It then fell into oblivion for three centuries; in 1904 it was revived for a Paris performance in concert form. Although it has not become part of the standard repertory, many stage and concert performances since then have proven the appeal of Monteverdi's *favola in musica* (fable set to music) to today's listeners.

To the casual observer, Monteverdi's work may seem little different from those of Caccini or Peri. It deals with the same classical subject, and the pastoral landscape is again populated by nymphs and shepherds given to much choral singing and dancing. It is not surprising that the story of Orpheus and Eurydice should have been such a favorite among early opera composers: according to the legend Orpheus, who is usually pictured playing the lyre, was a musician of extraordinary power. To represent dramatically how his singing and playing affected others has challenged many composers down to our own day. Significantly enough, the scene in which Orpheus pleads with Charon and succeeds in crossing the river Styx forms one of the high points in Monteverdi's opera.

Further similarities exist in the organization of the plot and some of the dramatic devices. Striggio's poem includes a prologue in which again an allegorical figure, Music, appears to inform the listeners of what they will hear. Again important developments do not take place on stage but are related by a messenger, and again the opera has a happy ending, in violation of the ancient myth. The appearance of the printed score is not unlike that of Peri's opera: it is little more than a sketch of what was actually sung and played, especially with regard to the participation of instruments. Similar also is the emphasis on monodic singing as a way of clearly representing the text. In Monteverdi's view, as in that of the Camerata, "L'orazione sia padrone dell'armonia e non serva." ("Let the text be the master of the music, not its servant.")

But while based on similar premises, even this early opera by Monteverdi goes considerably beyond its predecessors. He knew how to combine text and music in a greater variety of ways. His emotional scale ranges from great happiness to profound grief, with many affective contrasts. As a result his work is moving, at least in some scenes, and seems credible as musical drama—timeless, not a museum piece.

Throughout the opera the role of Orpheus is emphasized, far more than that of Eurydice (whose name is not part of the title); he takes part in all important scenes, and it is his participation in events or his reaction to them that evokes compassion in the listener. From the dramatic as well as the purely musical point of view the many pastoral scenes of choral rejoicing seem long. Here Striggio's drama shows its indebtedness to the past—to the courtly intermedi of the Renaissance, in which singing and dancing rather than dramatic continuity were stressed.

Monteverdi's score begins with a toccata, or overture, as we would say today. It is extremely brief, little more than a fanfare

"to be played, before the curtain goes up, by all the instruments,"
with high trumpets being most prominent. It must have created an
imposing effect, for Monteverdi had at his disposal in Mantua
some forty musicians, a large orchestra which he used freely and
imaginatively. The skeletal appearance of the printed score is due
to the fact that only in a few places did it include the instrumental
parts, but specific instructions as to which instruments are to play
appear for many scenes.

Purely instrumental sections are plentiful. They serve structural purposes as well as providing contrast of tone color. Recurring instrumental interludes, or ritornelli, separate sections of the
larger musical complex. The prologue consists of five stanzas with
an almost identical bass for each. The stanzas contain enough
variation to produce an effect of climax in the last one. We hear
the ritornello six times in all. Unusual is its recurrence in several
dramatically important places later in the opera.

The attentive listener will discover much variety in the
soloistic music of *Orfeo*. Longer phrases, brought about by less
frequent cadences, distinguish it from Caccini's and Peri's recitative. Rise and fall of the vocal line, its pacing and phrasing,
depend on the emotion expressed: at times it is calm, at other times
excited and breathless. In Act I the preparations for the wedding
festivities call for choral expressions of general happiness, interrupted only by a few passages of solo singing. The idyllic mood
continues at the beginning of Act II, but the entrance of the
messenger brings a drastic change in the course of the drama—a
change expressed by a startling change of harmony:

EXAMPLE I

[*Messenger: Alas, dreadful event . . .*]

The effect is intensified by a well-calculated contrast in timbre. For the first time in the opera Monteverdi specifies the instruments to accompany the recitative: *organo di legno* (organ with wooden pipes) and *chitarrone* (large lute). The messenger's repeated exclamations of anguish, her voice falling and rising again, are convincing expressions of the tragic news she has to relate. Orpheus, as he listens to her tale, becomes increasingly aware that the terrible event, as yet undisclosed, concerns him. The composer expresses this concern by a succession of rising phrases:

EXAMPLE 2

[*Where do you come from? Where are you going? Nymph, what news do you bring?*]

At the words "La tua diletta sposa è morta" ("Your beloved wife is dead") her voice drops abjectly, as if overcome by the shattering impact of her message. The harmonic progression resulting from this may still startle us today; surely its effect on Monteverdi's audience must have been stronger yet:

EXAMPLE 3

EXAMPLE 3   (*cont.*)

Orpheus is all but speechless—capable of only the exclamation "Ohimè." Such economy of means, such stylized but intense expression of grief may seem more convincing and modern to us than the portrayal of similar sentiments through the carefully constructed verses and coloratura arias of many later operas. Orpheus' moving lament is characterized by much chromaticism; to express intense grief in this way was to remain general musical practice throughout the Baroque era.

It is said that Monteverdi had to work hard to obtain from his singers the desired intensity of expression, a style of singing and acting not yet familiar to performers and audiences of his day.

In some scenes of this early opera the *stile recitativo* approaches the musical quality of an aria. Such condensation characterizes the crucial scene from Act III, mentioned earlier, in which Orpheus' singing succeeds in soothing Charon, the harsh ferryman. To the composer this encounter, a turning point in the action, presented a special challenge; he met it by providing a well-wrought musical structure. Charon's earlier refusal, composed as a set of strophic variations, is answered by Orpheus' "Possente spirto," a song cast in similar form (four stanzas) but rendered far more imploring in two ways. Orpheus' melody here is appropriately elaborate—he is "pulling all the stops"—and for once the score contains an alternate version of the voice part, showing the embellishments that could or should be added according to vocal practices of the time. Further weight is given to this scene by the inclusion of obbligato instrumental parts, the only solo singing in the opera to be distinguished in this way, and probably the first occurrence in operatic history.

Opposite: Orfeo's "Possente spirto": a page from the score, printed with movable type. Two versions of the vocal part are printed: one with, one without ornamentation.

Orfeo al fuono del Organo di legno , & vn Chitairone ,
canta vna fola de le due parti.

Violino.

Violino.

Pollen   te fpir   to   e formi   da

Potente fpir   to   e formida-]

bil nu   me   fenza

bil   nu   me   fenza cui

Choral scenes are more prominent in this opera than in the Florentine works, though they function in a similar manner. Monteverdi's chorus has the classic function of commenting, musically as well as textually, on what has happened.

Dances of many kinds, including choral dances, are included in *Orfeo*. To the historian the sixteenth-century dances may seem incongruous: should gods and heroes of antiquity perform Renaissance dances? The question is equally relevant to later operas on classic themes, e.g., the *Orfeo* of Gluck with its gavottes and chaconnes. It is unlikely that Monteverdi's audience was bothered by anachronisms of this kind, the less so since their knowledge of the nature of Greek dance was even more limited than their knowledge of Greek music. A look at costuming of the Baroque age confirms that this lack of concern with historical realism was widespread and not restricted to opera. Many illustrations have come down to us in which Greek, Roman, or Oriental characters appear in seventeenth-century costume, complete with hoopskirts and powdered wigs.

Monteverdi ends his opera with a popular dance of the sixteenth century, the morisca. With it he leads us back from the Greek tragedy-with-happy-end to the atmosphere of Mantuan court festivity.

Orpheus and Eurydice acclaimed by shepherds.

In its early stages, opera was an aristocratic entertainment, performed for the prince who had commissioned it, for his family and invited guests. A large hall in his palace might serve as theater, or there might be an open-air theater in the park surrounding the castle. The ruler and his immediate family sat on a raised platform in the center, with courtiers, attendants, guards, and others behind and flanking them. From its very beginnings, then, opera performances were important social as well as musical events—a state of affairs that has continued to affect many aspects of operatic life to the present day (see below, Chapter 17).

Throughout the Baroque era ancient mythology continued as the favored subject matter for opera. This should not surprise us, for a similar interest in the civilization of Greece and Rome, awakened during the Renaissance, continued to be manifest in painting, sculpture, and other arts. But aside from the classicizing intent of the Camerata, an explanation can be seen in the nature of Greek drama with its concentration on basic conflicts, involving both gods and mortals; on tragic situations in which intense emotions were displayed. Historical subjects were gradually added to mythology, at first with an emphasis on ancient history.

Monteverdi's last opera, *L'incoronazione di Poppea,* 1642, is an early example of the historical opera—a remarkable one at that, its main characters being drawn with surprising realism. Nero, Ottavia, Poppea, and Seneca appear as men and women of flesh and blood (though, in keeping with a convention of the time, the part of Nero was written for a castrato, a male soprano), involved in a drama of strong passions, rather than as personifications of courage, wisdom, and other virtues. Nor does virtue or justice triumph in the end, for Nero banishes his wife and has his mistress, Poppea, crowned as empress. An ardent love duet for Nero and Poppea provides the happy end.

A few years before *Poppea* appeared in Venice an event occurred in that city that was to be of great consequence for the future of opera: the Teatro S. Cassiano opened its doors to the public. Other theaters soon followed. Perhaps as a result, Venice in the seventeenth and early eighteenth centuries developed an operatic life of a vigor and dimensions that we can hardly imagine today. At times the visitor could choose among the offerings of seventeen opera houses, with little if any duplication of repertory. Venice had been a republic for some time, and it seems fitting that in her theaters all classes of society should mix, from princes and foreign ambassadors to the gondoliers whose witty, scathing, or obscene remarks often interrupted a performance.

This does not mean that class distinctions were altogether disregarded in the public theaters of Venice and other cities. Opera houses continued to be owned and financed by members of the nobility who insisted on attending performances in privacy. To achieve this and particularly to protect their ladies from contact with the common crowd, the box theater gradually replaced the amphitheater of the Renaissance.[13] Boxes, arranged in several tiers, were rented by noble families, for the season or longer periods, while admission to the main floor was open to anyone willing to pay.[14] The boxes often were quite comfortably furnished, provided with anterooms in which refreshments might be taken and with curtains to give complete privacy when desired. In contrast to these comfortable arrangements, the main floor provided no seats or benches. Here again the social aspects of opera are in evidence: the opera house was a place where one could meet friends and make the acquaintance of well-chaperoned members of the fair sex.

Once operas were performed for an admission-paying public, the profit motive tended to affect many aspects of its presentation

[13] The change is traced by Herbert Graf in *Producing Opera for America* (New York, 1961), pp. 19 ff.

[14] Slightly different arrangements were observed in some places. In Berlin under Frederick the Great, the first-tier boxes were reserved for the court; the second tier for other nobility, with citizens admitted to the third tier. All were to dress according to rules laid down by the King. Helmut Schmidt-Garre, *Oper— eine Kulturgeschichte* (Cologne, 1963), pp. 102 f.

The Teatro Olimpico in Vicenza, Italy, showing the amphitheater seating plan typical during the Renaissance. Engraving by F. Zucchi, ca. 1730.

and even its composition. The manager now might look for works that would bring in the crowds, that contained startling incidents and provided opportunities for spectacular staging. Hand in hand with this went the desire to present singers with strong popular appeal: the age of the virtuoso, the star performer, had begun. The profit motive showed itself in other ways, uncomfortably reminiscent of modern practices: while considerable sums were spent to hire a famous *cantatrice,* corners would be cut elsewhere to save money. Many operas of this period lack a chorus altogether, have a small cast, and use an orchestra of modest size. Handel, in his Italian operas, treated the chorus in a very perfunctory way, while in his oratorios, written for different performance conditions, large (eight-part) and long choruses occur.[15]

A curious mixture of history and fiction characterized the treatment of historical subjects for some time to come. An incident from history usually provided the librettist with a point of departure; to this he freely added intrigues, love affairs, and other *accidenti* of his own invention. Many a Hollywood drama has appropriated this procedure, with good results at the box office. Plots often were extremely complicated, with many secondary characters. Only toward the end of the era, for instance in the librettos of Metastasio (1698–1782), did a reduction in their number and a concentration on the essential dramatic conflicts bring about a tightening up of librettos.

But unlike *Poppea's* principals, the heroes and heroines of many Baroque operas fail to convince us because they display rigid emotions and character qualities rather than the mixture of feelings, the more subtle and conflicting emotions that would make them truly human in our eyes. Many plots impress us as contrived and stereotyped, constructed according to formulas in which the solution is easily predicted, or seems forced and poorly motivated. Myths and other plots served to glorify the ruler; the wisdom, virtue, and magnanimity displayed on stage were represented as qualities that he also possessed. The prologue, in which the attending prince might be addressed directly and obsequiously, made this quite clear.

These dramatic shortcomings exist not only in retrospect. Of the many aspects of Baroque opera that were criticized at the time, the weak plots and their unconvincing solutions received their full share of attention. Benedetto Marcello's satire *Il teatro alla moda*

---

[15] It has been claimed that in the London of Handel's time the chorus parts were sung by the soloists, i.e., as ensembles. This could lead to a situation where the singer of the title role, a king, would have to sing along, backstage, with the "chorus" of those who were plotting against him. J. Eisenschmidt, *Die szenische Darstellung der Opern G. F. Händels auf der Londoner Bühne seiner Zeit* (Wolfenbüttel, 1940/41), Vol. II, p. 87.

A contemporary cartoon by Hogarth testifying to the popularity of "The Beggar's Opera" by John Gay (1728). No one pays attention to the Italian opera being performed on the adjoining stage. "Harmony" turns her back on the (by implication) coarse "Beggar's Opera."

(Venice, ca. 1720) contains scathing and frequently witty remarks:

[The impresario] should urge the librettist to write truly stunning scenes, to be sure to employ the bear at the end of each act, to close the opera with the usual wedding scene or with the finding, at long last, of a certain person whose identity may be established through the aid of oracles, a star on his chest, a band around his ankle, or moles on his knees, tongue, and ears.[16]

Strange to say, to have one of the principal characters turn out to be someone's long-lost son, recognized by a mole or birthmark, continued to be a popular device in operas well into the nineteenth century (Mozart's *Figaro;* even Smetana's *Bartered Bride,* 1866). The only thing to be said for them is that such sudden revelations result in strongly emotional situations and hence are good for music. Or one might try to understand them by remembering that mixups and revelations of this kind were more

[16] English translation in *The Musical Quarterly* (hereafter abbreviated *MQ*), July, 1948, and January, 1949.

likely in ages when travel and other forms of communication were arduous and uncertain, and when birth certificates, passports, and other documentation were not insisted upon.

The intervention of a *deus ex machina* as a way of bringing about a happy ending is, of course, based on classic precedents. Peri's and Monteverdi's librettists made use of it; we find it in much Baroque opera after that. Even Kurt Weill's *Threepenny Opera* (1928, text by Brecht; based on Gay's *Beggar's Opera*, 1728) reminds us, in jesting fashion, of this practice: the king's messenger arrives on horseback, in the nick of time, bringing a totally unmotivated pardon for the about-to-be-hanged prisoner.

Baroque opera continued to favor the elaborate scenery of the earlier intermedi. As opera acquired a larger, admission-paying public, the desire to attract and please an audience by rich decor and stunning machines may already have influenced the writing of an opera, as well as its production. Venetian operas by Marc Antonio Cesti (1623–1669) and his contemporaries have innumerable scene changes and give opportunities for much display. When Cesti was appointed to the imperial court in Vienna this style became well established there. His *Pomo d'oro*, 1666, was one of the most splendid productions in operatic history.

Italian stage designers acquired fame with their lavish productions at many European courts. Among the best known were Giovanni and Lodovico Burnacini, active in Vienna, Venice, and

A performance of Cesti's "Pomo d'oro" in Vienna, 1667, upon the occasion of the wedding of Emperor Leopold I and Margarita of Spain. The theater was built by Ludovico Burnacini, who also designed the sets and costumes. The opera, in three acts, with sixty-seven scene changes, employed a cast of a thousand.

elsewhere: Giacomo Torelli, who went to the court of Louis XIV, and, in the eighteenth century, several members of the Galli-Bibiena family who designed sets in Berlin, Dresden, Munich, and other cities. Architects and engineers outdid themselves in constructing machinery to make possible the appearance of gods and goddesses on clouds or in flying chariots, to produce earthquakes, volcanic eruptions, great floods, naval battles, and a wealth of other spectacular effects. Entire books written on this subject testify to the vogue and importance of theatrical machinery.[17] The scenic requirements of Italian Baroque opera must have taxed the ingenuity of stage artists, the financial resources of the manager, and, because of the time required for scene changes, the public's patience, although in a less sophisticated and hurried age spectators may have found these attractions breathtaking and well worth waiting for.

For festive occasions at court, productions often were specially lavish. Fux's opera *Angelica vincitrice,* 1716, is a good example, to judge by the eyewitness account by Lady Montague:

I have, indeed, so far wandered from the discipline of the Church of England, as to have been last Sunday at the opera . . . and I was so much pleased with it, I have not yet repented my seeing it. Nothing of that kind ever was more magnificent; and I can easily believe, what I was told, that the decorations and habits cost the emperor thirty thousand pound sterling. The stage was built over a very large canal, and, at the beginning of the second act, divided into two parts, discovering the water, on which there immediately came from different parts two fleets of little gilded vessels, that gave the representation of a naval fight. It is not easy to imagine the beauty of this scene, which I took particular notice of: but all the rest were perfectly fine in their kind. The story of the opera was the enchantment of Alcina, which gives opportunities for great variety of machines and changes of the scenes, which are performed with a surprising swiftness. The theatre is so large that 'tis hard to carry the eye to the end of it; and the habits in the utmost magnificence, to the number of one hundred and eight. No house could hold such large decorations; but the ladies all sitting in the open air, exposes them to great inconveniences; for there is but one canopy for the imperial family; and, the first night it was represented, a heavy shower of rain happening, the opera was broke off, and the company crowded away in such confusion, but I was almost squeezed to death.[18]

In the course of the seventeenth century the continuous style of early operatic monody gave way to a separation of functions: the action of the opera unfolded in recitative while arias presented

---

[17] E.g., Nicola Sabbatini's *Pratica di fabricar scene* (Ravenna, 1639).
[18] Letter of September 14, 1716, as quoted by J. H. Van der Meer, *Johann Josef Fux als Opernkomponist* (Bilthoven, 1961), Vol. I, p. 147.

points of rest in the dramatic continuity. They were given over to the expression of the basic affections—the reaction of the person or persons involved in the situation that had arisen. Librettos soon were tailored to this convention.

Differences of function were coupled with musical differences. Just as the recitative became increasingly simple, losing much of the expressiveness of the measured *stile recitativo,* the arias developed in the opposite direction, becoming self-contained musical structures. *Secco* (Italian, "dry") recitative, in which the singer was accompanied only by sparse chords on a harpsichord or other chord instrument, was the musical vehicle for most of the dialogue. In moments of great emotional significance, the recitative was accompanied by the orchestra. Secco and accompagnato recitative have the more or less speechlike, nonmetrical voice part in common (see Examples 4 and 5).

Secco recitative (Handel, *Serse,* 1738, II/6)   EXAMPLE 4

[*Since my grief will not give me death, this sword shall kill me!*]

Accompagnato recitative (*Serse,* II/5)   EXAMPLE 5

EXAMPLE 5   (*cont.*)

for- se sa-per bra-ma-te   la mia fu-ria cru-de-le   o - ra chi si - a?

[*But you who hear my raving—do you wish to know the cause of my cruel suffering?*]

Arias varying greatly in length and structure and treating the voice and the accompaniment in many different ways appear in operas from Monteverdi's time on. A growing concentration on the aria, by composers and public, characterizes opera through the Baroque period and beyond. Composers were known to turn over the writing of recitative to their pupils; audiences, according to many descriptions of the time, frequently paid no attention during the recitative and would interrupt their visiting and conversing only when the orchestra was heard in the introduction to the next aria.

Secco recitative may seem strange and downright unmusical to the modern listener who hears it for the first time, especially if it is sung in a foreign language. But there must be reasons that it should have remained so firmly established for almost two hundred years. For one thing, it has advantages for the singer-actor. To sing secco recitative requires less expenditure of physical energy than to render an aria. To have the action—and therefore the singer—come to a stand-still for the aria makes it possible for the singer to devote his attention and energy to singing. (To some extent he must remain an actor even while singing an aria, as we noted in Chapter 2 above.) Nor does the speechlike reciting tone of secco recitative differ very drastically from another type of singing with which audiences, especially in Roman Catholic countries, were well familiar: the various styles of Gregorian chant, including the recitation tones for psalms and other parts of the liturgy. It is true that secco recitative often is sung so fast as to render it practically unintelligible and musically meaningless, but this need not be so. In Vienna the secco recitative of Mozart's operas is sung quite deliberately. To hear it is to realize how closely it expresses the textual meaning.

In many performances of Italian operas today the secco recitative is cut considerably, particularly if sung for audiences who do not understand Italian. This is also done in the interest of the swifter dramatic pace expected by twentieth-century audiences. Similar cuts are customary in operas with spoken dialogue, e.g., Beethoven's *Fidelio*. Many stage directors believe that what remains unsaid can be expressed equally well through gestures or facial expression.

It is part of the general stylization of Baroque opera that its foremost musical ingredient, the aria, also developed certain favored formal arrangements—aria types that are found again and again. Baroque arias have been listed and classified by many writers,[19] not only according to structure and musical style but also according to subject matter. The da capo aria represents a basic structural concept, subject to many refinements, that was widely and increasingly accepted during this age. A typical da capo aria of the middle and late Baroque starts with an orchestral introduction, the beginning of which may anticipate the singer's first few notes. At the end of the first main section a full cadence in the tonic key is reached, often indicated by a fermata or the word *"fine"* (end). A section in a contrasting key follows; it may be in a related minor key if the first part was in major. The contrast may extend to the mood of both text and music of this middle section, at the end of which the letters "d.c." (*da capo*, "from the head," i.e., repeat from the beginning) indicate a return to the opening, which is then repeated. In performance it was this repetition of the first section which called for the greatest virtuosity. Here the singer was expected to display his skill by introducing variations and embellishments.

The ritornello, i.e., the instrumental opening and conclusion of the aria, admittedly had a practical dramatic function as well as a musical one: it served as a signal for the singer to come on stage and it gave him time to exit with music.

Isolated applications of the da capo principle can already be recognized in Monteverdi's *Orfeo,* but the vogue of the da capo aria begins in the second half of the seventeenth century. Many operas by Alessandro Scarlatti and his contemporaries consist of a virtually unbroken succession of secco recitatives and da capo arias, the latter sometimes structures of large dimensions, containing several subdivisions and instrumental interludes.

---

[19] Grout quotes several eighteenth-century descriptions. *SHO,* pp. 185 ff.

Along with the da capo aria other types continue to be found, among them the short strophic aria. It is easy to see why the aria, musically concise and hence easier to remember, should have had greater popular appeal than the continuous style of the earliest musical dramas.

Arias with an instrumental obbligato were frequent. Trumpet arias seem to have had much appeal; at times they led to a virtual contest in which the singer and the instrumental soloist would match their skill and endurance, especially in embellishing the da capo section.

Arias were also classified according to their function and place in the drama. "Exit arias" occur in most Baroque operas: the singer, having finished his aria, leaves the stage. Their popularity is a commentary on the reign of the singer, since an effective exit was almost certain to bring applause, then as now. Exit arias still occur in Mozart's time and beyond; there are several in *Figaro*.

Comparison arias, to mention one more type, also were frequent. The term refers to a poetic rather than musical characteristic: a person's state of mind is compared to an object or activity from the world of reality, especially from nature. Comparisons of this kind were very popular. They may seem hackneyed to us, but their imagery usually provided the composer with an opportunity for tone painting. We shall find examples in Handel's *Julius Caesar:* others, again, occur in Mozart.

Convention also regulated to a large degree the number and kinds of arias that were to appear in an opera seria. Stendhal's description of conditions in the late eighteenth century are valid for the late Baroque as well, being based on the typical Metastasian libretto.

The operas of Metastasio have charmed not only Italy but all that is intellectual in every court of Europe, merely by the observation of the following simple, and commodious rules. In every drama six characters are required, all lovers. The three principal actors, namely, the *primo soprano,* the *prima donna,* and the *tenore,* must each sing five airs: an impassioned air (*aria patetica*), a brilliant air (*aria di bravura*), a tranquil air (*aria parlante*), an air of mixed character [somewhat less serious]; and, lastly, an air which breathes joy (*aria brillante*). It is requisite that the drama should be divided into three acts, and not to exceed a certain number of verses; that each scene should terminate with an air; that the same personage should not sing two airs in succession, and that two airs of the same character should never follow one another. It is necessary that the first and second acts should conclude with the principal airs of the piece. It is required that, in the second and third acts, the poet should reserve two suitable places, one for a *recitativo obligato* [i.e., accompagnato], followed by an air for display [of virtuosity] (*aria di tranbusto*); the other for a grand duet which must always be sung by the hero and heroine of the piece. Without attending to these rules, there can be no music.[20]

With the function of an aria thus regulated by convention it was only natural that an aria of a certain type might be lifted out of one opera and transplanted to the appropriate place in another, with or without the composer's consent. Substitutions of this kind were frequent in the Baroque and continued into the Classic era. Some later operas still provide a place for the insertion of another composer's aria; Rossini's *Barber of Seville* does so in the "Lesson Scene."

A tendency toward purely soloistic writing characterized Italian opera after the mid-seventeenth century. Ensemble and choral scenes were on the decrease. In duets the participants alternated rather than singing together. By the time of Scarlatti or Handel, choruses, if any, consisted of little more than simple, homophonic exclamations, usually reserved for the ends of acts. Except for important performances at court the orchestra was small; only a few woodwinds, trumpets, and eventually horns were

---

[20] *The Lives of Haydn and Mozart, with Observations on Metastasio . . . translated from the French . . .* (London, 1818), pp. 445 f.

added to the strings. Many arias, especially before 1700, had basso continuo accompaniment only. The sinfonia or overture was an independent instrumental piece, not thematically related to the opera that followed. Here, too, a formal pattern was favored: a rapid, vigorous opening section is followed by a contrasting episode, frequently in minor; this once more leads to a rapid section, often in one of the dance rhythms of the time. The dance may be purely instrumental, or it may constitute the opening scene of the opera, with dancing on the stage.

OPERA SERIA AND OPERA BUFFA

Our survey of Baroque opera so far has dealt only with the serious subject matter of religion, myth, and history—with *opera seria*. But lighter fare soon found its way to the operatic stage. Just when or why the first comic sketches with music, called intermezzi, were presented between the acts of opera seria cannot be determined accurately. They may have served to entertain the audience during the time needed for scene changes, for they were given in front of the curtain. A three-act opera would bring two sketches; a five-act work might have room for four. At first each intermezzo was self-contained; in time they presented a continuous plot, forming a small opera within the opera seria. Dramatically they stood in welcome contrast to the lofty subject matter and flowery language of the latter, which they parodied at times. They dealt primarily with amusing incidents from everyday life, of a kind well-known to the audience.

The growing popularity of *opera buffa* may have had a sociological basis. Opera drew a growing portion of its audience from the middle, and occasionally even the lower, classes. To these the glorification of a prince, by way of allegory drawn from ancient myths, offered nothing with which they could identify, whereas the marital squabbles of a Neapolitan fisherman, or the chambermaid who outwitted her mistress, or the clumsy farmer speaking thick dialect all belonged within the realm of their experience. To watch the wit or stupidity of these characters on stage delighted the audience; at times it provided them with an outlet for making fun of their aristocratic masters.

In many ways we can look at the rise of opera buffa as an aspect of the Enlightenment—a reaction to the "unnaturalness" of opera seria. Comic opera presented ordinary people, speaking naturally, often in dialect. It is to be expected that their music should be simple and natural, avoiding coloratura and lengthy arias, all the more so since the singers (at least in the early history of intermezzo and opera buffa) were not highly trained musicians. Nor was the unnatural voice of the castrato heard there.

Pergolesi's *La serva padrona* (*The Maid as Mistress,* Naples, 1733), one of the earliest examples still performed today, was originally heard between the acts of the same composer's opera seria *Il prigioner superbo.* Like most intermezzi it requires a very modest cast: three actors, of whom only two sing. The accompaniment also is simple. A characteristic of the music, aside from the lightness mentioned above, is the rapid declamation, with many word repetitions, suggesting the "patter song" we know from nineteenth-century light opera. Secco recitative is consistently used in eighteenth-century opera buffa, while spoken dialogue characterizes contemporary French and German light opera. An important soliloquy in *La serva padrona* calls for accompanied recitative. In general the accompaniment remains in the background; the violins are often led in unison with the voice.

Baroque opera buffa usually included roles for the bass voice, largely absent from opera seria, and ensemble scenes, particularly at the end of an act. These ensembles were both dramatically and musically lively; i.e., they advanced the action and provided a rousing finale. Mozart's masterful finales, especially in *Figaro* and *Don Giovanni,* stem from this tradition; in fact, most writers of light opera since then have found it effective to bring all characters back on stage for such an ensemble-finale.

With opera flourishing in so many cities and theaters, the number of works written and produced was staggering. Only in exceptional cases would a work be repeated in successive seasons; the normal procedure was to bring out a new work, to perform it until public interest began to lag, then to bring out something else composed for the occasion. Audiences expected this large turnover; as a result there was no such thing as today's standard repertory. "Everything was instantly staged, cheered, plundered for the coming seasons, and then thrown away" (Kerman). Since no copyright protection existed, composer and librettist were virtually forced to provide new works each season; they would not have profited from performances elsewhere, at a later date. Often the impresario "owned" an opera for two years, taking in any profits, and paying the composer a flat fee.

The opera's libretto was usually printed, while the score was not. The poet's name appeared in the libretto; only rarely the composer's. For the poet the sale of librettos was a welcome source of income. By dedicating his work to the local prince or to some other dignitary he could expect an additional fee. The extremely flowery and subservient language of many dedicatory prefaces to librettos make this intent all too obvious.

If he decides to dedicate his work to some personage of high position he should be sure that that gentleman has money rather than culture. . . . He should sing hymns of praise to the glory of that person's family and ancestors, and he should not fail to use as frequently as possible terms such as *magnanimity* and *generosity*. . . . He should close with a phrase of utmost reverence, saying, for instance, that he "kisses the leaps of the fleas on the legs of the dogs of His Excellency.[21]

[21] Marcello, *Il teatro alla moda,* "Instructions for Librettists" (see above, footnote 16).

In the hierarchy of Baroque opera neither composer nor librettist equaled in importance the famous singer of either sex. This state of affairs persisted for some time to come, so that a soprano at the Vienna court opera around 1780 received more than twice the salary of Gluck, the court composer. Male sopranos and altos, the castratos, achieved fame in both opera and church music. Their vogue can in part be explained by edicts at various times and places against the appearance of women singers in church or on the public stage. One of the most famous castratos was Carlo Broschi, better known as Farinelli (1705–1782). He possessed a voice of exceptional range, agility, and penetrating power, and earned a fortune as well as the admiration and friendship of poets and kings. That the role of a mighty ruler or valiant general should be entrusted to a soprano voice reflects on the Baroque aesthetic of opera: a lack of concern with dramatic realism and an overwhelming interest in the purely musical appeal of the voice. This outlook applied to opera seria only; in opera buffa, based on subjects from everyday life, castratos did not appear.

Operas often were written and produced with amazing speed. An impresario might buy a libretto for a modest fee and turn it over to a composer, at the same time assembling a troupe of singers. They would learn the individual arias as they were readied by the composer, frequently out of context. Within a few weeks the production would be ready and the first performance, anxiously awaited by the townspeople, could take place, with the composer directing from the harpsichord. If the opera was successful many would go to hear it every night—it was "the thing to do." Under these circumstances it is no wonder that audience interest was focused chiefly on the music and its performance, with its daily imponderables, changes, and surprises, rather than on the drama or on the dialogue, carried on in recitative.

Stage rehearsals were apt to be few, and devoted to the working of gadgets and machinery more than to acting, which was regulated by many conventions. Singers customarily entered from the wings and remained on the side from which they had made their entrance. As more singers entered they would appear alternatingly from right and left, arranging themselves symmetrically. There was little moving around on the stage; singers would "deliver" their arias from the position they originally assumed. Acting was stylized: certain body positions, motions of hands, etc., traditionally expressed certain emotions. A lady's handkerchief held before her eyes sufficed to indicate grief. The prima donna not only made certain that her part contained more lines and more arias than that of the seconda donna; she often insisted on precedence on the stage, standing on the right side, preferably one step forward.

Costuming, it has already been said, was fantastic rather than realistic. Warriors were apt to appear in more or less Roman attire regardless of the period or locale in which the opera took place. In general, a hero was recognized by a plume on his helmet; its excessive size may have caused worry and discomfort to the actor. The prima donna sometimes had a small page boy with her on the stage (though he was not one of the characters in the drama) merely to arrange her train. To be allowed the services of such a page boy became a status symbol fought over by rival singers. These and other conventions of costuming and acting provided welcome targets for satirical criticism. Even during this age it seemed incongruous to have a queen engage in motions and gestures of despair while the page boy dutifully tried to make her train look pretty.

Stage lighting, dim by our standards, was not expected to be realistic. Chandeliers served to light up the stage even if the scene represented a forest. Though the equipment of the age was limited, special effects such as multicolored revolving lights contributed to the overall dazzling impression of many a finale. The auditorium was not completely dark, for many spectators followed the libretto with the light of a candle.

The tremendously vigorous operatic life of the Baroque was

The famous castrato Senesino singing a duet with Francesca Cuzzoni. An anonymous satirical print, possibly by Hogarth, ca. 1725.

ruled by Italy. Italian maestri, virtuosi, and prime donne were in evidence everywhere, setting the style and the mannerisms. Italian composers held the leading positions at most European courts, and Handel, a German, wrote Italian operas for London audiences. Metastasio was court poet in Vienna; he was universally admired though he never mastered the German language. The general fondness, not to say craze, for Italian opera was furthered by the intermarriage of royalty: an Italian prince might reign in Austria, while a German-speaking ruler over an Italian province might have acquired a taste for opera there—a taste that he would also wish to indulge when he returned to his home land.

Italy's leading position lasted through the Classic era. It was successfully challenged in the nineteenth century, but to the present day Italian opera holds the most prominent place on stages and in the repertory of singers all over the world.

OPERA IN FRANCE

The highly developed political absolutism of seventeenth-century France affected her cultural life as well. In a society in which a monarch ruled by divine right, court life served to reflect his glory, through much ceremonial and display, from the ritual of the *lever* to elaborate festivities of many kinds. Opera, as a specially lavish and expensive form of art, figured prominently among the entertainments in Paris and Versailles.

When Cardinal Mazarin, an Italian by birth, rose to a position of political importance at the French court, he soon used his influence to bring Italian opera to Paris. Among early presentations was Luigi Rossi's *Orfeo* in 1647. Cavalli, the Venetian composer, was called to Paris, writing his *Ercole amante* for the wedding of Louis XIV (1660). But the principal figure in the colorful history of French Baroque opera was Jean-Baptiste Lully (1632–1687), a Florentine by birth whose phenomenal career at the French court began around 1653. Lully was asked to write ballets for several Cavalli operas, thus making them more palatable for Paris audiences, but these works aside, Italian opera did not succeed in Paris. To develop a characteristically French operatic style became a patriotic issue. The opening of the Académie Royale de Musique, as the opera house was called, with Robert Cambert's *Pomone* (1671) forms a milestone in this development. French opera remained much closer to spoken drama than Italian opera had. Significantly enough it was Molière who bought the privilege to present operas in Paris. Lully, who collaborated with the famous playwright in a number of works, eventually succeeded in pushing back all competitors. After Molière's death he was the undisputed ruler of French opera until his own death.

During this age French opera was characterized by more carefully fashioned drama, by noble, elevated language, by the absence of castratos and of the comic roles that had found their way into opera seria, and by arias that were short, simple, and lacking in coloratura display. Airs in AAB form, rather than da capo arias (ABA form), predominate, and secco recitative is altogether absent.

Lully studied the delivery of actors and actresses at the Comédie Française; in his own works he paid careful attention, in both airs and recitatives, to the prosody of the French language. The recitatives, as a result, have frequent changes of meter. A demanding director of his own works, he insisted that his singers take no liberties with his music and pay close attention to clarity of diction. High standards of performance, also in the well-drilled orchestra, contributed to the success of Lully's *tragédies en musique*. During his time ballet continued to be cultivated at the French court; the operas themselves also included much dancing. Arias and instrumental pieces in dance rhythms were frequent. The many choral scenes also added to the magnificence of processions, sacrifices, and other massed scenes—*divertissements* more or less closely connected with the main action.

The typical Lully overture begins with a slow passage in dotted rhythm, followed by a lively section with some imitation, and usually concluded by another stately part, briefer than the first. Eventually this kind of overture, which came to be known as a French overture, served as the opening of other, nonoperatic kinds of music as well, e.g., the instrumental suite of Bach's time.

Favored by royalty and the public, Lully's operas remained popular in France for some time.[22] *Armide* (1686), one of his most celebrated works, maintained itself in the repertory for 78 years. After Lully's death his style at first was widely imitated, but Italian elements again found their way into opera in Paris, adding a lighter quality. Lighter instrumentation and more da capo arias are among these Italian features.

Outside of France Lully's operas failed to establish themselves, perhaps because they were so closely connected with court life under the Sun King. Music is an international language, and while the predominantly musical attractions of Italian opera prepared the way for its worldwide acceptance, French Baroque opera, appealing (through its language) to the intellect as well as the senses, could not duplicate this success.

The popularity of opera buffa sparked many rounds of lively literary criticism and debate in the French capital, causing a sharp division of public opinion and leading to the celebrated "War of the Buffoons," in which partisans of French opera and opera buffa attacked each other violently in hundreds of pamphlets. It

---

[22] The scores, by royal command, were printed—hence the magnificent early editions of opera scores from France.

also accounts in part for the limited success of the last major composer of French Baroque opera, Jean-Philippe Rameau (1683–1764). Known also as a composer of instrumental works, an organist and theorist, Rameau turned to the writing of opera rather late in life. *Hippolyte et Aricie,* 1733, his first opera, caused widespread criticism from those who wanted to see Lully's style perpetuated. Other works did poorly because of inferior librettos. While incorporating many typically French qualities, Rameau's scores display greater harmonic variety and expressiveness than do Lully's, partly because of their far-reaching modulations. Essentially harmonic, chordal thinking is noticeable in Rameau's many substantial choruses. A well-developed sense for colorful and effective orchestral writing further characterizes his style, manifest in many ballet scenes and purely instrumental pieces descriptive of some stage action. Rameau's operas and opéra-ballets[23] still are expressions of the magnificence and pomp of eighteenth-century French court life. Though they are period pieces they characterize their period well enough to have been successful in some recent revivals (e.g., *Les Indes galantes* at the Paris Opera).

OPERA IN ENGLAND

In the first hundred years of its existence opera did not become fully established or acclimated in England. The scarcity of English operas, and certain characteristics of those that were written, can be related to developments in seventeenth-century English history.

In the masque, popular as court entertainment in sixteenth- and seventeenth-century England, prominence was accorded to staging and dancing rather than to music. The spoken dialogue and simple airs customary in the masque affected the style of opera as well, and recitative was slow in becoming established.

Under the Commonwealth and Protectorate (1649–1660) the theaters were closed, but private performances continued to take place. Actually, the ban of spoken plays somewhat furthered the cause of opera, since with the addition of music theatrical performances could be considered "concerts." William Davenant, a playwright and successful producer of masques until the theaters were closed, thus was able to present his *Siege of Rhodes* (1656; the music is lost). In the preface he expresses regret that recitative is "unpracticed here, though of great reputation among other nations." Davenant had lived in Paris, where he had become acquainted with Italian opera, supported there by Cardinal Mazarin.

Some of the works performed during the Commonwealth are

---

23 In an opéra-ballet the action is not continuous, each act being a dramatic entity and containing insertions (*divertissements* of singing and dancing) having only a tenuous connection to the plot.

not easily classified. Matthew Locke's *Cupid and Death* (1653) contains elements of both masque and opera, with recitatives, songs, choruses, and much dancing.

Following the accession of Charles II in 1660, England witnessed a general orientation to French culture and court life, with Louis XIV setting the style. Stage plays were allowed again, but plays with incidental music, often splendidly staged, proved more popular than opera. (Matthew Locke, for instance, wrote music to accompany Shakespeare's *The Tempest* and *Macbeth*.) John Blow's *Venus and Adonis* (ca. 1682), though called a masque, actually is a small and simple opera, showing a mixture of Italian, French, and English characteristics. Purcell's *Dido and Aeneas* appeared a few years later—the only English opera of the century generally known today. As Blow's pupil and successor at Westminster Abbey, Purcell probably knew *Venus and Adonis*.

Henry Purcell, *Dido and Aeneas* (London, 1689)

The brevity of *Dido and Aeneas* (approximately an hour) and small instrumentation (strings and harpsichord) put it into the category of chamber opera, a category in which there is renewed interest today. Purcell wrote the work for a girls' school in Chelsea; practical considerations in all likelihood account for the chamber qualities and for the predominantly female cast.

Purcell's librettist, Nahum Tate, eventually became poet laureate. No successful stage works of Tate survive, and it is doubtful that he had real dramatic talent. His verses for *Dido and Aeneas* certainly do not reveal any, though it has often been pointed out that they inspired Purcell to write an opera of consummate beauty.

The story of *Dido and Aeneas* is found in Vergil's *Aeneid*. In essence Tate's libretto follows the Roman poet; a prologue, invented by Tate, was not set to music. A seventeenth-century flavor is imparted to the classic tale by various additions, principally the witches' scenes. Brevity and extreme concentration, perhaps demanded by the occasion, result in a plot that is unusually simple for serious Baroque opera, yet this very simplicity contributes to the opera's appeal today. Economy of language is the chief strength of Tate's libretto. Aeneas' bow to fate, for instance, is expressed in a few simple lines:

> How can so hard a fate be took?
> One night enjoyed, the next, forsook.
> Yours be the blame, ye gods, for I obey your will,
> But with more ease could die.

The opera has no secondary plots. Since the tragic story is told so simply, Tate provided contrast and typical Baroque flavor in a number of lively scenes. Inserted in the right places they succeed in dispelling the serious mood. Being, for the most part, choral scenes, they also provide contrast of musical texture.

Stylization again is the key to Tate's portrayal of the protagonists, especially of Dido, the only one to emerge as a sensitive and complex individual. The essence of her emotions, which she hesitates to reveal fully, even to herself, is contained in but a few lines:

> Ah, Belinda, I am prest
> With torment not to be confest;
> Peace and I are strangers grown,
> Yet would not have it guessed.

Her "yielding to love" at the end of Act I is apparent from no lines of her own; only Belinda sings that Dido's "eyes confess the flame her tongue denies." Pleading with Aeneas, she urges and demands that he leave her: her faith has been disappointed and her pride injured. After his exit her disconsolate state is revealed by simple words movingly set to music.

EXAMPLE 6

But death, a-las!__ I can-not shun: Death__must come when he is__ gone.

The brief choral interpolation that follows does not dispel that mood; it reigns throughout the famous final scene, Dido's farewell.

Aeneas' part rarely even approximates this intensity; his is largely a supporting role. Only in his last encounter with the queen, after the appearance of Mercury, does he rise to comparable stature. Purcell gave him no arias, a musical indication that the part was conceived on a lower emotional level. (Perhaps the singer's ability also was involved.) Belinda's function in the drama, as the queen's lady-in-waiting and confidante, likewise is one of support; she has few opportunities to display any individuality. In several scenes she acts as the leader of the chorus.

Among the choruses, those of the witches achieve greatest dramatic importance. Conjuring scenes were frequent in both Italian and French Baroque opera; Purcell's work follows this tradition, including the apparition of an evil spirit, here disguised as Mercury. Neither the sailors nor the several choruses of courtiers or "people" are as close to the dramatic action.

Dido and Aeneas contains no spoken dialogue. The recitative is accompanied throughout, pointing to French rather than Italian models. Purcell's manner of treating the recitative is well adapted to English prosody, carefully articulated and measured. It moves swiftly, though a more deliberate pace is implied where the solemnity of the occasion might demand it. It avoids the numerous word repetitions found, for purely musical reasons, in the arias. Occasional affective words ("storm," "valor," "fierce") are emphasized by coloraturas.

As Dido's reproaches of Aeneas increase in fervor, the pace of their exchange accelerates. Dido angrily repeats his words and music—"by all that's good." Shorter phrases and a faster harmonic pace give a realistic quality to the scene. Words or thoughts with strongly emotional significance are, in accord with custom, given dissonant harmonies (see, e.g., "weep," "hate"). And abrupt changes from major to minor, often found in Purcell's music, serve to establish new situations musically.

Much of the incantation scene (Act I, Scene 2) is carried on in recitative. The entire scene shows the composer's skill at establishing, with restricted means, an atmosphere of the weird, enchanted, and grotesque. A somber prelude in f minor is followed by the sorceress' incantation, which contains several melodic leaps ("Appear! appear!"). This leads into the witches' brief chorus, contrasting in speed, meter, and key; the sorceress then continues (in a return to f minor, with a dissonance on "hate"). To the revelation of her fiendish plan the witches react with laughter that surely was intended to sound diabolical, though its ho-ho-ho's, in precise $\frac{3}{8}$ time, may provoke mirth rather than horror in twentieth-century audiences. Here is another example of what is meant by stylization taking the place of realism in Baroque opera.

Arias are brief and show formal simplicity. Only one da capo aria, of modest dimensions, occurs: Belinda's "Pursue thy conquest." For other arias Purcell uses as a structural device a ground bass: a bass melody, several measures in length, that is repeated again and again. Dido's opening air, "Ah, Belinda", is an example. This ground bass is stated 21 times, including the transpositions to a related key in the aria's middle section. Widely used in many kinds of Baroque music, the ground bass was one of Purcell's favorite form-giving devices. In this and other arias from *Dido and Aeneas* the listener may barely be aware of the bass repetitions since above them the composer provides melodies of great variety and beauty. Musical lines in the voice part develop freely and subtly; phrase ends in melody and bass seldom coincide. Dido's lament at the end of the opera, justly famous, consists of an especially expressive and varied melodic line over a chromatically descending ground bass.

EXAMPLE 7

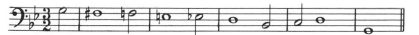

In these and other arias from the opera the orchestral introduction is quite short; later (especially Italian) Baroque operas may contain much more extensive ritornelli: preludes, postludes, and interludes between sections of an aria.

Variety is also displayed in the ways in which arias and recitatives are connected with other music. "Oft she visits this lone mountain," a ground bass aria, leads into an instrumental dance on the same bass. A recitative may conclude with a brief rhythmic passage ("the greatest blessing fate can give," Act I, Scene 1).

In this as in many other Baroque operas, ensemble scenes serve primarily to provide contrast of musical texture rather than characterization of the individuals taking part. Belinda and the second woman sing the same music, in parallel thirds, throughout their duet "Fear no danger to ensue"; the music is then repeated by the chorus. The two witches' plan to "conjure up a storm" is revealed in a contrapuntal duet. The two lines, though independent, are similar, beginning in canon, but the parts might as well be exchanged: there is no attempt to draw two individuals.

Among the choral scenes those dominated by the assembly of witches have already been mentioned. A chorus may enter into the action, or it may serve as commentator, expressing sentiments generally applicable to the situation ("When monarchs unite, how happy their state") or repeating what has already been sung by one or several individuals. Belinda's advice to seek shelter quickly is taken up by her fellow courtiers. Their decision to "haste, haste to town" is dwelt upon for some time, in a lively chorus. Critics of opera have often poked fun at choruses or arias in such situations, where real haste would have precluded any musical elaboration. But for Purcell and many successors the basic concept of haste provided sufficient reason for a lively piece of music.

Echo effects were a favorite device of Baroque music which Purcell does not fail to include. The echo chorus "In our deep-vaulted cell" is followed by an "Echo Dance of the Furies." A second orchestra backstage provides "echo" effects which, on close examination, turn out to have more independence than nature would provide—once more a case of purely musical considerations taking precedence over realism.

Purcell saved his most elaborate and moving chorus for the end of the opera: "With drooping wings, ye Cupids come." Its opening in imitative, madrigalesque style contains flowing lines, generally descending because of the image suggested by the text. The final portion, more chordal and solemn, is an expression of subdued grief. Dido, the gentle, beautiful queen, has died of a broken heart.

Strings and harpsichord (basso continuo) constitute the entire orchestra for Purcell's opera. The smallness of the group probably was required by the occasion; certainly the libretto contains a number of situations in which larger forces would have been effective. But the composer managed well with these resources. The string writing changes character as the dramatic situation requires. When hunting horns are to be heard in the distance, repeated triadic figures in the orchestra suggest the sound. While recitatives call for orchestral accompaniment throughout, most of the arias have basso continuo accompaniment only—an unusual practice which Purcell may have favored in order to have untrained voices stand out sufficiently. Thus the orchestra achieves prominence in the short overture, based on French models, and in the dances that occupy prominent places throughout, in keeping with the tradition of the masque and with contemporary French operatic practice.

Dido and Aeneas provides numerous opportunities for colorful staging, though in the original performance at a girls' boarding school these may not have been fully exploited. Yet it is not a "machine" opera; many modern productions without elaborate staging or costuming have proven its lasting visual and musical appeal.

HANDEL'S OPERAS

George Frideric Handel's popular reputation today rests chiefly on a few of his many oratorios and on his instrumental works. Many admirers of these do not know that he also had a colorful career as a composer of Italian operas and as an impresario—a career which, at various times, brought him fame and fortune but also financial ruin.

Handel (1685–1759) had come to the genre early in life, writing *Almira* at the age of twenty. Its success caused him to compose two more Italian operas for Hamburg; he then (1706) journeyed to Italy for some closer contact with opera in its home land. Several years there yielded valuable experience and brought further successes, so that when he settled in London the German composer, still young, could hold his own in the face of intrigues and rivalries with famous Italian composers and singers. Italian operas had been given in London before Handel's arrival there, mostly in English translation. Handel's *Rinaldo* (1711) was the first Italian opera written for London by a resident composer, with a specific stage and cast in mind. [24] Italian opera now flourished there for several decades in spite of much opposition. Since few of the spectators understood the language in which it was sung, opera was criticized as a snobbish, unnatural entertainment.[25] Reasoning of this kind did not prevent Handel and other composers from reaping considerable success in the field. Only late in his life, as a result of financial setbacks and other disappointments, did Handel turn from opera to oratorio.

Handel's operas, and Baroque opera in general, were virtually forgotten until the twentieth century. A veritable Handel renaissance took place in Germany in the 1920's. At that time several of his mature operas, including *Julius Caesar* (1724) and *Rodelinda* (1725) were given in versions that were heavily edited and adapted with a view to making them dramatically palatable. There have been presentations since then, in other countries as well,[26] but there are numerous barriers to a general acceptance, by today's audiences, of late Baroque opera seria. Not the least of these is the difficulty of casting roles originally written for castratos. Should modern performances reproduce the *sound* of the original, which would require that the parts be played by women, or should the roles be rewritten (requiring changes in tonality and accompaniment) to be sung by a tenor or bass? Other obstacles have been considered earlier in this chapter. Although Handel's music continues to sound vigorous and fresh, an appreciation of his operas as dramas demands considerable adjustment to early eighteenth-century conventions.

George Frideric Handel, *Julius Caesar* (London, 1724)

Julius Caesar, one of his most successful operas, shows the typical Baroque mixture of history with fiction, especially with amorous intrigues. Caesar appears as an individual, much wrapped up in his personal affairs, rather than as a brilliant and victorious statesman or warrior. Love and desire are first among the basic affections that

[24] Eisenschmidt, *Die szenische Darstellung der Opern G. F. Handels . . .*, Vol. I, p. 7.

[25] Thus Addison in *The Spectator,* 1711: "In the beginning of the Eighteenth Century the Italian Tongue was so well understood in England that Operas were acted on the publick Stage in that Language."

[26] *Julius Caesar,* for example, was given by a professional cast in Kansas City in 1965 and opened the 1966–67 season of the New York City Opera Company.

govern the conduct of each character. The opening of Act II thus becomes one of the key scenes of the opera: Cleopatra, as Lydia, has made elaborate preparations to attract Caesar's attentions and affection: "Love inspired me to devise an ingenious plan . . . to make him who has stolen my heart the prisoner of love."

The libretto, quite typical for its time, is constructed in such a fashion that each scene leads up to an aria characterizing the emotional situation in a general way, without reference to details of plot or to individuals. Since an aria usually is placed at the end of the scene, it provides the singer with an effective exit. *Julius Caesar* contains many arias of the types mentioned earlier, including a number of comparison arias. Here is Caesar addressing Cleopatra:

> Non è si vago e bello il fior nel prato
> quant'è vago e gentile il tuo bel volto.
> [No flower in the meadows is as beautiful
> and charming as your countenance.]

Recitatives and arias alternate in the previously described fashion, though there are some modifications of this norm. In Cleopatra's famous aria "V'adoro pupille" a brief recitative in which Caesar expresses his admiration for her singing is interpolated before the da capo section. Many arias are in da capo form, though their original dimensions are obscured by cuts in some editions. Sesto's vengeance aria "Svegliatevi nel core" contains a middle section in contrasting tempo as well as key.

Great rhythmic drive distinguishes many of the arias; others express tender sentiments in a lilting *siciliano* rhythm (Cleopatra's "Tu la mia stella sei"). In "Se pietà di me non senti" Cleopatra makes an impassioned plea that represents one of the musical and dramatic high points of the opera. Its emotional significance caused Handel to introduce it by an accompanied recitative. The aria contains an abundance of coloraturas on affective words. Here they strike us as expressive and well integrated with the melodic line; elsewhere in Handel's vocal writing (including the famous oratorio arias) they often consist of note patterns that are sequentially and rather mechanically repeated. Regardless of their level of emotional intensity, his arias are distinguished by harmonic fullness and inventiveness. Most of them are based on one or two short melodic figures, rhythmically distinct, which are continued and developed throughout the main portion of the aria. Occasionally they return in the middle section as well.

Aria accompaniments present much variety in orchestration and a good deal of tone painting. Thus Sesto, in another comparison aria, sings of the deadly serpent that will relentlessly pursue its victim. The animal's violent, gyrating motions are vividly reproduced in the orchestra. For arias of special significance an obbligato instrument is sometimes pitted against the voice (violin in "Se pietà"), often with pictorial connotations (hunting horn in Caesar's "Va tacito e nascosto," an aria describing a hunter's persistent stalking of his prey).

The small number of ensembles and the perfunctory nature of the choruses in late Baroque operas has been mentioned before. *Julius Caesar* is typical in this respect, too. Its two duets reveal an effective plan, found in other operas as well. A solo phrase at the beginning is echoed and then modified by the other singer before the duet proper gets under way. This variety is maintained later in the duet, though unanimity of thought or sentiment is musically expressed through much motion in parallel thirds or sixths.

The aesthetic of late Baroque opera, so different from modern dramatic concepts, is well analyzed by Grout.[27] To the modern listener who is able to make the adjustment, Handel's operas in particular may offer a rewarding experience—an introduction to a realm of musical drama that should be better known in an age in which other kinds of Baroque music are so widely enjoyed.

[27] *SHO*, pp. 159 ff.

The Queen of the Night, in a production of "The Magic Flute."

4

CLASSIC OPERA

"Classic music" is a term that has a variety of meanings, some more precise than others. In its historical sense it refers to the music of the second half of the eighteenth century—the period of which (for today's public) Haydn, Mozart, and to some extent Beethoven are the outstanding representatives. Several reasons exist for applying the label "Classic" to the musical style of this age, including the analogy to the fine arts. The art of ancient Greece and Rome, particularly its architecture and sculpture, was explored, admired, and imitated during this time as it had not been for several centuries. Nineteenth-century art historians applied the terms "classicism" or "neoclassicism" to the late eighteenth century; music historians availed themselves of the convenient label. They also detected in Haydn's and Mozart's music qualities which they admired in Greek and Roman art: serenity, balance, elegance without gaudiness or frivolity, simplicity, and dignity.

That the various arts share common characteristics in any particular period is often true, though it is a point that at times is overstated. Neoclassicism in painting and architecture reached the greatest flowering in the early nineteenth century, *after* the age of Haydn and Mozart. In drama, subjects from classical mythology had been favored not only in Baroque opera but also in spoken drama, especially in French tragedy of the seventeenth century.

Partly because of the towering figures of Haydn and Mozart we think of Austria as the land of musical classicism par excellence. It is true that Vienna became one of the foremost musical centers of the age, but it is also true that musical activity there as in other cities continued to be directed if not dominated by Italians.[1] Italian opera continued to be favored at almost all European courts, including those of ecclesiastical rulers such as the Archbishop of Salzburg. As an entertainment of the ruling class, eighteenth-century opera frequently was scrutinized for politically objectionable content. Da Ponte's libretto for Mozart's *Figaro* furnishes a well-known example, but such censorship was by no means restricted to the theaters of Vienna or Paris. While the old social order lasted, opera seria continued to fulfill its traditional function of glorifying its princely sponsors. But the ideas of the Enlightenment spread steadily, were widely discussed by the aristocracy, and, in some instances, found some acceptance even there.

Understandably, these ideas were reflected in eighteenth-century drama. The early part of the century had witnessed the rise of opera buffa, democratic rather than aristocratic, based on subjects from everyday life. During the Classic era opera buffa continued to make inroads on the popularity of opera seria. On its road to success it acquired new characteristics: it lost much coarseness of language and humor, it used less dialect, and its plots came to be set in middle-class rather than peasant surroundings. Elements of farce were replaced by more subtle wit and by dramatic ingenuity, and a good dash of sentimentality was frequently added. Opera buffa was to be taken seriously as drama, with plots that were imaginative and at times quite complicated, Mozart's *Figaro* being a case in point. While secco recitative continued to serve for the dialogue, the arias increased in musical substance. Finales became longer, consisting of several musical sections, and sometimes brought further dramatic developments. By the time Mozart wrote his mature operas the serious and light genres had fused to some degree. *Don Giovanni* particularly exemplifies this

---

[1] As late as 1842 an Italian, Donizetti, earned great triumphs there and was appointed Imperial Court Composer and Kapellmeister.

trend. When, in 1791, Mozart composed *La clemenza di Tito,* an opera seria on a Metastasian libretto, he did so because the subject had been chosen for him. Conventional opera seria had lost much of its appeal for him as it had for the public of this revolutionary age.

Since Italian opera continued to be composed and performed everywhere, its style in a sense became international. Few if any attempts were made to impart local or regional flavor to Classic opera. Mozart's works once more illustrate the point: both *Figaro* and *Don Giovanni* take place in Spain, yet except for the fandango in Act III of *Figaro* they contain nothing that sounds Spanish. Might the international appeal of Mozart's operas today be related to this absence of specifically national qualities? Certainly, as performed today in New York or Vienna, Mozart's operas are examples of international art: a cast of Austrians, Yugoslavs, and others sing, in Italian, for an audience that is largely English-speaking. But to some degree this applies to Verdi and Puccini as well. It remained for the coming age of Romanticism to give to opera national or regional characteristics, in ways to be discussed in the following chapter.

Sporadic attempts to create national opera were made during the Classic period, in both Germany and Austria. *Günther von Schwarzburg* (libretto by Anton Klein, music by Ignaz Holzbauer), was a patriotic German opera given in Mannheim in 1777. In his preface the poet urged his countrymen to look to their own past for suitable dramatic subjects, but his example was not widely followed. Mozart, on rare occasions, was capable of uttering patriotic sentiments, and at least once he expressed the wish that serious German opera might flourish.[2] Some hope that that might occur had been aroused when the Austrian Emperor Joseph II decided to support the cause of a national German theater and opera at court and established a National Theater in 1776. Unfortunately the emperor's interest soon lagged. While it lasted it was focused on lighter German opera—the Singspiel.

In some ways the eighteenth-century Singspiel can be compared to opera buffa: it is a musical play, light if not comical, with simple melodies usually close to the style of folk and popular song and at times borrowed from them. Works of this kind were performed publicly, not normally at court, by traveling troupes of actors. Since the Singspiel was musically less demanding than opera, it did not require professional singers. Spoken dialogue rather than recitative was used—a trait which the Singspiel shared with French opéra comique (see below) and English ballad opera, both of which were known in Germany through translations and

[2] Letter of March 21, 1785.

adaptations. As time passed, the Singspiel became increasingly sentimental.

The social changes of the declining eighteenth century furnish some reasons for the decline of opera seria. Diminishing revenues forced many of the lesser princes to live on a more modest scale. As the philosophy of political absolutism was more and more loudly challenged, some rulers felt morally inclined or obliged to curb extravagant spending. In either case the spectacular and expensive opera seria no longer was appropriate. In effect many court theaters functioned as public, municipal theaters, depending on an admission-paying, middle-class audience which preferred spoken and musical plays in its own language.

The term "Singspiel" is often applied to Mozart's German operas, yet neither *The Abduction from the Seraglio* nor *The Magic Flute* exemplifies it in the mid-eighteenth-century sense of the term. In the former work the part of Constanze is quite serious and substantial, as shown by the famous "Martern" aria with its taxing coloratura passages, or by the deeply felt "Traurigkeit ward mir zum Lose." Other roles likewise require vocal equipment and ability that one would hardly find among actors for whom music was only a sideline. Mozart may have been encouraged to write on this level by the avowed intentions of his emperor, who wanted the Viennese Singspiel to rise from the level of suburban comedy to something first rate, performed by virtuosos at court.

In France, Lully's noble and lofty tragédie lyrique had set the tone at the court of Louis XIV. Tolerating no interference or competition in this field, Lully watched with a jaundiced eye the activities of various Italian troupes that were playing their lighter, tuneful fare in Paris. Royal edicts forbidding singing on their stages resulted in subterfuges: actors might speak the lines while instruments played the melody, or the audience would sing popular tunes (*vaudevilles*) for which new texts had been supplied. Local troupes also played in the capital, though they were banished, as a rule, to suburban fairs. With the death of Louis XIV a Théâtre de l'Opéra-Comique was formed. Continuing the practice of opera buffa, opéra comique frequently parodied the serious operas performed at court, especially the successful ones. Italian troupes continued to appear in Paris; the popularity of opera buffa led to spirited discussions and pamphleteering (in the celebrated "War of the Buffoons"). Around the middle of the century French composers, inspired by the successes of Pergolesi and other composers of opera buffa, began to develop a distinctive style of comic opera with spoken dialogue and with airs that were no longer adapted from popular tunes, though they were generally simple and concise. An opéra comique customarily ended with a vaudeville finale: every participant in turn sang a stanza, followed each time by the refrain sung by all. Many later composers, not only in France, availed themselves of this effective closing device: Mozart in the *Seraglio,* Rossini in *The Barber of Seville.* During the Classic era opéra comique drew on a growing range of sentimental and semiserious subjects and attracted many first-rate composers, among them André Grétry (1741–1813) and Gluck.

The career and works of Christoph Willibald Gluck (1714– 1787) once more exemplify the international aspects of eighteenth-century music, especially of opera. Born in Bavaria, he spent his youth in Bohemia, a province famous for the musicality of its people, where he received a thorough general and musical education. At the age of twenty-two he entered the employment of a princely family in Vienna, having by this time already gathered much experience as a singer, organist, and cellist. Here he was exposed to much Italian opera, a genre which strongly fascinated him. Like Handel a generation earlier, he availed himself of an opportunity to go to Italy. In Milan he made the acquaintance of G. B. Sammartini, a successful writer of operas who befriended and instructed him for several years. Gluck's first opera, on a libretto by Metastasio, was successfully performed in 1741. He became thoroughly familiar with the traditions of both serious and comic opera in Italy and contributed several works before journeying to Paris and London in 1745. After five years, most of which had been spent as conductor for a traveling Italian opera company, Gluck settled in Vienna, though further trips for the production of new works soon took him to Prague and Naples. His reputation as a composer of Italian operas grew steadily and led to his appointment as Austrian court conductor in 1754. Several French comic operas well as additional opere serie, dramatic serenades, and ballets appeared in Vienna before *Orfeo ed Euridice* was produced at the court theater in 1762.

GLUCK AND OPERATIC REFORM

Gluck's setting of this favorite operatic subject is generally considered the first of his "reform operas." It does differ substantially from traditional opera seria, including his own earlier works, but these differences did not come about overnight. All through the century critical voices had been raised against opera seria; a substantial body of essays, pamphlets, letters, and parodies indicated widespread dissatisfaction with its "abuses."

Some criticism from the beginning of the century was mentioned in the preceding chapter. Among later essays Francesco Algarotti's *Saggio sopra l'opera in musica* (*Essay on Opera,* 1755) is particularly clear and succinct, dealing with virtually all aspects of the works themselves and with their performance.[3] Algarotti demands greater equality of all the constituent arts. Drama above all must not be neglected: it is the opera's center, and the other arts must contribute to it. Music also contributes; it should not rule. Algarotti maintains that in the past composers and singers have tried to "please too much," with arias containing excessive ornamentation; at the same time they neglected the recitative, which, in order to be expressive, should be accompanied. The overture should anticipate the drama's basic mood; chorus and dance should be an integral part of the drama; stage sets and costumes should be historically correct and appropriate.

These and other demands were not voiced by Algarotti alone—they were in the air at the time when Gluck established himself in Vienna. Other composers showed their concern with some of the same questions. Tommaso Traetta (1727–1779), whom Algarotti may have known in Parma, and Niccolo Jommelli (1714–1774) are but two of Gluck's contemporaries whose operas accord greater importance to dramatic effectiveness. Accompanied recitatives, choruses, ensembles, and orchestral music are enlisted to this end, modifying the traditional succession of secco recitative and aria.

French opera likewise came in for its share of criticism: what had seemed beautiful, noble, and dignified at the time of the Sun King no longer satisfied listeners who had come in contact with the light, tuneful, ingratiating style of Italian opera buffa. To be sure, French opera had not remained static since Lully's days. The principal figure in French opera of the mid-eighteenth century was Jean-Philippe Rameau, whose accompanied recitatives, arias, and especially choral scenes anticipate features for which Gluck often is given credit. Generally speaking, some of the reforms of Italian opera seria amount to an adoption and modification of practices found in tragédie lyrique.

Christoph Willibald Gluck, *Orfeo ed Euridice* (Vienna, 1762; Paris, 1774)

In Gluck's own case, concern with dramatic effectiveness and truthfulness exceeded all other considerations. In Raniero Calzabigi, an Italian poet who had arrived in Vienna in 1761, Gluck at once found a librettist after his own heart. Calzabigi had previously lived in Paris; his dramatic concepts were shaped by his acquaintance with Greek drama and the tragedies of Corneille and Racine. Simplicity and clarity of action were his chief concern, and

[3] Excerpts in *SMH*.

he believed that the inner action—the development of characters—
should be the drama's essence. Similar demands had been voiced in
France by the Encyclopedists, among them Diderot: opera "can
never be good unless it intends to imitate nature." Gluck's own
words reflect this view: "All art must imitate nature; therefore I
have always endeavored to be simple and natural."

Applying this view to the simple drama of Orpheus and
Eurydice, Gluck's musical purpose was to serve the drama constantly, even to refrain from writing "beautiful" music where it
would be dramatically out of place. "The greatest beauty of
melody and harmony can be a fault if it occurs in the wrong place"
(preface to *Paride ed Elena,* 1770). Gluck often studied a libretto
for a long time before writing any music, his aim being to understand each character completely, then to look for the appropriate
means of musical expression.

With restraint and economy of language Calzabigi's text fulfills the purpose of opera on which he and Gluck agreed: it does
not merely tell a story but expresses noble, ethical, humane sentiments. In place of the amorous intrigues so common in Baroque
opera, love, devotion, and self-sacrifice are glorified. The poet
does make a concession to the convention of Metastasian opera: the
happy ending, brought about by Amor, the *deus ex machina.* As
with earlier Orpheus operas, external circumstances of the performance (in this case the emperor's name-day) account for this.

With the outer action reduced to the basic development, long
narrative recitative is altogether absent from *Orfeo,* from *Alceste*
(1767), and from Gluck's later reform operas.[4] Simplicity of
action also makes possible many static scenes in which situations
are described rather than developed. The entire opening scene of
Orfeo belongs here; a *tombeau* scene in the tradition of French
tragedy, with choral singing and pantomime. When the curtain
goes up, the essential dramatic development has already taken
place: Eurydice is dead. Monteverdi's librettist, 150 years earlier,
had handled this scene in a far more dramatic fashion, with the
sudden appearance of the messenger. Calzabigi and Gluck depict
profound but restrained grief. In other scenes also, emotions are
purified and controlled. After the opening chorus, with Orpheus'
brief exclamations, Orpheus addresses the mourners in a short
passage of recitative. Here a comparison of Gluck's original Italian
version of the opera with the French version prepared for Paris
twelve years later is useful.[5] In the former, the recitative is con-

---

[4] Gluck's (or Calzabigi's) preface to *Alceste* is a famous document stating
their reform aims. Translation in *SMH.*

[5] The Paris version is the one more frequently performed today; unless otherwise specified, the discussion that follows refers to it.

siderably longer. Both in the inflection of the vocal line and in the punctuating chords of the accompaniment it comes much closer to the quality of secco recitative than does the later version, in which the prosody of the French language is reproduced by measured declamatory writing. Orpheus' air "Objet de mon amour" illustrates the simple, dignified melodic style, the Classic "noble simplicity" that Gluck had now adopted. In place of coloratura, which he generally avoided, there is a flowing, evenly paced line, diatonic and of moderate range. This is all the more remarkable since the part of Orpheus (a tenor part in the Paris version) was originally written for a male alto and since castratos traditionally had been favored with florid parts. Echo effects, so dear to Baroque opera, still occur. The aria is strophic, with recitative passages of increasing intensity separating the stanzas. In the last recitative section Orpheus appears disconsolate, addressing his reproaches to the lords of the realm of the shades in recitative that displays dramatic and musical power. To this Amor responds with an air that sounds hopeful, confident, and cheerful—moods to which the flowing, graceful accompaniment contributes. Orpheus asks the god of love to give him strength, for the sake of her who set his heart on fire. here the word "enflamme" supplies one of the opera's few occasions for vocal passage work.

Orfeo contains extensive and dramatic duets, especially in the third act, where Eurydice's happiness gradually gives way to doubt (that Orpheus still loves her, since he refuses to look at her) and despair. Her changing mood is reflected in the harmony, with bright D major for "Ah, grands dieux, quel bonheur!" Soon her anxiety is expressed in words and melody, but especially in the accompaniment. Successive dissonances (seventh-chords) express tension; a painful-sounding phrase issues from the violins, rises higher when repeated, and higher yet the third time. An ominous brief orchestral figure points up the crucial significance of her demand:

EXAMPLE 1

[*Just one glance from you . . .*]

(This subtle touch is lacking in the earlier version.) After this dramatic exchange the following duet seems weak at first, but soon its emotional intensity increases. Again the accompaniment contributes to the dramatic effect. Changing patterns match the changing emotions of both singers. In all, this is one of the opera's most forceful, dramatic scenes. The mood continues in the next recitative, but Gluck's skill prevents the scene from becoming static. Eurydice is gripped by fear; she is breathless and trembles. All this is convincingly expressed in her recitative. The following aria, "Fortune ennemie," is in da capo form, a duet being the middle section. Gradually the action approaches the crux. Another carefully instrumented recitative, with several tempo changes, brings Orpheus to the point where he can no longer refrain from looking at his spouse: he turns to her, and she dies at once. The scene, masterfully treated by Gluck, has not lost its impact today. The recitatives are on the artistic level of Mozart's accompagnatos in *Figaro* and *Don Giovanni*.

Orpheus' "J'ai perdu mon Euridice" follows immediately—an aria in rondo form that acquired greater popularity than any other part of the opera and led, not surprisingly, to a travesty in Offenbach's *Orpheus in the Underworld*. Gluck's melody, it has often been pointed out, is an extremely composed, controlled expression of grief—a simple, evenly flowing melody in C major. Compared with the first part of the act it seems serene rather than disconsolate.

Distinctive and sure handling of the chorus is apparent throughout the opera, with much variety in its involvement in the drama. Most successful, then and now, is the opening scene of Act II, in which chorus, ballet, and solo singing are freely mingled. The sound of Orpheus' lyre is heard backstage; when he appears, the Furies and monsters interrupt their dance, and a choral scene begins, in which both singing and dancing are intended to frighten the mortal who has dared to enter the underworld. Gluck's orchestra again provides ample support, including a realistic imitation of the barking of Cerberus, the three-headed guardian-dog:

EXAMPLE 2

To these wild, menacing sounds Orpheus responds with an imploring song of great purity, accompanying himself on his lyre. His plea for pity brings forth a succession of stern "No's," sung in unison, forte. The dramatic effect of such contrast is fully exploited. Gradually Orpheus' legendary musical power (and Gluck's increasingly persuasive music) softens the Furies' response: as they sing each of the successive choral stanzas they show "a little more compassion." Their words as well as their music accomplish this: at first they merely threaten, but later they ask Orpheus who has brought him to this place of "sighs and torments," and they wonder why and how he succeeds in calming their fury. At the end their earlier united front, symbolized by unison singing in the opening stanza, with strictly chordal texture, deteriorates: their final admission that "il est vainqueur" is whispered successively by each section of the chorus. The scene ends, as it started, with dancing. Similar scene complexes occur elsewhere in the opera; they exemplify the trend away from the earlier "number opera."

Numerous dances occur in the original version; many others were added for Paris, following local taste and tradition. This was the period during which new concepts of the ballet and its dramatic function were formulated and put into practice. Jean-Georges Noverre was the principal figure in this reform. His *Lettres sur la danse et les ballets* (1760) advocated a return to simplicity and naturalness in ballet—an art form which, in his eyes, could move as strongly as great tragedy and which therefore should rise above being merely beautiful spectacle and entertainment. From 1767 to 1774 Noverre was active at several theaters in Vienna and as ballet master to the imperial family. Two years later he went to Paris. His notion of subordinating the individual dancer to the effectiveness of the ballet as a whole paralleled Gluck's views and practices. In *Orfeo* and in Gluck's later operas, especially those written for Paris, there is much dancing. Chorus and ballet often are combined, as in the opening scenes of Acts I and II of *Orfeo*. The second scene of Act II contains an even larger proportion of dancing, beginning with the well-known Dance of the Blessed Spirits. Two other ballets follow before the first aria with chorus which, in the postlude, provides for further dancing. After the dramatic opening scene of Act II this essentially choreographic scene appears all the more static. Orpheus himself, after another dance interpolation, begs the shadows to make haste and restore Eurydice to his embraces.

Gluck's careful accompaniment to arias and choruses has already been noted; he shows equal care and mastery in the dance music. For the Paris version he took advantage of the large orchestral resources available there, adding clarinets and trombones and giving more prominent treatment to the trumpets. In both versions his intent to provide the right tone color for each dramatic occasion is evident. He supplied the right timbre for serene and delicate moods (opening of Act II, Scene 2, with flute and cello solos); he used cornetti and trombones in the opening scene—instruments which in Austria were traditional for funeral music—and he placed a second orchestra behind the scene to achieve dramatic contrast (opening of Act II). Minute care was also devoted to all details of production; Gluck's rehearsals in Paris became famous, often stormy affairs in which the master demanded far more than opera singers had been accustomed to give.

Though one of the leading and honored opera composers of his day, Gluck also was the target of much criticism and of intrigues in which personal and political considerations played a part, especially in Paris. The score of *Orfeo* was published there in 1764; in various versions and translations it soon was performed in all parts of Europe. It is one of the earliest operas to have maintained itself with some regularity in the repertory, through the nineteenth century and to the present day.

Gluck's collaboration with the French librettist Du Roullet resulted in several operas written specifically for Paris. *Iphigénie en Aulide* (1774), based on a tragedy by Racine and rehearsed under the composer's close supervision, was highly successful. Encouraged, Gluck prepared the French version of *Orfeo* (*Orphée,* 1774) and *Alceste* (1776). Though Gluck acquired an enthusiastic following, another faction of the Paris public loudly expressed its preference for Italian opera, especially for the works of Niccolò Piccinni (1728–1800). *Iphigénie en Tauride* (1779) represents a high point in Gluck's career—a tragedy in which his dramatic and musical ideas are most successfully put into practice.

Eventually Gluck returned to Vienna. Until his death there in 1787 he was the city's most famous musician.

MOZART'S OPERAS

Throughout his short life Mozart was actively and intensely involved in dramatic music. Opera, especially Italian opera, was the genre in which one could make a name for oneself everywhere, and Mozart's father, recognizing his precocious talent, wanted to give him the best possible musical education. In those days this still meant much travel: in music as in other callings an apprentice became a journeyman. Seeing just how things in one's field were done in other places was a necessary step on the educational ladder, before mastery could be achieved. There were trips from his native Salzburg to Vienna, Italy, Paris, London—always to centers of opera. Mozart not only heard much, absorbing various styles, but also made contacts with important musicians of the time. He soon began to compose works that, though following the dramatic and musical conventions of the age, yet already showed increasingly the measure of his genius. Though as a child prodigy he earned the admiration of royalty and the public, mostly as a performer, success was not so easy for the growing young man. His letters reveal his constant hope to be asked to write an opera, or to be offered a substantial court position. The latter never developed, but commissions for operas repeatedly provided badly needed encouragement.

Not all of Mozart's "mature" operas were successful at once, though *The Marriage of Figaro, Don Giovanni,* and *The Magic Flute* became classics soon after his death—classics in the sense that their appeal was international and lasting, surmounting changing trends of fashion. In the first part of the nineteenth century these operas more than other music established Mozart's fame. The twentieth century has seen growing appreciation of all of Mozart's œuvre, with the operas of his youth as well as the late *Tito* receiving occasional performances. Fewer listeners today than in the last century think of Mozart's music as simple or easy; rather they detect, behind frequently simple means (e.g., the small orchestra, some conventional dramatic devices, or naïve dialogue) wealth of imagination and profundity of meaning.

Mozart's lifelong interest in people, so evident from his letters, made him a keen observer of human nature. Though at times excessive optimism caused him to make mistakes in judgment, by and large he sized up and described people, with their strengths and their foibles, quickly and precisely. With such an interest it was natural that Mozart should be attracted to the kind of drama in which lifelike, ordinary human beings, rather than mythological or historical characters, are the protagonists: to opera buffa and its German and French counterparts.

Mozart's chief contributions in this field came about through his collaboration with Lorenzo da Ponte, an Italian poet who had settled in Vienna around 1782. His life story is more than colorful; he was an adventurer after the manner of Casanova, whom he knew, and he seems to have had much in common with the Don Giovanni of his own libretto. His memoirs, though highly colored and hence not an accurate source of information, still make absorbing reading today. The many ups and downs of his career include ordination as a priest, a calling which he soon found to be incompatible with his interests and disposition. He tried his luck as a dramatist and managed to arrive in Vienna at the opportune time, when Italian opera again was favored at court over the Singspiel. With a talent for making the right connections he succeeded in gaining an appointment as court theater poet. *The Marriage of Figaro* (1786) was the first product of his collaboration with Mozart. His reputation as a librettist was not based exclusively on this successful working relationship: Da Ponte was much in demand by other composers, including Salieri, often considered Mozart's rival.

Figaro established their mutually satisfactory working relationship, which continued with *Don Giovanni* in the following year and *Così fan tutte* in 1790. Soon after, Da Ponte was forced to leave Vienna. Eventually we find him in the New World, engaged in such diversified activities as owning a grocery store and teaching Italian at Columbia University. In 1825 he once more made musical history, for he was instrumental in bringing about the first New York performance of *Don Giovanni*.

Wolfgang Amadeus Mozart, *Don Giovanni* (Prague, 1787)

The suggestion for an opera based on Beaumarchais's comedy *Le Mariage de Figaro* probably had come from Mozart. The opera, though well received in Vienna, was soon dropped there. Its subsequent great popularity in Prague was heartening to Mozart: when he journeyed there early in 1787, everyone was singing its tunes. Mozart, loudly acclaimed, conducted several performances. Before returning to Vienna he agreed to write another Italian opera for Prague. This time Da Ponte apparently suggested the Don Juan story as a suitable subject. With accustomed speed Mozart wrote most of the work in Vienna, finishing it in Prague, where he had returned in October, 1787.

The production ran into various difficulties. Mozart complained that the company was smaller and less skillful than the Vienna one. *Don Giovanni's* premiere had to be postponed; even so the orchestra had to perform the overture at sight since Mozart, according to a famous story, did not commit it to paper until the early morning hours of the day of the first performance. Again he conducted and played the secco recitatives. A newspaper review that appeared a few days later commented on the opera's success but also on its difficulties of execution.

Don Giovanni was given in Vienna the next year, on the emperor's order. Curiously enough substantial changes were made, though the Prague success had been the main reason why the emperor wished to have it presented in Vienna. One of the additions, a long slapstick scene for Leporello and Zerlina in Act II, is hardly ever heard today; other changes have maintained themselves. Don Ottavio's aria "Dalla sua pace" was written for the Vienna performance of 1788, to take the place of "Il mio tesoro," which proved too difficult for the local tenor. Today we often hear both arias: the latter is sung in II/2, its original place, while the former is interpolated, now as then, in I/3. Interpolations of this kind once more throw a light on operatic conventions of the time:

the first consideration was to give a singer an attractive aria; only then did one look for a suitable place for it. For "Dalla sua pace" the spot chosen is none too effective; the dramatic "Or sai" just before would provide a better ending for the scene.

Donna Elvira's "Mi tradi quell'alma ingrata" (II/2), preceded by a moving, powerful accompagnato, was also added for Vienna; in this instance the singer had felt slighted and demanded an additional aria. Mozart supplied an effective showpiece for the purpose.

The story on which Da Ponte based his libretto exists in numerous earlier versions. Both Dent[6] and Newman[7] give detailed accounts and comparisons of these literary sources. The great number of differing versions indicates the wide appeal of the tale; like the Faust legend, it has been dramatized and interpreted in a great variety of ways, from a simple but spectacular ghost story to a tale of profound philosophical and psychological meanings. In fact, there are similarities between the Faust and Don Juan legends: both men are strong personalities pursuing activities that meet with the disapproval of society; both violate sacred laws; and in the end both receive their just punishment. Both Goethe's Faust and Da Ponte's Don are represented as successful, up to a point, in their pursuits, though during the brief time span of the opera's action Don Giovanni is continually thwarted in his attempts to seduce the various women in the cast. It is interesting to note that Goethe esteemed *The Magic Flute* and *Don Giovanni* above all other operas and felt that only Mozart could have done musical justice to his *Faust*.

The Don Juan story, of course, has appealed to many writers since Da Ponte; it held special fascination for the writers and artists of early Romanticism (witness E. T. A. Hoffmann's short story *Don Juan*[8]); and in Da Ponte and Mozart's setting it has continued to have strong audience appeal to the present day. In a psychology-conscious age this is not surprising, for the authors created a drama the principal characters of which lend themselves to a variety of fascinating interpretations.

As the licentious nobleman, Da Ponte's Don has something in common with his (and Beaumarchais's) Count Almaviva in *Figaro;* both are represented in an uncomplimentary way as members of the ruling class. Yet Masetto's challenge of the Don's superiority is not as effectual or as strongly worded as Figaro's in the earlier opera. Nor is Masetto as clever as Figaro, who outwits his Count on several occasions. Still, Masetto's "Ho capito, Signor,

6 *Mozart's Operas* (New York, 1947), Chapters 8–10.
7 *Great Operas*, Vol. II.
8 English translation in *MQ*, Vol. 31 (1945), pp. 504 ff.

The cemetery scene.

si!" tastes of rebellion, and some of Zerlina's lines also are uncomplimentary.

With *Don Giovanni* Da Ponte again provided Mozart with an effective libretto. There are, to be sure, loose ends—details of the action that he does not bother to explain. The sources from which he borrowed so hastily and heavily do better in some instances. Da Ponte, for instance, does not make it clear just where certain scenes take place, and at what time of day or night. Even Elvira's relationship to Don Giovanni is unclear: she is not represented to be his wife, as she had been in earlier versions of the story. Da Ponte's Elvira accuses the Don that at one time he had "declared her to be his spouse"—the word *sposa* ("bride," "betrothed") can have several interpretations—and then left her after three days. Some observers have pointed to another inconsistency of the plot. Less than twenty-four hours elapse between the Commandant's slaying and the cemetery scene, and it is unlikely that a statue, complete with inscription, could have been erected in so short a time. In realistic drama such ambiguities might be considered serious flaws, but it is doubtful that eighteenth-century audiences took such a view. Nor are today's audiences likely to see a need for explaining this kind of telescoping in a legendary plot, though commentators defending Da Ponte have attempted such

103

explanations. The several disguises, accomplished through masks or a mere exchange of cloaks, are, of course, quite in keeping with conventions of the time. But there are other inconsistencies. At the end of Act I the Don is obviously caught and cornered, yet (since another act must follow) he manages to get away, in spite of all the men closing in on him and the repeated shouts of "Tremble,

The finale: Entrance of the Statue.

villain!" Leporello's and Elvira's appearance in the courtyard of Anna's house (II/2) is difficult to explain; the subsequent arrival of Masetto and Zerlina even more so. Another scene for Anna and Ottavio, interpolated between the cemetery scene and the finale, is expendable from a dramatic point of view but provides the occasion for Anna's great coloratura aria "Non mi dir."

In all, Da Ponte's libretto is long, though in a properly paced performance it will not seem so. It also is complicated, with its division into so many scenes, but it is less complicated than *Figaro*. For many opera lovers *Don Giovanni* comes closer to perfection than any other work, and in spite of the foregoing remarks the libretto has a share in this. Strong effects are created in many ways, chiefly through a constant variation of the emotional climate or level of intensity, never allowing the listener to settle down. Tragic and comic elements are perpetually intertwined, and to this day there is disagreement about which of the two is the essential mood of the opera. Not only are there frequent shifts—a serious scene followed by a light one, as at the opening—but there are startling mixtures of the two that may seem grotesque in a Shakespearean way. Examples are numerous: the humorous and cynical asides by the Don and his servant in several of Elvira's scenes ("Ah, chi mi dice mai," I/2; "Ah taci, ingiusto core," II/1), or Leporello's comical remarks and behavior in the presence, both times, of the statue. The nature of the opera's finale also has a bearing on the listener's overall interpretation of this play, which Da Ponte called a *dramma giocoso*. After his final exchange of words with the stone guest the unrepentant Don feels the grasp of invisible demons and is engulfed by the flames of hell. His and Leporello's anguished outcry end this dramatic scene and might well have formed the opera's end, but the authors provided an epilogue during which the air is cleared of hellfire and demonic threats and a lighter mood returns, in the traditional manner of opera buffa. To those who wish to interpret *Don Giovanni* as an essentially tragic work, this conclusion is a thorn in the flesh—a scene that should be omitted in performance. They point to the Vienna production of 1788 as a precedent, since Mozart then did omit it. He did so, however, to compensate for the several lengthy additions mentioned above; not, as far as is known, because of any change of heart about the *giocoso* finale.[9] It continued to be cut in many performances, including those under Mahler in Vienna. In our own day the tendency has been to restore the finale, to view its omission as stylistically wrong. Opera of this type and period

---

[9] Da Ponte, later in America, is supposed to have claimed that Mozart wanted the opera to be altogether serious, but that he convinced him otherwise, for the sake of greater success.

customarily had a happy ending, with an ensemble finale. Earlier Don Juan plays also include a moralizing epilogue. An awareness of this eighteenth-century tradition caused Stravinsky to provide a similar conclusion for *The Rake's Progress* (see Chapter 14).

Mozart's opera, then, defies classification; it is a work *sui generis*—as is *The Magic Flute,* where a mixture of serious and comic elements provides quite different results. In *Don Giovanni* the uniqueness and strong appeal of the drama are also due to the complexity of its principal characters, beginning with the title role. The Don's actions mark him as dissolute, cynical, and cruel; his single-mindedness appears selfish unless one considers it patho-logical, an obsession. Yet to an extent he is drawn sympathetically, as some listeners may have discovered to their surprise. There is something appealing about his determination, though we disap-prove of its application, and there is a calm cold-bloodedness that is shaken only in a few moments. Courage is one of his attractive qualities, most evident in the cemetery scene and the finale, where it contrasts with Leporello's behavior. At one point in the finale Mozart (rather than Da Ponte) shows the Don to be at least somewhat unsure of himself: the repeat of his exclamation "Che cos'è?" ("What is going on?") is marked *piano* in the score. Don Giovanni's gaiety (as in the toast "Fin ch'han dal vino") has something eerie about it, and he transmits some of this mood to the opera in general, not only in the "ghost" scenes. The Don has very few arias to himself, and for a good reason: a lengthy aria would most likely reveal too much about his thoughts and feelings, dispelling the subtle aura of mystery that envelops him.

Some of this quality extends to the person on whom his attention is centered at the beginning of the opera: Donna Anna. In the opening scene, she rushes from the house pursuing the Don, the masked intruder, struggling with him, presumably trying to establish his identity. But whether he has succeeded in his mission, with Leporello standing guard, is not clear. According to Donna Anna's own account she "finally" mustered enough strength to free herself, and since in other versions of the story she escapes unharmed, this is the outcome most widely accepted. Others have been considered possible; whether rape, seduction, or neither took place would affect the interpretation of her role for the rest of the opera. There are those who believe in her being strongly attracted to the Don, consciously or subconsciously, an attitude said to explain her coolness to Don Ottavio. Such a view may in fact go back to E. T. A. Hoffmann's story. If she is in love with Don Giovanni she may, in typically Romantic fashion, consider herself the woman who is destined to save him—but this again is an interpretation not clearly supported by Da Ponte's lines. Others may consider such psychological interpretations out of place in eighteenth-century drama. In any case, we must assume that she did not establish the identity of the intruder and murderer; else the dramatic moment when it dawns on her that Don Giovanni's voice is that of the killer would be a deception of Ottavio. This is unlikely: Mozart's music makes the recognition scene one of the high points of the drama.[10]

Of the two principal female roles, that of Elvira lends itself less to complicated interpretations. Is Elvira a tragic figure? Abandoned by Don Giovanni, she is always seeking him—"quel barbaro, dov'è?" ("that monster, where is he?")—his degrading treatment of her is not enough to discourage her. After she is serenaded by him and Leporello in disguise, tender feelings once more get the better of her, and she appears as a pathetic rather than a tragic figure. Actually we pity her for the infatuation that makes

[10] For a different interpretation, see Alfred Einstein, *Mozart* (New York, 1945), p. 439.

Donna Elvira serenaded by Leporello and the Don.

her hope again and again. Only in the finale does she rise above this: presumably (Da Ponte does not make this clear) she knows what is about to happen—did she see the stone guest approach?—and her main concern is for the Don, whose deceptions she is willing to forget if only he will reform. But she soon sees the futility of her attempt. In earlier scenes she shows up with exasperating regularity, determined to prevent her erstwhile paramour from committing further misdeeds. There is something comical about all this, and about her succumbing once more to feigned protestations of love. One wonders whether librettist and composer of this *dramma giocoso* expected the audience to react this way.

No such problems exist for the singer who plays Leporello. The comic servant is a traditional figure in Italian opera; Leporello, in word and deed, follows the tradition. Even Leporellos, however, differ in appearance and behavior. Often the character is portrayed as short and fat (the latter a reflection of the gluttony which, along with cowardice, is one of his outstanding traits), so that his physical appearance makes him ridiculous as a stand-in for his master. Though the libretto says nothing to suggest his appearance, one way or another, it is obvious he should not be phlegmatic, but agile and alert. He may be young. Even in critical situations, when retreat under a table seems advisable, or when he trembles with fear, he has a capacity for seeing the humorous side; he makes excuses to the statue that his master is "too busy, very sorry," to keep the appointment for supper. With the strenuous life led by his master, Leporello, too, has to "wear himself out night and day." They have several quarrels because of this—a standard opera buffa routine. Still, there is something like secret admiration or relish in his enumeration of the Don's conquests in many countries—the lovingly reiterated "mille e tre" of the Catalog Aria.

All other characters are secondary in importance, and are drawn with less distinction and finesse by the librettist and composer. Ottavio belongs to this group; though he is present much of the time, he says and does little that would place him among the principals. Most listeners will agree with Dent, who considers him the weakest character in the opera,[11] good and loving as he may be. Many of his lines are not only ineffectual but anticlimactic, and his complete lack of temperament may have led to the claims that Donna Anna really is attracted to Don Giovanni. Was Ottavio intended to appear comical? He seems so to present-day listeners, when he goes so far in his gallantry and bravery as to consider informing the police of his suspicions. His blandness, at any rate, makes his fiancée, but also Don Giovanni and Elvira, appear all the more vigorous and warm-blooded.

[11] *Mozart's Operas,* pp. 160 f.

Zerlina and Masetto, the simple, young country people, also have predecessors in comic opera. Zerlina is charming and naïve. Masetto at one point does utter some rebellious thoughts, but he is a slow-witted country bumpkin, easily outfoxed by his lord. Mozart's music characterizes them perfectly. In accord with tradition he wrote complex music—dramatic, and with some coloratura display—for those of higher social standing, while providing simple music for Masetto and his bride-to-be. In the duet for Don Giovanni and Zerlina, the famous "La ci darem," Mozart shows consistent observation of this principle, for the Don, intent on succeeding with Zerlina, addresses her in her own musical language, with graceful melody and simple accompaniment. The same applies to the canzonetta—a simple melody with mandolin accompaniment with which Don Giovanni serenades Elvira's maid.

To back up these soloists and several choruses (country people, servants; the chorus of demons in the finale), Mozart supplies an orchestral accompaniment with great variety of texture and tone color. It reveals the same consummate craftsmanship and imagination found in his orchestral works from the same period. Among the woodwinds, clarinets are much in evidence—instruments of which the composer was especially fond and which were not yet generally available. Mozart liked to use them in lyrical and sentimental moments, often playing in parallel thirds. The prominence of woodwinds generally distinguishes Mozart's opera scores from those of many of his contemporaries. He uses them to good effect in the overture, where their rising scale passages, crescendo, repeatedly lead to a sudden piano, conveying a ghostly effect both here and in the corresponding place in the finale:

EXAMPLE 3

Brass instruments are all the more effective for their sparing use, the treatment of trombones being a case in point. Because of their traditional association with church and funeral music they were seldom heard in symphony or opera. Mozart does not use them at all in the overture and first act; their somber tones are heard for the first time in the cemetery scene. Their timbre thus creates a specially startling effect as they provide a harmonic, hymnlike accompaniment to the Commandant's ghostly voice. Mozart may have intended them to be played on the stage, hidden behind or beneath the statue. Trumpets likewise are employed with moderation. After the overture they are not heard again until Donna Anna's dramatic accompagnato "Don Ottavio! son morta!" in which they add to the mood of agitation and urgency. Full, festive scoring distinguishes the Don's rousing "Fin ch'han dal vino," which soon follows (though without trumpets or timpani), and the larger ensembles and choruses, especially in the act finales.

Stage orchestras are introduced on several occasions, each time with distinctive touches. In the first act finale Mozart is not content with having one dance orchestra appear on the stage but provides three. At one point, after some tuning, they perform three different dances simultaneously. A minuet ($\frac{3}{4}$ time, Ottavio and Anna), contradance ($\frac{2}{4}$, Don Giovanni and Zerlina), and waltz ($\frac{3}{8}$, Leporello and Masetto) reach the listener's ear from three locations on the stage. Each dance is self-sufficient, yet they all go together perfectly. Was the effect intended to be humorous? More likely Mozart was aiming for a moment of musical and dramatic realism. The complexity of the music goes with the involved action and confusion which it accompanies: Don Giovanni, dancing with Zerlina, is trying to lead her away from the crowd; Leporello, on

The finale: Leporello, having seen the Statue approach, warns his master: "Don't go out there!"

his master's orders, attempts to lead Masetto in the opposite direction, while the three masked spectators can hardly conceal their rage.

The stage musicians in the second act finale are there simply to supply dinner music, but a special touch again is provided. Mozart has them play tunes from two operas popular at the time. Leporello recognizes them both; when, for their third selection, they strike up the "Non più andrai" from Mozart's own *Figaro,* Leporello laconically remarks: "This one I know only too well!"— words that surely brought down the house in Prague, where this and other tunes from the opera were heard at all streetcorners.

With the first bars of the overture the serious aspect of the *dramma giocoso* is emphasized: the music which later accompanies the statue's appearance is heard. Tempo and mood then change, however, and the opening andante does not return. The overture fulfills the function, stipulated earlier by Gluck, of preparing the audience by establishing the basic mood of the opera. Mozart anticipates both the serious and light moods encountered in the opera itself. Starting in d minor, the overture ends inconclusively on a C major chord that leads into the F major of the opening scene.

The structure of this scene immediately sets it apart from

Leporello and Donna Elvira: The Catalog Aria, Act I.

earlier Italian opera, buffa or seria. After Leporello's short introduction ("Notte e giorno faticar") a trio develops at once, fast
and vigorous, the vehicle for important dramatic developments.
The pace that is set here, and the manner in which ensembles carry
the action forward, remains typical of the entire work. Ensembles,
often with a fluctuating number of participants, may occur any-
where in the drama, though, as was customary, they achieve their
greatest importance and complexity in the finales. In *Don Giovanni,* and even more in *Figaro,* they take up a larger proportion
of the opera than do the arias. Ensembles, even more than secco
recitatives, are the pillars of the drama, and since so much of the
action is lively, the trios, quartets, etc., are mostly allegros. Particularly in the act finales the number of singers increases steadily,
creating a kind of dramatic and musical crescendo that is most
effective. Da Ponte himself, in his *Memoirs,* gives a description of
this particular operatic convention. In an operatic finale "all
singers must appear on stage, whether there are two, three, six, or
sixty of them, and they must sing arias, duets, trios, sextets, or
sessantets. If the plot makes this implausible it is the librettist's
task to *make* it plausible, somehow, even if all the rules of Aris-
totle and of good sense have to be violated. Then, if the finale
does not succeed—worse luck for him."

Mozart probably was the greatest master of the operatic
ensemble, yet there are times when the music gets in the way of the
acting, or, at least, presents difficult tasks for the singer-actors and
the stage director. *Don Giovanni's* opening scene is a case in point:
it is well-nigh impossible for Anna to throw out the intruder
quickly and resolutely; there is so much music that their struggling
is apt to occupy too much time. When, after her father's slaying,
she again emerges from the palace it takes her too long—several
seconds too long, especially on a small stage set—to realize what
has happened. But in most instances Mozart's stage sense and
experience provide the kind and amount of music that results in
ensemble scenes with much drive. In the opening scene and in
many others the dramatic implications of the situation are masterfully exploited through music: the agitated Donna Anna is engaged in verbal and physical struggle with the intruder while
Leporello, the onlooker, comments in his usual calmer fashion on
the developments. The later trio, after the Commandant has been
mortally wounded, is worth close examination. Don Giovanni
calmly observes that the old man is dying; at the same time we
hear the Commandant's weakened voice and gasps—an entirely
different musical line—while Leporello, in characteristic parlando,
expresses disapproval and fear.

Among the many ensembles of action, the final scene in

which the statue arrives is most startling, though musically not the most complex. Others are contemplative and static, including the trio "Protegga il giusto cielo" in which the three participants voice similar (though not identical) emotions in an elaborate passage of great lyrical beauty.

Concern with dramatic effectiveness is also shown in the arrangement of successive arias. Often a whole complex of short arias provides rapid changes and brings unexpected developments, freely shifting between recitative, aria, and ensemble. We find this in the long and involved Scene 3 of Act I. The Don meets Zerlina, and just as she agrees to leave with him, he is thwarted by Elvira, who takes her away ("Ah! fuggi il traditor!"), upon which Anna and Ottavio enter to ask the Don, of all people, for help. But before they can specify their request Elvira once more appears to expose the *dissoluto* (in the quartet "Non ti fidar"). As Anna listens to him try to extricate himself, the horrible truth dawns on her. The arias which support all this are short: Masetto's "Ho capito," the duettino "La ci darem," Elvira's "Ah! fuggi il traditor!" The climax comes with Anna's dramatic accompagnato, followed by "Or sai."

Don Ottavio's pleading with his fiancée (following the cemetery scene) is carried on in secco recitative up to the point at which he calls her cruel, an epithet Donna Anna denies fervently. Mozart therefore switches to accompagnato, with orchestral interpolations of the principal theme from the following "Non mi dir." In that aria she expresses, in not altogether convincing coloraturas, the hope that some day perhaps the heavens will feel pity for her. Those who favor the theory that Donna Anna does not really want to marry Don Ottavio may point to the bravura qualities, to the self-assurance expressed by this grand aria, as evidence of her insincerity. But the point is debatable; similar criticism may be applied to Elvira's "Mi tradi." Both of the arias just mentioned, like most others, are addressed to someone directly. Soliloquies are rarer in Mozart than in earlier Italian opera; in *Don Giovanni* the only examples are Leporello's "Notte e giorno" and Ottavio's "Dalla sua pace."

A number of expressive accompanied recitatives have already been mentioned; Mozart as a rule reserves them to prepare dramatically crucial scenes, charged with tense emotion. In doing so he followed traditions of both Italian and French opera. Passages such as Elvira's "In quali eccessi, o Numi," with the jagged interjections of the orchestra and the carefully indicated dynamics forming a pictorial representation of "la fatale saetta" (arrow or thunderbolt) striking down the evildoer, show Mozart's sure sense of the stage. Chromaticism, modulations, and abrupt harmonic

Masetto and the country people.

changes are freely employed to create feelings of agitation and tension, as in Anna's "Don Ottavio! son morta!"

How Mozart, who did not intend to "reform" opera, towers over the writers of conventional Italian opera, is well expressed by Dent in a comparison of Gazzaniga's *Don Giovanni* (1787) with Mozart's: "Gazzaniga's music is certainly dramatic, and it is also reasonable. . . . But from beginning to end there is not a single theme of any real musical significance. Every figure, vocal or instrumental, is a stock pattern. . . . Compared with Mozart's, it suggests a rehearsal at which the actors walk through their parts in their ordinary clothes, on an empty stage in daylight."[12]

Da Ponte's and Mozart's collaboration proved eminently rewarding because their talents complemented each other. Mozart's own awareness of what kind of texts and words are well suited for composition contributed to the success. In an often-quoted letter he said that in opera, poetry should be "the obedient daughter of music." The statement is easily misunderstood, leading to the assumption that he considered the text to be unimportant. The libretto for *Don Giovanni,* which he in all likelihood helped to shape, belies this, and the letters he wrote while composing *Idomeneo* and the *Seraglio* further clarify his view. Words, especially word repetitions, may at times be adjusted to the requirements of a musical phrase, but Mozart considered it his foremost

[12] *Mozart's Operas,* pp. 154 f. Printed by permission of Oxford University Press.

114

musical task to bring into relief, through appropriate musical means, the characteristics of each person and each dramatic situation.

The Magic Flute
(*Die Zauberflöte*, Vienna, 1791)

In the spring of 1791, some ten years after the *Seraglio*, Mozart received a proposal to write another German opera. The librettist was an old acquaintance, Emanuel Schikaneder (1751–1812), who by that time had seen many ups and downs in his theatrical career. In his youth he had been a serious actor—Hamlet had been one of his roles—but later he assembled and directed a traveling troupe of players. In 1789 he settled in Vienna, writing and producing plays and operas. Schikaneder was a man of the theater, well versed in practical matters and anxious to produce the kind of spectacular play that would bring in the crowds. His libretto for *The Magic Flute* had the qualities that had proven successful in Viennese suburban theaters: a fairy-tale plot that offered much opportunity for stage display and machines; a colorful, exotic setting, a resplendent and haughty queen, a beautiful, sad princess, a wise priest, a virtuous prince—and, last but not least, a comic part which Schikaneder had tailored for himself with loving care.

Mozart is said to have accepted the invitation reluctantly, never having written a *Zauberoper* before. Perhaps he wanted to help Schikaneder, a fellow Mason; perhaps he hoped for some financial success himself.

The extent to which *The Magic Flute* libretto is Schikaneder's own invention has been repeatedly investigated.[13] Certainly he was inspired by and borrowed freely from a variety of sources —rather generously by modern standards but in a manner that did not go beyond the custom of the time. Once Mozart had agreed to the venture his collaboration extended to the text as well. Quite likely it was the composer's influence that lifted the libretto above the world of magic and slapstick.

Opinions about the libretto have always varied. It has been called inane, inconsistent doggerel by some critics who find that only Mozart's music makes the opera bearable. Others have marveled at the profundity of thought hidden behind Schikaneder's verses. Goethe held that in spite of some obvious faults the libretto was dramatically effective; he was fond enough of the work to write a sequel to it.[14]

Persuasive arguments can be advanced for both views. Schikaneder's drama is curiously constructed: passages expressing lofty

---

[13] See, especially, Dent's detailed study, *Mozart's Operas*, pp. 218 ff.
[14] *Der Zauberflöte zweiter Teil* (fragment, 1798).

The appearance of the Queen of the Night. From an early nineteenth-century design by Schinkel.

sentiments are interrupted by Papageno's antics and puns. The spoken dialogue in particular is full of platitudes. Often it is Schikaneder's choice of words rather than the thoughts expressed that appear childish. He was no great poet, and cuts in the dialogue are customary today, even in Austria.

Certainly there is much to delight the unsophisticated spectator: a large serpent is slain, wild animals dance to the sound of Papageno's bells, the three Genii descend in a flying machine, a table with food and drink rises out of the ground. The "star-flaming" Queen appears with thunder and lightning, and an ancient hag, "eighty years and two minutes" old, turns into beautiful young Papagena. But underneath the fairy-tale incidents, and curiously intertwined with them, the allegory of Tamino's purification and initiation unfolds. Many of the ethical concepts of Freemasonry are expressed through this story of the struggle between the forces of darkness and light.

Masonic ideas, ritual, and symbolism clearly inspired some scenes. Among these ideas, expressed primarily by Sarastro and the Speaker, are the belief in tolerance ("In diesen heil'gen Hallen") and in the dignity and goodness of man (Speaker: "He is a prince"; Sarastro: "What is more: he is a human being"). The three Genii remind Tamino and Pamina of the Masonic virtues ("Be steadfast, tolerant, silent"), and Pamina admonishes Papageno to tell "the truth, even if it were a crime." The powers of darkness are represented by women, whom the Masons generally distrusted. The Queen of the Night "deceives her people through superstition"; Tamino should not believe her, for "a woman does little but chatters much." The number three, a frequent symbol in Masonic ritual, appears everywhere in Schikaneder's libretto. Mozart provides trios for the three ladies and the Genii; there also are the three-times-repeated chords in the overture and in Act II, Scene 1. All these allusions to Masonic beliefs and practices must have been fairly evident in Mozart's time. Masonic symbols decorate the title page of the printed libretto, while the Egyptian setting is less strongly suggested by references to Isis and Osiris and by a few stage directions.

It is generally claimed that this Masonic orientation was an afterthought, introduced after much of the first act had already been written, and that for this reason the characters of Sarastro and the Queen of the Night are inconsistently drawn. In the first scenes, it is argued, the good Queen, widowed and helpless, suffers

The frontispiece and title page of the original libretto. Note the Masonic symbols in the frontispiece engraving.

because of Sarastro, the wicked magician who has robbed her of her power. Later on the roles are reversed: the Queen clearly represents the forces of darkness. Sarastro is wisdom personified, and at the end of the opera "the rays of the sun drive away the night." An objective examination of the libretto yields little evidence for the alleged inconsistency. The only references to Sarastro's wickedness are found in remarks by the Queen and her Three Ladies. Her own recitative and aria, in which she appoints Tamino to rescue her daughter, tells us little about herself, but we already can infer that she is determined to regain her power by any means whatever. As Walter Felsenstein says, the Queen is a liar. Her grief is faked, calculated—no real sorrow could be expressed by such coloraturas[15] Masonic sentiments are expressed quite early in the first act, in the Quintet, No. 5. There the Three Ladies, Tamino, and Papageno reflect on the advantage of padlocking the mouths of all liars: "hatred, slander, and venom would then be replaced by fraternal love."

The mixture of the ridiculous and the sublime—dignified temple scenes followed by Papageno's clowning and asides—has led to attempts to rearrange the sequence of some scenes, so that, for instance, the rites of Tamino's and Pamina's purification would not be interrupted by the "Pa-pa-pa-pageno" duet. But the constant changes from the gay to the serious are characteristic of the fairy-tale opera so popular at the time. To eliminate them would mean to impart a different flavor to the opera, undesirable and unnecessary in view of its lasting appeal.

On the original playbill *The Magic Flute* was called a *Grosse Oper*. The term seems appropriate, not only for musical reasons to be discussed presently, but also in view of its stage possibilities. It is the kind of opera that gains, today as then, from colorful, elaborate staging, from an approach that does not play down the spectacle as something to be ashamed of. A *Magic Flute* production should not be an economy item in the budget of any opera house.

It may be in the nature of Schikaneder's subject that the characters are not as subtly drawn as they had been in *Figaro* or *Don Giovanni*. Whether we interpret *The Magic Flute* on the level of a fairy tale or an allegory, its main concern is not the individual human being, involved in true-to-life situations. Hence the subtle psychological touches are missing. Tamino is an idealized prince, beautiful and good. He is manly (though he faints at the sight of the serpent!), generally calm and determined. His love of Pamina, at the first sight of her picture, is ardent, and he soon vows to save her. Tamino's music, beginning with his first, most important aria, expresses these qualities: it is dignified and of great lyrical beauty.

[15] *Musiktheater* (Bremen, 1961), pp. 49 f.

EXAMPLE 4

Dies Bild-'nis ist be-zau-bernd schön, wie noch kein Au-ge je ge - sehn!

[*O picture of magic beauty, such as no eye has ever seen!*]

Pamina is the expected complement. She displays the same virtues, except that, being a woman, she is weak, at least momentarily. Normally an obedient daughter, she is horrified by her mother's command to murder Sarastro. The serene side of her nature is most beautifully portrayed in her duet with Papageno, "Bei Männern, welche Liebe fühlen." When she approaches Tamino and he refuses to answer her, bidding her to go away, her feelings find expression in an aria not of violent despair but of profound sadness and resignation, and she longs for death:

EXAMPLE 5

Ach, ich fühl's, es ist ver-schwun-den, e - wig— hin mein gan-zes— Glück, e - wig

[*Ah, I feel that love's bliss has vanished forever.*]

Her mind clouded with despair, she weakens so far as to consider ending her own life, but she is deterred by the three Genii, who remind her that "suicide is punished by God." In the end she shows sufficient virtue to be allowed to undergo the trial.

To these two lyrical roles, dramatic and musical contrast is provided chiefly by the Queen of the Night. Her appearances are few and of short duration, yet she must be dramatically convincing as the determined, wicked queen. Since she has little opportunity to act (she sits on her throne throughout her first aria), her character somehow must be communicated through her posture, a few gestures, through lighting and makeup. Her voice must have the appropriate timbre, and her coloraturas must be "queenly"—sure and seemingly effortless. Both of her arias (and only hers) contain florid passages in the best Italian tradition; Mozart may have intended them to impart a glittery, unreal quality to the role. Her coloraturas, incidentally, are one reason why this opera cannot be classified as a traditional Singspiel.

Sarastro, the high priest, again is the representative of moral, ethical values and beliefs, rather than a human being of flesh and blood. His wisdom, tolerance, and magnanimity relate him to the Bassa Selim of the *Seraglio*. For Sarastro's arias Mozart employs a consistently noble and simple, hymnlike style, with an essentially homophonic accompaniment:

EXAMPLE 6

[*Strengthen them with patience in the hour of danger.*]

This style, also found in the March of the Priests and in some choral scenes, is very similar to what Mozart employed in several compositions written for his Masonic lodge in Vienna. The choice and treatment of wind instruments (including basset horns) in the ritual scenes reinforces the similarity. The key of E flat major, in which *The Magic Flute* begins and ends, likewise is Mozart's favored tonality in these Masonic compositions.

To all these exalted characters contrast and comic relief is provided by Papageno. Schikaneder was not modest: many of Papageno's scenes are dramatically unnecessary but provided the

Papageno: An illustration from the original libretto, 1791.

author–actor with opportunities to display his comic talent. Papageno is the simple child of nature. Unaware of the world except for his immediate surroundings, he lives for the pleasures of food and drink and longs for female companionship. He also is a coward. In some of these ways he resembles Leporello, but he lacks his worldly experience and cynicism. Papageno's wishes are simple, and in the end his human weaknesses are forgiven. While Tamino and Pamina are rewarded with "beauty and wisdom," Papageno's reward is a girl just like him—hence her name Papagena. His contrasting nature to the serious characters is reflected in his music. His two arias (Nos. 2 and 20) come close to the style of folk song. Melodies consist of short, simply constructed phrases:

EXAMPLE 7

Der— Vo-gel-fän-ger— bin ich ja, stets lu - stig hei - sa hop-sa -sa! ich

[I am the bird-catcher, always gay.]

Their rhythm is pronounced, simple and dancelike. Both of his songs are strophic. While No. 2 consists of identical stanzas, the accompaniment in No. 20 contains variations for the Glockenspiel in each of the three verses.

Secco recitative is not found in either the *Seraglio* or *The Magic Flute,* but accompanied recitative takes the place of spoken dialogue in some important scenes, notably the dialogue between Tamino and the Priest (finale of Act I). In keeping with the seriousness of the topic, it has a stately quality. Its somewhat slower pace also reflects the prosody of German as opposed to Italian.

The less individualistic character drawing in this opera affects the nature of the ensemble scenes as well. Generally speaking they are simpler, serving for the most part to express unanimity of thought or feeling. The three ladies in the Queen's service sing several trios, of which the first is rather long for its position so early in the opera. The three Genii—to be sung by boys, preferably, rather than women—likewise sing as a group, not as three individuals. Other ensemble scenes, for instance the quintet, No. 5, which begins with the padlocked Papageno's humming, also lack the complex part writing of *Figaro* or *Don Giovanni.* The song of the Two Men in Armor represents yet a different style: here Mozart gives to both voices an ancient German chorale melody, surrounded, in the manner of a Baroque cantus firmus, by a polyphonic web provided by the orchestra:

EXAMPLE 8

Two Men in Armor (CHORALE: "Ach Gott, vom Himmel sieh darein")

Der, wel-cher wan-delt die-se Stra-ße voll Be-schwer-de,

[*Who wanders on this toilsome road*]

The hymnlike nature of some of the choruses has already been mentioned; others serve, in the traditional manner, to announce Sarastro's arrival or to praise the wisdom of his decisions.

Papageno and the three Genii.

Monostatos, Pamina, and Papageno.

The Magic Flute begins with Mozart's most substantial overture, in which an extensive contrapuntal main section follows the stately opening, with its repeated wind chords. Aside from these, the overture contains no thematic material from the opera itself. Throughout the opera, instrumental color is provided chiefly by those instruments which are associated with the principal characters: Tamino's flute, Papageno's Panpipe and bells. When Monostatos, the wicked Moor, sings his "Alles fühlt der Liebe Freuden," a piccolo provides a subdued but sparkling accompaniment—a kind of weirdly Oriental effect. Mention has already been made of the wind instruments in the scenes involving Sarastro: trombones, trumpets, and the dark-colored basset horns.

HAYDN'S OPERAS   Having reached the end of a chapter on Classic opera the reader may wonder why there has been no mention of Mozart's great contemporary, Joseph Haydn. It is true that the list of Haydn's operas is substantial, and many of them were performed successfully during his lifetime, but for a number of reasons they have not maintained themselves in today's repertory. Asked why he did not continue to write operas, Haydn pointed out that his style was suited to the special performance conditions at Esterháza, the secluded country estate of his prince. His operas, he stated, could not have been successful at the large court opera houses of Vienna, Prague, or other capitals. Haydn's explanations may in part have been rationalizations. After becoming acquainted with Mozart's operatic masterpieces, he freely acknowledged the superiority of his young friend and colleague in this genre. Admittedly this caused him to cultivate other forms, such as symphony and quartet, in which he knew he could excel. Unlike Mozart, whose father took him on several extensive journeys to Italy, Haydn did not have the opportunity to soak up opera at the source. This inability to gain first-hand familiarity with Italian opera he often deplored; combined with differences of personality it may in part explain Haydn's lack of international success in opera while reaping honors all over Europe with instrumental music and his late oratorios. Today, almost two hundred years later, some Haydn operas are occasionally revived and increasingly appreciated, while several lost works have been rediscovered.

To divert Dr. Bartolo's attention, Figaro, in shaving him, uses a generous amount of soap. From a Metropolitan Opera production of "The Barber of Seville."

5

EARLY NINETEENTH-CENTURY OPERA

THE POLITICAL DEVELOPMENTS OF THE eighteenth century that culminated in the French Revolution brought about sweeping changes in the structure of European society. In many countries monarchies and other aristocratic forms of government continued to exist, but often their economic foundations were shaky. When expenditures for court entertainment were curtailed, opera, being specially expensive, was among the first to be affected. As the aristocracy's role as patron and sponsor of music diminished, public presentations of concerts and operas became more frequent. The educated middle class had participated in various musical activities of the Baroque and Classic ages (e.g., the *collegia musica* of the universities); now it came to have greater influence on the general musical repertory, even at court establishments. Similarly, the private nature of court performances—for the ruler's family and invited guests—changed to our present-day concept of public presentation. Audiences were anonymous, since admission was open to anyone willing to buy a ticket. Paid admissions, rather than princely munificence, now were essential to meeting expenses; the profit motive consequently caused managers, impresarios, and administrative directors to give greater consideration to the tastes of an audience, hoping to attract and please a larger public than had been in attendance under the old social order.

These conditions reinforced the traditional tendency of opera to stress the spectacular. They also caused bigger opera houses to be built, with seating capacities of 1,500 or more,[1] larger and sumptuous foyers, restaurants, and other public rooms. In writing for these houses composers, in turn, kept different performance conditions in mind. The orchestra increased in size, making heavier demands on the singers, while spacious stages invited the monumental effects and crowd scenes associated with grand opera, discussed later in this chapter.

The nineteenth century became the age of the virtuoso performer. Though there had been famous singers before, their "box-office potential" now was of particular concern to managers. Billboards sometimes advertised a performance by printing the prima donna's name in bold type and by referring in equally large letters to new sets "painted expressly for the occasion," while the names of librettist and composer were barely visible.

Though popular appeal was a consideration, nineteenth-century opera was not "for the people." It continued to be patronized predominantly by the educated upper middle class, rather than by the workers and artisans of a rapidly expanding industrial society. Wagner, it is true, had visions of Germans from all walks of life united by attending performances of music drama at Bayreuth, but in practice it was only after the First World War, and especially under totalitarian regimes, that opera performances were arranged for large numbers of workers.

The social changes that affected the makeup of nineteenth-century audiences also had important consequences for the composer. No longer content to be a lowly servant to a music-loving prince, the artist gained social acceptance and importance, frequently (as in Beethoven's case) considering himself an equal, by virtue of ability and "genius," of the nobleman who may still have provided his economic support. A composer wrote for audiences of his own social and educational standing, and therefore felt free to communicate on a more personal level than the old order would have condoned.

[1] Graf, *Opera for the People,* pp. 116 ff., gives statistics.

Middle-class patronage meant changes in subject matter: there was more middle-class drama. Still, subject matter, as in previous ages, continued to be socially limited. Just as in eighteenth-century opera seria a middle-class hero (say a merchant) would have been most unusual, in nineteenth-century bourgeois opera we do not find the proletariat represented—no factory workers in important roles; not, at least, until the age of naturalism and verismo. Protagonists in serious opera were on a social level comparable to that of the audience—perhaps higher, but not lower.

As the opera composer's social standing increased, he became a person of greater authority in the profession as well. His scores contained specific directions about matters of interpretation. Exact tempi were indicated, especially after the introduction of Mälzel's metronome (ca. 1816); embellishments were written out, and a great variety of dynamic markings was supplied. Singers, as a result, no longer could take the accustomed liberties. An eighteenth-century composer's contract may have stipulated that he was to take charge of rehearsals and stay for the first few performances of the new opera, present in the orchestra pit though not conducting. After his departure the concertmaster (leader of the violins) would be in charge. In the nineteenth century the opera *conductor* made his appearance, at first in Italy, as the person responsible for rehearsals and performances, charged with the observation of the composer's intentions and with general precision of execution. Inevitably this meant that singers came to take more seriously their function as interpreters of someone else's music. Composers with strong personalities, Verdi and Wagner among them, did much to bring about this different state of affairs.

Ludwig van Beethoven, *Fidelio* (Third Version, Vienna, 1814)

As harpsichord player in the Bonn orchestra, young Beethoven (1770–1827) had ample opportunity to become acquainted with the repertory of his time. Much of it was light and superficial, but it also included operas by Mozart and Cherubini—works that made a strong impression on him. Though *Fidelio* was to remain his only opera, he had plans and hopes for others.

Of all the arts other than music, drama attracted Beethoven most. He read the important German and French writers of his time, and he was constantly on the lookout for librettos that would suit him. As an ardent champion of the ideas of the Enlightenment he was most readily attracted by subjects embodying these, glorifying humane, noble, heroic thoughts and deeds. *Fidelio* furnishes an example, as does his other dramatic music and the choral finale of the Ninth Symphony.

Beethoven held lofty views about the theater; its purpose to him was the presentation of highly ethical, moral subjects capable of improving and educating an audience. Hence he disliked plays or operas that were mere entertainment, all the more so if subject or treatment were frivolous. Much of the repertory performed in Vienna (to which city he had moved in 1792) thus incurred his displeasure. He may also have been somewhat envious of the successes of fashionable Italian composers, especially Rossini, and he blamed the Viennese for liking this light music better than his own works. In spite of his general admiration for Mozart, he said that he could never compose operas like *Figaro* or *Don Giovanni;* "scandalous" subjects to him were a desecration of art.

A composer in whose operas Beethoven found dramatic qualities conforming closely to his views was Luigi Cherubini, then highly esteemed in Vienna. During the 1802–3 season three of Cherubini's operas were given there; of these *Elisa* impressed Beethoven greatly—the story of a devoted woman who attempts to save her beloved one from the perils of Alpine storms and avalanches. The plot of *Les Deux Journées* (known in German as *Der Wasserträger*) involves the daring rescue of a politically persecuted nobleman, a rescue in which his wife takes part. It contains marked similarities to the subject and literary style of Beethoven's own opera, the full title of which is *Fidelio, Or Conjugal Love.*

Operas in which courage, love, and devotion overcome injustice and villainy were much in vogue during and after the French Revolution; the genre is sometimes called "horror and rescue opera." It was popular because people still retained vivid memories of acts of violence and heroism that had occurred during the stormy political upheavals of the late eighteenth century.[2]

Beethoven's opera belongs to this category. Its author was the French lawyer J. N. Bouilly, who had also supplied the libretto for *Les Deux Journées.* He had based the play, titled *Léonore,* on events that had taken place while he held public office during the Reign of Terror, 1792–94. To avoid troubles with the censor, he changed the locale to Spain. Bouilly's text had been set by Pierre Gaveaux in 1798; the topical and effective story was soon seized by other composers. Emanuel Schikaneder, whom we have encountered as Mozart's librettist, suggested the subject to Beethoven; a German adaptation of the text was then prepared by Joseph Sonnleithner. To avoid confusion with other Leonore operas,

2 Menotti's *The Consul* (see below, Chapter 15), achieved great popularity in Europe right after World War II, possibly for similar reasons.

Beethoven (or others) eventually decided on the title *Fidelio*.

That work on the opera progressed slowly and tentatively can be seen from Beethoven's many sketches. Over the years this "favorite child" caused the composer much grief. The original version in three acts turned out to be too long. Its failure was due in part to the adverse conditions in Vienna shortly after Napoleon had occupied the city. Several friends urged Beethoven to revise and shorten the score; although he was at first furious at the suggestion, he eventually complied. But the second version (1806, now in two acts) was also soon withdrawn, owing to a number of disagreements and personality clashes. Not until eight years later did another version appear, with numerous revisions of text and music. This is the form in which the opera is almost always heard today.

The highly moral aspects of the plot are evident. Its main theme, wedded love, assumes added significance against the political background: love leads to the triumph of justice over tyranny. Noble sentiments are voiced in several scenes: they lead to the brief release of the prisoners; they are expressed by Florestan, who

Anton Dermota as Florestan.

is comforted by the knowledge that he has done his duty; and they permeate the entire finale, particularly the words of the minister: "Tyrannenstrenge sei mir fern. . . . Es sucht der Bruder seine Brüder." ("Far be it from me to be a ruthless tyrant. . . . A brother seeks his brothers.")

Opinions about the dramatic effectiveness of *Fidelio* are divided. The opera is still in the standard repertory, especially in Austria and Germany, but the fact that it is the only opera by the great Beethoven in part accounts for this. The subject continues to have strong appeal, but the pace of the drama is uneven. In view of the lofty subject, the domesticity of the opening scene seems trite: Marzelline is busy with her ironing, at the same time warding off the amorous Jaquino and his talk of marriage. Dramatically and musically this opening duet, much of the spoken dialogue, and Rocco's aria about the necessity of money impress us as bows to the conventions of the eighteenth-century bourgeois Singspiel. The lyrical quartet so close to the opera's beginning also retards the pace, which quickens only gradually: not until Pizarro's entrance and his great vengeance aria, "Ha! welch' ein Augenblick!", is the full dramatic tension established. The first part of Act II, with Florestan's recitative and aria, the grave-digging scene, Pizarro's "Er sterbe!", and Leonore's revelation of her identity bring the climax and denouement. But now, before the final scene, an intermission must take place—long enough, at least, for the change of sets. A break at this point is dramatically unfortunate, for in essence the drama is over when the arrival of the rescuing minister has been announced and Pizarro has been foiled. That he now will meet his just deserts will cause little excitement; that Jaquino will marry Marzelline seems all too conventionally operatic.[3] The final scene, though long, thus accomplishes little with regard to the external action but provides the composer with an opportunity for the expression of moral sentiment. Beethoven did so with sincere, brilliant, and moving music, largely choral, in praise of justice, mercy, and marital love and devotion, in a scene that anticipates the mood of the Ninth Symphony finale.

Technically speaking, *Fidelio* is a Singspiel, consisting of spoken dialogue,[4] arias, ensembles, and choruses. Unusual and effective is the use of melodrama (see the Glossary) in the dungeon scene. The generally serious and somber subject, as well as several intensely dramatic scenes with accompanied recitatives and florid arias, lift *Fidelio* above the Singspiel as it was usually

---

[3] Marzelline's change of heart is clearly implied in the 1806 libretto; less clearly so in the later version.

[4] Recitatives occasionally have been substituted, at the Metropolitan Opera and elsewhere. No valid reasons exist for this practice, which has largely disappeared today.

understood in the later eighteenth century, moving it closer to French opera of the revolutionary era.

To remedy some of the dramatic weaknesses modern producers have occasionally modified the spoken dialogue (as had already been done in 1806 and 1814)—not only by shortening it but also by bringing it somewhat closer to modern usage and taste. One might debate whether this is artistically defensible; the question is worth thinking about since the principle involved applies to other operas. On the affirmative side one might remember that better, idiomatic *translations* of operas are generally welcomed today, and that these also result in texts not known by the composer. Furthermore, the textual changes mentioned for *Fidelio* extend only to Sonnleithner's spoken parts, not to the words set by Beethoven.

The opera's principal characters are drawn with simple, bold strokes, black or white, villainous or heroic. Leonore—once more a trouser role, with all its problems of casting, acting, and singing—is all virtue, steadfast devotion, humility, and courage. (*Illustration,* p. 6.) But she is not a lifeless personification of *virtù* in the manner of Baroque opera. Her doubts of her own strength to endure the ordeal, her sudden display of cold-blooded courage, and her happiness to be reunited with Florestan—all these make her appealing as a human being. These qualities, incidentally, were not as prominent in the two earlier versions. By comparison Florestan's part is but a small one, simply and nobly drawn. Pizarro, on the other hand, is one of the blackest villains in the annals of opera—a character who would strike us as exaggerated in a spoken play. But in this opera as in others (*Der Freischütz, Tosca*) a completely evil nature is somehow rendered credible through music—an art, as has been said before, that succeeds well in expressing such basic emotions or qualities of character. Just how readily we accept Pizarro also depends on his acting. I remember one Pizarro who, after the great vengeance aria, No. 7, *immediately* continued with spoken dialogue, calling for the captain of the guard. In the interest of the drama, he thus deprived himself of one of the traditional opportunities for receiving applause. An interruption by the audience—worse yet, Pizarro's acknowledging the applause with a bow—indeed destroys the mood that Beethoven creates here.

Rocco is a slightly more complex character; a simple person, to be sure, but caught up in a situation that brings him into conflict with his own conscience. The figure, and the dilemma, are only too familiar from more recent pages of history: living in an environment of political despotism, Rocco inwardly rebels but follows all orders short of murder. He wants to stay out of trouble. "For the

*Pizarro and Rocco. From
a recent Vienna produc-
tion.*

likes of us it is best to know as few secrets as possible." He balks
at Pizarro's order to kill, but he cooperates with him, telling
himself that death will be a relief to Florestan. Giving in to
Leonore's entreaties, he allows the prisoners a few minutes of air
and sunshine, but when Pizarro returns, Rocco, fearful of his
wrath, quickly assures him that Florestan will die. Even in the
dungeon scene, when Leonore boldly steps between Pizarro and
Florestan, Rocco still urges her to desist.

Marzelline and Jaquino both have minor parts, on the
drama's periphery. Her fondness for "Fidelio" serves to justify
Rocco's interest and confidence in the "young man," thus motivat-
ing Fidelio's presence during the dungeon scene.

Though the prisoners appear only twice, they are important
actors, essential in establishing the atmosphere of tyranny and
oppression that is the opera's underlying mood. Their appearance
and acting must be profoundly moving. As they first emerge from
their dark cells, weak and cowed, they can hardly believe that they
are breathing the gentle, fresh air. Hope returns for the first time:
with the word "freedom" their singing reaches a fortissimo. A

guard appearing on the wall serves to remind them of their condition, and soon they revert to their former, terrorized state. Good acting is imperative here; the audience must never gain the impression that "twenty gentlemen of the chorus are performing a four-part composition by Beethoven" (Hans-Georg Hoffmann).

The middle-class family environment of the opening scenes is reflected in the relatively simple music, closer to the Singspiel tradition than what follows. Much repetition characterizes the opening duet; the repeated knocking at the gate results in musical repetitions as well. Melodic phrases are short; the accompaniment is simple and unobtrusive. Rocco's song about money both textually and musically comes close to being trivial. It was eliminated from the 1806 version but restored to please the singer of Rocco's part in 1814. Today it is often omitted. More substantial is the lyrical quartet, No. 3, in which we hear Leonore's singing voice for the first time. The quartet is in canon; i.e., the four voices enter successively, with the same music. Modifications are largely rhythmical, to accommodate the different words sung by each participant. Another ensemble, the trio for Rocco, Marzelline, and Leonore, further delays the unfolding of the principal action. With Pizarro's aria an ominous mood takes over. Sweeping, frequently angular melodic lines, irregular accents, and agitated

The chorus of prisoners.

accompaniment reveal Beethoven's dramatic talent more than anything up to this point in the score. He modifies the immediate
repetition of the text in a number of musical ways that create
heightened tension. With a fortissimo outburst of D major the
peak of Pizarro's frenzy is reached, and his shouts of "Triumph!"
are forcefully underscored by the orchestra. The guards overhear
him; their fear and awe is expressed by subdued choral interjections while the villain's raving continues. The duet between Rocco
and Pizarro that follows is much less intense. This is as it should
be in order to set off Leonore's great scene, the recitative and aria
"Abscheulicher! wo eilst du hin?", one of the high points of the
opera.

Four bars of orchestral introduction, allegro agitato, express
Leonore's feelings as she emerges from her hiding place, horrified
by the conversation just overheard. Every line of her recitative
expresses a different emotion; the changes are minutely observed in
the music with tempo changes, tremolo accompaniment ("Doch
toben auch des Meeres Wogen"—"Though the ocean may rage"),
and expressive orchestration that anticipates some of the favorite
effects of Romantic opera (modulation and woodwind writing at
the mention of a bright rainbow: "So leuchtet mir ein Farben-
bogen"). The aria itself begins adagio, with an accompaniment
distinguished by prominent writing for three French horns—again
anticipating practices of Weber and later Romantics. Some vocal
passage work is echoed in the horn parts. With the allegro con brio
section Leonore's sentiment changes to courage and determination,
aptly expressed by a new theme:

EXAMPLE 1

Characteristically the aria's second section, providing the climax,
stresses the words "mich stärkt die Pflicht der treuen Gattenliebe"
("strengthened by my vows of faithful conjugal love"). We have
here an effective "exit aria," ending with a flourish—coloratura
writing, to be sure, but for dramatic emphasis rather than mere
vocal display.

Following the prisoners' chorus, Rocco reveals to Leonore
that she must help him dig the grave of "that man." Her anxiety
and impatience—might he be her husband?—appear from several
intensely emotional phrases, but the duet ends conventionally:

EXAMPLE 2

[Let us not delay any longer; we must follow the call of duty.]

Beethoven's introduction to Act II, a masterpiece of instrumental writing, evokes the mood of desolation and horror visibly established by the stage set, the dark and dismal prison. Contrasts of string and wind color in the opening chords, an expressive unison figure in the strings, sudden, off-beat accents—these and other devices so frequent in Beethoven's symphonies and other instrumental music here are used with telling effect. They carry over into Florestan's recitative, where tremolos in the lower strings and restless, irregular timpani figures accompany his exclamations. A striking and beautiful modulation lends importance to his resignation that God's will be done:

EXAMPLE 3

[I shall not complain: the measure of my suffering is in God's hands.]

The opening theme of the aria

EXAMPLE 4

[Good fortune left me in the springtime of my life.]

137

is familiar to concertgoers from the overture *Leonore No. 3* (see below). Florestan's aria rises in intensity, in a way that reminds us of Leonore's great scene discussed above. In the poco allegro section the starved, feverish prisoner experiences a vision, calm at first though intense, eventually "bordering on madness." Both the voice part, with short, breathless phrases, and the accompaniment express this most persuasively. At the end Florestan sinks down exhausted, while the accompaniment dies down to a whisper, a last flickering of life.

Musically, Leonore's and Florestan's scenes are the high points of the opera. The dramatic climax is reached in the quartet, No. 14, beginning with Pizarro's "Er sterbe!" ("Let him die!"), proceeding rapidly to Leonore's "Töt' erst sein Weib!" ("First kill his wife!") and to the trumpet signal from the tower.

At the end of this scene, and preceding the opera's finale, the overture *Leonore No. 3* is often played, a custom going back at least to the end of the nineteenth century. Beethoven had realized that it was too weighty a symphonic composition to serve as the traditional overture; hence for the 1814 version he substituted the far shorter and simpler *Fidelio* overture. To "rescue" *Leonore No. 3* by playing it after the dungeon scene can hardly be justified on dramatic grounds. Much of its musical material—the trumpet calls are the most glaring example—refers to earlier scenes and hence appears regressive, weakening the impact of the finale. Conductors who insist on playing the overture at this point are apt to do so for musical reasons alone. It is a brilliant composition in its own right. It has the added advantage that it connects perfectly with the preceding scene, beginning with the same note on which that scene had ended.

We have already alluded to the ceremonial character of the opera's finale, an ending necessary for the expression of Beethoven's ethical views. Though its position as a separate scene may be awkward, it complements, emotionally and musically, the rapid developments preceding it. The scene change was added for the 1814 version. Broad daylight contrasts with the gloom of the previous scene, symbolizing the victory of "the powers of light" in a manner that reminds one of the *Magic Flute* finale. For the combined choruses of the people and the prisoners Beethoven writes majestic music, harmonically and rhythmically simple. Nobility of sentiment prevails in the ensuing scene, which essentially belongs to Don Fernando, the minister. Once more the orchestra serves to express the unspeakable—the joy of Leonore and of Florestan, whose chains are at last removed. Soloists and chorus then alternate and join in varying vocal combinations for the final expression of praise: "Nie wird es zu hoch besungen,

Retterin des Gatten sein" ("To be the husband's rescuer can never be praised too highly").

Fidelio followed Mozart's great operas by less than twenty years. Given Beethoven's views of the purpose of drama, *Fidelio* is a sincere, generally effective, and frequently moving realization of his goal. Yet Leo Schrade's estimate of the two composers as dramatists is to the point:

Beethoven's understanding of man moved entirely within the moral, metaphysical and philosophical realms. Mozart's understanding went deeper and was more realistic and universal, for he wished to exclude no aspect of human nature. Thus he necessarily was the greater dramatist.[5]

Gioacchino Rossini, *The Barber of Seville* (*Il Barbiere di Siviglia*; Rome, 1816)

Though Rossini (1792–1868) composed an impressive number of serious and light operas, only *The Barber of Seville* is perennially popular today. In the composer's own day several of his serious works were highly regarded: the early *Tancredi* (1813) and *Otello* (1816); *Mosé in Egitto* (1818; revised 1827), the later *Semiramide* (1823) and, especially, *William Tell* (1829). It is well known that with the last-mentioned work Rossini stopped writing operas, for reasons that have never been fully explained. Dramatic weaknesses may explain the disappearance of his other works (though *La Cenerentola,* 1817, and some of the works mentioned above are occasionally performed today), but *The Barber of Seville,* while not free of such weaknesses, has proven its vitality for some 150 years.

Like many popular generalizations, the notion that it is a "singer's opera" has some factual basis. The tremendous vogue of Rossini's operas caused much unhappiness to Beethoven and other contemporary composers, who attributed this popularity to Rossini's tuneful and effective vocal writing. Indeed *The Barber*'s greatest appeal has always been the sparkling beauty of its melodies, offering many opportunities for the display of vocal dexterity. But it would be unjust to overlook the composer's skillful exploitation, in many places, of the text's dramatic possibilities, or to deny his mastery in handling the orchestra.

The story of *The Barber* still amuses today's audiences—an indication that slapstick episodes, no matter how often seen or how heavily handled, are apt to induce welcome laughter, and that the opera's basic theme, given in the subtitle as *L'Inutile Precauzione*

[5] Leo Schrade, *Mozart* (Bern, 1964), p. 168. My translation. Copyright 1964 by A. Francke A. G. Verlag, Bern, Switzerland.

(freely paraphrased as "Love Conquers All Obstacles")—has timeless appeal.

The subject had proven its effectiveness in a variety of earlier dramatizations. For centuries audiences had laughed at characters like the old suspicious doctor, outwitted by a smart young thing, or the drunken soldier, the complaining chambermaid, the scoundrelly music master. Such figures were common in Italian commedia dell'arte (see above, Chapter 3) and can be met in plays by Molière, Cervantes, and others. They reached their greatest literary fame in Beaumarchais's comedy *Le Barbier de Séville,* on which Sterbini's libretto for Rossini is based.

The transformation of a stage play into an opera is not unusual, but Beaumarchais's first version (1772) had been an opéra comique for which he himself had written some music, based on Spanish folk songs. It was never given in that form. Before it could become a success as a spoken play it underwent further modifications, largely because of its daring political, revolutionary implications. In his prose play the French dramatist made lifelike human beings out of the commedia dell'arte types. The dialogue contains much food for thought, political and otherwise. When the play was transformed into a libretto the usual simplification of action and characterization took place. As a result Sterbini's characters, with the exception of Figaro, again are "types," amusing and sympathetic though they may appear.

Rossini's *Barber* was not the first opera on the subject. In 1782 Giovanni Paisiello's *Barber of Seville,* on a libretto by Petrosellini, had been successfully performed. (Paisiello's opera thus antedates Mozart's *Figaro,* based on Beaumarchais's sequel to

The multiple-scene set of a San Francisco production of "The Barber of Seville."

Le Barbier.) Rossini, over thirty years later, was well aware of Paisiello's opera. In writing another *Barber* he was paying traditional homage to the effectiveness of the subject, just as numerous *Tito* operas had preceded Mozart's. Out of respect for the older composer—or so he stated in his preface—Rossini changed the title to *Almaviva, Ossia l'Inutile Precauzione,* but this was soon discarded. Sterbini provided a number of episodes not found in Beaumarchais (or Petrosellini), thinking them to be effective in an opera: the serenade of the opening scene and the appearance of the guard at the end of Act I.

At its first performance Rossini's opera was a dismal failure. The story that this was due to intrigues engineered by Paisiello is discredited today; a series of mishaps, as described by the Rosina of the first performance, are the more likely reasons. Subsequent performances brought enthusiastic audience approval, and *The Barber* has been one of the most durable operas.

Its slapstick episodes and broad humor certainly have contributed to this. Doctor Bartolo is a caricature; crotchety and suspicious, full of plans and precautions that fail. In the shaving scene soap traditionally is scattered over most of the doctor; the drunken soldier, sword in hand, staggers around the stage and constantly mispronounces Bartolo's name. Servants are lazy and sleepy (their yawning and sneezing are given broader play by Paisiello); the music master is unctuous and slovenly. When his return threatens to upset the lovers' scheme, Figaro and the Count convince him of his own illness, and he staggers away, yellow and shaking. His description of calumny and its devastating effects, listened to by the awed doctor, can be extremely humorous.

Broad comedy of this kind does not try to win an audience by subleties of characterization. Neither Rosina nor the Count nor Figaro is drawn in any profound manner. Rosina is young, determined, uncomplicated—she has not yet had time to grow up into Mozart's Countess. Count Almaviva is revealed as the ardent young lover—little more. Rossini's Figaro, unlike Mozart's, is best characterized by what we first hear of him: his offstage "la, la, la's," followed by the well-known "Largo al factotum" with its light-hearted patter.

The overture that introduces us to this carefree comedy is appropriately sparkling, even though it had done duty for two of Rossini's earlier operas. In his view of an overture's function such a substitution was entirely in order—the music was to set the mood for what followed, without showing, through its musical material, any more specific relation to the work.[6] The overture thus is an

---

[6] According to Francis Toye, Rossini wrote a new overture for *The Barber,* based on Spanish popular themes, which soon became lost. (*Rossini,* New York, 1947, p. 46.)

abstract piece of music. It has always been a standby of concert programs, incorporating some of Rossini's most characteristic features. There is much drive in the allegro, rhythmic vitality, and a typical "vamp" bass. The gradual increase in volume found here occurs in so many of his orchestral and ensemble passages that the nickname "Signor Crescendo" was bestowed on him. The overture ends with numerous repetitions of a cadential passage—also a trademark. Later in the opera the orchestra once more is prominent during the storm music of Act II, which Rossini also borrowed from an earlier opera.

The Count's first aria, "Ecco ridente," with which he serenades the invisible Rosina, is a vocal showpiece of considerable difficulty. In the opera's first performance Rossini allowed the tenor to substitute a Spanish song and to accompany himself on the guitar. For a number of reasons this proved disastrous, and ever since then Rossini's own cavatina (also taken from an earlier opera) has been used. A guitar, rather than a harp, should supply the accompaniment, even if it emanates from the orchestra pit. The numerous embellishments written out by the composer and a high range make this scene taxing and at times precarious—a vocal tour de force that reveals little about the Count himself but presumably impresses Rosina. With this coloratura aria we find ourselves in an entirely different medium from Mozart's *Figaro,* though coloratura singing was by no means unknown to the Viennese public.

Almaviva's cavatina leads into several bars of secco recitative, sometimes obscured by applause. The musicians (on stage) now are paid and dismissed. In many productions the stage business here implies that they are dissatisfied with their fee. Sterbini's libretto does not call for this interpretation, though the players' noisy obsequiousness might well annoy the Signor Conte. The little bit of dialogue is drawn out in typical Rossini fashion, through endless repetition and sequential passages, with a light, staccato accompaniment:

EXAMPLE 5

Ah ma-le-det-ti an-da-te vi-a, ma-le-det-ti an-da-te vi-a, ah— ca-ne-glia, vi-a di qua!

[*Cursed people, go away!*]

Later on, encouraged by Figaro, Almaviva begins another serenade (No. 5, "Se il mio nome"), in a less spectacular vein but revealing Rossini's facility of melodic invention, with characteristic expressive modulations:

EXAMPLE 6

Io son Lin - do-ro che fi - do v'a - do-ro, che spo-sa vi bra-mo,che a no-me vi chia-mo, che a no - me vi chia - mo, di voi sem-pre par - lan-do co - sì...

[*I am Lindoro who faithfully adores you / Who wishes you to be his wife; / You, whose name he is calling; / Who always speaks of you thus . . .*]

Before this canzona we hear what is perhaps the most effective "entrance aria" in all opera—Figaro's "Largo al factotum." It is prepared by a long orchestral introduction during which Figaro is

143

still backstage, giving out several "La, la, la, lera's." His very entrance often is greeted with applause. In this aria Rossini provides a brilliant characterization of the title role—one of the best examples of the patter song so typical of opera buffa. The tempo, as rapid as humanly possible, does much to establish the mood of ebullience, youthful exuberance, and optimism. Several harmonic excursions (from C to G and E flat, and the outburst in A flat on "Ahimè!") help to maintain the pace and audience attention. Lively acting, insofar as the torrent of words permits, accompanies the singing. Traditionally Figaro engages in several bits of stage business suggested by the text, e.g., looking around everywhere as though people were calling him from all sides. This brilliant aria gains from Rossini's typical accompaniment patterns, light in texture, with numerous repeated-note figures, staccato. Patter songs of this nature, also found occasionally in Mozart, remained in fashion long after Rossini. Their vogue reflects an essentially musical rather than dramatic orientation. Proceeding at breakneck speed with numerous word repetitions, they could be counted on to create a humorous effect. Gilbert and Sullivan created famous examples in their operettas; the effect there may be even funnier since very rapid speech is more normal in Italian than in English.

Once Figaro's effervescent personality traits have been revealed, Rossini does his best to sustain the image. An insignificant question provides the opportunity for further light-hearted singing: in a gay, lilting passage in $\frac{3}{8}$ time the barber informs Almaviva of his street address. The tune appears in the woodwinds, while Figaro's parlando concentrates on one note:

EXAMPLE 7

[*Number fifteen, on the left side*]

As in other Rossini arias, melodic and rhythmic qualities are most appealing here; there is little harmonic inventiveness. When the Count responds to Figaro's remarks, a new accompaniment pattern is established, now in sixteenth-notes, resulting in a "crescendo of rhythm" that leads to the end of the scene.

Along with "Largo al factotum," the cavatina that introduces Rosina has become famous as a display piece. "Una voce poco fa" today is a favorite of coloratura sopranos, though Rossini composed the role for a mezzo. Here he was evidently willing to let the singer display all possible vocal splendor. After a thirteen-bar introduction the orchestra recedes completely into the background, until the appearance of a violin melody causes the voice to turn to parlando. The next section, moderato in $\frac{4}{4}$ time, has its own introduction. Rhythmically it is not as free as the opening, though there are several fermatas, which singers at times embellish with additional cadenzas. Again there is faster motion in the accompaniment, and the familiar repetitions of the final cadence:

EXAMPLE 8

fa - rò gio - car, fa - rò gio - car, fa - rò gio - car,_ fa - rò gio - car!

[*(A thousand tricks) I shall play!*]

More than a prima donna showpiece, the aria does represent the basic moods of the text. The opening andante is lyrical and amorous: Lindoro's voice has thrilled Rosina. In the moderato section, more lively, we have a fair musical portrayal of her temperament: if necessary she can be cunning like a viper and she can play a thousand tricks.

In "La calunnia" Don Basilio also is given an opportunity to shine. The text reminds one of the comparison arias so popular during the Baroque; the metaphor of the gentle breeze growing into a storm provides, once more, a great opportunity for a long crescendo. A typical Rossini figure serves as an ostinato:

EXAMPLE 9

EXAMPLE 9   (*cont.*)

In order to stretch out the effect, the initial crescendo is reduced to a piano and then gradually rises once more. A startling harmonic device is enlisted: D major and closely related keys are stubbornly adhered to until the "explosion," fortissimo, on an unexpected E flat major chord, followed by E major and the return to the principal key area.

Doctor Bartolo, as a principal, is given somewhat greater musical prominence. He vents his anger, mixed with triumph and a dash of smugness, in the aria "A un dottor della mia sorte." The piece is difficult and long but fits the dramatic situation well. Doctor Bartolo's role, like opera buffa bass parts in general, does not feature coloratura singing. Here the doctor's sentiments are voiced in rapid patter, mostly in sixteenth-notes, over an accompaniment that contains some variety. This aria, too, ends effectively with an allegro vivace section. In all it is quite taxing for the "old fool." During the nineteenth century an aria by Pietro Romani (1791–1877) was often substituted here; this is less often done today.

Substitutions also were the order of the day in the "Lesson Scene" from Act II. The composer's own music—an aria which Rosina identifies as from *L'Inutile Precauzione*—fits the dramatic situation well: its text has a bearing on her own predicament and calls forth several interpolations from the Count, the supposed music master. For some time, and for several reasons, this music disappeared from the opera. Many nineteenth-century prima donnas did not deem it showy enough. The tradition of singing other music in its place was firmly established for several generations, including substitutions that were anachronistic, in a style that contrasted glaringly with the rest of Rossini's opera.[7] Nellie Melba is reported to have favored *Home, Sweet Home; The Old Folks at Home,* and, on at least one occasion, *The Star-Spangled Banner.*

Berta, the doctor's old maidservant, may be of little importance to the plot, but she is a standard character in this sort of comedy, and she must have an aria. Somehow the lighthearted

[7] Krehbiel, in the preface to the G. Schirmer vocal score, lists some of these. See also G. Jellinek, "The Barber's Mad Scene," *ON,* December 20, 1954.

accompaniment prevents us from taking her complaints seriously, and this may have been the composer's intent.

With most of the dialogue carried on in recitative, true duet or other ensemble writing is rare. A spirited exchange of words between Rosina and Figaro starts with her "Dunque io son"; it consists predominantly of brilliant passage work for the lady. Except for the end there is no simultaneous singing. Dramatically the duet accomplishes little: Figaro informs Rosina that she is the "beautiful object" of Lindoro's affections; she remarks, in repeated asides, that she knew it before. He asks her to write a few lines for Lindoro; she already has done so, and she is happy because she is about to see him. Much musical effort is made to get this across; much bel canto with little dramatic motivation.

In his finales Rossini shows a different approach, somewhat resembling the architectural sense of Mozart. The Act I finale is especially complex, showing careful overall planning toward a climax. It starts with Bartolo, and the Count in disguise; gradually

Figaro and Rosina.

Rosina, Basilio and Berta, then Figaro are added. A theme recurs throughout the first section:

EXAMPLE 10

As the events become more and more complex, Rossini's ensemble writing does the same, though the texture remains light throughout. With Figaro's entrance a new key and theme are reached in the orchestra, and the pace quickens up to the unexpected arrival of the guard. At this point we return to an andante; but the pace once more quickens. The vivace section is a comical fugato: beginning with Doctor Bartolo ("Questa bestia di soldato"), everyone proceeds to give to the officer his own version of what has happened, a wild, incomprehensible chatter, ended by the officer's "ho inteso" ("I've got it"). He is about to arrest the Count, who then reveals his identity—again an unforeseen turn of events calling for an abrupt change of key and a drop in the dynamic level to piano. Bartolo is "struck like a statue"; everyone else is "speechless," or so they sing. Figaro is the first to recover and see the comic side of the situation: pointing to the speechless Bartolo he "nearly dies laughing." With a not very ingenious modulation C major is reached again, along with a new allegro—the customary stretta-finale, here continued over many pages. Starting pianissimo the six principals, joined later by the chorus, sing in unison that they are utterly stunned by what has happened. But consternation hardly is the basic musical mood of this finale; its rhythmic vigor and determination seem to spell out a happy ending regardless of what the text implies.

For the end of Act III a complex finale, perhaps in the Da Ponte–Mozart manner, might be suggested by the plot, with each character commenting on the turn of events from his point of view. But Rossini does not avail himself of this opportunity. The Count does most of the singing, with the chorus chiming in briefly here and there. The finale itself (No. 20, "In somma, io ho tutti i torti!") is far shorter than that of Act I, and less complex. It consists of a brief vaudeville: Figaro sings the first stanza, the group has the refrain, Rosina and the Count provide the second and third couplets, slightly embellished, separated by the choral refrain. The other soloists are not given couplets of their own but merely participate in the ensemble that soon brings down the final curtain.

"Music is the most romantic of all arts."
——E. T. A. HOFFMANN

Many qualities of romanticism in literature and in the fine arts are reflected in early nineteenth-century music, including opera: the turn to subject matter from the Middle Ages and other remote periods; manifestations of patriotic and nationalistic consciousness; a fondness for religious and supernatural subjects, and a response, frequently sentimental, to the beauties of nature.

Dissatisfaction with the universal reign of Italian opera had made itself felt before this, as we noted in the case of Mozart and other late eighteenth-century German composers. As a result of the Napoleonic occupation, politicians, writers, and other intellectuals in the many German states again felt drawn together, conscious of their common German heritage. Much patriotic poetry was inspired by the Wars of Liberation, which not only caused a wave of nationalistic sentiment in the political sphere but stimulated further interest in the common German cultural past. Weber, by 1814, had written patriotic songs and choruses, while Herder and others, in their demands for a new German opera, had pointed to the Middle Ages as a source for subjects that would be suitable, preferable to those of Greek and Roman mythology. Folk tales, fairy tales, and legends inspired many Romantic writers; their fondness for the supernatural is reflected in novels, short stories, and dramas, including opera librettos. It was this fondness for stories of bygone days that caused the brothers Grimm to undertake their well-known collection of fairy tales. Others, too, collected folk songs and folk poetry: *The Youth's Magic Horn,* a collection published by Arnim and Brentano beginning in 1808, inspired Romantic writers to the time of Mahler.

Romantic literature also is characterized by a new receptivity to nature, both idyllic and stormy, but always "natural," untamed by man. Nature afforded solitude, inspiration, and often consolation. The restless wanderer, whose agitated feelings are matched by the untamed forces of nature, is a characteristic Romantic figure, Wagner's Flying Dutchman being a well-known operatic example.

These attitudes, especially pronounced among German Romantics, found expression in many kinds of music. The resources of a larger orchestra, particularly the woodwind and brass sections, afforded composers additional colors to express the moods of nature. French horns, traditionally associated with forests and with the hunt, were effectively used for this purpose throughout the nineteenth century.

Some of the literary qualities that appealed to the Romantics they discovered in Shakespeare's plays. A Shakespeare revival took place in the early part of the century, in time affecting musical drama in both France and Germany. Berlioz, Thomas, and Gounod; Nicolai and Wagner; but also Verdi and Boito in Italy were among the composers who wrote operas based on Shakespearean dramas; others supplied incidental music or concert overtures for stage plays.

The concept of the fusion of the arts, to be discussed in connection with Wagner, also made its appearance now, and numerous painters, writers, and musicians showed a lively interest in arts other than their own. E. T. A. Hoffmann provides an example: he was successful as a writer of novels, short stories, and essays, many on musical subjects, and he composed in various genres, including a Zauberoper, *Undine* (1816). Close cooperation between librettist and composer now became the rule, and a desire for unified, homogeneous works caused some composers to write their own librettos.

Carl Maria von Weber,
Der Freischütz **(Berlin, 1821)**

Though other Weber operas exemplify the Romantic fondness for the "far away and long ago"[8] and though others too have forest settings, it is *Der Freischütz* which to a larger measure than any other opera of the first third of the nineteenth century epitomizes the ingredients of romanticism. The mysterious, dark forests form more than a backdrop; the moods of nature are vividly present, entering into the action and affecting dialogue and music. Religious sentimentality pervades many scenes; medieval superstitions are essential to the plot and supply colorful detail. Much of the music comes close to the folk idiom so cherished by the German Romantics.

While the rising tide of German national sentiment finds no direct expression in *Der Freischütz,* its initial success must in part be credited to patriotic feeling. Perhaps this outspoken quality has at the same time been responsible for its continuing success in German-speaking nations and its lack of popularity on stages elsewhere. The opera made a profound impression on the young Wagner, who became an ardent champion of Weber's music and, indeed, some years after the composer's death in England took it upon himself to have Weber's remains brought back to his native soil, delivering a eulogy on the occasion.

Carl Maria von Weber (1786–1826) received an appoint-

---

[8] Especially *Oberon* (1826), scenes of which are set in Tunis and Baghdad in the ninth century.

ment as court composer in Dresden in 1816. From the beginning he espoused the cause of German opera there, in the face of strong opposition from the firmly entrenched champions of Italian opera. Offended by what he considered to be a hostile attitude, Weber offered *Der Freischütz* to Berlin, where it served as the opening production in the newly built court theater. Yet in Berlin, too, an Italian reigned at the court opera—Spontini, whose *Olympia* had reaped considerable success just a few weeks before the *Freischütz* premiere. Spontini had the support of the Prussian court, which did not attend the new German opera, but all of Berlin's intellectual leaders were present: E. T. A. Hoffmann, Heine, and Mendelssohn among them. The evening turned into an unprecedented triumph for Weber and for the cause of German opera—*Der Freischütz* was an instantaneous success. Weber's reputation as a writer of patriotic songs and choruses had preceded him to Berlin. In Heine's words, "the bridesmaids' chorus was so popular that it could be heard in every home; the dogs seemed to be barking the tune in the streets."

Der Freischütz was soon given all over Germany; within four years of its premiere it had reached New York. For a long time it attracted large audiences in Paris, though in a pirated and extremely mutilated version that aroused Wagner's ire. Later on it was given at the Opéra, with recitatives and ballet music (based on other Weber scores) supplied by Berlioz.

Weber's colorful, well-paced Singspiel uses a text by Friedrich Kind (1768–1843). It has been widely criticized for its alleged triteness; the librettist was an easy target for puns on his name, *kindisch* meaning "childish" in German. Kind had found his subject in a collection of ghost stories—the *Gespensterbuch* published by Apel a few years before. In that version of the tale the hunter kills his bride and goes insane—an ending which Kind decided to change by introducing the hermit and the blessed roses that protect Agathe, thus bringing about a happy ending. Kind at first had written an opening scene in which the hermit blessed these flowers and another scene during which he prayed for Agathe's protection from Caspar. Both of these were dropped in the final version—wisely so, for the last-minute revelation of the roses' protective powers is far more effective, coming at the opera's dramatic high point.

Kind's libretto once more shows that verses of no remarkable literary quality can serve music well.[9] The spoken dialogue is simple and natural enough, but banalities do show themselves in some of the verses, as in the finale:

[9] Goethe was more charitable than most of Kind's critics, remarking that more credit should be given to him for his treatment of a good operatic subject.

Der Jäger stürzte vom Baum,
Wir wagen's kaum nur hinzuschau'n,
O furchtbar Schicksal, o Grau'n!
[The huntsman fell from the tree;
We hardly dare look!
O dreadful fate, O horror!]

The arch-Romantic nature of subject and plot have already been discussed; it appears in numerous small details as well. Various incidents reinforce the ghostly, supernatural character: the forester's picture falls off the wall and almost kills Agathe at the very moment when, miles away, Max downs an eagle with a charmed bullet. A funeral wreath instead of the bridal wreath is delivered before the wedding. Max's last magic bullet, directed by Samiel, misses its mark because Agathe is protected by the roses; instead it strikes down the villain, Caspar. The venerable old hermit emerges briefly but then loses himself in the crowd—the author's not too ingenious way of "saving him" for an effective entry later.

In the wolves' glen scene, librettist and composer enlist all the forces of nature—eerie lights, thunderstorms, driving wind and rain, a lunar eclipse—and a host of supernatural forces. Ghostly choruses, riders in the sky, apparitions of the dead, all contribute to a colossal Romantic finale. Weber became quite engrossed in the stage problems. He wanted the effects to be as realistic as possible and wrote detailed memoranda about props, lighting, etc. Sixty-five stagehands were required for this scene.

If the principal characters of the opera appear overdrawn to us, the blame may be the composer's rather than the librettist's. Weber had strongly moralistic views about opera plots and wanted the principals to represent clearly the forces of good or evil. At times he demanded changes in the text to accentuate these contrasts. These views certainly find expression in *Der Freischütz:* Agathe is pure, holy, and sweet while Caspar is all dark, evil, and villainous. Caspar, to be sure, is helpless and frantic: his pact with the devil (i.e., Samiel, the "Black Hunter") will be up the next day unless he can find another victim. Evil he remains to his end, expiring with a curse on his lips.

Max displays no strong character traits. He, too, is a victim: knowing that he must succeed as a marksman to win Agathe, he is an easy target for Caspar's machinations. In the end he repents his weakness; like Don Ottavio in Mozart's *Don Giovanni* (whom he resembles in other ways) he must wait for a year before he may win his bride. Aennchen is consistently drawn as the typical soubrette, though she is a young relative rather than a servant. She

Opposite: The wolves' glen scene: Max and Caspar.

resembles Blondchen, Constanze's maid in Mozart's *Seraglio*: coquettish, light-hearted, and forever trying to cheer up her lady. When everyone else expresses horror at the thought of Max's entering the wolves' glen at night (in the terzetto *"Wie?* was? Entsetzen!"*), Aennchen refers to the Black Hunter in a phrase that trips along lightly, as though she refused to take the superstition seriously.

The other characters in the opera are of minor importance except, of course, Samiel himself. His is a speaking part throughout—a most effective way of distinguishing this emissary from the lower regions, particularly in the wolves' glen scene, where he is engaged in a "duet" with Caspar. As a supernatural creature he materializes out of nowhere on several occasions. With modern lighting effects these appearances can be startling and ghostly.

Der Freischütz has been called the first Romantic opera—a statement that is correct only from the vantage point of our own repertory, for it disregards quite a procession of earlier, now forgotten works. E. T. A. Hoffmann's *Undine* and Spohr's *Faust,* both of 1816, are among them. Hoffmann himself had misgivings about the vogue of such plots and predicted that the kind of Romantic story "in which the devil is invoked, ancestral ghosts appear, and gypsies put curses on the murderers of brothers" would be short-lived. If *Der Freischütz* were to be buried with the rest of them, Hoffmann thought, it would be no great dramatic loss; but Weber's music, he predicted, would save the work from oblivion. "Since Mozart's operas nothing of greater significance has been written than *Fidelio* and *Der Freischütz."*

Contributing substantially to this success was Weber's handling of the orchestra. Four French horns receive prominent assignments in the overture and throughout the opera, not only to conjure up a romantic picture of the forests but to provide special accents and color in some of the ghostly moments. Sudden tremolos and accents in the strings, and pianissimo rolls on the timpani serve similar purposes. Horns also lend a characteristic touch to the peasant music of the opening scene. At times Weber's vocal writing seems to follow the horn patterns of the accompaniment:

EXAMPLE 11

[*Let hope give you new life.*]

Other wind instruments make prominent contributions, with the expressive qualities of the clarinet receiving special attention. In all, Weber's orchestra provides many different color combinations, takes advantage of every opportunity for tone painting, and expresses a great variety of moods. The theme associated with Samiel always occurs in a specific orchestral color: string tremolo with offbeat pizzicato notes in the basses reinforced by timpani:

EXAMPLE 12

Aside from this, one of opera's first "leading motives" in the later, Wagnerian sense, there are instances in which themes from earlier scenes are ingeniously recalled by the orchestra, especially in the wolves' glen music.

As the curtain rises on the first act, the proximity of Weber's music to folk style is evident: the rousing chorus of country people, the peasant march played by a stage band, and Kilian's mocking song with the heckling chorus as its refrain. A rousing hunters' chorus is heard in the second scene; another one, also loosely related to the drama, precedes the second-act finale. Choral writing of this kind had occupied Weber before he wrote *Der Freischütz;* his hunting choruses remained popular for generations to come in Germany, where the tradition of male choruses is still strong today. In Scene 3 a waltz, heavy and peasant-like, is introduced with the tuning of fiddles. Its rustic strains disappear gradually until only the afterbeats of the accompaniment are heard faintly, as from a distance. The people have disappeared, leaving the stage clear for Max's soliloquy.

Weber most successfully captured the spirit of German folk song in the bridesmaids' chorus, "Wir winden dir den Jungfernkranz." It is simple, naïve, yet charming. Four brief solo verses are heard, each followed by the choral refrain. After some further dialogue the bridesmaids exit, once more singing the refrain, which is followed by a quiet postlude. This melodious simplicity more than any other feature has contributed to the success of Weber's opera, from his own day to our own.

The arias show great variety in their ancestry. Max's "Durch die Wälder, durch die Auen" opens with a sweeping phrase, characteristic of German song of the time:

EXAMPLE 13

Durch die Wäl - der, durch die Au- en   zog ich leich-ten— Sinns— da - hin!

[Through the woods, through the meadows I roamed, light of heart!]

As he believes himself abandoned by Providence, the mood changes and the Samiel motive appears in the orchestra. A brighter mood returns (change to G major, woodwind accompaniment) as he thinks of faithful Agathe waiting for him, but the c minor of despair returns (allegro con fuoco), and the Black Hunter is visible once more, until Max's outburst "Lebt kein Gott?" ("Is there no God?") causes him to vanish. The scene is well constructed in spite of the many repetitions of text and music toward the end.

Caspar's song "Hier im ird'schen Jammertal," its three stanzas separated by dialogue, has a heavier, boisterous, Germanic quality. Its shrill piccolo trills impressed Hoffmann as "the gaiety of hell." Contrary to the conventions of opera, another aria by Caspar follows at once, but this one is a great vengeance aria in the Italian tradition. A pianissimo accompaniment by strings and woodwinds accentuates Caspar's invocation of the spirits of darkness, leading to the D major section in which victory and vengeance are acclaimed, fortissimo, with vocal flourishes.

In the duet that opens Act II Agathe and Aennchen are introduced; the lightheartedness of the latter speaks through her phrases in lilting sixteenth-note motion. Her arietta about meeting a nice young lad, in polonaise rhythm, sustains this mood. Light oboe passages and a lyrical, amorous cello melody represent the girl and boy. This is followed by Agathe's great "scene and aria," "Wie nahte mir der Schlummer." The term "scene" in this context refers to the length, complex structure, and dramatic significance of the song. At the opening, woodwinds and strings provide accompaniment for her recitative, which is free, with several tempo changes. Mood and setting are genuinely romantic; all through her soliloquy we are aware of the setting—the forest looking in through her window, the beautiful, starlit night. Weber evokes the mood with a modulatory passage that has become famous:

156

EXAMPLE 14

[*How beautiful a night!*]

Nature's beauties, and her concern for Max, have put Agathe in a prayerful mood. She kneels down in supplication ("Leise, leise"—"Softly, softly"; adagio, accompanied by muted strings). All these sections are short, interrupted by passages of recitative. Her mind is not on praying: she thinks she hears Max's steps in the distance (repeated notes for two horns, pianissimo). Jubilantly the music returns to the original bright key of E major, vivace con fuoco; Agathe is confident that now all will go well for Max and for herself.

Her later "Und ob die Wolke" (III/12) is short, lyrical, sincere, and simple; it provides needed relief from the turbulent finale of the previous act. Agathe, in her wedding gown, kneels at a *prie-dieu*. Her mood—and hence the mood of the scene in general—is described as "mit wehmütiger Andacht," or reverence mixed with melancholy. A cello obbligato, noble and warm, is heard throughout this scene. Aennchen's Romanze follows, a slight piece which has lost some of its appeal today—not because it represents an afterthought of the composer, added at the request of a singer, but because of its arch, coy quality. It apparently was intended as a parody on the many serious romanzas of the age, and it includes some overly dramatic passage work and ominous tremolos for the viola. More convincing is the allegro section that follows, a gay aria in $\frac{6}{8}$ time with which Aennchen tries to dispel the clouds on Agathe's face. The viola obbligato continues through this section.

Most successful among the ensemble scenes is the terzetto preceding the wolves' glen scene. While Agathe registers dismay, Aennchen makes light of the superstition, at the same time pleading with Max not to tempt fate by entering the haunted place. Max is apprehensive but determined. A storm is approaching; it is

*Agathe's house in the
forest: Max takes leave
to keep his appointment
with Caspar in the
wolves' glen.*

reflected in the accompaniment. Max nevertheless prepares to leave,
and with repeated farewells the scene might have ended. But he
returns and asks Agathe to forgive him. She feels nothing but fear
for his fate, while Aennchen, true to her part, complains in
chattering sixteenth-notes about the trials of a hunter's life. The

158

trio concludes with an allegro vivace that is completely conventional, its Italian clichés seeming uncomfortably out of place.

For most listeners the wolves' glen scene represents the high point of *Der Freischütz*. Musical and dramatic effects are closely and successfully correlated. With imagination and skill Weber exploits the possibilities of tone painting and leads up to the climax. For the opening chorus of invisible ghosts he supplies a sparse, subdued accompaniment in f sharp minor, with somber effects produced by trombones and with sudden outbursts by horns and woodwinds, including two piccolos. For the invocation of Samiel and for much of the dialogue, melodrama is used, as it is for the incantation that precedes the actual casting of the bullets.

Caspar's desperation as he pleads with the adamant Samiel is evident from the breathless accompaniment figure, repeated many times:

EXAMPLE 15

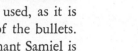

Max, when he appears at the rim of the gorge, hesitates: here the orchestra brings reminiscences from the heckling chorus. To remember that humiliating moment is enough: Max realizes he must go on, and as the orchestra quotes from his earlier aria ("mich fasst Verzweiflung"—"I am seized by despair") he joins Caspar for the ritual of the bullet casting.

At the cast of each bullet there is different stage business, which is reflected in the music. Bassoon and trombone have a prominent figure as a wild boar charges across the stage. While the sixth bullet is cast, a ghostly hunt is heard moving across the sky, with dogs barking and horses neighing (horns, fortissimo, $\frac{6}{8}$ time). Now all the orchestral resources are enlisted for the climactic moment: the sky is completely black as the two thunderstorms collide. Rising modulations lead back to the f sharp minor with which the scene had opened as Samiel appears and both Caspar and Max fall to the ground. Suddenly the storm has subsided—Samiel has vanished, and the nightmarish scene ends on a sustained pianissimo chord for strings and a timpani roll.

Given the opera's subject, the finale of Act III was likely to be sentimental. It starts out dramatically enough: everyone is stunned by the rapid and unexpected succession of events—"Er traf die eig'ne Braut" ("The bullet hit his own bride"). But Agathe awakens and opens her eyes—a great, rising C major arpeggio seems to represent this—and a chorus of thanksgiving

The finale.

issues forth at once. As Caspar dies, the Samiel motive once more appears. With characteristically Romantic humility, Count Ottokar turns to the venerable hermit and gladly abides by the holy man's advice. His entrance, with solemn brass chords in E flat major, brings back memories of Sarastro. Like Mozart's wise priest, the hermit exhorts all present to practice humility and charity. Even his melody, serious and noble, with several large skips, suggests this model.

EXAMPLE 16

[*Even a pious heart may falter.*]

After this, little else can happen except general approval of his wisdom. Following the hermit's example, all kneel down in prayer, and the opera ends with everyone's avowal to trust henceforth in the mercy of God. For no evident reason Weber chose the same melody which earlier had served to express Agathe's anxiety to see Max again. The sentimental ending, quite appropriate for the early nineteenth century, will seem less stirring today. Beethoven chose a similar mood to end *Fidelio,* but it is characteristic of the two composers that while religious sentimentality characterizes Weber's finale, *Fidelio* ends with praises of courage, devotion, and justice.

Weber's overture is the only part of *Der Freischütz* widely known in America. It is wholly satisfactory as an abstract instrumental composition (at the first performance it was repeated in its entirety), but actually it contains most of the important vocal themes. Thus we have what amounts to an instrumental, condensed version of the opera itself. To a lesser extent Beethoven had done this in his overture *Leonore No. 3.*

Except for the introduction, with its beautiful writing for four horns, virtually all themes of the *Freischütz* overture are taken from the opera itself. Their juxtaposition in the overture corresponds to the struggle between the forces of good and evil in the drama. Samiel's ominous theme is heard first, leading into Max's "Doch mich umgarnen" (c minor, molto vivace). Samiel's forces again are in command with agitated music from the height of the wolves' glen inferno. This gives way to Agathe's theme of hope ("Süss entzückt entgegen ihm," here in E flat major, dolce). For some time these elements struggle with each other. Samiel's theme is heard again, pianissimo, and a moment of suspense is reached (general pause). But a bright, fortissimo chord in C major proclaims that the forces of light will win: the remainder of the overture, based on Agathe's theme, introduces the exact music that will bring the opera itself to its jubilant end.

Violetta and Alfredo, in a Berlin production of "La Traviata."

6

MID-NINETEENTH-
CENTURY OPERA

Among mid-nineteenth-century Italian composers of operas Verdi's name stands
out above all others—indeed, the works of
Verdi's middle period are known wherever
operas are performed and are among the
best-known operas of any age or land. Verdi's
rise to fame cannot be understood without
some awareness of his immediate Italian predecessors who, successful at home and
abroad, contributed to the development of
the public's taste and of young Verdi's style.
Foremost among these writers of opera
were Bellini (1801–1835) and Donizetti
(1797–1848). Bellini's style is characterized
by carefully fashioned melodic lines—elegant, sweeping, and forceful, with an element of vocal display. The nobility of Bellini's arias has impressed discriminating
musicians down to the present time, Wagner
and Stravinsky among them. That some of

**ROMANTIC OPERA
IN ITALY**

his works (*La Sonnambula; Norma;* both 1831) have had recent revivals, especially in concert form, testifies to a renewed appreciation of bel canto singing, of the musical if not the dramatic appeal of the scores. Donizetti's *Lucia di Lammermoor* (1835) has of course maintained itself on the stage as well: it is a gruesome, typically Romantic tale, evoking the setting and atmosphere of Sir Walter Scott's novel. The famous coloratura passages with flute obbligato of the "Mad Scene" from this opera are more than vocal fireworks; they serve a definite dramatic purpose. And, indeed, the role of Lucia, offering histrionic as well as musical challenges, has established the reputation of some of the greatest nineteenth- and twentieth-century sopranos.

Donizetti succeeded in the realm of lighter opera as well. *L'Elisir d'Amore* (1832), *Don Pasquale* (1843), and other works generally make use of a simple dramatic scheme. A situation is established and then explained or reflected upon at length, in aria, duet, or ensemble. The aria text very quickly describes this simple situation and then relies on extensive word repetitions to "spin out" the music to the desired length. Practically every aria in *L'Elisir d'Amore* is of this nature, with a steady, rhythmical accompaniment and the cadential repetitions that had also been Rossini's trademark. The scheme worked well for Donizetti, a prolific writer who finished some of his opere buffe in little more than a week. His popularity lasted well into the second half of the century, until the even lighter fare of Offenbach took Europe by storm.[1]

FRANCE

From Lully's days to the time of Gluck and beyond, French serious opera had maintained a tradition of large and sumptuous spectacles. During the days of political absolutism these served to display the wealth and splendor of the ruler, but the tradition was firmly enough established to maintain itself in the nineteenth century as well. The term "grand opera" has been used rather loosely for any large-scale production; as a technical term it applies to French serious opera from about 1830 to 1850. Grand opera was sung from beginning to end. It favored historical subjects in which crowd scenes and spectacular stage effects were frequent and prominent. The large forces on stage called for a similar array of musical forces, including, often, music on or behind stage. Heroic subject matter was treated with a dramatic and musical pathos that may seem overblown today. The grand manner had already shown itself in Spontini's works, eminently successful in Paris (e.g., *La*

---

[1] Donizetti's popularity extended to the New World. Ronald Davis, discussing opera in San Francisco around 1850, states that Donizetti's *Daughter of the Regiment* (Paris, 1840) was more popular than any other opera. (*A History of Opera in the American West,* Englewood Cliffs, 1965, p. 87.)

Vestale, 1807; in *Olympie,* 1819, forty trumpets were used on stage). These works prepared the way for the operas of François Auber (1782–1871), Giacomo Meyerbeer (1791–1864), and for Rossini's last opera, *William Tell* (Paris, 1829). The last was based on a drama by Schiller, with additions that are significant for what was considered essential for grand opera: a march of the archers, a ballet of the peasants. Auber's *La Muette de Portici* (1828), based on a historical subject, is rich in crowd scenes, with battles on stage and behind the scenes, an eruption of Vesuvius, large choruses and marches. Through plot and music this fiery opera captivated the revolutionary spirit of the time. When it was given in Brussels in 1830, an excited, enthusiastic audience streamed out into the streets and staged a violent demonstration that eventually led to the overthrow of the government.

Meyerbeer was one of the most successful composers of the time. Like grand opera itself, he was cosmopolitan, international in outlook—a German Jew so celebrated in France that Napoleon had the street leading to the opera house named Rue Meyerbeer. Honored and decorated by several Prussian kings, Meyerbeer eventually succeeded Spontini in Berlin. He tried his hand at both Italian and German opera before he succeeded in Paris with *Robert le Diable* (1831) and *Les Huguenots* (1836). Supernatural and religious subjects are treated in a manner that relates grand opera to the Romantic movement, then flourishing in all the arts, with Paris as the center to which artists flocked from everywhere. Rossini's *William Tell* soon was eclipsed by Meyerbeer's grand creations.

And grand opera continued to flourish well into mid-century. An imposing crowd scene that is not part of the literary sources still characterizes Verdi's *Don Carlo* (1867), an opera also written for Paris and also based on a play by Schiller. In this libretto the auto-da-fé, the public burning of heretics, furnishes the occasion for a long procession of nobility and clergy, with much pomp and pageantry, all of it watched and commented upon by a large crowd. Similar grand effects are found in Berlioz's *Les Troyens* (1858)[2] and in the triumphal march, ballet scene, and finales of Verdi's *Aida* (1871).

As the events of the French Revolution faded into the distance, opéra comique replaced the "horror and rescue opera" in public favor. Much of it eschewed any pretensions to political criticism or satire but was merely intended to be good entertainment. The principal composers, now largely forgotten except for a few of their arias, were Boieldieu (*La Dame Blanche,* 1825), Auber (*Fra Diavolo,* 1830), and Adolphe Adam (*Le Postillion de*

---

[2] For a discussion of Berlioz's operas, see *SHO,* pp. 323 ff.

Longjumeau, 1836). Plots and music tended to be sentimental rather than strictly comical, with melodies and dance types approaching the simplicity of folk or popular idiom. Their designation in the score as chanson, romance, or barcarole reflects this. The borderline between this kind of sentimental opéra comique and what soon became known as operetta is by no means clearly defined. It became a rigid policy that any work containing spoken dialogue was excluded from the Paris Opéra and had to be performed at the other house, the Opéra-comique, even if its subject could by no stretch of the imagination be considered comical: the original version of Bizet's *Carmen* furnishes an example.

NATIONALISM AND REALISM

Many of the Romantic traits found in Weber's *Freischütz* also characterize opera of the later nineteenth century, from Spohr and Lortzing in Germany to Gounod and others in France. The Romantic movement ran its course more quickly in literature and painting than in music, though precise delineation is not possible in any of these fields.

Nationalism, an important ingredient of Romanticism, produced different artistic results in various countries and regions. The rise of political nationalism in Germany was kindled by the Napoleonic oppression and occupation. Inhabitants of the separate German states, suffering the same degradations and hardships, discovered or rediscovered common bonds of language and culture and thought fondly of the great Germany of the past. In both Germany and Italy attempts to create national states were made through most of the century, until the German empire and the Italian kingdom were established in 1871. Among the intellectual leaders in this struggle for national unity were the two foremost opera composers of the time, Richard Wagner (1813–1883) and Giuseppe Verdi (1813–1901).

Wagner's political activities included participation in the unsuccessful revolution of 1848—activities that might have cost his life had he not left Saxony before a warrant for his arrest had been published. He already had voiced patriotic sentiments during his days of poverty and loneliness in Paris (1839–1842), where he barely eked out a living writing salon arrangements of French operatic airs. To him the musical life of the French capital seemed superficial and commercial, and he felt all the more strongly attached to his own musical heritage. "Oh my magnificent Germany, how much I love you . . . if only because *Der Freischütz* grew from your soil!"

Weber's Romantic operas had already exerted a strong influence on Wagner in his formative years. Success came first to him with *Rienzi* (1842), in subject matter and treatment closely related to grand opera of this period, especially to the style of Meyerbeer. After *The Flying Dutchman*, to be discussed below, Wagner turned to more specifically German subject matter. Both *Tannhäuser* (1845) and *Lohengrin* (first performed 1850) are based on German medieval legends containing strongly religious (Christian) elements. *The Ring of the Nibelung*, a monumental cycle of four music dramas on which Wagner now set to work, is based on several pre-Christian Germanic myths. It is in these later works, to be taken up in the following chapter, that Wagner's ideas about the nature and function of music drama found their expression.

Aside from the Germanic subject matter itself, expressions of patriotic sentiment occur in several Wagner works, notably in *Lohengrin* and *Die Meistersinger*. Much of Wagner's extensive prose writing also is patriotic and nationalistic. In retrospect Nietzsche, who at one time had been an ardent Wagnerite, saw a "deep significance in the fact that the rise of Wagner coincided with the rise of the German empire." Wagner's patriotism, intense nationalism, and anti-Semitism, documented in his prose writings, were among the reasons for Hitler's enthusiasm for Wagnerian music drama.

The ups and downs of the Risorgimento, the movement for unification of Italy, were close to Verdi's heart. He was on terms of intimate friendship with several of Italy's political and intellectual leaders, and believed strongly in the cause of Italy's freedom from foreign political domination. Though at first reluctant, Verdi accepted nomination for a seat in the first national parliament, a seat that he won and held for many years. A story that illustrates the composer's general popularity during these stormy years has often been told. The slogan "Viva Verdi" could be found written on many walls, testifying, if the writer was caught, merely to the popular love of his operas, but actually intended as an endorsement of V.E.R.D.I.—*Vittorio Emanuele, Re* (King) *d'Italia*.

In spite of this intense political involvement, comparable to Wagner's, Verdi expressed his nationalism less tangibly in his operas. Their music may sound Italian to the core, but the range of subjects and locales is far wider than Wagner's. Many of his plots have general revolutionary implications that caused difficulties with the censors—but none of the successful Verdi operas are direct expressions of Italian patriotism or nationalism.[3]

By the mid-nineteenth century, realism in the arts, including drama, had brought a widening of areas from which subjects were drawn—beyond the mythical and historical, the glamorous and

[3] Though *The Battle of Legnano*, 1848, deals with the insurrection of the Lombards against a foreign ruler.

high-flown. Realism in all the arts was characterized by concern for the present and future rather than the past. Political and especially social problems of the day were taken up. Works of art, including paintings as well as operas, were set in everyday surroundings, in the large city rather than in a court milieu, and they dealt with subjects related to the life of the middle or lower classes.

Realistic drama achieved its impact with subjects that were close to the heart of the public; with conflicts strikingly put into relief rather than with display of elegant, beautiful language or oratory. Many writers held that drama should be a plea, for or against some issue. One play by Dumas *fils* (1824–1895) is an appeal for more liberal divorce laws; another tries to win compassion and understanding rather than scorn for girls of the demi-monde (a term which he coined) by presenting them as victims of society.

While the drama's subject matter became realistic, its literary treatment often remained traditional. Sentimentality continued to be an important ingredient, as it had been in Romantic drama. Dumas's stage play which became Verdi's *La Traviata* is a good example. In time an increasing amount of true-to-life detail in character drawing, language, and staging was added. In the second half of the century the social-message approach of realism gradually gave way to the stark presentation of "things as they really are." Novels, plays, and paintings dealt with the seamy side of life, with poverty, vice, and disease. To avoid preaching, to let the glaring, unwholesome facts speak for themselves characterizes naturalistic drama. We shall see how this development affected late nineteenth-century musical drama as well.

Richard Wagner, *The Flying Dutchman* (*Der fliegende Holländer*; Dresden, 1843)

Wagner's inspiration for writing an opera on the theme of the eternal wanderer came from several sources. He may have known the ancient legend before he became acquainted with the version included in a story by Heine, published in 1834. The plan to write an opera on the subject already existed in Wagner's mind when, in 1839, he embarked on a sea voyage from East Prussia to London—a voyage that turned out to be stormy and exciting. The little group of travelers came close to being shipwrecked and sought protection from a furious storm in a Norwegian fjord. Such close contact with the elements, coupled with the sailors' talk about the Flying Dutchman, made a strong impression on the young composer. The story, as Wagner developed it, included several aspects of Heine's version, notably the idea of the Dutchman's salvation through a woman. This became the central theme of the opera; similar concepts figure prominently in his later music dramas. Other details as well, e.g., the sailors' calls in Act I, echoed by the fjords, go back to impressions Wagner received during that stormy voyage.

As was to be his custom henceforth, Wagner wrote his own libretto. Composition progressed rapidly, the overture being written last. By this time (1842) Wagner had found his first major position, as court conductor in Dresden. *The Flying Dutchman* was produced there early in the following year.

We can easily see a number of strongly Romantic traits in this story. As in *Der Freischütz* we have an ancient legend, with supernatural aspects and religious undertones. Once more the untamed forces of nature enter into the action rather than merely providing the setting. Nature and its many moods was to inspire Wagner as it had inspired the earlier Romantics: most of the *Ring* operas, *Die Meistersinger,* and *Parsifal* take place outdoors and show countless instances of musical representation of nature.

The supernatural aspects of the legend of the Flying Dutchman are evident, and Wagner provided a number of additional effective touches. From its first appearance on the horizon, the Dutchman's ship makes a ghostly impression, with its blood-red sails and invisible crew. In the last act a strong wind shakes the phantom ship and whistles through its rigging while all remains calm around Daland's vessel. Feverish activity develops on the Dutchman's ship, accompanied by the crew's eerie singing and diabolical laughter. After Senta's leap into the sea, the ship "sinks at once with all the crew. The sea surges up, then recedes as in a whirlpool. In the glowing red of the rising sun the figures of Senta and the Dutchman appear, transfigured, from the sea and rise toward heaven." A more Romantic apotheosis can hardly be imagined.

A division of the opera into several acts had not been Wagner's original plan, but even in that form his desire for uninterrupted development of the action can be realized with modern stage equipment. Acts II and III can be performed without a break: the entr'acte music provides sufficient time for a quickly executed shift of sets.

The plot moves at a good pace and is well constructed, though there is much that is dramatically and musically conventional. Wagner saw fit to add the tenor role of Erik—the traditional young lover. A number of dramatic situations are decidedly "operatic," especially the grand revelation by the Dutchman of his identity. Coming so late in the opera, it can hardly surprise anyone. And there is the apotheosis already mentioned. Set musical numbers occur in all acts: the steersman's song, the spinning chorus, Senta's ballad. The telescoping of the action also is operatic—in Act I, the speed with which Daland, impressed by the treasures on the Dutchman's ship, offers him his daughter; in Act II, the pace from the initial meeting of Senta and the Dutchman to their mutual vows.

A dramatic weakness might be seen in the finale, the outcome of which is based on the Dutchman's eavesdropping. Senta, we are led to believe, fully intends to be "true unto death"; she denies Erik's accusation that she was already promised to him. But the Dutchman, who overhears this conversation, despairs and gives orders to his crew to make ready at once for their departure. All of this, then, is based not on an inevitable, tragic conflict. We might interpret the Dutchman's despair either as feigned, which is unlikely, or as a necessary move leading to his ultimate testing of Senta's faithfulness.

The ghostly crew of the Dutchman's ship.

In the subject matter and mood of this opera there is much to suggest *Der Freischütz,* but Wagner's characters are more interestingly drawn. There is no villain to remind us of Caspar, and Senta is a more complex heroine than Agathe. The Dutchman himself is more fascinating than any of the male characters in Weber's opera. He is a typical Romantic figure: the restless wanderer with whom Wagner identified himself. Such a figure reappears in several of his later music dramas.

The composer's own ideas about the interpretation of the principal roles are known to us from an essay he wrote in 1852. According to this, the Dutchman himself is to appear intense but outwardly calm and controlled—a calmness interrupted only for a few brief moments. His opening monologue in particular must show great restraint and a certain lassitude—as though he only reluctantly goes through the motions, once more, of going ashore and looking for the one person who can break the curse. His first conversation with Daland brings a brief, impulsive outburst of hope—"May she be mine!" In the second act duet with Senta that hope has become more fervent. When he exclaims "Allmächtiger, durch diese sei's!" ("Almighty God: let her be the one!"), he kneels down. Wagner's intention here was to express the Dutchman's "love for Senta which at the same time gives rise to terrible fear—concern for the fate to which she exposes herself by offering her hand for his salvation." Throughout, the Dutchman must evoke the audience's compassion. Even in the prosaic setting of the second act he must not lose the aura of gloom and mystery. In the same essay Wagner gives explicit instructions about the coordination of steps and gestures with specific notes, chords, and accents in the orchestral accompaniment—a fusion of dramatic and musical elements so characteristic of his later works.

Senta's role is easily misinterpreted. Hers is not a sentimental infatuation with a storybook hero but the strong obsession of a sturdy and essentially simple nature. Her exclamation, at the end of her ballad, that *she* will be his salvation, is sudden and causes general consternation. To have Erik enter at this very moment makes for an effective dramatic situation. Her decision is forceful and determined, not a sentimental impulse. During Erik's account of his dream she sits with her eyes closed, as hypnotized ("in a magnetic sleep" are Wagner's directions). From this state she turns to "highest exultation," seeing in his dream the sign that she must "find him and perish with him." The sudden entrance of the Dutchman creates the opportunity for an effective bit of staging: the door opens, covering up his picture, and the Dutchman himself steps into its place. Senta stands motionless, her eyes fixed on the man who appears so suddenly. To make this role fascinating and convincing requires a talented actress.

Her father, Daland, Wagner tells us, is not a comic type like so many sailors in operas, but the level-headed captain of a small vessel, uncomplicated, toughened by years of hard work gaining a livelihood from the sea. He is quite willing to avail himself of the material advantage that such a marriage might present, and he makes no secret of his materialism. He has hardly presented the stranger to Senta when he shows her some of the jewelry to induce to marry him. The introduction over, Daland's function in the drama is accomplished; he barely enters into the developments from this point to the end of the opera.

Erik likewise is an uncomplicated character. Wagner insisted that he should appear strong and impetuous, even when he pleads with Senta, reminding her of her earlier promises and asking her to speak to her father in his favor. Erik, like everyone else, knows the identity of "the man in the picture" about whom Senta thinks too much; gradually his fear of losing her for himself gives way to fear for her soul: "you are in Satan's claws!"

Although Wagner, at the time of writing *The Flying Dutchman,* already theorized against traditional opera, many of its

Arrival of the Dutchman's ship, Act I.

formal features are still present in this work. It does lack the
spoken dialogue of *Der Freischütz* and the consistent alternation
between recitative and aria. But not until some years later did
Wagner arrive at the characteristic continuous musical style of his
works of maturity—the "endless melody" of the *Ring* and *Tristan*.
The Flying Dutchman still is a "number" opera, and most of these
self-contained arias, ensembles, and choruses clearly reveal their
ancestors in eighteenth- and nineteenth-century opera. Senta's ballad, among the first pieces composed, is an example. Having
written it, Wagner found that it formed the center, musically and
dramatically, of the opera. Its thematic material then spread
through the entire work. To have one of the characters suggest that
someone sing a song may not be a very imaginative way of
introducing an aria, but Wagner resorts to that device. The
ballad's traditional strophic form is ingeniously modified. In the
second stanza the girls, moved by Senta's narrative, softly join her
in the refrain. After the third stanza Senta, emotionally exhausted,
sinks back in her chair, and the chorus alone softly sings the
refrain, interrupted by Senta's sudden "Ich sei's, die dich durch
ihre Treu' erlöse" ("I shall be the one to save you through my
faithfulness").

It is true that the several themes of the ballad are the most
important ones of the opera, among them the Dutchman theme

EXAMPLE 1

Jo - ho - hoe ! Jo - ho - ho-hoe ! Ho - ho - hoe !

with which the ballad opens, and the salvation theme

EXAMPLE 2

Doch kann dem bleich-en Man-ne Er - lö - sung ein-stens noch wer - den,

[*Some day salvation may come to the pale man.*]

that forms the refrain. These and several other themes in the opera
are leading motives, in some ways similar to those in his later
music dramas, but it is to be noted that most of them are vocal in
origin and phrase design, that their number is still small, and that
they do not undergo the symphonic development and transforma-

tion found in his later works beginning with *Lohengrin*. Some modifications of the principal themes do occur. Senta's above-mentioned "Ich sei's"—her determination to save the man from his curse—is related to the salvation theme:

EXAMPLE 3

Ich sei's, die dich durch ih-re Treu'___ er - lö - se!

[*I shall be the one to save you through my faithfulness!*]

Likewise the melody shared by both at the end of their duet

EXAMPLE 4

Was ist's, das mäch - tig in___ mir___ le - bet,

[*What is the strong feeling that stirs me?*]

grows out of the salvation theme. With its rhythmic determination it forms a fitting conclusion to this scene, for the Dutchman has just sung "Mein Heil hab' ich gefunden"; salvation now seems assured.

The Dutchman motive, being very concise, foreshadows Wagner's later *Leitmotive*. At times it appears very subtly, as during Erik's narration of his dream, when the strange ship and its captain are mentioned. In the overture Wagner made use of all the important motives from the opera. They are introduced and combined in a way that comes close to being a presentation of the essential dramatic development, with the salvation motive providing a victorious conclusion.

Another self-contained musical number is the steersman's song. Its strophic form also is modified by orchestral interludes representing the restless sea, with sudden gusts and waves shaking the ship. The last stanza remains unfinished as the steersman is overcome by sleep.

The monologue of the Dutchman is more freely constructed, beginning with an expressive accompanied recitative. In the several sections that follow, the musical style is determined by the changing sentiment of the text. His final outcry is echoed by his invisible crew.

Daland's introduction of the Dutchman in Act II is marked "aria" in the score. It has the regular phrases and accompaniment patterns of much early nineteenth-century opera. The four-bar theme forming the orchestral introduction recurs several times.

EXAMPLE 5

EXAMPLE 5   (*cont.*)

er,   gleich mir,   das Gast - recht spricht   er   an.

[*Extend your welcome to the stranger, my child. He is a sailor, as I am, and asks for our hospitality.*]

Here as elsewhere in the opera, words and phrases are repeated for textual emphasis or to round out a musical phrase (e.g., "Glaubt mir, wie schön sie ist, so ist sie treu"). Daland finally realizes that it would be best to leave the two of them alone. As he leaves, the bright thematic material and the D major tonality disappear as well. "The Dutchman and Senta are alone; they remain motionless, lost in contemplation of each other." With repeated statements of their two themes the aria leads without break into their great duet. Here, too, conventional operatic features can be found. The first section ends with a cadenza for both singers:

EXAMPLE 6

[*May such an angel grant it (salvation) to me!*]

The spinning chorus that opens the second act may appear dramatically contrived and "operatic" to us, especially if the girls with their spinning wheels are seated in orderly rows, facing the conductor. But it achieved greater immediate popularity than any other excerpt from the opera. Choruses are prominent in all three

The spinning chorus, Act II.

acts. Dramatically the opening of Act III is most convincing, with Daland's crew and their girls being merry. Their compassion for the strangers is expressed with chromatic harmonies

EXAMPLE 7

[They are already old and pale, not ruddy, and their sweethearts are dead.]

quite different from their otherwise robust music. They try to arouse the Dutchman's crew. When they finally succeed, and ghostly activity breaks out on the other ship, the sailors try to reassure themselves by once more intoning loudly their "Steuermann, lass die Wacht." Compared with this, the opening chorus of Act I lacks conviction—Daland's crew trying to make the ship fast and safe in

Choral scene, Act III.

stormy weather, singing their "hojoho's." When, later in the same act, they all repeat the steersman's song, we are right in the theatrical tradition of the many soldiers' and hunters' choruses of earlier opera.

With all these ties to tradition, *The Flying Dutchman* shows enough individualistic and effective traits to have earned it a lasting place. Colorful, typically Romantic orchestral writing contributes a large measure of this success. Agitated chromatic passages for the strings paint a vivid picture of the stormy sea, while added brass (including the tuba) characterizes the awe-inspiring Dutchman and his ghostly, unsinkable ship. English horn and harp are effectively used in the more lyrical moments; pianissimo rolls on the timpani produce a subdued atmosphere of anticipation and suspense (in the overture and at the arrival of the Dutchman in Act II). As he was to do often in his later music dramas, Wagner has the orchestra express the emotions experienced by one or several characters who are silent on the stage. Senta and the Dutchman gaze at each other intensely for some time. They are silent, but an eloquent figure in the strings speaks for them:

EXAMPLE 8

The scene and its treatment anticipate similar moments of long, significant gazes in *Die Walküre* and *Tristan*.

In a few places Wagner still assigns to the orchestra a subordinate function of vocal support; even to the regular, rhythmic bass patterns which he later criticized in Italian opera:

EXAMPLE 9

Detailed stage directions appear in both libretto and score, a practice to which Wagner adhered in all his later works. Some of the specified scenic effects undoubtedly were difficult to execute realistically in the 1840's, yet Wagner became even more demanding in the *Ring* operas. Projection and other lighting effects are used extensively today to picture the stormy sea, the rapid approach of the phantom ship in Act I, or its destruction. Regardless of the means employed, the visual effects obtained should produce the intense, gloomy, and ghostly atmosphere which Wagner demanded for his "Romantic Opera."

Giuseppe Verdi, *La Traviata*
(Venice, 1853)

We have already seen that by the time Verdi had established himself, opera was outgrowing its function of entertaining a small segment of society, the aristocracy of birth or wealth. In Italy especially, opera, while not losing its social connotations, addressed itself increasingly to a large public from all walks of life. Even in present-day Italy many an elderly shopkeeper or office worker displays an enthusiasm for and knowledge of opera that are not equaled elsewhere in Europe, let alone on other continents. Enthusiasm of this kind does not, as a rule, extend to more recent works than the operas of Puccini; it is apt to afford a place of special affection to the works from Verdi's middle period. The operas in question chiefly are *Rigoletto* (1851), *Il Trovatore* and *La Traviata* (1853), *A Masked Ball* (1859), *La Forza del Destino* (1862), *Don Carlo* (1867), and *Aida* (1871)—works which for a hundred years have formed a substantial portion of standard operatic fare all over the world. There is no other composer whose operas have had such a long, substantial, and uninterrupted hold on the public's favor.

Early in his career Verdi composed with great speed, in the manner of many eighteenth-century writers whose operas were written according to established formulas and conventions, often for a specific occasion. As success came to Verdi, leading to a betterment of his financial position, the pace more frequently was determined by his own artistic requirements and tended to be slower. Nevertheless *Rigoletto, Il Trovatore,* and *La Traviata* all were composed within less than three years. By this time the composer had much popular following. Of *Il Trovatore's* first performance a newspaper reported that "the public listened to every number in religious silence"—behavior quite different from that of typical audiences of an earlier day.

Of these operas, *La Traviata* is most apt to move us as drama, aside from the beauty and persuasiveness of its musical language. Plot and libretto may have faults, but these do not remove the drama from our realm of experience. *La Traviata* does not impress us as *Il Trovatore* or *La Forza del Destino* do—dramas in which accidents, poorly and unconvincingly motivated, determine the course of the action.[4] Unlike *Rigoletto, La Forza del Destino,* and

[4] After the first performances of *La Forza del Destino* Verdi, still wanting to make changes in the work, wrote to his librettist: "We must find a way to avoid too many deaths." Years later he still admitted that the opera contained "many weaknesses and absurdities."

Il Trovatore, La Traviata does not involve violence: it is human drama. The subject is timeless even if it is presented within the framework of certain mid-nineteenth-century conventions.

Many of Verdi's operas brought him into conflict with censorship. Some of the realistic detail found in *Rigoletto* brought forth strong objections, both from official quarters and from some of the public. To have the father discover Gilda's body in a sack was too much, and the censor rebuked the librettist as well as "the famous maestro, Verdi, for . . . having chosen a plot so revoltingly immoral, so obscene and so trivial." In the case of *La Traviata*, the subject itself caused sensation and scandal.

Alexandre Dumas *fils* wrote his novel, *La Dame aux Camélias*, in 1847. If the subject itself, dealing with the life of a Paris courtesan, seemed shocking to some, this effect was increased by the general knowledge that much of Dumas's account was autobiographical, that the Marguerite Gautier of the novel and the Violetta of the opera were modeled on Marie Duplessis, well known in Paris at the time. In 1849 Dumas decided on a stage version of his novel. It was written quickly, but difficulties with the censor kept the play from being performed until 1852. Predictably it caused a sensation—a *succès de scandale*. To elevate the story of such a woman to a dramatic subject implied, in the eyes of many, a condoning of her character and actions. In time, the part of Marguerite became a vehicle for many great nineteenth-century actresses, Sarah Bernhardt among them. The play, though generally outshone by Verdi's opera, is still performed today.

Verdi saw Dumas's play in 1852; he was at once impressed with its musical possibilities and asked F. M. Piave, with whom he had collaborated on earlier operas, to fashion a libretto for him. Both Piave and then Verdi worked with incredible speed—the composer working on *Il Trovatore* and *La Traviata* at the same time—and the first performance took place in March, 1853. The story of its fiasco, based in part on remarks in Verdi's letters, has often been told, but there is evidence to the contrary. At least one critic wrote a very complimentary review, and there were ten repetitions during the first season.[5] Flaws certainly must have marred the first performances, especially poor casting of the title role.

For many readers and listeners of the mid-nineteenth century the subject was specially shocking because it was contemporary—operas, generally speaking, had dealt with events (historical or otherwise) from the past. The claim that *La Traviata* was first staged in contemporary costume, however, has also been challenged, though modern performances of the opera do customarily use an 1840 setting. More recently there have been attempts to

[5] M. J. Matz, "The Truth about La Traviata," *ON*, January 11, 1964.

stress the timeless nature of the subject by using twentieth-century dress.[6]

If the play and opera shocked their first audiences, the subject itself, rather than the dramatic treatment, must account for it. True, a woman who has "strayed from the narrow path" (*traviare* means "to stray") becomes the heroine of an opera, and, further, she is drawn sympathetically—more so, in fact, than any of the other characters. But there is nothing in the libretto that can be construed as a defense of her former life. The story is conventionally moral in a number of ways: Violetta's death is the result of a life devoted to pleasure alone. Neither her fate nor the life of others in her company, whose charms are already fading, is presented as attractive. Similar portrayals of women of her kind, who find and give real love, occur in some earlier and much later literature, but Verdi's interpretation of this theme remains one of the most moving.

Today's audiences are not likely to see in *La Traviata* an example of shocking realism. Rather they will be aware of the Romantic manner in which the subject is treated, both textually and musically. Much of the drama is intended to tug at the heartstrings in the best sentimental, Romantic fashion. Above all, there is Violetta's noble resignation, her sacrifice of love to convention, to the happiness of Alfredo's family. The sacrifice is accomplished by actions calculated to lead Alfredo to believe that she no longer loves him and has gone back to her former life. Out of this situation grow many dramatically effective if extremely sentimental situations, notably in Act II. When Alfredo publicly insults her in Act III,[7] her fainting is the appropriate reaction of a mid-nineteenth century heroine. Soon after, also in typically Romantic fashion, she nobly forgives him and expresses hope that God will help him when the inevitable remorse sets in. There are numerous other situations, of greater and lesser importance, in which Romantic sentiment is displayed: her realization, in Act IV, that "it is too late"; followed by her farewell to past days of happiness; the entire deathbed scene, especially her wish that Alfredo should give her portrait to the fair young maid whom he will one day marry. Verdi was fond of a musical device that increases the poignancy of such scenes: the increasingly serious dialogue of Act I is carried on against a background of gay dance music. Similarly the gloom pervading all of Act IV is contrasted with the merriment of the Mardi Gras crowd in the street.

Verdi's treatment of many scenes leads one to believe that he

---

[6] The numerous dramatizations of the subject include a film (with Greta Garbo) and, more recently, a ballet (with Margot Fonteyn and Rudolf Nureyev).
[7] This would be the second part of Act II in the original division of the opera; what is usually considered Act IV consequently is the earlier Act III.

was attracted to "The Lady of the Camellias" by the possibility of portraying through music the complex character, especially the psychological conflict, of Violetta. In a special sense of the term, then, Violetta is the opera's heroine. To have a heroine rather than a hero is characteristic of much nineteenth-century opera, from the Romantic works of Weber and Wagner to Gounod's *Faust* (1859), in which Marguerite is the central figure, and on to Puccini's operas. Verdi's Violetta not only is present on the stage through most of the opera; as the chief protagonist her emotional development, from "Ah fors'è lui" on, holds our attention and influences the drama's course more than do any external events. In this sense *La Traviata* can be considered a turning point in Verdi's own development.

Piave's libretto simplifies and condenses the stage play in expected ways. There are fewer characters, and the general dramatic pace is more rapid. As so often happens, the condensation results in the omission of some essential detail, so that some of the action is not as clearly motivated as it is in the play. Germont *père*'s appearance at Flora's party in Act III, just in time to hear his son insult Violetta, is one of Piave's less fortunate changes; it is unconvincing and adds nothing to the scene's effectiveness. Yet the libretto, and Verdi's music, also provide dramatic touches beyond the reach of the stage play, as at the end of Act I when Alfredo's singing, offstage, imparts special poignancy to Violetta's "sempre libera"—to her determination to remain emotionally uninvolved.

Conflicting emotions are Violetta's outstanding characteristic, and throughout the opera Piave and Verdi succeed in making these conflicts absorbing and believable. They already lend dramatic impact to Act I. Knowing her own disposition, her health, and her need for continuous, ever changing pleasure, Violetta fights her own incipient affection for Alfredo. Much can be, and has been, read into her motives. Some actresses have played Violetta as a basically unsophisticated country girl, incurably ill, who turned to a life of pleasure to drown out her fear of death. Such an interpretation would make her renunciation of Alfredo appear in a different light, considerably less sentimental than usual. Her conflicting emotions determine the style of her music from the beginning: it vacillates between coloratura ("sempre libera"), characterizing the lighthearted, frivolous side of her personality, and the lyricism of "Ah, fors'è lui," with its realization that "love is the heartbeat of the universe." With coloratura she tries to convince Alfredo that she "does not know what love is," and that heroic feelings are beyond her capacities. As the drama moves on, situations become more and more serious so that there are few occasions

Alfredo and Violetta.

for displaying lightheartedness. Instead, Violetta is presented as increasingly generous and self-sacrificing. We are moved by these qualities, though perhaps less so than audiences of the mid-nineteenth century—an age in which tears were more universally cherished and melodrama was not yet a time-worn cliché of radio and motion picture. As a person Violetta remains convincing; often, however, in spite of Piave's language. She is most effectively characterized through music, beginning with the prelude, where an intense, warm melody (Violetta's principal theme, later sung to the words "Amami, Alfredo") is combined with a light, ornamental line expressive of the frivolous side of her nature:

EXAMPLE 10

Alfredo likewise has one important theme, heard for the first time in his important scene with Violetta, Act I:

EXAMPLE 11

Di   quel - l'a - mor,   quel - l'a - mor____   ch'è   pal - pi - to

[*Out of such love, love that pulsates*]

Its similarity to Violetta's above-mentioned theme has often been noted. Verdi reintroduces it in her "Ah, fors'è lui"; also, quite consistently, while she reads his letter in the opera's last scene (violin solo), and once more, *pppp,* as she dies. This kind of "recollection," especially of a sentimental theme, became a sure-fire device, used effectively by many composers, Puccini among them (e.g., in the last scene of *La Bohème*).

In comparison with Violetta, the opera's other characters appear less fascinating. Alfredo's attitude changes, but only because of Violetta's noble deception. Since we know her true motives, his violent reaction does not make him more absorbing to us. More interesting is Germont *père,* because in him we witness a significant change. In Act II Germont enters with a preconceived attitude, with resentment against this woman who has endangered not only his son but the happiness of his family as well. As he listens to Violetta he gradually realizes that he has misjudged her, and his attitude and tone change. The growing intensity of his music reflects this—he is pleading with Violetta. Eventually compassion breaks through his original façade of reserve and scorn. When he sings "Piangi, o misera" he has met Violetta on human, equal terms. This, rather than the finale, in which he is all remorse and repentance, is his great scene.

Much of the popularity still enjoyed by *La Traviata* (and other operas from Verdi's middle period) is due to felicitous melodic invention. Verdi's melodies have a power of projection and propulsion that defies description. He was well aware of his talent for writing captivating melodies, irresistible and of immediate popular appeal. In the case of "La donna è mobile" from *Rigoletto,* Verdi wished to insure what he felt certain could be a spontaneous success, and so insisted during rehearsals that no one

"La Traviata": The end.

in the cast sing or whistle the tune outside the theater. As he predicted, it drew tremendous applause at the premiere.

Several melodies in *La Traviata* have these characteristic qualities, beginning with the *brindisi,* the toast proposed by Alfredo and then Violetta in Act I. Its cantilena is anticipated in the orchestral introduction, which ends abruptly, thereby making us all the more aware of the rhythmic momentum of the aria:

EXAMPLE 12

[*Let us drink from cups of happiness.*]

Verdi uses this device often. Other arias display the same melodic sweep and vigor, combined with rhythmic vitality: Violetta's "Sempre libera" later in the same act, and the "Addio del passato" of Act IV. In these and other instances Verdi's accompaniment has a subordinate function, supplying a rhythmic foundation and little more. Critics have often pointed to these stereotyped accompaniment patterns, comparing them unfavorably with Wagner's accompaniments from the same period. Granted that Verdi's voice-and-accompaniment patterns lent themselves more successfully to barrel organ transcriptions (a form of massacring operatic favorites that fortunately disappeared with the advent of radio), the criticism is valid only to a limited degree. Some Verdi melodies are practically self-sufficient; for these a more complex accompaniment would only serve to cover up and to confuse. In other instances the composer did provide accompaniments that are varied and expressive, employing specific tone color for heightened effect, as in "Addio del passato," or in the melodrama of the preceding letter-reading scene.

Verdi's more substantial arias comprise several sections, with changes in mood, texture, and tempo. Far from conforming to the earlier Italian practice of alternating recitatives and arias, Verdi frequently wrote complex scenes in which solo singing is interrupted by short passages of accompanied recitative[8] which may lead into small or large ensembles. The entire first act is a continuous structure. Alfredo's "Un di felice," as a declaration of love, brings a slowing down from the brilliant and nervous waltz rhythm. Violetta's answer leads into a duet, eventually returning to the former tempo. The orchestra then provides a transition, bringing back the music of the introduction as Flora and the other guests return (chorus). Later in the act Violetta's great soliloquy (recitative and aria) is interrupted by Alfredo's offstage singing. With such changes in texture the drama unfolds in a natural manner, and the pace (especially in Act I) is more rapid than had been customary in the earlier "number opera." Some of the longer lyrical arias end with the traditional cabaletta—a rapid, vigorous, and rhythmical section.

Tradition still caused Verdi to provide arias commensurate in number to the importance of a role. Father Germont's "Di Provenza il mar" appears to serve such a purpose; dramatically it is weak, and its two verses might have been dispensed with otherwise. Verdi seems to have realized this: at least once he tried to remedy matters by moving the aria to a place earlier in the act, soon after Germont's entrance. In this way the end of the act belonged to Violetta; her music here provides a far more satisfactory climax.

Most of the arias, it has been shown, are not musical display pieces interrupting the action but are integrally related to the drama. In this way *La Traviata* is more modern than the contemporary *Trovatore,* where arias frequently are static, "delivered" to the audience. There is a good deal of word repetition in *La Traviata,* but much of it is credible in context: the meaning of "follie," "amore" and like words is thus stressed; the repeats do not merely serve to round out a musical phrase.

The ensembles in *La Traviata* also are distinctive in this regard. Other Verdi operas, e.g., *A Masked Ball,* contain ensemble and choral scenes that are there for purely musical reasons. Endless

---

[8] Secco recitative no longer is found, though the sparse accompaniment early in Act II comes close to it.

word repetitions have no other function than to emphasize a basic mood and to bring a scene to a desired musical length. In *La Traviata* such choral pronouncements are rare, while ensembles of action predominate. Since the opera is intimate, the small ensemble is most in evidence. All of Act II is carried on in this way. There are aria-like sections ("Pura siccome un angelo"; "Dite alla giovine"), but these are no more important or expressive than the give-and-take of free dialogue. Tension steadily mounts through the first part of this act. Here, too, there is a cabaletta, beginning with Violetta's "Morrò! La mia memoria." After Germont's departure Violetta's feelings once more surge up, culminating in her outburst "Amami Alfredo." The emotional upheaval of all these developments is expressed by Verdi's accompaniment, which is harmonically and rhythmically sensitive, ever changing, with modulations and numerous dynamic contrasts closely related to the text.

Two orchestral preludes, related in thematic material and mood, open Acts I and IV of Verdi's opera. Far shorter than the average nineteenth-century overture, they do not function as symphonic synopses but establish, with economy of means, the emotional climate of the opera. A delicate opening, played *ppp* by divided violins in a high register, suggests Violetta's frailty. This opening theme is common to both preludes and is heard repeatedly during the opera's last scene. Prelude I then presents Violetta's principal theme, "Amami, Alfredo." It rises pleadingly to a forte, but a mood of lassitude and resignation returns soon, and the end is marked *morendo* ("dying away").

Act III had ended vigorously: the scandalized Germont had led off his son amidst loud expressions of indignation by all. To this the mood of the following prelude stands in the strongest possible contrast. Violetta's theme is missing this time, and so is the light, flirtatious counterpoint that had accompanied it in the Act I prelude, but some trills and grace notes still faintly suggest that quality. Since the entire short prelude establishes the mood of the scene that follows, it is sometimes played *after* the curtain has risen: the prelude, in a sense, accompanies and reinforces our visual impression of this extremely subdued scene.

In *La Traviata* Verdi responded with great musical sensitivity to the challenge of subtle dramatic and psychological characterization. The opera's continued popular appeal today is not merely due to the attractiveness of a few arias but to Verdi's convincing musical interpretation of the principal characters' emotional lives.

Beckmesser's interrupted serenade: a Metropolitan Opera production of "Die Meistersinger."

7

WAGNERIAN MUSIC DRAMA

No COMPOSER EVER WAS GIVEN MORE TO theorizing—to verbal expression on a great variety of subjects, not all of them closely related to music. Wagner's collected writings fill a dozen or so substantial volumes. We may agree with Ernest Newman, who would gladly have sacrificed three-fourths of them for another opera from his pen, but within the remaining fourth Newman no doubt would have included two treatises in which Wagner expounds his views on the nature and purpose of music drama: *The Art Work of the Future* (1849) and *Opera and Drama* (1850–1851).

Ever since the beginnings of his musical career Wagner had felt increasingly dissatisfied with the operatic life of his time— with its superficiality, aimed at entertaining the luxury-loving upper classes. And he had been equally critical of characteristics of the operas themselves. Whether the undesirable qualities of the works caused the objectionable attitudes of the public, or vice versa, was a question Wagner did not attempt to answer.

In Wagner's opinion, the trouble with opera for a long time had been that music, a means of expression, had become an end—the *raison d'être* of opera—while drama had been relegated to the role of providing an occasion or excuse for music. This confusion he found to be most flagrant in Italian opera. He severely criticized many of its features, some of which we noted in earlier chapters: a small range of subjects, poorly constructed plots, trivial language, coloratura singing, hackneyed tunes with barrel-organ-like accompaniment, harmonic poverty, and rhythmic monotony. Diversion and entertainment, he believed, were all the public sought and received—purposes completely at variance with his own views of the nature of music drama. He continually stressed the task of the poet who inspires and "fertilizes" the musician and his art. True music drama—he avoided the term "opera" because of its association with the hated tradition—represents a fusion of equally important contributions from many fields: poetic language, vocal and instrumental music, dance, acting, and stage design. The art work of the future must not neglect any of these; it must appeal to the eye as well as to the ear. This is Wagner's *Gesamtkunstwerk,* the total work of art, the purpose of which goes beyond entertainment, involving the audience on an aesthetic and spiritual level comparable to participation in a religious rite.

Other Romantics before and after Wagner believed in some kind of fusion of the arts. That Beethoven should have felt it necessary to introduce words in the final movement of his Ninth Symphony appeared significant and inevitable in Wagner's eyes: Beethoven *had* to burst the bonds of conventional symphonic music to achieve his mission. Programmatic symphonies and tone poems further exemplify the nineteenth-century trend toward an amalgamation of the arts, a tendency also evident from the extensive literary activities of many musicians. Romantic painters, writers, and musicians often were interested in each other's fields and moved in the same artistic circles. But the concept of the total art work became essential to Wagner's artistic creed. He theorized about it at great length and applied his theories to his own works. The fusion was most likely to be successful if accomplished by one artist, and Wagner put this belief into practice. Not only did he write his own texts, a task he approached with great seriousness, but wherever possible he took charge of all other aspects of the production of his music dramas. He directed, he collaborated with stage designers and painters, he provided sketches for costumes and properties, often after painstaking historical research. If he could not be present to supervise, he wrote letters with detailed instructions.

Realizing that a completely unified and integrated presentation was next to impossible under existing conditions, Wagner with great determination made plans for the creation of the right setting. He envisioned a theater, preferably away from the great cities, where a company of devoted artists could work hard and at length, under his direction, to achieve performances in which all artistic aspects received appropriate prominence and care. The theater, built to his specifications, was to be a temple of the arts to which worshipers would flock from far and wide to see and to hear German music dramas written for the occasion.[1]

The plan certainly was grandiose and unheard of; but even more remarkable is the fact that ultimately it was realized. Convinced of the importance and rightness of his undertaking, and an unusually vocal spokesman for his own cause, Wagner obtained the spiritual and material backing of King Ludwig II of Bavaria. Eventually the secluded small town of Bayreuth was decided upon as the site for his Festspielhaus. In spite of many difficulties,

[1] Wagner had not intended that only his own works should be staged there; this was the decision of his widow, who also attempted, unsuccessfully, to have *Parsifal* performed at Bayreuth only.

The Festival House, Bayreuth.

financial and other, the first Bayreuth festival took place in the summer of 1876. With some interruptions the festivals have continued since then—every summer since 1951.[2]

The building itself is apt to disappoint the visitor who expects an architectural masterpiece. Wagner had hoped that in time the structure would be finished in a more imposing manner, but the funds that he had expected to be contributed by an enthusiastic nation had failed to come forth. Nevertheless, the acoustics of the hall benefited from the use of much wood and a canvas ceiling. Tiers of boxes, found in most traditional opera houses, are absent. They would have been reminiscent of class distinctions, of opera as aristocratic entertainment, while Wagner's audiences, like those of classical Greek drama, were to be united, sharing a great experience.

One mechanical innovation deserves special mention since it grew out of the *Gesamtkunstwerk* idea. The orchestra pit in Bayreuth is partially covered, and the platform on which the players are seated can be raised or lowered. Wagner felt—and many operagoers today will agree—that the visual impression of a stage set often was marred by the orchestra's activity, taking place

[2] See the article "Bayreuth" in *Grove's Dictionary* for complete dates.

Bayreuth: The covered orchestra pit.

in full view. In Scenes that called for subdued lighting this became especially annoying, for the bright lights on each music stand interfered with the total effect. In Bayreuth the stage apron extends sufficiently over the orchestra pit to minimize this disturbance. Gradually rising rows of seats enable the audience to look over, rather than into, the pit. (This was another reason for not providing tiers of boxes). These arrangements resulted in good views from every seat; they also improved the balance in volume between orchestra and singers. The *Ring* orchestra is large, especially its brass section, yet the volume of its sound can be subdued sufficiently not to overpower the singers.

Floor plan and general shape of the Festspielhaus were not generally copied, though the Prinzregententheater in Munich, which opened in 1901, resembles it. King Ludwig II had intended to build a festival opera house in Munich for the performance of Wagner's works, but the project never materialized.

Over a period of almost a century the popularity of Wagner's operas has fluctuated, but the festivals at Bayreuth continue to be among the major musical events of the Western world. While the whole concept of Wagnerian music drama has repeatedly been challenged, a large public continues to listen in a spirit of reverence and considers Bayreuth a shrine. (To others it may merely be a "must" item on any grand tour of Europe.) With contagious enthusiasm for his own exalted cause Wagner managed to instill a spirit of cooperation and devotion in this company. Famous singers from near and far considered it a privilege to participate, even in small roles. Such subordination, in an age of stars, was quite an achievement in itself. The conductor's name now tended to become as important as the name of the singer—a change reflected in billing and advertising.

To Wagner, it has been said, drama was of paramount importance. He referred to his Bayreuth cast as actors (*darstellendes Personal*) rather than singers. This may seem puzzling to a person who, going to see the *Ring* operas or *Tristan*, expects fast-moving dramatic action on the stage. Quite to the contrary, these works contain many passages, some of them long, during which little or no outward action takes place on stage. The entire second act of *Tristan* serves as an example; the drama, here and elsewhere, lies in the emotions experienced by the characters on stage. What goes on in their hearts and minds may be reflected in the lines they sing, but frequently it is revealed by the orchestra. In Wagner's view, instrumental music can express the unspeakable. It may emphasize a gesture; it may bring back to memory a previous event or emotion; or the orchestra may by itself establish a new mood. In these and other ways Wagner wanted his orchestra to be more than the accompaniment—the "monstrous guitar"—of Italian opera.

As he increased its dramatic and musical contribution he reduced the traditional difference between vocal and instrumental melody. Quite often the chief melodic line reaches us from the orchestra pit rather than from the stage.

To a public and to critics accustomed to clearly defined arias with subordinate accompaniment, Wagner's melodic style was unsettling. Eduard Hanslick, his most vocal and often vicious critic, again and again attacked this absence of clear-cut melodies, the "endless music without pause or contrast . . . shapeless . . . a musical jellyfish that drifts on and on." In a sense Wagner's "endless melody" is related to the *stile recitativo* of the early Florentines: the prosody of the voice line, while generally slow, is that of spoken German, and the style is continuous. There is, however, no vocal ornament, and the harmonic implications of melodies as well as the harmonic language in general are of a complexity unheard of before. *Tristan* represents Wagner's chromaticism at its extreme; it has been called the last step in the development of tonal harmony. In most Western music the degree of chromaticism is related to the intensity of emotions expressed; thus it is fitting that *Tristan,* rather than the *Ring* operas, should contain it to such an advanced degree.

The principle of the *Leitmotiv,* already operating in *The Flying Dutchman,* was expanded considerably in the later operas, especially the *Ring.* Since this cycle of four works has a continuous plot, some motives are heard in several or all of them. Many are presented in the first work (Wagner calls it a prelude), *Das Rheingold,* and at their first occurrence are clearly related to persons or objects. When a motive recurs later in the cycle its function may be associative: it reminds the listener of someone or something (or of an abstract concept) not present or even mentioned at the time. It may be modified or developed to correspond more closely to the situation where it is now reintroduced. At times a specific key may also be associated with a certain character.

Wagner held that the cast of a music drama should be small, including only roles essential to the plot. For *Tristan* and the *Ring* this meant the absence of any chorus, though in his last work, the "consecrational play" *Parsifal,* choral scenes once more appear. Ensembles tend to be dialogues rather than duets.

Wagner the poet was attacked almost as widely as the musician. Hanslick complained about "the unnatural, stilted progression of his diction, which offends every feeling for fine speech." Steeped in the milieu of Germanic lore, Wagner set out to capture the flavor of its poetry. To do this he resorted to *Stabreim,* the poetic device of alliteration which, rather than end rhyme, characterized early Germanic poetry. Alliteration to Wag-

ner was expressive of feeling; end rhyme was more intellectual—
the result of understanding rather than feeling. His poetic language today often seems involved, hard to understand, and self-
consciously archaic, but it is another manifestation of a desire to
achieve historical correctness in the expression of any and all
detail.

A similar attitude characterizes the approach to staging taken
by Wagner and his collaborators. The concept of the *Gesamtkunstwerk* required that meticulous care be devoted to its visual aspects.
In choosing his singers Wagner considered appearance, acting
ability, and diction as well as purely musical qualifications. He
once drew up a detailed plan for the establishing of an academy in
which singers would obtain more substantial training in these
related fields than was customary, and he deplored the fact that
most conductors lacked nonmusical, i.e., dramatic, training.[3]

Keeping in mind that this was the age of realism in all

[3] Wagner's proposals for reforms of opera training are summarized by Herbert
Graf in *Producing Opera for America,* pp. 62 f.

*An early Metropolitan
Opera set for Wagner's
"Das Rheingold," Scene
I.*

matters of staging, we only have to read some of the directions in Wagner's scores to be aware of the formidable tasks faced by his stage designers and machinists. For the opening scene of *Das Rheingold* Wagner provides the following description:

> On the bottom of the River Rhine. Greenish twilight which is lighter above and darker at the bottom. On top, water flows ceaselessly from right to left. Towards the bottom these floods dissolve into an increasingly fine damp mist, so that the bottom of the stage, up to a man's height, seems to be completely free of water. . . . Jagged cliffs rise up from the depths everywhere. . . . Around one cliff in the stage center one of the Rhine maidens is circling with a graceful swimming motion.

Just as difficult to realize is the last scene of the *Ring*—the end of *Götterdämmerung*. Here Brünhilde must mount her horse and charge into the burning funeral pyre. Flames rise up high at once; soon the entire stage is aflame. Now the River Rhine overflows its bed, and on its waves the three Rhine maidens swim near.

We may well doubt that with the equipment then available scenes of this kind could be made to look convincingly real, but up to the time of the First World War such realism was at least attempted at Bayreuth and elsewhere.[4]

In practice, most people agree today, Wagner did not succeed in bringing about a successful fusion, and certainly not the equality, of all the contributing arts. Music dominates—and most Wagnerites probably prefer it that way. "His music will always be a thousand times more potent than his machines" (Romain Rolland).

Die Meistersinger von Nürnberg
(Dresden, 1869)

Though the planning and writing of *Die Meistersinger* was interrupted by work on the *Ring,* Wagner here created an entirely different atmosphere. In *Die Meistersinger* we are in the real world; its protagonists are human beings, warmly and appealingly drawn. Wagner provided a lively picture of a period and place, rich in detail that is historically accurate and that at the same time blends in smoothly with the principal action. *Die Meistersinger* is Wagner's only opera in which humor is prominent; yet, as we shall see, it provides far more than light entertainment. Numerous choruses and several ensemble scenes, along with colorful finales and festive pageantry, distinguish it from the *Ring*

[4] See Chapter 13.

operas. Though among the longest operas in the repertory it holds our attention well; quite likely it is Wagner's most beloved opera today.

Wagner's plans for the work ripened slowly. As early as 1835, during a visit to Nuremberg, he received impressions that were to find their way into the drama. His interest aroused, he began to study the practices of the sixteenth-century mastersingers. A prose sketch for the opera was ready in 1845, but further work was interrupted by the composition of *Lohengrin*. The subject was taken up in earnest in 1861; in a letter of the following year Wagner expresses his certainty that *Die Meistersinger* will be his "most perfect masterwork." His earlier intention had been to write a small work—one that could conveniently be performed by smaller companies, but as the subject grew from pure comedy to something far deeper, the dimensions of the score likewise increased.

What is *Die Meistersinger* all about? There is the action itself—a good plot, with many amusing touches. Certainly the work can be enjoyed on this level, without looking for a more profound interpretation. But it is just as certain that beneath this outer action Wagner wanted to tell something of his own philosophy of art, especially about the artist in relation to a society that does not understand him. The composer's own difficulties in a musical world that to him seemed populated with Beckmessers caused him to write from the heart, with intense personal feeling. Like Walther von Stolzing, whose violation of musical tradition brings him into conflict with the masters, Wagner had been the target of widespread attack. That strong personal feelings were directing his pen is evident from sketches for the opera in which the Marker's name was Hans Lick or Hanslich!

Walther von Stolzing represents the artist, young in spirit, who creates freely, finding his inspiration in life around him, in nature, in love. As an outsider he is unfamiliar with the numerous rules of poetry and music by which the mastersingers abide. Living away from society, Walther tells us, he learned the art of singing from "an ancient book" by Walther von der Vogelweide, one of the medieval Minnesingers. It seems ironical that Beckmesser should be the first to object to this teacher, dead for a long time, since Beckmesser personifies the conservative, tradition-bound, and rule-conscious musician.

Viewed from this angle, the general validity of artistic rules becomes the chief issue of the opera. Wagner (who frequently speaks through Hans Sachs) does not deny the need for rules in art but submits that they should be revised from time to time, even by the people—a thought at which Beckmesser shudders. Sachs stands for open-mindedness. He is willing to make an effort to understand what is new and different, willing to grant that a work of art may incorporate its own rules and principles, and willing to look for these. Thus he instructs Walther, who is anxious to begin his song "according to the rules," to set his own and then to follow them. The song turns out to be "a little free," but to Sachs this is not necessarily a fault. Beckmesser, on the other hand, only knows one set of rules and prides himself on their knowledge. Here Wagner's animosity caused him to be inconsistent in his drawing of the Marker, for Beckmesser's own serenade violates many of these same rules, as Sachs is quick to point out with hammer strokes and words. That Wagner was able, in this scene and elsewhere, to treat the opera's theme with humor was all to the good: the preaching is subtly disguised but the message comes across just the same.

We have seen that Wagner undertook some historical studies to provide authenticity in general setting and detail. One of his sources, a book on the art of the mastersingers by Wagenseil (1697), contained several mastersinger tunes that found their way into the opera. Wagner's treatment of the Lutheran chorale in the

Beckmesser emerges from the Marker's Booth, his slate showing the many mistakes he noted in Walther's song.

opening scene also reveals some knowledge of sixteenth-century practice: the congregation sings, with instrumental interludes after each line. (In addition to the organ Wagner uses orchestral instruments, chiefly to express Walther's emotions.) A cobbler and poet named Hans Sachs lived in Nuremberg around 1560; the "Wach auf!" with which Wagner's Sachs is greeted in the opera's final scene is one of the historical Sachs's poems. We learn a good deal about customs and procedures in the guild of amateur musicians. David's account of the long and arduous road to becoming a master may affect us as it does Walther, who is awed as well as amused. Many scenes and bits of dialogue fill in our picture of life in a sixteenth-century town—the night watchman singing his little ditty; the reference to Dürer, Nuremberg's most famous painter–engraver. Beckmesser's lute, however, is out of place in the finale: in the historical contests no accompaniment was allowed.

The formal arrangement of a master song, described in the book of rules (*Tabulatur*) and read aloud by Kothner, also agrees with sixteenth-century practices. Two similar sections (*Stollen*) of several lines each are followed by a contrasting section (*Abgesang*). This so-called bar form is best known today (in abbreviated form) from a number of Protestant chorales. Several songs in the opera display this bar form, including Walther's "Am stillen Herd" in Act I.

According to Wagner's own standards a good opera text should make good reading, and *Die Meistersinger* easily passes that test. It was Wagner's custom to invite an audience of friends for the reading of a new libretto; he introduced *Die Meistersinger* this way in 1862. Warm and frequently subtle humor pervades the entire text. Some of the humor extends to Wagner's rhymes, at times purposely awkward ("Junker—sprung er") as in some of the authentic mastersinger poetry.

The plot is well constructed and generally convincing, though one may wonder why the mastersingers should even *consider* that Walther, an outsider and not a burgher, so quickly might become a master. Nor is it ever made clear who among the bachelors in the guild will compete. Beckmesser, as the oldest, sings first, but we are told of no others. As the plot unfolds, Sachs and Beckmesser emerge as the most interestingly drawn characters. Sachs in particular is drawn with loving care. He shows wisdom and warmth; he meets difficult situations with calmness and restraint. In his beautiful scene with Eva (III/4) their affection for each other is subtly revealed—not only by words but by what remains unsaid; by their acting; and, of course, by the music. The absence of pathos (Sachs's expression of philosophical resignation is combined with a touch of gaiety) can make this a very moving

scene. In the "Wahn" monologue and in his preceding remarks to David, Sachs reveals similar qualities of wisdom and humaneness. Wagner's first sketches of the text do not yet show Sachs to be such a complicated human being. He is merely the robust shoemaker, given to the kind of practical joke that we find in the cobbling scene of the final version.

Beckmesser at times comes close to being a caricature, but in all he is convincingly drawn. Though not an old man, he is sour, crotchety, and overly suspicious of others. As Marker he prides himself on his knowledge of poetry and music, yet underneath he is unsure of himself, particularly as he assumes the role of Eva's suitor.[5] No one who makes such a fool of himself can be a real villain. As already mentioned, his serenade in Act II violates both rules and common sense to a greater extent than is believable. Apparently Wagner could not resist including this comical exaggeration, which always brings the house down. Thoroughly thrashed at the end of Act II, Beckmesser cuts a sad, pathetic figure from then on. Having picked up Sachs's manuscript of Walther's song (III/3), he at first feels triumphant—"Now all is clear!" Triumph soon gives way to embarrassment: Sachs's words make him feel like a thief. He registers surprise and delight when the sheet is offered to him, but abruptly and comically his delight and gratitude give way to suspicion—perhaps Sachs has already memorized the song? Convinced finally that all is well, he stumbles off stage happily, forgetting the very manuscript from which he expects his salvation.

Die Meistersinger reveals a number of differences in musical style from the *Ring* operas and *Tristan*. Subject and milieu chiefly account for this. To evoke the world of Nuremberg's sturdy, respectable citizens Wagner chose melodies and harmonies a good deal less chromatic than had seemed right for the ancient Germanic myths or for the emotion-drenched atmosphere of *Tristan*. A certain sturdiness also characterizes the rhythm of many passages and themes. Songs and a singing contest are essential to the story; these are self-contained compositions that contrast with the "endless melody" of Wagner's other music dramas. Besides the Prize Song and Beckmesser's serenade there are other musical "numbers," both solo and choral, including the cobbler's song, David's *Sprüchlein* (III/1), and the "Wach auf!" chorus of the last scene.

Though these style differences may suggest simplicity, *Die Meistersinger* is a finely wrought score, a delicate polyphonic web

---

[5] That Beckmesser, a contestant himself, should have been allowed to officiate as Marker in Act I is hardly proper—a flaw to which Sachs calls attention, but only after the trial.

Opposite: Hans Sachs (Act III, Scene 1).

Beckmesser and Hans Sachs (Act III, Scene 1).

containing much variety. Leading motives are more numerous and more ingeniously employed than they had been in *The Flying Dutchman*. Indeed, they are so numerous that several editions of the score include an "index of motives." Their abundance has prompted analysts and commentators to provide a name for each motive—a label indicating its meaning in the drama. Here is the "cobbler's motive":

EXAMPLE 1

and here the "motive of resignation" (*Entsagung*):

EXAMPLE 2

Few listeners will be aware of the meaning in each case, except after repeated hearing and careful study of the score. Wagner himself said little on the subject, but it stands to reason that this awareness normally is not conscious, any more than a casual listener's awareness of formal details in a sonata movement or fugue. In *Die Meistersinger,* some motives are so prominently and extensively stated and developed that one will soon recognize them and understand their meaning. A leading motive usually appears in the orchestra. When we hear it for the first time its meaning is made clear by the dialogue. Later appearances recall this meaning, providing commentary on the action, amplifying, explaining, or even contradicting a thought expressed by one of the singers.

Wagner knew well how to fit a musical theme to the person, object, or concept in mind. Thus the principal motive representing the stately assembly of the masters has a weighty, majestic quality:

EXAMPLE 3

while the motive of Walther's longing and striving is appropriately intense and restless:

EXAMPLE 4

The free-for-all at the end of Act II is announced by what sounds like a bugle call to battle:

EXAMPLE 5

To see how motives are intended to recall important characters and events from earlier scenes we may look at the beginning of Scene 3 in Act III. Beckmesser appears outside the cobbler's shop, peeks in, and, noticing that it is empty, quickly enters. He is nervous, excited, and suffering acutely in body and spirit from the thrashing and humiliation he received the night before. His entrance is signaled in the orchestra by the theme of his serenade, followed by the "battle motive." The "Wahn" (folly) motive, heard in the celli, is prophetic of the foolishness that will cause him to fall into a trap before long. As he contemplates the cobbler's bench the appropriate motive appears: unpleasant memories result in his mounting excitement. He limps around restlessly and wipes perspiration from his brow (to several of the above-named motives, especially the "battle" motive, faster and faster). Eventually he spots Sachs's manuscript on the workbench (Prize Song motive). There is no singing up to this point, but the motivic work in the orchestra, combined with Beckmesser's actions, clearly bring out Wagner's intentions as contained in the stage directions.

In the opera's instrumental prelude some of the principal motives are combined in a way that makes it possible to interpret the piece as a musical summary of the opera's basic dramatic conflict. The opening section is in C major; both the key and the motivic material are that of the mastersingers' guild. The next section, in E major, brings Walther's music (second part of Prize Song), but this is soon interrupted. In the contrasting key of E flat major Beckmesser's world is now evoked. His narrow, critical nature, his "small" view of art, is aptly suggested by a small, somewhat grotesque version of the mastersinger motif:

EXAMPLE 6

These elements are then combined in a number of ways: they are developed, they struggle with each other. Another motif is introduced:

206

EXAMPLE 7

with which in the opera's final scene the people express their dissatisfaction with Beckmesser: "He is not the right one!" But eventually the bright C major and the mastersinger theme win out, as they do at the end of the opera itself.[6]

Wagner's fusion of text and music is accomplished in various ways, not only through his *Leitmotiv* technique. Through many subtle devices the music underscores or gives added meaning to the text. A reference to King David brings forth a few prominent notes on the harp, the instrument traditionally associated with the biblical king. At times the humor of a situation is evident from music rather than text, as when David (the apprentice), still under the spell of the free-for-all the night before, begins to sing his St. John's Day song to the tune of Beckmesser's serenade. Even a pun on the words *Bar* and *Paar* is brought to our attention (at least for German-speaking audiences) by a laughing figure in the orchestra.

Musical changes in the several versions of the Prize Song are textually and dramatically justified. With Sachs's encouragement and advice, Walther sings two complete verses (bars) in III/2 but is unable to provide a third one—the interpretation of his dream. During the following scene Beckmesser appears and eventually makes off with the manuscript. Walther then returns (Scene 4); inspired by the sight of Eva he adds the third verse. What poor Beckmesser tries to sing in the finale starts out as an utterly garbled version of Walther's first verse. After a few measures he sees the futility of struggling with this unfamiliar kind of song and, in desperation, falls back on the tune of his own serenade from the previous night. At last Walther's opportunity has come to show to the masters and assembled people how his song really sounds. Wagner was wise enough to avoid the anticlimax of a literal repetition: this second version contains several modifications, including a temporary modulation to the remote key of B major.[7]

[6] See Philip Kepler, "Clash Before the Curtain," *ON*, January 23, 1956. Wagner's prelude was written before the rest of the opera, but its form and use of motives may well have been intended to have such a meaning. The matter is discussed in Newman, *The Wagner Operas* (New York, 1949), pp. 299 f.

[7] Lest he be accused of dramatic inconsistency Wagner provided the appropriate stage directions. Kothner at first follows the song manuscript which Sachs had given him, but he soon "drops the paper, deeply moved," and merely listens. Walther, noticing this, now feels free to depart from the original version.

Ensembles and choral scenes of great variety occur in all three acts, from the congregational singing of the opening scene to the rousing popular acclaim of Sachs at the end. A quintet in which the participants simultaneously express different thoughts and emotions occurs in III/4 ("Selig wie die Sonne")—traditional in concept and dramatic function, yet musically original and moving. Act I ends with an intricate, large ensemble scene: Beckmesser argues excitedly with the other masters; Walther, with determination, attempts to finish his song; while the apprentices, dancing around the Marker's booth, sing their mocking chorus. The brawl scene that concludes Act II so effectively has already been singled out in an earlier chapter as one of the most complex crowd scenes in all opera. Curiously enough, in the agitated crowd of neighbors, apprentices, journeymen, and masters it is this last group that takes up in unison Beckmesser's serenade melody, though the words now have the correct accentuation:

The final scene.

EXAMPLE 8

[*Who is quarreling and fighting there?*]

Compared with these two scenes, the finale of Act III is conventional but nevertheless effective. Certainly all three act endings contribute to the opera's great and lasting audience appeal.

Carmen and Don José in a Berlin production of the opera.

8

THE LATER NINETEENTH CENTURY

Both nationalism and realism continued to affect musical drama in the second half of the century. The Shakespeare revival continued with considerable force in France, Germany, and other European countries. Nationalistic dramas, often based on historical subjects, and containing crowd scenes and other large-scale stage effects, became increasingly popular (Sardou's *La Patrie*, 1869, is an example). Controversial subjects, including those involving middle-class morality, were treated with some frankness, (Sardou again provides an example with his *Divorçons*, 1880). Charpentier's opera *Louise* (1900) is a late example of a trend already represented by *La Traviata*. Dealing with the subject of free love, it shocked audiences of the time, though the treatment is frequently sentimental rather than realistic.

Realism in painting at first had implied

a return to nature as a model. Artists moved their easels outdoors, painting nature as it was rather than painting imaginary (and always beautiful) landscapes in the studio. Realism of this kind gradually gave way to naturalism, which favored the stark and frequently the shocking, and pulled no punches. As Marek points out,[1] Manet's *Olympia,* first shown in 1865, drew such widespread criticism because its portrayal of a nude woman was unashamed, true-to-life, and in no way idealized. Its effect on contemporary audiences was similar to (but probably stronger than) that of Bizet's opera *Carmen* some ten years later. Manet later turned to impressionism, a movement characterized by quite different techniques of painting, though it too considered any subject, no matter how ordinary or prosaic, as appropriate for artistic treatment (Monet, for example, painted the St. Lazare railroad station). But naturalism, in literature as well as in painting, meant selectivity of subject matter, emphasizing the dark, problematic side of reality. In French literature naturalism made its mark more through the novel (with Zola the major figure) than through the drama. Naturalism grew out of the social upheavals of the nineteenth century: it frequently mirrors materialism and Marxism. Its novels and dramas frequently accuse and intentionally shock. Ibsen was among those who indicted the

[1] *Opera as Theater,* p. 105.

Manet's "Olympia."

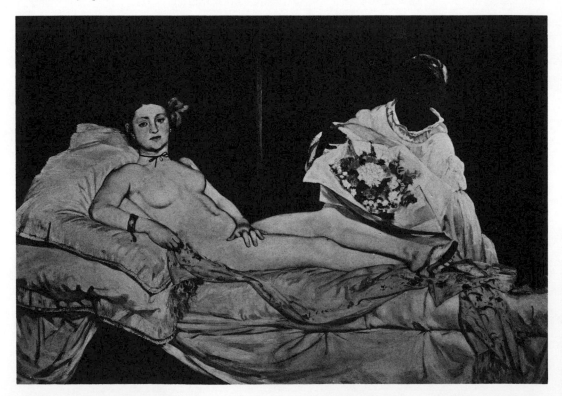

bourgeois world around him, with its façade of respectability covering up greed and corruption (see his *Pillars of Society,* 1877; *Ghosts,* 1881; *An Enemy of the People,* 1882). Much late nineteenth-century drama, too, concerned itself with social problems and with disease, both physical and mental (see Ibsen's *Ghosts;* Strindberg's *Miss Julie,* 1888).

Naturalism in musical drama, especially in late nineteenth- and early twentieth-century Italian opera, is generally called verismo. It is the subject of the following chapter.

Historical accuracy in all details of staging had been the concern of Wagner and some of his associates. In some places, such as the Court Theater in Meiningen, this approach, essentially realistic, continued to be in vogue until the end of the century. Realistic staging owed much to the introduction of electrical stage lighting late in the century. Strong light was not kind to painted backdrops, and more three-dimensional scenery was needed. With technological advances stages became better equipped to accommodate heavy and complicated sets and props; rapid scene changes could now be accomplished with revolving stages, elevator stages, and other equipment.

The striving for ever greater realism eventually came to be considered a dead-end road. After the turn of the century more and more stage designers and directors raised their voices against excessive realism, especially in opera, a genre which they and others considered to be not basically realistic (see Chapter 13).

Georges Bizet, *Carmen* (Paris, 1875)

With the possible exception of some of the operas of Puccini, no opera written after *Carmen* has equaled its general and lasting popularity. *Carmen* is the kind of work which many opera enthusiasts consider to have been done to death, of which they believe themselves to be tired. Yet on re-hearing it they may discover details of which they had been previously unaware, and to their own surprise they may respond anew to some of its familiar charms.

Unlike Bizet's earlier works, *Carmen* is sure-fire opera. It boasts a good and taut plot, with few secondary complications. Much of the action is obvious and clearly motivated, thereby lending itself well to musical treatment. Ample opportunities for colorful stage effects exist in every act, and there is good character drawing. Added to these dramatic assets is the quality of Bizet's virtually indestructible music. To call it obvious would be an unfair generalization, applicable to the Toreador Song, the Habanera (one might argue about this), and to Micaëla's "Je dis," but

The Act II set of a San Francisco production.

not to many of the other solos and ensembles. Depending on the dramatic situation, obviousness in music is not necessarily a vice, and subtlety need not always be a virtue.

Carmen is so robust that it has weathered countless adaptations and arrangements.

It possesses a unique balance of the picturesque and the lyrical, the romantic and the savagely realistic. . . . We have had Carmens subtle and wanton, coquettish and coarse, suggestive and realistic, Carmens of every shade of dramatic emphasis and variety of characterization. We have seen productions of the opera as far apart as that of "Carmencita and the Soldier," by the Moscow Art Theatre Musical Studio, done in Russian, with constructivist scenery . . . and the "Carmen Jones" . . . with a Negro cast . . . with a scenario which departed even more than the Russian one from the original text.[2]

At the first performance *Carmen* was not a resounding success. The audience, we are told, thought the work was daring and shocking. But was it really shocking, twenty-two years after *La Traviata?* In plays and in novels Parisian audiences had been exposed to equally realistic, brutal happenings and to characters even more lacking in conventional morality than the Carmen of Bizet's opera. More likely it was the critics who expressed disapproval (without necessarily being shocked) of this kind of drama. At least one critic objected to a general trend: that members of the

[2] Olin Downes, *Ten Operatic Masterpieces* (New York, 1952), p. 170. Copyright 1952 by Charles Scribner's Sons. An adaptation for television is described in *ON*, November 1, 1954.

lowest social class, especially courtesans, now appeared as "the heroines of our dramas, our comedies, and even our opéras-comiques. . . . Once an author has become fouled in the social sewer, he is forced to descend . . . to the lowest level for a choice of models."[3] What really was considered shocking, then, was that this kind of "low" subject matter, which already had scored with the common audiences of the boulevard theaters, now should gain respectability at the Opéra Comique. Its director considered *Carmen* unsuitable for performance there—a "nice" theater, to which middle-class families took their daughters—because a violent death takes place on stage. Certainly some details of the opera may have caused head shaking. The girls emerging from the factory smoking cigarettes may have shocked some, though more knowledgeable Parisians must have been aware that smoking among women and children was quite common in Southern Spain.

The colorful subject itself must have helped the opera on its road to quick success. Carmen is a gypsy, and gypsies had held a powerful fascination for Romantic composers: their colorful customs, their exotic appearance. Gypsies and their music had inspired Liszt, Brahms, and other nineteenth-century composers before Bizet. Spain had not been much in evidence in concert music before the mid-nineteenth century, but the longing of the Romantics for far-away, sunny, "exotic" places led to a succession of Spanish rhapsodies, symphonies, etc.—many by French composers. Some modern producers of *Carmen* have moved away from the essentially Romantic, pretty, and colorful nineteenth-century Parisian concept of Spain, attempting instead to convey the real atmosphere of Andalusia—hot and dry, with bright light that hurts the eyes. They stress the poverty of the factory girls and bring out the atmosphere of gloom, fate, and melancholy—all more in keeping with reality than the prettied-up, glittery Spain of the tourist posters. The success of such greatly diverse interpretations only shows how basically sound the opera is.

Carmen's libretto was written by Henri Meilhac and Ludovic Halévy, whose successful collaboration had begun with texts for several Offenbach operettas (*Orphée aux enfers,* 1858; *La Belle Hélène,* 1864). This time their literary source was a story, *Carmen,* by Prosper Mérimée (1803–1870), which had appeared in 1845. Most of the opera plot is based on Mérimée's third chapter, in which Don José relates to the author the events that led to his being condemned to death. Details of the plot vary, but Carmen and José are essentially the same in story and libretto. The Carmen of the story is less attractively drawn—a thief, a woman with no scruples whatever. She is married to an old, ugly bandit who is

[3] Mina Curtiss, *Bizet and His World* (London and New York, 1959), p. 399. Printed by permission of Alfred A. Knopf, Inc.

eventually killed by José. In the story José also kills Zuniga; in the opera bloodshed is avoided until the finale, which thereby gains greater impact.

The opera's original version contained spoken dialogue. For the Vienna production later in the same year (after Bizet's death) recitatives were written by the composer's friend Ernest Guiraud and substituted for most of the dialogue. The change has often been regretted, for it resulted in the omission of some relevant detail.[4] The longer spoken dialogue makes Carmen appear in a somewhat different light: her behavior in Act II is less impulsive and less cruel. Micaëla's appearance (in the middle of the night!) in Act III also is better motivated. In the recitative version it seems altogether absurd—and so, consequently, does her aria.

One need not dwell on the libretto's effectiveness. To enhance the impact of the serious drama the authors have provided a number of lighter scenes and touches: Micaëla's banter with the soldiers in Act I, the children's chorus, the chatter of Frasquita and Mercédès in the card scene of Act III, the festive procession that precedes the final tragedy. At the end of Act III a powerful dramatic touch, not found in the novel, is added: Carmen wants to rush off in the direction of Escamillo's singing, but José blocks her way. Nothing is said by either, but the incident ominously points to the final moments of the opera.

For theatrical effectiveness and for practical considerations the last act is arranged to take place all in one locale—a change from Mérimée's story. The square in front of the arena was a wise choice: offstage singing and noise from the bull ring give the impression of a larger set and actually exert an influence on both Carmen and Don José as events move on to the catastrophe.

Though there are several sentimental and trivial passages (José and Micaëla's duet "Parle-moi de ma mère!"), on the whole the libretto reads extremely well. How hard it is to capture the flavor of Halévy's lines, say, for the Seguidilla, in translation! Ruth and Thomas Martin's translation is in idiomatic English but somehow sounds too facile and too neat:

> Who wants my heart? Who comes to claim it?
> Here is your chance, it still is free.
> You can have it for the asking.
> With my new love I'm on my way.[5]

---

[4] A return to the original version has often been advocated—e.g., by Edgar Istel. ("Carmen . . . A Dramaturgic Analysis," *MQ,* Vol. VII, 1921, pp. 493 ff.) This has been done at times, but generally speaking the recitatives continue to be firmly entrenched.

[5] Copyright 1958 by G Schirmer, Inc.

Opposite: The unglamorous approach (a Berlin production directed by G. R. Sellner with sets by Raffaelli).

At her first appearance Carmen's chief character traits are clearly established by her own remarks. "Quand je vous aimerai? ma foi, je ne sais pas" ("When will I love you? Heavens, I don't know!") at once tells us a good deal; the thought is elaborated in the Habanera which follows. She is calm when others are excited: questioned about the quarrel in the factory, she is amused and shows her impertinence by singing. She then deliberately sets to work on Don José—partly because of the lack of interest he shows at first. Later, when José has fallen for her completely, he no longer interests her. The text of the Habanera, early in the opera, thus is prophetic. Her infatuation with José is consistent with what we know of her temperament. Both in Mérimée's story and in the opera the attachment is slightly more than a passing fancy. In the opera she refuses to go with the smugglers because she is in love. When they laugh at this, she insists that this time "love comes before duty." A sense of loyalty also is involved, since José had gone to prison for her. But when the bugle sounds and José wishes to leave, her feelings change quickly.

Mérimée's Carmen was "a wild, strange kind of beauty . . . [her] eyes had a voluptuous and at the same time wild expression." Bizet's Carmen makes a similar impression, though she is somewhat tamer. (In the short story she had urged José to stab her husband and had enlisted his help in robbing an Englishman whose mistress she had been.) Even so, shortly before the opera's first performance Director Du Locle was seriously worried about Carmen's vulgarity and tried in vain to have the authors agree to some major last-minute changes. A strong belief in fate characterizes her, both in the story and in the opera. In the former she allows José to take her to a lonely mountain region, where, admitting she had always known he would kill her, she faces death calmly, as she does in the opera. While her wildness and impulsiveness may fascinate, her bravery is one of her most appealing qualities—somewhat like Don Giovanni's bravado when he defies the statue. Carmen dominates and gives high dramatic tension to the opera's last scene. Knowing what José is about to do, she admits her love for Escamillo, and in a final, impulsive gesture of defiance, to words more spoken than sung, she throws the ring at his feet.

Neither Carmen nor José is a profound or complicated person, but their motives, desires, and fears result in enough conflicts to enlist our attention and sympathy. Of the two, José is less subtly drawn. Once ensnared by Carmen, he is guided by one basic emotional force: to hold on to her, though he disapproves of much of what she does. His soldier's sense of honor is only a weak counter-current, and his jealousy of Zuniga once more causes him to run afoul of the law, with the result that he is chained all the more closely to Carmen.[6] Now he has little choice but to join the smugglers, but at the act's end he isn't terribly happy about it. In Act III his infatuation continues, against his will and better judgment. He does not really want to continue the smuggler's life, but now he can no longer give up Carmen—again because someone else has appeared, this time Escamillo. Only Micaëla's revelation that his old mother is dying finally brings him to tear himself away. Strangely enough he expresses no concern or grief, but turns to Carmen with a grim "We shall see each other again." Several earlier scenes reveal José's strongly sentimental attachment to his mother—a trait that probably found warm approval among audiences of the 1870's.

Micaëla's role was invented by the librettists. In a sense she takes the place of José's mother, who never appears in the opera. As Ernest Newman puts it, Micaëla is there for musical rather than dramatic reasons, but she does supply the normally expected contrast: "a regulation stage blond ingénue symbolizing virtue." Next to Carmen, Micaëla is such a pale character that there can be no question of her competing for the audience's attention or sympathy; today even less than in Bizet's day. She is more convincing if acted as a simple, sturdy country girl, without the overly sweet manner (and the golden tresses) affected by most of her interpreters. Some people tolerate her; few *Carmen* buffs are really fond of her.

Bizet's large orchestra and colorful scoring contribute substantially to *Carmen*'s success.[7] He never confronts the singer with the problems that Wagner's music, written at about the same time, poses. The accompaniment is lively and multicolored (cornets replace trumpets; castanets and tambourines are effectively used), and often contains essential thematic material, but it does not compete with or spell potential ruin for the voice. The score has been called a veritable textbook of orchestration, worth close study in spite of the supposed familiarity of the music. The overture at once shows off the orchestra to good advantage; it is a short but rousing introduction, based on some of the principal themes. We first hear music that will be associated with the gay, festive crowd in the last act:

[6] His jealousy is better motivated in the dialogue version, where Zuniga, in Act I, had quite clearly indicated his interest in Carmen. José then is understandably bothered by his return in the tavern scene.

[7] See also "The Scoring for *Carmen*," in George Martin, *The Opera Companion*, pp. 82 ff.

EXAMPLE 1

There follows the Toreador Song from Act II, too familiar to need quotation here, after which the crowd music returns. Now there is a complete break in preparation for the first presentation, fortissimo, of what is generally called the "fate" theme:

EXAMPLE 2

Its full statement leads to a syncopated, abrupt ending, on an ominous diminished seventh chord:

EXAMPLE 3

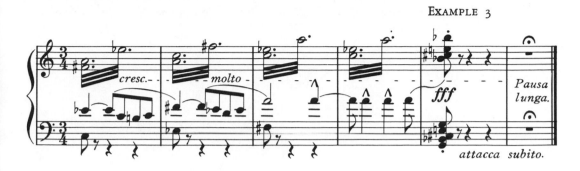

While not a summary of the action, the overture does acquaint the listener with material heard later at some of the dramatically most important moments. At several points in the opera the "fate" motive occurs in the orchestra, all the more prominently since no one is singing at the time. We hear it just before José's aria "La fleur que tu m'avais jetée" and again in Act III, when Carmen predicts that José will kill her. Other themes or entire melodies are used in similar fashion, for instance the theme heard at Carmen's first entrance and always associated with her:

EXAMPLE 4

Allegro moderato

Tenors

La voi-là!

(Note its relation to the "fate" theme.) Guiraud, in his recitatives, goes along with Bizet's *Leitmotif* technique. At the opening of Act III, for instance, José refers to "a woman who believes me to be an honest man," and the orchestra quotes the "mother" theme from Act I:

EXAMPLE 5

espressivo

Et_____ tu lui di-ras   que sa mè - re   Son-ge nuit et jour_____ à l'ab-sent_____

[*Tell him that his mother thinks about him day and night.*]

The fate motive is heard just before Carmen says "Tu me tuerais peut-être" ("Perhaps you would kill me")—a thought that is echoed by low, ominous, quite Wagnerian chords in the brass.

Three entr'actes further reveal Bizet's skill at orchestral writing. The first one is based on José's song about the Dragoon of Alcala. Since that song occurs in the third act, one might think that a more logical place for this entr'acte would have been preceding *that* act, instead of the lyrical andantino in which flute, clarinet, and harp figure prominently.

Bizet took the principal theme of the third entr'acte from a tonadilla (light opera) by Manuel Garcia (1775–1832), a beautiful melody, with a catchy, syncopated polo (southern Spanish dance) rhythm over a steady pizzicato accompaniment. Contrary to popular belief such quotations of actual Spanish music are rare in *Carmen.*

EXAMPLE 6

Allegro vivo

In spite of the manner of quoting motives described above, *Carmen* has little in common with Wagnerian music drama. It is a "number" opera, and owes much of its success to the effectiveness of its arias. Except for Micaëla's "Je dis," Bizet avoids arias that are addressed to the audience. This quickens the dramatic pace and makes for greater realism. The dramatic motivation of the Habanera (a last-minute addition) is weak, but it is there: the soldiers ask Carmen when she will bestow her favors on them; her answer leads fairly smoothly into the famous aria with choral refrain. Based on a song by Sebastián Yradier,[8] the Habanera, as the title makes clear, is Cuban rather than Spanish in character. Though the melody is not Bizet's own, its languid quality goes well with the text, the final version of which *is* Bizet's, not the librettists'.

EXAMPLE 7

[*Love is a rebellious bird that no one can tame; if he does not want to come, one will call him in vain.*]

[8] The source was freely acknowledged in the original vocal score.

Olin Downes cites Bizet's source melodies for comparison.[9] They show that Bizet followed Yradier and the other models closely but not slavishly. Whether Bizet's melodies are "more interesting" is debatable, especially in the case of the tonadilla, which became the main theme for Bizet's entr'acte. The version quoted by Downes certainly is more characteristically Spanish.

At the end of this scene Carmen throws away her flowers, aiming them at José. Nothing is said, but as he picks them up an intense melody rises from the orchestra, leading into a fragment of the fate motive. The effect of this ending is far from casual: we know that there will be repercussions.

Carmen's next song, the Seguidilla, appeals for many reasons. A fascinating situation has been established as Carmen, about to be taken to prison by Don José, cleverly exerts her charm. Constant chromatic motion and shifting harmonies add to the seductive effect of her description of where she will be and what will happen. The basic key is b minor, but the opening bars only vaguely suggest it:

EXAMPLE 8

and it is not established for about thirty measures. Bass line and melody both have frequent chromatic shifts, and there are excursions to remote keys (b flat minor, D flat major). The rhythm remains steady throughout, though it varies in dynamic force, with effective buildups.

The opening of Act II brings one of the opera's most colorful scenes, with singing, instrumental music, and dancing. Carmen's Gypsy Song (chanson bohème) has three stanzas; at the end of each, Frasquita and Mercédès join in the refrain. Here, too,

[9] *Ten Operatic Masterpieces*, pp. 172 ff.

everything moves to a well-planned climax. Each refrain has a faster tempo; as the singing becomes louder the accompaniment becomes correspondingly fuller.

"So they want some garbage—here it is." Bizet's famous remark about the Toreador Song most likely was whimsical, not to be taken at face value or preserved for posterity. The song may have been written reluctantly, as an afterthought, to provide an effective entrance for Escamillo. This it accomplishes to perfection; Escamillo usually is applauded before he sings a single note. The couplets, again with refrain, are a vivid description of a bullfight. At the end of the refrain Frasquita and Mercédès repeat "l'amour," as does Carmen, looking at Escamillo. His reply, repeating the same word, has a slightly stronger inflection—enough to give us an inkling that Carmen soon might turn to him. Bizet makes the most of the catchy refrain. It recurs in several scenes, so well integrated that one would hardly suspect it to have been an afterthought. As Escamillo exits in Act III the song appears in the orchestra, scored for woodwinds, viola, and divided cello parts, with beautiful chromatic harmonization, suitable for the different mood of the situation.

EXAMPLE 9

A little later, at the end of the act, Escamillo sings it offstage, bringing about the tense moment we saw earlier. In the last act it is sung by all, in unison and fortissimo, to different words. More subtle and convincing is its recurrence at the very end of the opera, gay and victorious, at the precise moment of Carmen's death—a stark, characteristically veristic touch.

Don José's music does not approach the effectiveness of any of the arias discussed so far. The Flower Song in Act II is dramatically well prepared and motivated—José's last effort to convince Carmen that even though "honor and duty" call him back to quarters he really loves her. A full accompaniment (including four horns, English horn, and harp) is used with typical restraint. The aria has good pace and structure; it rises, tapers off, and then rises once more to a high B flat. Surprisingly enough the phrase is marked pianissimo, an indication which many tenors find not only difficult but also inconvenient to observe, since it is less likely to result in applause.

The Act II quintet.

Micaëla's "Je dis" has already been mentioned as the opera's only aria "delivered" to the audience, i.e., a monologue. The entire scene lacks dramatic persuasiveness; musically it seems old-fashioned (a rather formal da capo aria), sentimental (with Romantic horn fifths and cello obbligato), and generally out of place. It can only be compared to the equally sentimental duet, No. 7. There Micaëla pulls all the stops. José's mother sends a letter and "a little money"; she thought of her son as she was walking home from church. The duet proper ("Ma mère, je la vois") then follows, saccharine to the end, when José refers to the "demon" whose prey he is about to become. No name is mentioned, but the audience by now is apt to recognize the Carmen motive which appears in the orchestra.

Among the numerous other ensembles the quintet in Act II, in $\frac{6}{16}$ time, is more formal and self-contained than most. The humor of the text led to a light, rapid musical setting of considerable difficulty. A similarly light touch prevails later in the act, when El Remendado and El Dancaïro politely disarm Zuniga. Other gypsies arrive on the scene so that ensemble and chorus are joined, as happens elsewhere in the opera. Before this act's finale Carmen and José join in a realistic duet scene. As she dances, the bugle "call to quarters" is heard offstage, leading to her quarrel with José. Most other ensembles also are dramatic rather than lyrical, even the card scene in Act III, where the delighted babbling of Frasquita and Mercédès is cleverly combined with Carmen's gloomy realization that the cards, for her, predict "toujours la mort."[10]

Choruses likewise are woven into the dramatic action; frequently they are part of a larger musical structure. Street scenes like the one that opens *Carmen* were popular in late nineteenth-century opera (e.g., the second act of *La Bohème*); the boulevards of the growing cities suggested such settings, with all sorts of people coming and going and others watching them.

The repeat of the opening chorus, after Micaëla's exit, seems a little forced. Morales says "Let's resume our pastime of watching people as they stroll by," and the chorus promptly repeats "Sur la place. . . ."[11] After the stabbing and screaming inside the factory, Bizet provides a comic chorus: all the girls talk at the same time, explaining to Zuniga what has happened. The situation recalls a similar scene in *The Barber of Seville* (see above, p. 148).

[10] The construction of this ensemble scene is discussed in Hamm, *Opera*, pp. 79 ff.

[11] In the original version another scene followed here, with an aria for Morales. It was cut in an 1883 performance and is no longer found in modern scores. See Winton Dean, *Georges Bizet* (London, 1965), pp. 215 f., for these and other modifications of Bizet's first version.

Choral refrains lend brilliance to several arias. Other choruses merely add to the spectacle—e.g., the children's chorus at the opening, announced by trumpet calls, first backstage, then in the orchestra. The urchins (they should be very small) sing mostly in unison, with some spoken counting of their marching steps. During their singing the guard changes, and the boys imitate this ceremony.

The idea of having a chorus of factory workers who sing the praises of cigarette smoking might appear realistic; actually the librettists and Bizet handle it in a sentimental and romantic fashion, with numerous word repetitions. This chorus and others involving action caused difficulties during the rehearsals. Halévy, the librettist, reminisced about these:

After two months of rehearsal [the singers] insisted that the two first-act choruses were unperformable: the entrance of the cigarette girls and the scuffle around the officer after the arrest of Carmen. These . . . necessitated not only singing, but . . . motion, action, coming and going —life, in short. This was without precedent at the Opéra-Comique. The members of the chorus were in the habit of singing the ensembles, standing motionless in line, their arms slack, their eyes fixed on the conductor's baton, their thoughts elsewhere.[12]

A large orchestra supports this delicate chorus. Harp and string arpeggios help to create the "volatile" affect.

Other choruses are less realistic and more conventionally operatic. At the opening of Act III the smugglers prepare for the precarious and clandestine descent, yet the music rises to a fortissimo, and there are much-repeated admonitions that "one false step" may lead to their doom.

For the end of the opera Bizet provided a scene complex in which chorus, ballet, aria, and ensemble contribute to the stirring climax. The crowd scene in front of the arena calls for much display. A ballet usually is interpolated here, though it is not included in the score. Colorful processions lead up to Escamillo's entrance, and the chorus sings the refrain of "his" song. Here, too, his appearance could hardly have been prepared more brilliantly. His "Si tu m'aimes, Carmen" *can* be piano espressivo: he easily has everyone's attention at this point, and the lyrical duet comes off all the better, contrasting with the preceding and following music.

Greatest intensity is reached, understandably enough, in the final exchange of words between Carmen and José. Here the excited comments of the offstage chorus—the crowd watching the bullfight—increases the emotional heat. Carmen is cornered by

[12] Curtiss, *Bizet and His World*, pp. 381 f.

Opposite: The final scene.

José, but she is delighted by the cries emanating from the arena. The chromatic agitation in the bass (allegro fuocoso) has become a favorite "melodramatic" device since Bizet's time. Again the chorus and offstage fanfare interrupt the argument, announcing Escamillo's victory. Carmen has died, and the orchestra, for the last time, fortissimo, announces the "fate" theme, as though a prophecy has finally come true.

Grout's characterization of the operatic situation in France a generation before *Carmen* can do duty for the last quarter of the century as well: "The adoration of Meyerbeer, the neglect of Berlioz, and the craze for Offenbach." Meyerbeer's operas continued to be performed regularly, Berlioz continued to be neglected, and Offenbach held his own. In addition there were some composers who excelled in the genre of lyric opera—works of a somewhat more intimate nature than grand opera, yet not light enough to be considered comic opera. Of this extensive repertory a few works have maintained themselves to the present day: *Mignon* (1866) by Ambroise Thomas; *Faust* (1859) and *Roméo et Juliette* (1867) by Charles Gounod. Sentimentality is much in evidence in Léo Delibes' *Lakmé* (1883) and in the operas of Jules Massenet, of which *Manon* (1884) and *Thaïs* (1894) continue to be heard with some regularity. Gustave Charpentier's *Louise* (1900) has already been mentioned as containing a number of realistic traits, close to the verismo of Puccini, whose *Tosca* (see below, Chapter 9) appeared in the same year.

Modest Mussorgsky, *Boris Godunov* (First Complete Performance, St. Petersburg, 1874)

Nineteenth-century musical nationalism, it is often said, was strongest in those countries that did not have a long heritage of art music. During the eighteenth century Russia indeed had produced little music that was both indigenous and lasting. In music as in the other arts and sciences, the Czar and his court were strongly oriented toward the West. Italian opera, which had dominated the scene in the eighteenth century, continued to be favored at Moscow and St. Petersburg well into the later nineteenth. Russian musicians continued to go to Paris, Berlin, Leipzig, and other Western centers to receive musical training. French and, to some extent, German were spoken in the homes of many educated families, both of the aristocracy and the fairly well-to-do bourgeoisie. Popular acceptance of the works of Glinka, Borodin, and other Russian composers of the mid-nineteenth century was slow. Though good performances of their works (including their operas) were given, it was not considered fashionable to attend. As in Western Europe, Italian opera and its prime donne (e.g., Adelina Patti) exerted a strong fascination on a large portion of the Russian public.

In Russian music of the later nineteenth century two "schools" are commonly distinguished—Western and Eastern. Representatives of the former include Anton Rubinstein (today largely forgotten) and Tchaikovsky, both of whom had received the traditional Central European conservatory training. Tchaikovsky's music, while not without characteristic Russian touches, to a large degree incorporates devices and styles of Western music, especially in the areas of harmony and rhythm. Much of it is cast in the traditional larger forms of symphony and concerto. Among members of the Eastern school Modest Mussorgsky (1839–1881) in particular lacked this Western-oriented training and did not, in fact, receive any systematic musical instruction until after he had resigned his army commission in 1858. Lessons with Balakirev, the mentor of several of the younger, consciously Russian composers, were discontinued when the teacher decided that Mussorgsky did not have sufficient talent for composition. Thus Mussorgsky was essentially self-taught and especially lacked technical training in instrumentation and orchestration. Yet his writing shows imagination, originality, and force. From the vantage point of a century later, we tend to credit much of this originality to his very lack of familiarity with devices and techniques that had already proven their effectiveness. His compositions are not numerous, and several major works, including operas, remained incomplete, but they reveal a flair for expressing vigorous, dramatic moods.

The political upheavals of his time absorbed Mussorgsky's interest. He was in sympathy with the movement that brought about the liberation of the serfs in 1861, even though this event reduced his family's land holdings and income. Mussorgsky had to go to the country to straighten out the family finances. He continued to live there during summers and came to know the peasants well, gathering impressions and material for later use. His artistic creed was that of a realist—he wanted to portray "life, no matter where and how manifested; truth no matter how unpleasant." If much of his music was unconventional, this too was due to a desire for direct, realistic expression, not simply to the shortcomings of his musical training.

Boris Godunov for several reasons represents a landmark in modern opera. Aside from its powerfully realistic plot and style, the work dwells on the representation and probings of Boris' mind—his ever increasing fears and hallucinations, his physical and mental deterioration as a result of oppressive guilt feelings. *Boris* was written before *Carmen* or *Aida,* but both dramatically and musically this highly original musical drama has much more in common with twentieth-century expressionism than with contemporary late Romantic opera. Nor did *Boris* come into its own before the twentieth century. With Chaliapin interpreting the title role (for the first time in 1898) the opera became widely known in the 1920's, both in Europe and America. More recently, especially through the interpretations of Boris Christoff and George London, it has won new audiences, through live performances and through recordings.

Mussorgsky prepared his own libretto, basing it on historical sources (especially on a work by N. M. Karamzin) and on Pushkin's dramatic chronicle by the same title. Work on the opera was begun in 1868, and the full score was completed by December, 1869. Mussorgsky offered *Boris* to the Imperial Theater in St. Petersburg. It was rejected, partly because of the absence of an important female role. Though keenly disappointed, the composer undertook extensive revisions, including the addition of the entire "Polish act." From here on the history of *Boris* becomes quite complicated, since other revisions followed, made by the composer, by his friend and fellow-composer Rimsky-Korsakov, and (after Mussorgsky's death) by others. The composer's own revisions of 1872 led to a private performance of excerpts in 1873 and to the first complete performances in 1874, quite successful in spite of critical disapproval. This version (published in 1926) ends with the forest scene. Minor revisions were added in 1877, but the opera disappeared from the repertory until Rimsky-Korsakov's complete revision was published in 1896. It was performed that year and again in 1899 and 1904. Further changes were made, especially in the coronation scene, between 1906 and 1908. This version remained the most performed for many years.

The pros and cons of Rimsky-Korsakov's modifications have been widely discussed. They were drastic, including many changes of actual notes, of melody, harmony, rhythm, and orchestration. He even supplied some additional music and made some cuts, which he, however, restored later. His intention had been to help the opera achieve popular understanding and appreciation; to express Mussorgsky's frequently unconventional musical thoughts through more effective language. Above all he saw obstacles to success in Mussorgsky's scoring. As an acknowledged master of orchestration he in effect rewrote many sections, providing a sound which undoubtedly is more polished but at the same time may lack some of the impact and force of the "cruder" original. Rimsky-Korsakov was aware of this; his hope was that some day the public would understand the original and then would discard his own version.

Even today few people are in a position to make a fair comparison, since an authentic rendition of Mussorgsky's own first and second versions hardly ever can be heard. Though Rimsky-Korsakov's version still serves as the basis for most performances, further changes, especially in the orchestration, have been made by Karol Rathaus and Dmitri Shostakovich.

In spite of its original difficulties and its complicated history, *Boris Godunov* is the most popular Russian opera today, more popular than Tchaikovsky's operas *Pique Dame* and *Eugene Onegin*,[13] more popular than the operas of Prokofiev or Shostakovich.

Except for the Polish act there is little in *Boris* that is conventionally operatic, dramatically or musically; but it is a colorful treatment, broadly conceived, of a historical subject. There is much variety in mood and in emotional intensity. Comical elements are present even in some essentially serious scenes; pomp and display alternate with the lyrical and intimate. The subject itself (as well as its musical treatment, to be discussed below) obviously and strongly is related to Russian nationalism. The historical Boris reigned from 1598 to 1605. He had succeeded in gaining the

[13] Tchaikovsky is said to have considered *Boris* the "vilest and messiest of operas."

Boris and Feodor.

confidence of Czar Ivan IV, "the Terrible," and had further secured his position through the marriage of his sister to the feeble-minded Czarevitch, Feodor. When Feodor, who had become Czar in 1584, died without a direct heir, his half-brother Dmitri would have been the rightful successor. Pushkin's (and Mussorgsky's) interpretation of the historical account assume Boris' implication in Dmitri's death—historically questionable but essential for the chief theme of the opera, which is Boris' guilt. Many details of the libretto are in accord with the known historical events.[14]

In preparing his libretto Mussorgsky followed the basic dramatic arrangement of Pushkin's *Boris,* which was a series of loosely connected scenes or tableaux rather than a tautly constructed continuous action. Pushkin's drama (1825) consists of twenty-four scenes, a leisurely pace suggesting the epic quality of other nineteenth-century Russian writing. The episodic structure is maintained in the libretto, though numerous characters were eliminated and though there are only nine scenes, divided, usually, into four acts and a prologue. An episodic arrangement may have been suggested by the span of time covered by the action, which extends over seven years, and by the division of the plot into two streams, one dealing with Boris and his growing feelings of guilt, the other, more outwardly dramatic, tracing the career of the monk Gregory up to his appearance, on horseback, as the "rightful" pretender to the throne. In the opera, Boris and Gregory never meet. The episodic nature of the text leads to another remarkable feature: in several versions of the opera, the order of scenes in the last act is reversed—something impossible in most dramas.

It is evident that Mussorgsky, for all the criticism of his first version, did have a feeling for theatrical effectiveness. The very absence of the love element of the Polish act makes that version particularly taut. There is no coronation scene in Pushkin, but this addition is most successful in the opera. For comic relief Mussorgsky added various touches to Varlaam's role. In the opera, Pimen's account of the miracle takes place in Boris' presence; in the play the miracle is related by someone else. Boris is not on stage, and the account therefore does not contribute directly to his final collapse. Here, too, Mussorgsky accomplishes a dramatic condensation.

Mussorgsky, according to his own account, transplanted many of Pushkin's verses into the libretto, which, nevertheless, is not "wordy." In the coronation scene (and elsewhere) Mussorgsky gets along with a minimum of text. There is no attempt to be discursive, philosophical, or "poetic"—and the scene is all the more impressive for it.

---

[14] The "false Dmitri," in history, succeeded after Boris' death and was proclaimed Czar. But after a few years he, too, was murdered, at the instigation of Shuisky, who then succeeded him as Czar.

To call the dramatic structure episodic does not imply any lack of cohesion in the individual scenes, all of which are well paced dramatically and musically. The coronation scene again serves as an illustration. The forest scene moves along even more rapidly, and the cumulative effect is powerful. The chorus is in command from the beginning of that scene. The crowd brings in the Boyar in chains—the mocking chorus; and Varlaam and Missail appear, inciting the crowd. Excitement grows steadily. After a pause a new buildup starts with the arrival of two Jesuits. They are dragged away, the "false Dmitri" arrives, with trumpets and bells heard from a distance. Finally all disappear except for the fool who, lonely and sad, bewails the fate of Russia and her people.

"The people" indeed are at the center of Mussorgsky's opera: next to Boris they can be considered the chief "protagonist." Their role has been compared in importance to that of the peasants in Tolstoy's *War and Peace*. It was Mussorgsky's avowed purpose, in this opera and elsewhere, to portray them. "They alone are great and real."[15] Compassion for the masses, downtrodden and cowed by ruthless officials, pervades much of the opera, even during some of the lighter moments. During the inn scene two guards consider relieving the monks of some of the alms they have collected. Later

[15] See Gerald Abraham, "Tolstoy and Music," in *Studies in Russian Music* (New York, 1936).

Reading the warrant for the fugitive's arrest.

on the leader of the guards, without authorization, adds to the written warrant that the fugitive should be hanged. The people's portrayal is realistic, not glamorized. In the prologue they are immediately characterized as being bullied by the police, and on command they resume their clamoring for Boris to become their Czar. Yet as soon as the police officer leaves, they begin to quarrel among themselves. They hardly know what they are shouting for—there is some joking among them about this—but they obediently resume their "spontaneous" demonstration when the police are seen again.

The people, then, are the "heroes" of the opera, without being "heroic." In the revolution scene the mob, incited by Varlaam and Missail, seizes the two Jesuits and drags them away, though they really are on their side—but the mob does not like Jesuits and "Romans" in general.

Mussorgsky lavished much care on the portrayal of the title role. The audience does not meet Boris right away, but he and his might dominate the opening scene. Though his stature is imposing, he is characterized from the beginning as a sad person, weighed down by untoward events of both his public and private life: conspiracies in various parts of the realm, and his daughter's loss of her fiancé. Evidence of disloyalty has made him suspicious of the people around him, especially of the Boyars, who, in fact, are plotting against him. His attitude is strongly affected by the all-pervading sense of guilt which causes him to interpret bad news as God's punishment. In spite of his crime Boris is religious; we are led to think so by many of his utterances. His monologue in Act II ends with an outcry for God's mercy, as do the clock scene and his death scene. When the fool tells him to his face that he, Boris, has killed the Czarevitch, Boris, to everyone's surprise, merely asks the fool to pray for him. He is a believer, and his conscience troubles him all the more, in the end contributing to his death. Psychological characterization of this kind was of paramount importance to Mussorgsky. He resorted to some quite modern devices to accomplish his purpose: in the opera's most famous scene, the persistent whirring and ticking of a mechanical clock help to unnerve Boris completely.

Different interpretations of Boris' character are possible: the degree to which he is mentally deranged, the way in which his fears and suspicions take visible form. Depending on the way in which Boris' role is acted and sung, the audience may see in him either villain or hero, and their view of Gregory–Dmitri will vary accordingly.

Shuisky's part is drawn with special care. Mussorgsky seems to have studied the historical sources, giving an accurate portrayal of Shuisky as a "cool, smooth, artfully dissembling intriguer, hiding his ambitions under a mask of modesty and humility" (Newman). The contrast between the irascible Boris and the controlled and purposeful Shuisky exists in their music as well as in their dialogue. Boris, beside himself, mutters all kinds of imprecations in short, breathless phrases:

EXAMPLE 10

Per-jur'd, doub-ly per-jur'd, yet un-a-sham'd, trea-son-ous flatt-rer, hy-po-crite,

to which Shuisky answers calmly, supported by a smoothly flowing accompaniment:

EXAMPLE 11

Tsar! my er-rand is ve-ry grave, the news I bring will vex thee.

Soon Boris' ire turns into fear. His question then gives Shuisky the opportunity to give an account, with carefully chosen details, of what he saw in Uglich. All the while he observes Boris closely and dispassionately; he therefore can give a detailed account of Boris' behavior to the Boyars in Act IV. Shuisky knows how to drive Boris to madness. His deliberate manner of doing so brings to mind similar scenes from naturalistic stage plays.

None of the other characters stands out with comparable clarity. Pimen, the venerable monk, is simply drawn—an old man to whom Mussorgsky gave appropriately subdued music. His calmness and holiness set the tone for the monastery scene in Act I, in which he gives sage advice to the troubled Gregory. Pimen does not reappear until the Duma scene. Why he arrives at that time to demand an audience with Boris is not explained further. Significantly enough his arrival is announced by Shuisky.

Boris' fear increases as he listens to Pimen's story.

Gregory, the "false Dmitri," appears to be young, innocent, and impressionable in the monastery scene. He has grown up somewhat when we meet him again at the inn near the Lithuanian border. There he largely minds his own business, saying and doing little until circumstances—the reading of the warrant—force him into action. Little similarity exists between this Gregory and the Gregory of the Polish act, where he appears in a moonlight-by-the-fountain setting, anxiously awaiting a rendezvous with Marina, the noble Polish lady of his affections. He is all ardor, all tenor, an easy target for Rangoni's and Marina's sinister plotting. He may regain some sympathy later in this scene when he reminds Marina

of his destiny and showers contempt on her—but he soon suc-
cumbs again to her entreaties (larghetto amoroso in the Rimsky-
Korsakov version), and the scene ends with a love duet. His appearance in the revolutionary scene, triumphant, on horseback,
forms an impressive climax. He now is a politically successful
figure—a symbol rather than a human being.

Varlaam and Missail, with whom Gregory meets in the inn
scene, are much different. Their simplicity is reflected in their
unsophisticated, straightforward music and in their speech. The
melody with which they introduce themselves repeatedly makes us
wonder about the sincerity of their piety:

EXAMPLE 12

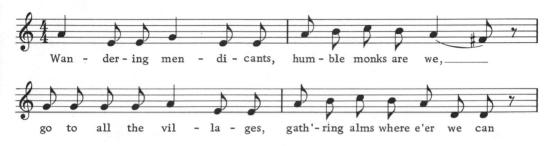

Wan - der - ing men - di - cants, hum - ble monks are we,_____
go to all the vil - la - ges, gath'- ring alms where e'er we can

These two vagabond monks have much in common, but their
temperaments differ, with Varlaam being the more impulsive,
uninhibited, and robust. Through his reading of the warrant, halt-
ingly, our impression is confirmed that this monk hardly was given
to the "clerical" occupations of reading and writing. Neither he
nor Missail has any scruples—they readily join the revolutionary
crowd (in the forest scene) and loudly demand that the two Jesuits
be hanged.

Rangoni is a conventional, oily villain—not evil enough to
fascinate. No such character exists in Pushkin's drama; he was
invented by Mussorgsky. The unsympathetic portrayal of Rangoni,
who represents the interests of the Roman church, a foreign power,
adds to the opera's nationalistic bias. He is eager for Marina to use
all her seductive powers to bring Gregory under the Jesuit's spell,
thereby bringing Russia under the influence of Rome. Marina
appears as an intelligent, purposeful woman. Her collapse, as a
result of Rangoni's invoking hellfire and Satan, does not really
convince. Henceforth she remains under Rangoni's spell and, in
the "scene by the fountain," carries out his orders.

Specific motives and themes serve to identify several of the
leading roles, though not Boris himself. As pointed out in earlier
chapters, the *Leitmotif* principle most commonly associated with

Wagner occurs in much other nineteenth-century opera. A vigorous, repeated-note theme heard several times in the prologue is associated with the police officer:

EXAMPLE 13

More generally it may represent authority, for a similar figure is heard for the first time in the next scene, at the moment of Boris' first appearance. In the inn scene it accompanies the arrival of the guards. Another theme is associated with Gregory–Dmitri, heard when he is scrutinized by Varlaam. Later the guards ask Gregory who he is, and the orchestra answers

EXAMPLE 14

before Gregory identifies himself as "someone who lives nearby." The melody reappears, sometimes subtly disguised, at other times broadly stated, as during his first appearance in the revolution scene.

A short figure

EXAMPLE 15

is associated with Varlaam in the inn scene and on later occasions. In his "Song of Kazan" it is conspicuous throughout.

Short, recurrent chromatic figures are present in several instances when Boris is seized by intense feelings of guilt, as in the Kremlin scene:

240

EXAMPLE 16

He asks Shuisky whether it is true that murdered children rise
from their graves, and the orchestra expresses his agony:

EXAMPLE 17

After Shuisky leaves, this theme once more bursts forth, leading into the clock scene.

Rangoni's evil advice to Marina calls forth a descending chromatic passage in the orchestra. The figure characterizes him during several later appearances.

In this drama of the Russian people, folk material does occur, not surprisingly. Mussorgsky's melodic style frequently suggests folk song; both the nurse's song and the mocking song are examples: Actual folk tunes, however, were rarely used.[16]

EXAMPLE 18   Nurse's Song

Mocking Song

Like other Russian nationalistic composers of the nineteenth century, Mussorgsky found inspiration in the music of the Russian Orthodox church. The hymn sung in the coronation scene—a traditional melody that had been used by Beethoven in one of his "Russian" string quartets—and another one during Boris' death scene are examples. Several songs in a folk style are heard during the inn scene: the song of the drake and Varlaam's "Siege of Kazan" with its five-bar phrases. Varlaam's drinking song contains a realistic touch: while he sings, Gregory pumps the innkeeper for information about the frontier and the possibility of escaping into Lithuania. These and other songs are dramatically motivated; others, such as Boris' farewell, are arias—reflection, monologue— in the traditional sense. The fool's song is particularly moving. Its wailing motive is haunting and expresses most eloquently the sadness and hopelessness of the exploited and oppressed people whom he symbolizes.

Throughout the opera melodic lines suggest the patterns and the implied harmonies of Russian folk music. At the time of writing *Boris,* the composer was looking for a musical language that would respect the sounds and the prosody of Russian speech. (Janáček, a generation later, carried on similar studies in Czech language and music.) The distinctive quality of Mussorgsky's rhythm results from this. His "recitative" is quite different from Italian opera, far less regular, more forceful and direct.

---

[16] Calvocoressi indicates some of these. (*Modest Mussorgsky,* New York, 1956). The texts for the innerkeeper's song and Varlaam's song also were borrowed.

EXAMPLE 19

The same quality distinguishes many choral passages:

EXAMPLE 20

Tenors

Now seat him on this | log, my chil-dren! | That's | right!

Basses

Now lest he hurt his

throat, poor gen-tle-man, by shout-ing we'd bet-ter gag him to save his

Quite right!

voice!

When the vocal line expresses less vigorous emotions and becomes intensely lyrical, a similar concern for prosody is maintained. Irregular (i.e., three- or five-bar) phrases also occur in purely instrumental passages; they account for much of the distinctive quality of Mussorgsky's melody. This is one of the areas in which Rimsky-Korsakov, with the best of intentions, tried to improve on the composer, frequently forcing Mussorgsky's phrases into more regular but ill-fitting metrical patterns.

Mussorgsky   EXAMPLE 21

Rimsky-Korsakov

Comparison of the opera's several versions reveals numerous other changes, in harmony and doubling of notes, as well as actual note changes in melodic passages.

In both melody and harmony the Polish act is much closer to Western tradition than the rest of the opera—showing that Mussorgsky was not as isolated from that tradition as the rest of the opera might suggest. Sweeping and elegant melodic lines are harmonized and orchestrated in a manner that suggests Italian opera of a slightly later period. One wonders whether Puccini might have studied the duet in this scene, especially passages in which the violins double an expressive vocal line. Elsewhere the orchestration also relies on devices more typical of French or Italian usage (e.g., the opening of the "scene by the fountain"). Mazurka and Polacca (Polonaise) rhythms are brought in, somewhat self-consciously, to suggest the Polish setting.

Modality (instead of major–minor tonality) characterizes Russian folk music, and many of Mussorgsky's melodies have a modal flavor, de-emphasizing leading tones. For Western ears, modal melodies and harmonies suggest subdued, sad moods, even in those scenes of the opera that one might expect to be gay, as the tavern scene. Mussorgsky's harmonic procedures frequently are unorthodox; he avoids standard modulations in favor of abrupt changes of keys. Vacillation between two unrelated key areas is not unusual. In the coronation scene the successive entrances of the voices establish A flat major and D major, fitting in with patterns previously set up in the accompaniment.

EXAMPLE 22

loved!___   Thou___ our   Tsar!___

___   Thou___ art   our   Tsar!___

Thou___ our   Tsar,   our   Tsar!___

Thou___ our   Tsar,   thou   our   Tsar!___

Mussorgsky's advanced harmonic style is most evident in scenes of great emotional tension. The clock scene once more provides examples, as does the death scene, but also the agitated revolutionary scene in Kromy forest, an essentially choral scene with great dramatic and musical impact. It is no wonder that in this opera, in which the people hold such a prominent place, choruses are numerous and varied. From the people's clamoring in the prologue (with brief solo interjections) to the jubilant acclaim of the coronation scene, to the hymnlike solemnity of the death scene and the excitement in Kromy forest, Mussorgsky's choruses run a wide, expressive gamut.

Realism extends to the manner of choral singing as well, at least in Russia today. George London, who has performed and recorded *Boris* in Moscow, was impressed by the "cultivated vulgarity" of the chorus: accuracy of pitch and rhythm without refinement of tone quality.

Realistic mise-en-scène was sought after in early performances of Boris and of other nationalistic Russian operas of the time. In Soviet Russia today the social message of the opera—the plight of the people and their rebellion—adds official endorsement to the popularity of the work. Playing up the political implications may lead to interpretations and stage business that would not have passed the censorship of the Czarist regime. But the sincerity and generally human quality of Mussorgsky's drama appeal and succeed regardless of present-day ideological interpretations.

Giuseppe Verdi, *Falstaff* (Milan, 1893)

Forty years passed between Verdi's *La Traviata* and his last opera, *Falstaff*—years during which opera had flourished throughout Central and Western Europe and, increasingly, in the New World. During these years Wagnerian music drama had solidly established itself, exerting a strong influence on opera composers of other nationalities. On the other hand Wagner's tremendous success, coupled with the dominance of German music in the symphonic repertory, inevitably led to a reaction, causing other composers (such as Debussy in France) to take stock of their own national heritage. In Italy, as noted in a previous chapter, national feeling ran high during the second half of the nineteenth century, and Verdi, both politically and musically, held a leading position.

Verdi's travels had taken him to Paris, Vienna, and other centers of opera. Obviously he was aware of the strong impact of Wagner's style on European opera in general. To some extent he may have been afraid of succumbing to that influence.[17] Certainly his operas after *La Traviata* and *Rigoletto* show some stylistic similarities to Wagner's work, particularly in the handling of the orchestra, yet in no way does he imitate the German composer's style. Verdi's later operas remain unmistakably Italian—and Verdi.

A careful tracing of Verdi's development from *Traviata* to *Falstaff* cannot be undertaken here—but a development there was, not a sudden change. *Don Carlo* (1867) demonstrates this, containing much that was new along with characteristics of the earlier Verdi, such as the familiar rhythm patterns in the accompaniment. *Don Carlo* is believable as drama, powerful yet subtle. Vocal lines are rhythmically complex, with much chromaticism and modulation. There is less of the "La donna è mobile" tunefulness. A large orchestra is augmented by much stage music. Increasingly Verdi's scoring shows concern with diversity, with specific instrumental color. *Aida* (1871) became more successful than *Don Carlo,* though (or because) in some ways it is less subtle and more "theatrical." The basic dramatic conflict—love versus patriotic duty—had been an age-old favorite, even in seventeenth-century opera seria. Verdi's contrapuntal skill is increasingly evident, in the prelude and in several ensemble scenes.

For the librettos of his last two operas, Verdi was fortunate in obtaining the collaboration of Arrigo Boito (1842–1918), himself an opera composer and therefore all the more sensitive to

---

[17] Though Franz Werfel, in his novel *Verdi: Roman der Oper,* makes more of this self-consciousness than can be verified.

the special requirements of that genre. At one time Boito had been quite critical of Verdi: he was a Wagner enthusiast, dissatisfied with the musical emphasis in traditional Italian opera, with shallow treatments of dramatic subjects, and with the low literary quality of so many librettos. Boito wrote the words for Verdi's *Hymn of the Nations* (1862). A reconciliation took place, and years later Boito said that it had been "the greatest satisfaction of his life" to serve Verdi. Verdi admired his texts and demanded far fewer changes from Boito than he had from his earlier librettists. When *Otello* was first performed in 1887 an Italian writer predicted "from now on it will be impossible to have absurd plays and miserable verses set to music."

At the time of *Aida* Verdi had reached the pinnacle of success. Times had changed in Italy: a composer, rather than a prima donna, now could insist that his wishes, with regard to rehearsals and performances, be respected. Verdi was honored, feted, decorated—and probably paid more than any composer before him. His fee for *Aida* is said to have been the highest in operatic history. *Aida,* it was generally believed, was to be the crowning achievement of a busy and glorious career in opera. That it should be followed by two other masterpieces was a surprise to many; Verdi himself hesitated to make any promises about finishing either score. If he undertook and carried out both tasks it was due to his love for Shakespeare, admittedly his favorite dramatist, and to the harmonious working relationship with Boito. *Otello* turned out to be a work of powerful dramatic impact. To a larger measure than before this is achieved through continuous scene complexes in which duets and other ensembles, rather than arias, dominate. Again the large orchestra assumes a role that goes far beyond traditional functions of accompaniment, contributing continually to the description of action and to the portrayal of states of mind—underscoring, explaining, and reminding.

Otello once more had been a triumph for the master. Its first performance had been front-page news, with correspondents from all over Europe and from the United States attending, some of them telegraphing act-by-act reports to their papers. With this success behind him Verdi, aware of his age, hesitated to make further commitments. Boito had carefully suggested the Falstaff theme in 1889. The thought of writing a comedy—the first one since an unsuccessful early work—appealed to Verdi, and Boito's finished libretto pleased him greatly.

Boito fashioned his libretto by choosing characters, incidents, and lines from Shakespeare's *Merry Wives of Windsor* and the Henry plays, the rotund knight figuring in all of these. Many famous lines from *Henry IV,* Parts I and II, are preserved, ably translated; Boito wrote additional text where needed, with a fine feeling for style. Since he utilized portions of several plays he had to condense and consolidate even more than usual, and to omit altogether some secondary characters. Incidents taken from the several sources were arranged in a way that insured good dramatic contrast and climax. Occasionally parts from several Shakespeare speeches were fashioned into one. Thus Verdi set Shakespeare to music only in a very general way, but Boito's libretto, in the opinion of many (including Verdi's biographer Toye), amounts to an improvement over the original *Merry Wives of Windsor*.

Verdi was almost eighty years old, and his pace of composing had slowed down. He had doubts about finishing the score and told his friends and publishers that he was writing purely for his own amusement. Eventually he agreed to a performance date, but he reserved the right to withdraw the opera even after the dress rehearsal if that should dissatisfy him—conditions unheard of in the annals of opera.

Falstaff turned out to be a masterwork. Audiences and critics had not expected anything else, though the opera's finale pleased less than the rest. Most critics, in praising Verdi's score, drew comparisons to Mozart and Rossini. Some pointed, justifiably, to similarities to Wagner's *Meistersinger*. For Boito it was ample satisfaction to have "forged a hammer from Shakespeare that caused the bronze colossus from Busseto [Verdi's home] to ring again, at a time when age was about to silence him."

Much care went into preparations for the first performance. A stage designer journeyed to Windsor to study the setting and architecture and generally to absorb the local atmosphere. Such a procedure, not unheard of during the age of realism in staging, reminds one of similar journeys and studies undertaken and directed by Wagner.

Boito's and Verdi's comedy moves at a remarkable pace; it is boisterous and vigorous from beginning to end. Again there is no overture. With the first bars of the music the curtain goes up and we are *in medias res,* learning more, with every line, about people and events. Dr. Cajus' accusations are calmly confirmed by Falstaff, the culprit. Unable to obtain any satisfaction from him, Cajus turns on Bardolph for having gotten him drunk—which Bardolph also admits—and for then having picked his pockets. All this lusty dialogue moves along briskly, establishing a *joie de vivre* atmosphere reinforced by the music. Mutual name-calling leads to Cajus' oath: in the future he will get drunk only in the company of honest people. To this Bardolph and Pistol respond with their mockingly solemn "Amen," in which Boito, musician as well as librettist, creates the opportunity for a musical pun suggested by Shakespeare's lines. Soon we hear Falstaff's farcical praise of his tremendous paunch—"This is my kingdom"—and Bardolph and Pistol echo the sentiment—"tremendous Falstaff!"

Boito is a master of comic effects. A poetic, hymn-like passage serves to praise Bardolph's rubicund nose, which serves as lantern on their nightly journeys from tavern to tavern. The lines scan and rhyme—then two words are left over: "costi troppo" ("too expensive!"), and the effect is hilarious. Falstaff's famous speech about honor, a pronouncement addressed to Bardolph and Pistol, is in verse form, hardly noticeable in Verdi's free rhythmical treatment.

The rapid pace of this opening scene is maintained during most of the opera, with II/2 (Falstaff's dousing) and the finale in Windsor Forest forming high points of spirited activity. Absolutely nothing in the score is slow, uninspired, or in any way betrays the composer's age.

Leonard Warren as Falstaff.

Dramatically speaking, *Falstaff* is a period piece—Shakespeare's, not Boito's period—in which conventions of the earlier age are observed. Nannetta and Fenton, though given some delightful music, continually move at the periphery of the action. Much of the stage business, e.g., the episode with the screen, must be taken in the spirit of comedy of a bygone period, playful and unrealistic. As a hiding place the screen is not meant to be taken seriously, especially when Ford and the servants turn the rest of the house upside down in their search. Both text and music of the finale capture Shakespeare's fairy-tale flavor with felicity. To stage this well is no mean task, with so many people milling around in a small space. In this scene, as in II/2, they must seem busy and forever moving, pursuing—they must not stand around singing.

Within the context of farce and comedy Boito gives us well-drawn portrayals of several of the principal characters, notably of Falstaff himself. His age is not specified in Shakespeare or Boito. He is "vecchio John," but "old" is a stretchable term. His own actions and comments imply that he is a man of some vitality, in the Indian summer of life. Good-naturedly he laughs off Cajus' accusations without denying them. Boito's Falstaff, like Shakespeare's, does many foolish things, but he is not a mere fool. The good things in life he enjoys wholeheartedly and unashamedly. After scolding Bardolph for having ruined him by drinking so much, he calls on the host to bring another bottle. Money, along with wine and women, rates high on his scale of values. When Ford in disguise introduces himself, money bag in hand, Falstaff at once (there is hardly a break in the music) shows himself to be extremely cordial: "caro signor Fontana!" His exalted opinion of himself, of the fascination he holds for the ladies, is comical. The conceited oldster is a favorite character in farces of all ages. Gluttony and fearfulness (this latter demonstrated in the "spooky" finale) are additional stock qualities displayed by him as they had been by Leporello, one of the most famous representatives of the type. Conceit renders Falstaff gullible, as it did Beckmesser; therefore he is continually fooled by the "merry wives" and even by Bardolph and Pistol, who are none too bright. Falstaff's conceit results in his downfall (literally) and chastisement. If he seems appealing and sympathetic, not repulsive, that is in part due to his human weakness. In the finale he graciously accepts defeat, a touch not found in Shakespeare.

As the comedy moves on, Ford becomes an increasingly absorbing character. At first he does not seem sympathetic. There is some cunning in the way he sizes up Falstaff in II/1 (to do this may not be too difficult): he appeals to his vanity and virility (with a preposterous scheme for "conquering" Alice), but first to his love of drink (the gift of a large glass of wine precedes him) and money. But Ford becomes a more absorbing figure with the sudden turn in the plot—a fortissimo clap in the orchestra is the turning point—as Falstaff calmly informs him of the anticipated rendezvous with Alice. Now Ford becomes more interesting: we know a complication he doesn't know, and we wonder how he will react. This continues, to a lesser extent, in II/2, but everything is such a mad whirl then that we barely have time to think about anything except the on-the-surface happenings. In the third act, when Ford is in on the plot (though himself the victim of another plot), he becomes less fascinating.

Though the comedy of *Falstaff* is "full-length," the opera is short. George Martin has pointed out that the entire work is shorter than the last act of *Die Meistersinger*. The brisk pace of the opening has already been referred to. No time is lost: after Bardolph's and Pistol's "tremendous Falstaff!" the conversation abruptly turns to Ford and his beautiful wife. Pistol at once volunteers essential information: she has the key to the money box. In no time the letters are sent, and we are upon Falstaff's dissertation on honor. The second act opens in a similar let's-get-down-to-

Mrs. Ford, Dame Quickly, Meg Page, and Falstaff (Act II, Scene 2).

business manner, and the hectic finales of Acts II and III are unforgettable.

This pace is made possible by Verdi's melodic style, which goes a step beyond *Otello* in its concentration on dialogue, always mindful of text prosody. Little time is taken for leisurely, lyrical arias—just enough to insure sufficient contrast. A lyrical, sentimental line at times is intentionally at variance with the prosaic text, e.g., "Quel tuo naso ardentissimo" in I/1:

EXAMPLE 23

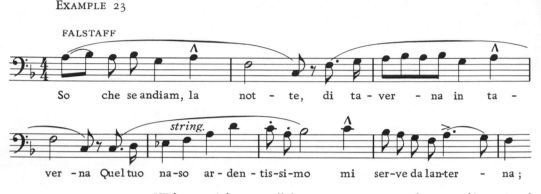

FALSTAFF

So   che se andiam, la   not - te,   di ta - ver   - na in   ta -

ver - na Quel tuo   na-so   ar - den - tis-si-mo   mi   ser-ve da lan-ter   - na ;

string.

[*When at night we stroll from tavern to tavern, that very shiny nose of yours serves as my lantern.*]

Such exaggeration is as comical as exaggerated gestures can be. In II/1 Dame Quickly really "pours it on": melody and harmony grow quite sentimental as she exclaims "povera donna" and as she delivers the message from Meg. To Quickly's exclamation "You bewitch them all!" Falstaff calmly and drily answers "I know." Things continue in conversational tone. Arias there are few, but Verdi writes neither conventional recitative nor Wagnerian endless melody. Though he allegedly said that there was too much singing in opera, Verdi consistently keeps the human voice in the foreground. It carries the chief melodic line. Passages that might be called arias include Ford's monologue on jealousy—an aria because it amounts to a longer, uninterrupted expression of thought and feeling by one individual, not because of any traditional melody-plus-rhythmical-accompaniment texture. Falstaff's reminiscence "Quand'ero paggio" is delightful but ever so brief and therefore hardly conveys the impression of a formal aria. The honor discourse also is brief, and without long-winded operatic gestures. Just two words, effectively contrasted, make a point: "L'onore! Ladri!" (Honor! You Thieves!). Verdi's phrases are short, uneven in length and structure, determined by the phrasing of the text. He provides a masterful rendering of Boito's words (here based quite closely on Shakespeare), continually bringing out their meaning.

The lyrical scenes for Nannetta and Fenton at times broaden out musically. Fenton's outpouring at the opening of the Windsor Park finale is another aria–soliloquy, ending with the by now familiar "Bocca baciata," answered, from a distance, by Nannetta.

As arias are de-emphasized, the ensembles in *Falstaff* loom all the larger in importance, a condition that makes for special problems of rehearsing and performing. As one director said, "If I am to do a *Tosca,* I want to know who is the Tosca; if I am asked to do a *Falstaff,* I want to know who is the conductor."[18] Ensembles of varying dimensions and lengths occur. Most of them are not self-contained set numbers but change and flow freely, as determined by dialogue and action. The final fugue, "All the world is a joke," is one of the exceptions. Verdi continued the tradition of writing his most complex ensembles for the act finales, creating wonderful scenes of excitement and confusion in which everyone sings different words at the same time. In I/2 the quartet of women leaves the stage to the quintet of men. Individuals come and go. For a while the stage is left to the young lovers. Then, repeatedly, all soloists join forces. At one point in the resulting nonet the women chatter away in $\frac{6}{8}$ time, as they did before, while the men continue in rapid $\frac{2}{2}$.

[18] Martin Mayer in *ON*, March 21, 1964.

*The quartet of women
(Act I, Scene 2).*

The overall design of the opera is in part determined by the distribution of ensembles. Kühner has pointed out that, in the three acts of two parts each, the ensembles always are prominent in the second parts. In I/2 a symmetrical arrangement is found:

a) four women (dialogue, then quartet)
b) joined by five men (quintet-nonet, then dialogue)
c) duet of the two lovers
d) return of four women (mostly dialogue)
e) return of the two lovers
f) return of five men, joined by four women (dialogue, then quintet-nonet)
g) four women (dialogue, then quartet)[19]

The finale of Act II is well characterized by Fenton's remark "It's a madhouse!" Here, too, as many as nine soloists sing simultaneously; added to this whirl are the comments of the chorus of neighbors. During much of this scene Nannetta and Fenton, almost oblivious to the world on the other side of the screen which hides them, have sweeping sustained melodic lines which contrast with the chatter of everyone else.

Verdi's orchestra in a number of places brings back motives that have a specific textual meaning, thereby reminding the listener of the earlier situation. The phrase "dalle due alle tre"

EXAMPLE 24

QUICKLY

dal-le due al-le   tre

[*between two and three o'clock*]

with which Quickly tells Falstaff that Alice's husband usually is out between 2:00 and 3:00, is the most conspicuous example of such a motive. Its importance is stressed by its being set off by rests as Quickly sings it, and by Falstaff's immediate repetition of it, as though he wants to make sure he has understood this important bit of information. The little motif recurs in the orchestra a number of times, always with the intention of recall. Sometimes it is stated clearly, sometimes subtly, as when Ford, in his monologue, sings "L'ora è fissata" ("The time has been arranged")—the hour in question being "between two and three." Falstaff's "Va, vecchio John" recurs once but then is forgotten until the last act, when it is sung once more. Quickly's humble greeting

[19] Hans Kühner, *Giuseppe Verdi* (Hamburg, 1961), p. 139.

EXAMPLE 25

[*Your servant!*]

returns a few times, but there is nothing particularly subtle about the use of this formula. No themes serve to represent specific characters in the Wagnerian manner, though certain keys are associated with certain people. Falstaff is most at home in C major; Nannetta's and Fenton's love scenes are scored in A flat major, and the merry wives chatter in the bright key of E major.

Verdi's rhythmic style helps to establish the basic mood of many scenes. The spirited opening brings a vigorous yet light bouncy pattern, just right for the boisterous discussion that begins as soon as the curtain opens.

EXAMPLE 26

Rhythms are freely varied to go with the changing dramatic situation, and there are few rigid repeated-note patterns maintained for longer periods. Steady rhythmic accents occasionally serve humorous purposes: the marchlike accents of "Va, vecchio John" give an exaggerated, march-on-to-victory flavor to Falstaff's self-encouragement. Lilting triple time adds an overly sentimental quality to Falstaff's duet with "Fontana": "L'amor, l'amor."

For those who consider *Falstaff* Verdi's masterpiece his imaginative handling of the orchestra has special attraction. It constantly underscores the text or in other ways offers commentary on the action. As one comes to know this score well one discovers some of the less obvious examples. Falstaff examines the bill,

Bardolph counts the few remaining coins in his master's purse—and its emptiness is reflected in the light accompaniment which descends to "rock bottom." Dr. Cajus' oath is rendered even more comical by a little fanfare in the orchestra:

EXAMPLE 27

[*I swear*]

The accompaniment to the dissertation on honor continually varies with the text. Honor is a word, air that vanishes—and in the orchestra we hear:

EXAMPLE 28

[*a word*]

After Quickly's exit we can hear Falstaff's joy in the orchestra's vigorous grace-note theme, rooster-like, almost. His virility and charm will triumph: "Alice is mine!"

EXAMPLE 29

Soon "Signor Fontana" enters and displays a large money bag, and the sound of jingling coins, sweet music to Falstaff, rises from the orchestra. Later, when Ford sadly complains "I love her, but she doesn't love me," the little woodwind echoes give it away as a fake. Horns in more places than one symbolize the cuckold, a symbolism already found in earlier opera, e.g., in Mozart's *Figaro*. When Falstaff tells Ford that he is about to deceive Alice's "loutish husband," horns are prominent in the orchestra. In Ford's great monologue, ending with his praise of jealousy, the orchestra gives a magnificent description of his emotions, his fierce rage and his sobs, his grim vow of vengeance. This ends with a great descending scale (horns are prominent) and leads into the graceful, trilly and frilly string music that describes Falstaff's reappearance, all dressed up for his appointment with *la bella Alice*. The huge orchestral trill in Act III has become famous: with the help of mulled wine a feeling of warmth and well-being gradually pervades Falstaff's whole body. The "thrill that shakes every fibre of the heart" grows in the orchestra, along with Falstaff's description. A study of the score (including the fairy music of the last act) will reveal numerous other instances of Verdi's ingenious orchestration.

Falstaff grows on the viewer and listener. If it is not heard as frequently as *La Traviata,* that is in part due to difficulties of production. *La Traviata* calls for a smaller cast and orchestra and therefore can be done in a smaller house. It is more of a soloist's opera, meaning that less time (and money) has to be allotted for rehearsing complex ensembles. But these production difficulties only in part account for the earlier opera's greater popularity. For many operagoers soaring melodies that can be easily remembered are a greater source of enjoyment than the rapidly moving music that gives sparkle to Boito's comedy. It has also been said that most opera fans prefer tragedy to comedy and are moved by works in which a strong love interest is central to the story. Erich Leinsdorf has made this point. The action that deals with Nannetta and Fenton is only loosely related to the main plot. It is touching and well handled, but the listener gets far less involved emotionally than he does with Violetta, or Tosca, or even Wagner's Eva. Nevertheless, many people rejoice in the fact that both Wagner and Verdi wrote at least one major comic opera.

So far this study has been almost exclusively concerned with European opera, performed in Europe. A brief summary of operatic developments in the United States, up to the twentieth century, may be in order at this point, if only to remind us that even before the days of the modern ocean liner and airplane, communication with the Old World was close, and that it extended to the field of music, including opera.[20]

Some operatic activity existed on American soil during colonial times. Its extent, and the kind of repertory performed, varied regionally. Due to religious objections Puritan New England, in the early and mid-eighteenth century, had less theater (and less worldly music in general) than the South. Quaker influences had similar consequences, especially in Philadelphia. Various subterfuges served to circumvent laws prohibiting theatrical performances: plays might be advertised as "moral dialogues" or, in the case of opera performances, as concerts or rehearsals. This practice still existed after the revolution, just as buildings were not called opera houses but "academies" or "museums" well into the nineteenth century.

According to Sonneck, prerevolutionary opera in America consisted almost exclusively of ballad operas and modernized versions of English masques. Gay's *Beggar's Opera* and Coffey's *The Devil to Pay* were especially popular in the 1750's and '60's; the masque *Comus,* with music by Arne, was given in Philadelphia in 1770. There also were adaptations of works by Gluck, Philidor, and other composers who had recently been successful in France. As the Revolutionary War broke out, an Act of Congress (1774) put a stop to most public entertainments. In all, the quantity of light opera performed in colonial days was considerable. Little factual information about the quality of performances exists, but amateurs participated frequently, especially in the orchestra. With few exceptions orchestras were small and inadequate, as were the buildings and halls in which opera was given.

Late in the eighteenth century, New Orleans became an important operatic center. The repertory, not surprisingly, favored French works and the French language. Cherubini's *Les Deux Journées* was given in 1811. High standards of performance ex-

---

[20] More extensive accounts of the subject include the following: O. Sonneck, *Early Opera in America* (New York, 1915), and H. Krehbiel, *Chapters of Opera . . . in New York* (New York, 1908). P. L. Miller, "Opera, the Story ·of an Immigrant," in *One Hundred Years of Music in America* (New York, 1961), deals with events after 1860. Further bibliography in Grout, *SHO,* pp. 490 f.

A performance in the Park Theater, 1822.

isted from this time on through most of the nineteenth century. Many well-known French operas had their American premiere in New Orleans, though the Italian repertory also was cultivated.[21]

Around the mid-eighteenth century ballad operas also enjoyed popularity in New York. Several theaters existed by then, including the Nassau Street Theater and the John Street Theater, where George Washington attended performances. The Park Theater opened in 1798; it burned down twice. As rebuilt the second time it seated 2,500. Around this time many operas were sung in English, a practice that changed in the course of the nineteenth

[21] R. Davis, *A History of Opera in the American West* (Englewood Cliffs, 1965), Chapters 1 and 2.

century as more and more European troupes came to the New World.[22] Numerous other theaters, in which opera was occasionally performed, existed in New York during the first half of the nineteenth century. The Academy of Music opened in 1854. By this time Italian opera had become well established. In 1825 Manuel Garcia, Spanish impresario and tenor, had brought his troupe for what was to be a particularly successful season. Among the stars was the famous Maria Malibran, his daughter, acclaimed as a singer with a remarkable voice range and as an accomplished actress. She had started her road to fame as Rosina in Rossini's *Barber of Seville*. This work also was the great success of Garcia's 1825–1826 season in New York, during which four other Rossini operas were given. In an earlier chapter we referred to the *Don Giovanni* production of the same season, in the presence of Da Ponte, Mozart's librettist.

Many well-known operas reached New York in a remarkably short time. *La Traviata* was given in 1856—three years after the Venice premiere and before it had reached Paris. This was the time when Walt Whitman was an enthusiastic operagoer in New York, with a special fondness for Italian opera—an interest that may surprise some of the poet's admirers. Whitman's article "The Opera," written for *Life Illustrated* in 1855, dwells on the social aspects of New York opera—aspects that were of considerable importance then as a hundred years later.

By this time, then, opera was solidly established on American soil—imported, not American opera, to be sure. In Chicago, opera developed rapidly after the middle of the century. Even San Francisco saw some performances, mostly by companies from Mexico, in the 1850's. The Crosby Opera House in Chicago opened its doors in 1865 but was destroyed by fire a few years later. The new house, the Auditorium, was opened with much celebration in 1889, only six years after the Metropolitan Opera House had been inaugurated in New York. In both New York and Chicago this was the period when opera functioned, on a grand scale, as a favored entertainment of a social elite recently come into fortunes in banking, railroads, and other branches of a rapidly expanding economy. At the same time there was growing and genuine enthusiasm for opera among the less wealthy, understandably so in view of the large influx of Italian and German immigrants. A visible result of this growth was the remodeling of the Metropolitan: the original 122 boxes proved to be too many and were reduced in number, making room for additional rows of lower-priced seats. Opera managements at times were criticized, then as later, for lavish spending on famous singers, for skimping on

[22] A. M. Lingg, "Old New York," *ON*, February 3, 1962.

other production costs, and for allowing insufficient rehearsal time.[23] The repertory's emphasis varied a good deal. German, especially Wagnerian, opera was much in demand during Leopold and Walter Damrosch's years of conducting for the Metropolitan and other companies (1884–ca. 1900). Walter Damrosch composed several operas as well, but neither his nor operas by other late nineteenth-century American composers[24] achieved more than temporary success.

[23] Large fees paid to artists, as well as elaborate decorations, resulted in a $600,000 loss during the Metropolitan's opening season.
[24] For some names and titles, see Grout, *SHO,* pp. 492 f.

*"And before him all Rome trembled": The Act II finale of "Tosca" in a
San Francisco production.*

9

NATURALISM IN MUSICAL DRAMA: VERISMO

THE PARTICULAR KIND OF REALISM AND naturalism found in late nineteenth- and early twentieth-century Italian opera is called verismo; it forms the subject of this chapter. Its foremost representatives were Ruggiero Leoncavallo, Pietro Mascagni, and, in some of his works, Giacomo Puccini.

In Leoncavallo's one-acter *I Pagliacci* (*The Clowns;* Milan, 1892, libretto by the composer) the audience is told by Tonio, the singer of the prologue, that the author has intended to give us "a slice of life"—a term that has often been used to describe one of the basic techniques of realistic drama. Yet the term "verismo" implies more than "truth" (Ital. *vero* = "true") to life. Typically, veristic opera contains a generous amount of violence; characters display uninhibited, elemental feelings of jealousy, hatred, passion, lust, and the like. *Cavalleria*

Rusticana (*Rustic Chivalry*) by Mascagni (Rome, 1890, based on a successful play by Giovanni Verga, the writer who had coined the term "verismo"), which in performance often is paired with *I Pagliacci,* displays many of these qualities. If one believes that music is especially suited to the expression of strong and basic emotions, including those mentioned above, one can see why veristic opera became so successful, at a time when naturalism in spoken drama was in vogue. It also represented a reaction to the sentimentality of much Romantic opera, especially to Wagner's brand of emotionalism.

Opera through the ages, it should be clear by now, has expressed basic emotions, and the presentation of scenes of violence was not new or restricted to verismo. Almost a hundred years earlier operas of the "horror and rescue" type (see above, Chapter 5) had pictured acts of cruelty and violence.[1] Veristic operas lack the moral undertones and the usually happy, or at least just, endings of the earlier type. They are meant to shock or stun the audience and therefore contain much that is sensational, or was at the time. Today's public has been subjected to heavy doses of melodrama through other media, especially the motion picture, and may react less strongly.

The passing of time has robbed an opera like *Cavalleria Rusticana* of some of its realistic impact. What seemed like stark, true-to-life drama in 1890 may seem quite sentimental and conventional today, especially to non-Italian audiences. The dialogue is partly to blame; the trite lines given to the chorus ("Let us now return to our ladies," or the workers singing about the joys of Easter), and the contrived situations calling for song, e.g., Alfio's singing, to everyone present, about the joys of being a coachman.

The veristic approach by itself did not insure success, even for such a well-versed man of the theater as Puccini. *Il Tabarro* (*The Cloak,* 1918) is his most veristic opera. The stark, melodramatic plot takes place on a river barge and involves simple, poor people: the skipper and his wife, a stevedore, and an old hag who makes a precarious living by collecting salvageable articles from trash cans. Yet *Il Tabarro* has never approached the success of *La Bohème* or *Madam Butterfly,* in which sentimentality rather than brutality dominates.[2] *Il Tabarro* belongs to a group of three

---

[1] Méhul's *Bluebeard,* for instance, was very successful in Dresden in 1826. It contains a long scene in which Raoul, knife in hand, drags his wife across the stage by the hair, to the death chamber, amid much screaming.

[2] *La Bohème* shows well the difference between realism and verismo. It contains numerous realistic touches in drama (Colline's farewell to his threadbare overcoat) and music (the child's voice, off-key, in the scene with Parpignol, the toy vendor). Musetta interrupts her prayer to the Madonna with practical instructions to keep a lamp from blowing out. Mimi, on her death bed, unlike Violetta in *La Traviata,* does not engage in taxing singing. Yet the overall effect of this opera is a mixture of lightheartedness and sentimentality—not of cruelty or sensationalism.

one-acters; of these, *Gianni Schicchi,* a light comedy, has been consistently more successful.

Late in his life Verdi had been aware of the then incipient movement of verismo. Though the Tosca subject at one time appealed to him, the veristic approach was not for him. He considered it "a copying of reality; but to invent reality is far better. . . . To copy reality is photography, not painting."

Giacomo Puccini, *Tosca* (Rome, 1900)

Of all the examples of verismo *Tosca* has had the broadest audience appeal, consistently from the day of its first performance to the present. It is based on Victorien Sardou's stage play *La Tosca,* first performed in Paris in 1887—one of a series of highly successful dramas by this master of realism. Sardou had become the leading light of the Paris theatrical world. His rise to the top was closely linked with the stellar career of Sarah Bernhardt, generally considered the greatest actress of her age—an opinion in which she concurred. The role of Tosca was written for her; according to some it became her favorite role.

Puccini saw the play, and though his knowledge of French was limited, his dramatic instinct told him at once that here was an operatic subject after his own heart. Luigi Illica (1859–1919), who had collaborated on earlier librettos for Puccini, had arranged Sardou's drama for another composer, Alberto Franchetti. Once Puccini's mind was made up that *Tosca* was his kind of opera he set out, with the help of his publisher Ricordi, to convince Franchetti that *Tosca* was not suitable for his talent. No sooner had Franchetti given up his claim than Puccini signed a contract for his opera with Ricordi.

Work on *Tosca* proceeded rapidly. It was decided to have it first performed in Rome since the action takes place there. After the success of the opening night the opera played to full houses for twenty further performances. It reached Buenos Aires within a few months; London and New York soon followed. Some unfavorable reviews, especially in London, failed to interfere with continued public acclaim for the work.[3] The opera came out in Paris, the scene of Bernhardt's triumphs, in 1903. Sardou took a lively interest in the production, taking charge at rehearsals with much enthusiasm. Later he is said to have remarked that the libretto was an improvement on his own play.

Illica's earlier text for Franchetti served as a starting point; later Giuseppe Giacosa (1847–1906) also collaborated. This three-

---

[3] A London reviewer asked "What has music to do with a lustful man chasing a defenseless woman, or the dying kicks of a murdered scoundrel?" In Kerman's more recent (and more carefully considered) opinion Tosca is a "shabby little shocker." (*Opera as Drama,* New York, 1956, p. 254.)

man team had worked together successfully on *La Bohème* (1896) —surprisingly enough, for Puccini was extremely demanding. At the time of writing *La Bohème* Giacosa complained bitterly about the endless changes the composer required, causing some text passages to be rewritten five times. Work on *Tosca* also brought disagreements, but though the librettists suffered, Puccini's theatrical flair brought about a number of improvements in what is by no means a flawless libretto. Perhaps the most fortunate change was made in Act II. Here the librettists had Cavaradossi sing an aria while being tortured. Puccini demanded and obtained other changes, replacing what would have been conventionally operatic with some startling veristic touches. Tosca's last line in Act II, "E avanti a lui tremava tutta Roma" ("And before him all Rome trembled"), is said to have been supplied by the composer.

Tosca is a fine example of the differences between a stage play and an opera—differences that occupied us in an earlier chapter. A brief comparison of Sardou's play and Puccini's opera may therefore be useful. Both take place against the historical background of Rome in the year 1800. The ups and downs of Napoleon's campaigns in Italy—alliances, battles won and lost, the short-lived republican governments in both Naples and Rome, secret-police terror—these form the backdrop for Sardou's drama of love and intrigue. Sardou took great pains to preserve accuracy in both general setting and detail. History and locale provide more than a backdrop, however, since political events and figures enter into every scene of the drama. Only with a knowledge of this background do we fully understand why people talk and act as they do. Sardou needed five acts and twenty-three characters to supply the needed detail. As usual, the librettists were faced with the task of reducing the number of lines sharply. In the process of fashioning a libretto of three acts and nine characters a good deal of information was eliminated that would be necessary if the listener were to understand all details of action and motivation. As it is, many details of the plot are left dangling in the opera; the first and second acts are full of unexplained names and allusions.[4]

It has often been said that the libretto is weak for this reason, and it is true that under close examination these flaws become evident. If the average listener does not seem to be bothered by them we must assume that the basic dramatic situations are clearly enough drawn, and supported by the music, to render the drama as a whole absorbing and credible. Much of the action was condensed and simplified. The character of Scarpia in particular suffers from this.

In some ways this condensation is beneficial for the dramatic

[4] Newman (*Great Operas,* Vol. II, pp. 219 ff.) discusses many of these.

impact. Queen Maria Carolina is a key figure in Sardou's plot. In the libretto she does not appear at all: through the open window we merely hear Tosca's singing at her party. For the opera this is enough, and Floria Tosca is the opera's only female role. Sardou's last act consists of two scenes, the first of which takes place in Cavaradossi's cell. During the other, the execution scene, Tosca is not present. Combining these two brings about a more gripping last act for the opera—melodramatic, perhaps, but certainly moving. The listener knows all along about Scarpia's fiendish plan, while Tosca and Mario hopefully think about their life together after the ordeal of the mock execution. By their condensation the librettists produced a text—whatever its faults—that makes *Tosca* one of the fastest-moving of all operas. The pace is such that cuts are never made (except for a few bars following "Vissi d'arte"), which is unusual today. Each of the three acts moves swiftly. From the moment the curtain rises after three bars of music—again there is no overture—to Tosca's leap to her death this pace is maintained. The great amount of action and violence is responsible for some of the criticism leveled against the opera. There are just enough lyrical moments to provide contrast and emotional relief. One such passage was criticized by Ricordi, though on musical rather than dramatic grounds. This is the scene in Act III, from Tosca's arrival to the unison duet "Trionfal. . . ." Puccini was sure of himself and did not make any changes, long as the scene may be in relation to the act as a whole.

Puccini's finales are masterfully handled. The Te Deum that ends Act I is of no great importance in Sardou. For the opera it provided possibilities of dramatic contrast closed to spoken drama: the expression of Scarpia's evil sentiments and, simultaneously, the dramatic and musical splendor of the religious ceremony, with organ, choir, spoken prayers, and bells. Here Puccini's veristic music drama is not far removed from the spectacular finales of earlier grand opera.[5] Equally effective, in a different way, is the end of Act II, after Scarpia's death. Here, too, the play has more words than the opera, where the orchestra speaks for the singer and reinforces the silent play on the stage.

Realistic detail is provided in abundance. We have already noted the setting for each act[6] and the fact that in each case it

[5] In a recent Vienna production incense was wafted through the auditorium during this scene, and the smell of gunpowder at the end of Act III.

[6] For some reason the opera's first act takes place in the church of S. Andrea della Valle, rather than the church indicated by Sardou, which, because of its location, would have made a more logical hiding place for Angelotti. On the other hand, S. Andrea della Valle is more spacious, providing a better setting for the Te Deum celebration that concludes the act. See Laird Kleine-Ahlbrandt, "The Hero as Revolutionary," *ON*, February 15, 1969.

forms more than a backdrop for the action. Puccini took this realistic setting even more seriously than Sardou, who was not bothered by the impossibility of Tosca's leap from the parapet into the Tiber, some fifty feet away.

In his music the composer displayed similar concern with accuracy of small details. He solicited expert clerical advice for the Te Deum scene; for the third act he wished to know the exact pitch of the large bell at St. Peter's, and he studied the effect of many church bells ringing simultaneously in the vicinity of the Castel Sant' Angelo. In a general way the music of the second-act cantata suggests the sound of late eighteenth-century music—Sardou had even introduced the composer, Paisiello—and the shepherd's song has the flavor of folk songs of the region. Cantata and shepherd song, coming from a distance, enhance our awareness of the locale, at the same time taking the listener beyond the confines of the stage set. So do various other sounds that reach us from offstage: the cannon shot announcing the prisoner's escape and the drum roll at the crucial moment in Act II, signifying Mario's imminent execution.

With all this attention to realistic detail some inconsistencies do occur—of minor significance since only the careful student of the plot is likely to notice them. The sacristan, it has been argued, ought to recognize the portrait of the Marchesa Attavanti: her chapel is in his church, and she often comes to pray there. After the cannon shot in Act I Scarpia appears in the church almost at once, fully informed of the details of the escape. Elsewhere in the opera time is also treated freely—a kind of dramatic license—for the benefit of pace. After Tosca has revealed Angelotti's hiding place Spoletta leaves for the villa in the country and finds Angelotti, who commits suicide. Spoletta then returns to the Farnese Palace and reports to Scarpia—all of which could not possibly happen within the few minutes allotted by Puccini. Some of these inconsistencies, and others, are due to the omission of details found in Sardou's play.

As a drama, then, *Tosca* has weaknesses and strength. Good drama, it might further be argued, succeeds without so much violence—torture, attempted rape, murder, execution, two suicides—but makes its impact in more subtle ways. Veristic stage plays of this kind may no longer appeal as they did in Paris during the 1880's; but the opera *Tosca* owes some of its success to a plot and to characters that represent strong, basic emotions and call for music of suitably strong, direct appeal. Certainly the unrelenting pace of the opera is one of its chief assets. Scarpia, in Act I, enters, surveys the scene, sees the painting (*he* does recognize the Attavanti at once!), quickly draws his conclusions, and, when Tosca

Opposite: The Te Deum, Act I: At the end of his soliloquy Scarpia joins in the singing of the solemn chant.

returns, decides on his strategy. She reacts just as he had expected
and promptly leads his agents to the villa. As she leaves, the finale
culminating in the Te Deum gets under way at once. Events move
with similar speed in the other acts.

In spite of the opera's title, Scarpia has been regarded by
some as the character who governs the opera's happenings from
beginning to end. The very first chords of the opera represent him
(see Example 1), and Tosca's last exclamation is addressed to him.
Certainly he is the opera's most forceful figure—a villain through
and through. His villainy is so complete that some listeners refuse
to take him seriously—yet history is not without monsters of his
kind, and he is consistently drawn. Sensuality combined with
bigotry are his outstanding qualities; the touch of religious hypoc-
risy is particularly repulsive. Typically his first utterance is censure
of the choir boys for their merriment in church. Several remarks
later in the act accentuate this trait. He reprimands Tosca for her
oath, in church, and in the end he joins enthusiastically in the
singing of the Te Deum. In a sense all this is echoed at the end of
the second act: Tosca, having stabbed and killed the lustful chief
of police, piously places two candles near his body and a crucifix
on his chest.

In drawing Scarpia's personality the play, again, provides
better motivation and clues. There the Queen threatens him: find
Angelotti, or else! His cruel and frantic efforts thus are more
understandable, and through much of the play this motive is
stressed more than in the opera, where his desire for the beautiful
singer is in the foreground most of the time.[7] The changed
emphasis is characteristic for Puccini.

The Tosca of the opera is somewhat more warmly drawn
than the play's heroine, but in most regards they are alike. In the
opera's opening scene we immediately observe her chief traits: her
strong jealousy, her piety, her warm, outgoing feelings toward
Mario, her coy sense of humor ("paint her with dark eyes!"). As a
devout Catholic she would predictably disapprove of Mario's
liberal views and activities, and he, at first, thinks it best not to let
her in on Angelotti's escape. Yet her religious devotion does not
make her overly serious or subdued. She is a temperamental artist
whose actions are guided by impulse. Scarpia knows her, or her
type, well; his schemes are based on such knowledge. Tosca is
admirably drawn—a young, vivacious woman, childlike in some of
her reactions, in need of protection, devoted to her Mario. It has

---

[7] Stage directions at the beginning of the opera's Act II state that Scarpia is
restless and "betrays a feverish anxiety"—but his remarks, and Puccini's music,
express complete confidence that he will find and hang Angelotti.

been said that subtle character drawing is not typical of verismo—that people act out of essentially simple, direct impulses. This is true of Tosca, but the lack does not make her less appealing.

Cavaradossi, the young liberal, comes from an aristocratic, wealthy family. Painting is an avocation for him. Sardou supplies many details about his background, explaining some of his remarks and actions—why he, a "Voltairean," should be painting in church. As a person he is a cut above many tenor-lovers because of his manliness and courage. Yet he is not a stereotyped, idealized hero—Puccini saw to this. Instead of a grandiloquent farewell speech, Mario sings the brief "E lucevan le stelle" ("The stars were shining"), the complete text of which shows us another facet of verismo. That the condemned man, just before his execution, should conjure up a vivid, erotic picture of Tosca is no "psychological improbability" (Carner) but a particularly realistic touch which may be lost in some of the more flowery translations.

When Cavaradossi recognizes Angelotti he refers to him as "Consul of the overthrown Roman Republic," yet Angelotti had been imprisoned because of his leadership, earlier, in a similarly short-lived Neapolitan Republic. Once more Sardou tells us a good deal more about his background, but for the purposes of a taut libretto the details were rightly omitted.[8] In the opera, Angelotti's appearances are too brief—an escaped prisoner desperately looking for safety—for him to emerge as a profound or complex character, important as he is to the plot.

With the sacristan's role some comic relief is introduced into these serious happenings. The result is not altogether satisfactory, for aside from greed—which seems to be a standard attribute of operatic servants—and some queer mannerisms the sacristan does not show himself to be particularly comic or otherwise attractive. He detests the painter because of his reputation as a liberal and agnostic; gleefully he wants to be the first to tell him the bad political news, though actually he does not get the chance. When Scarpia interrogates him he is all abject fear. His hiccuping and choking while he explains about the basket of food find reflection in the music.

Puccini's score contains a rich variety of musical ingredients. Of these his lyrical and warm melodies, typically Italian in their broad sweep, show his gift to best advantage—melodies that are essentially vocal but in many instances are equally successful when entrusted to the orchestra, especially the upper strings. Such mel-

---

[8] In the play the chapel belongs to the Angelotti, rather than Attavanti, family —a more logical hiding place for the fugitive but also, for that reason, more likely to be searched. See Newman, *Great Operas,* Vol. II, pp. 231 f.

While Cavaradossi sings his "Recondita armonia," the Sacristan mumbles.

odies can be heard throughout the work, not only in those places where they are lifted out of the general musical texture and amount to arias, such as Mario's "Recondita armonia," Act I. Passages like Tosca's "Non la sospiri la nostra casetta?" ("Aren't you longing for our little house?") and the cantabile duet that follows are but two examples of many.

A kind of hypnotic quality often results from insistent repetition of a melodic line, in this opera more than in Puccini's other scores. Appropriately enough the music of the execution scene, ominous and inexorable, is the most extreme example, from the appearance of the firing squad to the moment when, the last soldier having left, the melody also vanishes and is left dangling on an unresolved chord. Such insistent melodies ·may be treated sequentially, e.g., on a higher pitch level at each occurrence—a technique employed in the torture scene, affecting both vocal and instrumental melodic lines. In this instance it is coupled with a more and more "insisting" crescendo that only lets up with Tosca's exhausted "non posso più." Even the Te Deum ending Act I has this ostinato quality, achieved by the persistent bell sounds in the bass and the melodic line given at first to the orchestra and organ and later to Scarpia, in the end merging with the Te Deum chant.

Musical contrast goes hand in hand with the librettists' technique of contrasting violent and lyrical scenes. In Act II the music by turns grows ferocious and gentle. Scarpia gives instructions to his henchmen in the adjoining chamber; we hear Mario's

Act II: Tosca (Maria Callas) has not yet seen the knife.

exclamations, first of defiance, then of anguish, and the music rises to a pitch of frenzied agitation. Then the prisoner is carried in; there is a tender exchange of words between him and Tosca, interrupted by Scarpia's loud, triumphant instructions to Spoletta. Once more the music reaches a climax of excitement in Mario's shouts of "Vittoria!", but soon he is dragged away, and the music changes character completely as Scarpia settles down to resume his interrupted meal. After this the mood continues to fluctuate. Scarpia's pursuit is suddenly arrested by the drum roll, followed by Tosca's calm and imploring "Vissi d'arte." Events continue to move with the speed characteristic of this opera: during the subdued but intense music that accompanies the writing of the safe-conduct Tosca sees the knife on the table, conceives her plan and, within about eight measures, carries it out. Violent music accompanies this scene, but it soon is over, and the hushed remainder of the act once more makes its effect through musical contrast.

Variety of a different sort is introduced by Puccini's use, in a number of places, of a musical idiom other than his own. The cantata and shepherd's song have already been mentioned; the former is preceded by a gavotte in a stylized eighteenth-century idiom. This passage in Act II, and the calm, bucolic quality of the shepherd's tune in Act III, lend special impact to the violent developments to follow.

By the time he composed *La Bohème* Puccini had already developed his own technique of using themes and motives. Like Verdi he associated themes with specific persons; other themes represent concepts and events. He does not develop his "leading motives" in the Wagnerian fashion. Some of the themes are quite long, amounting to complete melodies. They may be repeated again and again, producing the hypnotic effect mentioned above. Not all themes are equally clear in their meaning. The Scarpia motive is distinctive, concise, and most obvious in its association:

EXAMPLE I

The composer subsequently not only modifies the theme as such but also recalls the characteristic whole-tone progression of its bass line. When Mario advises Angelotti to hide in the well, the orchestra, pianissimo, brings this progression:

EXAMPLE 2

Elsewhere the sound of whole-tone scales also is exploited, as in the interrogation scene of Act II:

EXAMPLE 3

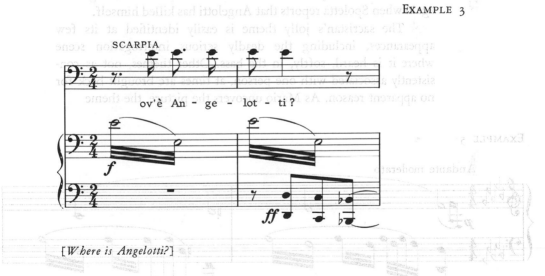

[Where is Angelotti?]

Once Scarpia has died, his theme for the first time appears in the minor mode (last bars of Act II). Though the villain no longer is present, his evil plans determine the outcome of the third act, and his theme hovers in the background during the opening of that act, just before the shepherd's song. At the very end, as Spoletta rushes up the stairs, the orchestra's harmonies once more imply the Scarpia theme—understandably so, for the murder has been discovered, and Tosca "will pay dearly for his life."

Equally concise is the Angelotti theme. Its nervous, jerky chords well represent the fugitive and his fear of detection:

EXAMPLE 4

Many listeners will correctly associate this theme with Angelotti at its later recurrences. Tosca, we learn later in the act, wants Mario to meet her that evening, and the Angelotti motive reveals to us Mario's secret—why he cannot be there. The orchestra brings it in again when Spoletta reports that Angelotti has killed himself.

The sacristan's jolly theme is easily identified at its few appearances, including the deadly serious interrogation scene where it is heard, softly, in the bass. Other themes, not as consistently associated with one person, at times are brought back for no apparent reason. As Mario uncovers the picture, the theme

EXAMPLE 5

is heard for the first time—an ominous sound. Is it meant to represent the beautiful Marchesa Attavanti? Musically it seems to have grown out of a portion of the sacristan's melody:

EXAMPLE 6

It reappears when Angelotti relates the escape plan, made with the Marchesa's help, but when Scarpia asks the sacristan where the Attavanti chapel is, the orchestra gives out the "escape" theme:

EXAMPLE 7

which had already been heard when Angelotti told of his escape and which now recurs a number of times. Nor do we hear Example 5 when Tosca identifies the Attavanti in the portrait or when she swears that the Marchesa never will have Mario as her lover, which would have been a logical place to introduce it. Instead, the orchestra both times quotes the Angelotti theme! Nor is there reason to introduce an "Attavanti theme" immediately before Mario's enthusiastic shout of "Vittoria!" Yet the Attavanti theme it is commonly called.

During Scarpia's questioning of Cavaradossi an extended theme is heard:

EXAMPLE 8

marcatissimo e sostenuto

It persistently accompanies this scene, with the cantata music drifting in at the same time, having first been introduced during Spoletta's announcement that he had taken Cavaradossi into custody. The torture theme

The firing squad (Act III).

EXAMPLE 9

also has an appropriately insistent quality. There are other melodies that seem to have specific dramatic connotations but cannot be so conveniently labeled. While Scarpia writes the safe-conduct a melody arises from the orchestra

EXAMPLE 10

too beautiful and not villainous enough to be considered a Scarpia theme. It returns as Scarpia breathes his last, with Tosca's words "Or gli perdono" ("Now I forgive him"), and again in the last act while Tosca relates these same happenings to Mario. There is a sadness to this theme; one might interpret it as signifying the futility of Tosca's desperate action.

It is part of the technique of verismo to favor continuous dramatic action, thus providing few opportunities for self-contained, formal arias. This applies to *Tosca,* and as a result only a few excerpts have been successfully extracted for concert performance. Mario's soliloquy in Act I, "Recondita armonia," is occasionally heard that way—almost too short to be effective, and containing muttered interruptions by the sacristan which have to be cut.

Tosca's "Vissi d'arte," equally short, is the most successful aria. Critics have objected to it on the grounds that it slows down the pace, but the action is so rapid and violent before and after that this is hardly a valid argument. Usually it is the audience that introduces an artificial interruption and destroys the mood of the scene by prolonged applause. The same applies to Mario's "E lucevan le stelle" in the third act. Dramatically it is well motivated; the danger is that the tenor will "deliver" it with too much exuberance, especially the end, in order to obtain the expected ovation. Its melody is persuasive in the best Puccini manner—a brief but impassioned farewell to life, somewhat reminiscent of the "Addio" in La Traviata. One has the feeling that Puccini wanted to make the most of it, having the orchestra anticipate it earlier in the act. As the dawn music dies away and the prisoner is escorted to the platform the melody is quoted in full—inappropriately so, for the mood of the scene so far still is quite subdued. We hear it again, presented by a clarinet, as an introduction to the aria itself. Again, as Tosca leaps off the parapet, the orchestra quotes a substantial portion of it—unison, fortissimo—implying, perhaps, the words that had earlier accompanied this phrase ("My dream of love has forever vanished," etc.). No doubt Puccini had found this kind of ending to be so successful in La Bohème that he once more availed himself of the technique.

Objections have frequently been raised against Mario's quasi-aria of victory, following his torture. Dramatic reason, it is said, speaks against it: by this outburst Mario dooms himself, and having just fainted from pain and exhaustion he could hardly have dragged himself to his feet and delivered the rousing, marchlike "L'alba vindice appar" ("The dawn of vengeance is breaking"). The scene obviously is weak, but neither of these objections is valid—assuming that dramatic realism is the basis on which such a scene ought to be defended. Tosca's confession had already sealed Mario's fate as a conspirator against the government who had concealed another conspirator. Furthermore, one might argue, Mario, as a result of the ordeal, is beside himself and not rational. As to the second objection: such a brief, frantic outburst need not be considered impossible under the strained emotional circumstances. It is soon over, and Mario collapses and is dragged away.

Instrumental solo passages, such as the one mentioned earlier, for clarinet, are infrequent in Tosca, but there is much variety in the orchestral scoring. The cello ensemble in Act III, as Mario is trying to put his emotions into the right words for a farewell letter, is ingenious and captures the mood extremely well. The dawn music at the beginning of this act is remarkable, not only for sheer musical beauty but for the realistic way in which the unrelated (in pitch and rhythm) sounds of numerous church bells are woven into a coherent musical texture. Clarity and coolness of the early morning hour were suggested before this through light chords by plucked strings and woodwinds. The chords with parallel fifths, in a high register, might remind some of the even "colder" sound at the beginning of Act III in *La Bohème*. In both instances Puccini provides an orchestral opening that sets the mood perfectly; just as at the end of the preceding act in *Tosca* the orchestra, synchronized with Tosca's silent acting, had provided an unforgettable scene. Puccini's orchestra is always active; without disputing the supremacy of the voice it maintains its own life through independent lines, themes, and rhythms.

Pelléas and Mélisande in the tower scene: a Berlin production.

10

IMPRESSIONISM AND MUSICAL DRAMA

Car nous voulons la Nuance encor,
Pas la Couleur, rien que la nuance!
—VERLAINE

THE SCHOOLS OF REALISM AND NATURAL-ism had put their stamp on many arts in the second half of the nineteenth century, including painting, literature, and music. A reaction first occurred among painters. Some French artists, including Monet, Manet, Renoir, and Dégas, came to abandon the traditional concern with exact representation, the detailed imitation of reality in which objects were clearly depicted in a manner that now came to be regarded as photographic. Perhaps it was due in part to the emergence of the science and art of photography that painters saw other purposes in art than realistic representation of nature. Paintings were to evoke moods—to suggest the atmosphere of a scene, especially a landscape, rather than to give a clear and complete picture of every tree, every rooftop, every person viewed. One of the first landscapes of this kind to attract public attention was Claude Monet's *Impression: Sunrise*, rejected for an exhibition in 1867 and finally shown in 1874. The term "impressionism" was coined at that time, at first with derogatory connotations.

Impressionistic painting is characterized by subtle nuances of light and color, by the absence of clearly defined lines and shapes, and by a generally hazy, veiled quality, leaving much to the viewer's imagination—"reality dissolved in a luminous fog."

It is easy to see how similar reactions to realism took place in other fields as well. The corresponding literary movement is often called symbolism rather than impressionism. Mallarmé, Rimbaud, Verlaine, and Maeterlinck were its chief representatives. In poetry, drama, and other genres of literature they avoided the obvious and squarely-stated. Instead the Symbolists wished to "evoke in a deliberate shadow the unmentioned object by illusive words." To name an object, Mallarmé held, was to sacrifice most of the pleasure of gradual realization. "To suggest, that is our dream"— to put words together in harmonious combinations that would convey to the reader a mood or a condition never actually mentioned. "I think there should be nothing but illusion." Symbolist poetry and drama thus deal with thoughts, sensations, and images with a meaning beyond what is actually said or directly implied. Words or events have a larger, symbolic significance, sometimes only vaguely implied and hence subject to different interpretations. Subtle and restrained, symbolism represents a reaction, also, to the full-blown emotion, the broad pathos and sentimentality of Romanticism, a reaction that assumed particular importance when the Symbolist creed was applied to musical drama. Furthermore, neither Impressionistic painting nor Symbolist writing had the social bias of realism: they did not accuse, condemn, or preach.

To describe musical impressionism one can well draw analogies to painting. As "color" is stressed and "line" is de-emphasized on the canvas, so musical color (referring both to tone color or timbre and to colorful harmony) is stressed over melodic line. The music of Claude Debussy (1862–1918) furnishes the best example. Vagueness of forms and shapes in painting can be compared to the vagueness of melody, of lines that meander, that have no clear-cut beginning or end. Debussy, who promulgated similar theories about harmony, shocked many of his teachers and elder contemporaries. In his music chords are freely used and combined, no longer in a traditionally functional manner (where certain harmonies lead to certain others and where dissonances resolve in expected ways to consonances) but for their characteristic, sensuous color effect. Rhythm likewise is subtle and vague, with frequent shifts of accent.

Artists and philosophers of the late nineteenth century displayed much curiosity about the Orient, showing sensitivity to the subdued and languid qualities of much art and to the mysterious, fatalistic aspects of Eastern thought and religion. For Debussy the different timbres, scales, and rhythms of Javanese music were particularly fascinating—music which he had heard at the Paris International Exposition of 1889 (though he may earlier have been familiar with the instruments of the Javanese gamelan).

Claude Debussy, *Pelléas and Mélisande* (Paris, 1902)

Maeterlinck's drama *Pelléas et Mélisande* was produced and printed in 1892. Debussy read the play soon thereafter and saw it performed the following year. He had already discussed his dramatic theories with friends several years earlier. Characters and action, he had said, must have a meaning, suggested rather than obvious, that goes beyond the particular situation of the play. "My dream is to find a libretto in which the characters will not argue but live their lives." The librettist should merely hint at his meanings; his characters should belong to no particular time or place. This intentional vagueness is not restricted to Debussy's dramatic theory but is part of the Symbolist and Impressionist creed. Maeterlinck's play appealed greatly to Debussy, who promptly went to see the author. Maeterlinck at first was quite willing to have his play used for an opera, though he later had a change of heart, largely for personal reasons.

Maeterlinck's prose speech had all the qualities which Debussy was looking for in a libretto, and he set it to music with only minor changes and some omissions.[1] The procedure—to set the text of a play almost verbatim, without fashioning it into a libretto—was unheard-of at the time and has remained rare since.

Debussy worked slowly and painstakingly. He soon realized the difficulty of this subtle approach to opera, in which the music deliberately "held back" and seldom was in the foreground, never getting in the way of the continuous dramatic action. At one time the composer had been an enthusiastic Wagnerite. He had made the pilgrimage to Bayreuth "and even cried, as was proper." Though he now pursued a different dramatic ideal, he still felt self-conscious and somewhat under the spell of "Klingsor" (the magician of Wagner's *Parsifal*).

After four solid months of rehearsing, including forty orchestra rehearsals, the opera was performed in 1902. Debussy was not satisfied and continued to make changes until his death. The

[1] See Edward Lockspeiser, *Debussy* (New York, 1962), Vol. I, p. 191, and *SHO*, p. 498, for a partial listing.

public dress rehearsal (amounting, in Paris, to a premiere) was a scandal and fiasco, largely engineered by Maeterlinck, who by this time had completely dissociated himself from the work and had publicly expressed his hope that it would fail. The first official performance was quieter; numerous presentations later during the same season showed that Debussy's unusual opera was obtaining some public success. This it has maintained to the present day. Understandably enough the unostentatious, subdued quality, the lack of arias and ensembles, have worked against its wider popularity, but it is worth noting that with Debussy's music *Pelléas et Mélisande* is Maeterlinck's only drama to have maintained itself in the general repertory.

Debussy's constant subordination of music to text, his concern with declamation at the exactly right pace, was bound to cause critical comments by those who had expected an opera along conventional lines. Camille Bellaigue noted that Debussy was "the first composer to have succeeded in writing a score without even a single measure of melody." Mélisande "forgets herself," i.e., sings, just once—as she combs her hair, in the Tower Scene. Many critics were helpless when confronted with the lack of clearly set-off musical forms, the vague rhythm, the unconventional handling of the orchestra. Some approved, and one critic was "overjoyed to find no imitation of Wagner, Gounod, or Massenet." Others realized that Debussy's style was not altogether without precedent. Attention to the spoken word indeed had characterized French opera, consistently more so than Italian opera, since its beginnings in the Baroque era.

Maeterlinck's play inspired a number of other major composers. Gabriel Fauré wrote incidental music (1898), as did Sibelius (1905). Schoenberg's tone poem of the same title was written in 1902 and first performed in 1905. Debussy's setting, begun in 1893, thus was the first.

The characteristic vagueness of Maeterlinck's text is evident everywhere, even in the *dramatis personae*. Arkel is King of Allemonde, "a legendary country." Mélisande is "a mysterious young princess," and the action takes place "in legendary times."[2] Nor do we learn much about the protagonists in the opening scene. Mélisande's answers to Golaud's questions are vague or no answers at all. Often in the course of the opera people seem to talk past each other. Act I ends with Mélisande's unanswered question, "Why will you leave?"

---

[2] Some of the details suggest the Middle Ages, but it is the flavor rather than a historical setting which is evoked. There are supernatural touches that have this flavor, such as Golaud's fall from his horse at the precise moment Mélisande loses the ring in the fountain (a similar incident occurs in Weber's *Freischütz*), or the kneeling of the servants who somehow know that Mélisande has just died.

someone who knew "the secret of expressive silences," a statement that would characterize Debussy equally well.[3] Even for their last

Mélisande and Golaud.

There is much about the story that is left unclear and dark. In the opening scene both Mélisande and Golaud are lost. The atmosphere is one of darkness, to which Mélisande, Genevieve, and others refer repeatedly. Darkness and mist are oppressive. Golaud describes the castle as old and gloomy; so are the surroundings, the caves and subterranean vaults. This darkness, symbolic like so much else, is hardly ever relieved. The motivation of various actions is left unclear—the characteristic technique of hinting or suggesting. Golaud does not say why he had brought Pelléas to the castle vaults (III/2), but there are implications, all the more ominous because they are only that. Golaud warns Pelléas to "take care." The on-the-surface meaning is that the stones are slippery, but symbolically the remark bears on Pelléas' relationship to Mélisande. This applies to the entire text of this short scene, with its comments on the "rising odor of death," etc., all reinforced by the music. The mood is dispelled in the following scene, which is (symbolically) sunlit. Pelléas remarks on the clean, fresh air and the flowers; the language and meanings now also are clearer. Nature is important in Maeterlinck's drama. This quality also may have rendered it attractive to Debussy, who shared the Impressionists' interest in expressing the changing aspects of nature, especially of light. Vagueness of language extends to the scene with a brief choral interjection (I/3): sailors are heard, dimly in the distance—but they sing no words, merely "Hoé! hisse hoé!", and a little later they only hum, à bouche fermée.

Accompanying this vagueness there is careful and clear structuring of the drama. Act III, for instance, is a well-planned architectural whole, each scene building on the preceding one. The tension reaches a high point toward the end of Scene 4, when Golaud's rising anxiety and jealousy is expressed through music that similarly has increased in intensity, through a rise in pitch level and through a slow but steady dynamic build-up.

Restraint and understatement are part of the poetic and dramatic style. After Goland has abused Mélisande (IV/1), she merely says "Il ne m'aime plus. . . . Je ne suis pas heureuse!" ("He no longer loves me. . . . I am not happy."), followed by Arkel's somewhat veiled answer (not really an answer), "Si j'étais Dieu, j'aurais pitié du cœur des hommes . . ." ("If I were God, I would take pity on the hearts of men"). Simplicity of language is part of this understatement, so well demonstrated by Pelléas' and Mélisande's confession of their love for each other. Debussy "never expanded the sentiment of a moment into an aria or a Liebestod" (Kerman). A critic once referred to Maeterlinck as someone who knew "the secret of expressive silences," a statement that would characterize Debussy equally well.[3] Even for their last impassioned moments together Pelléas and Mélisande speak few and simple words.

Symbolism pervades every scene,[4] giving a deeper meaning to often seemingly casual remarks. Mélisande has lost her crown, and loses her wedding ring, but is quick to point out that she does not want either back. The child Yniold tries in vain to lift the large stone, symbolic of the general helplessness of everyone in the face of events that have happened so far. "Your hair is all grey!" he says to Golaud, and the remark is all the more meaningful because Golaud is jealous of his younger half-brother. Hidden psychological meanings—some people today might refer to them as Freudian slips—are found elsewhere, more or less subtle and symbolic. When talking to Pelléas, Mélisande always refers to Golaud as "your brother," never "my husband." The recurrent image of blindness is a more general symbol: blind, inevitable fate governs all happenings. Much of the time the action is moved by forces beyond the characters themselves, who are merely existing in

---

[3] In a letter to Chausson Debussy wrote of silence as "perhaps the only means of throwing into relief the emotional value of a phrase." Quoted by Lockspeiser, Vol. I, p. 191.

[4] Martin, The Opera Companion, pp. 637 ff., gives possible meanings for each scene—some fairly obvious, others less plausible.

a world which is the way it is—beyond good and evil. The sequence of so many scenes, some quite brief, reinforces this impression. Debussy calls them *tableaux,* pictures or sketches, and some of them are sketchy indeed, in the Impressionistic manner. Impulses, subtle instincts, nervous reactions, rather than reason, guide and motivate the characters. Motives therefore are often only hinted at—we are to make our own inferences, with sensitivity and imagination. Virtually all the dialogue is emotionally subdued, with no outward pathos but, frequently, a burning intensity within. Yet in spite of or in addition to all this there are moments of very real action, of intense, on-the-surface drama. And, in time, the principal characters do emerge with some discernible qualities.

Pelléas, from the beginning, is gentle, sensitive, indecisive, and young. His are not the qualities of the usual young lover in opera; he is far removed from the stereotype. Genevieve's words "It is Pelléas, he has cried" introduce him. In some scenes he appears effeminate; at one time it had been considered to have the part played by a woman. The plan was abandoned, not from any consideration of realism but because of the change in the balance of voices that would result. In some scenes he and Mélisande do appear "like children," especially in comparison to Golaud. At the end of the opera Golaud, full of terrible remorse, still wonders whether their actions, even their kisses, had not been those of children.

Pelléas and Mélisande are similar in some ways, moving in but not really belonging to the real world. More than the others Mélisande is shrouded in mystery. There is the absence of factual information about her—where she comes from, and why she is here—but also as a person, as a human being she remains aloof. She is cold, lost, unhappy, weak and in need of protection; she laments her own cowardice. Debussy realized how difficult it would be to characterize her through music: "her fragility . . . her elusive charm . . . her long silences which a single gesture might frustrate or render meaningless."[5] Though Mélisande loves Pelléas—she says that she loved him from their first encounter— she appears detached, never being actively involved in the drama and rarely even in any conversation.

In comparison to these two Golaud is more strongly and clearly drawn. He is older than Pelléas, but he should not appear or act as though he were his father. His mounting doubts and his jealousy are real to him, to others, and to the audience. What he says is more articulate, and his actions *are* actions, surging into violence in the fourth act. He changes in his relation to the other

[5] Leon Vallas, *Claude Debussy* (London, 1933), p. 124.

King Arkel and Méli-
sande.

principals and for that reason is more clearly involved in the outer action. Golaud's portrayal shows that in Symbolist drama, with everyone moved by forces of destiny, beyond their control, an individual remains an individual. "Fate" also played an important role in many Baroque operas, but there people frequently did not emerge as individuals, being mere figures, personifying abstract character qualities.

Arkel, again, does not emerge as a real person. Debussy himself saw him as "coming from the world beyond. His is the disinterested, prophetic tenderness of those beings whose life will soon be extinguished. And to express all this with c d e f g a b ! What a profession!"

The generally subdued character of Debussy's score is evident

290

to the most casual listener. Subtlety, restraint, understatement—
they all result from the Impressionist–Symbolist aesthetic, which
abhors the obvious.[6] Somber colors dominate. Even when Golaud
speaks of joy (II/2), harmonies in the minor mode prevail, as
though the thought of happiness must be suppressed. In the scenes
that are the emotional high points of the opera we have few outbursts, few fortissimos for singers or orchestra. Most of the Tower
Scene is "low key"; only as Mélisande's hair falls down and
envelops Pelléas is there a surge of sound that soon subsides.
When Mélisande hears footsteps—"I believe it is Golaud!"—
there is only hushed fear and excitement. In this scene and elsewhere such musical understatement goes with the dramatic approach. Anger and incipient jealousy are smoldering under the
surface. "Laughing nervously," Golaud merely sings "What children!" and leaves. The basic mood of the later love scene is not
ardor or transport but tenderness, even sadness on Mélisande's
part. Sensitivity to gentle moods characterizes Debussy's orchestral
works as well. It is so very striking in his opera because of the
difference from what prevailed in contemporary German or Italian
opera.[7] The few outbursts of violence stand out all the more.
IV/2 contains one of these. As Golaud's jealousy grows he becomes almost incoherent, beside himself. The general musical style
here reminds one of Mussorgsky's *Boris Godunov*, especially the
Clock Scene, which Debussy knew and admired. But even at such a
moment Debussy avoids the aria, the grand gesture.

How sensitively the music follows explicit and implicit dramatic meanings is shown by countless passages. Even the pace of
singing has a bearing on this, being slower and somewhat more
forceful for Golaud than for Pelléas. In at least one instance the
pacing of the dialogue—regulated in opera as it never can be in
spoken drama—reveals Mélisande's innermost thoughts: her
overly quick "No" in reply to Golaud's question whether it was
Pelléas who made her unhappy.

Debussy's music may suggest dramatic action even where
such action is not specifically indicated in the score. At the end of
the Tower Scene, in one recent production, Pelléas glances back at
Mélisande longingly. Golaud observes this glance, at the precise
moment when the orchestra reaches a forte—a musical representation of the flash of jealousy that rises up in Golaud.

Concern with prosody results in a melodic style that comes

---

[6] Debussy once suggested that a "Society of Musical Esotericism" was what
was needed, rather than bringing art to the masses.

[7] Debussy, quite aware of this, somewhat jokingly said that his opera ought to
be produced in Japan.

close to recitation or chanting, frequently on one repeated note, with very sparse accompaniment.

EXAMPLE I

[*Is it you, Pelléas? Really, I never noticed it before, but you have the serious and kindly face of those who will not live much longer.*]

Rhythmic subtlety and flexibility recall the style of Gregorian chant—a kind of music which, after a decline of many centuries, was being studied and revived at Debussy's time, especially in Belgium and France. A rhythmic vagueness pervades most of the opera—a typically Impressionistic quality that was deplored by some critics and segments of the public as the abolition of rhythm or the dissolution of music.

Melodic intervals are small except in the few passages of great excitement, as they would be in spoken language. In a place of great intensity this excited declamation comes close in effect to the *Sprechstimme* employed by Schoenberg, Berg, and others not many years later.

292

EXAMPLE 2

[*All your long hair, Mélisande, has fallen down from the tower!*]

This manner of recitation lacks, of course, the purely musical charms of traditional operatic airs. Debussy was well aware of this; believing this style to be suitable and intimately tied to the drama, he would not permit a concert performance of excerpts from the opera. Later he explained and defended his melodic treatment:

The characters of this drama endeavor to sing like real persons, and not in arbitrary language built on antiquated traditions. Hence the reproach leveled at my alleged partiality for monotonous declamation, in which there is no trace of melody. . . . Dramatic melody should be totally different from melody in general. . . . The people who go to listen to music at the theater are . . . very like those one sees gathered around a street singer! There, for a penny, one may indulge in melodic emotions.[8]

And to his singers, during rehearsals for *Pelléas,* the composer said: "You must forget that you are singers before you can sing the music of Debussy." Since Debussy's melodic lines are so intimately tied to the prosody of spoken French, performance in translation presents special difficulties.

Somewhat more plastic and clearly outlined are melodic themes that occur in the orchestra. Wagner's concept of the *Leitmotif* was not rejected by Debussy, but it was not imitated either. Specific motives do occur and recur in the opera, but they are more diffuse and developed than had been Wagner's custom. Nor can they be as unequivocally and systematically identified with persons or objects. The theme quite consistently connected with Golaud's appearances

[8] Quoted by Victor Seroff, *Debussy* (New York, 1956), p. 204. Copyright 1952 by G. P. Putnam's Sons.

EXAMPLE 3

is called the "Fate" theme by some analysts, including Gilman,[9] who distinguishes and labels fifteen other themes. Most listeners will find them far less easy to remember than those of the *Ring* operas or *Die Meistersinger*. Debussy's belief in avoiding the obvious extends to his use of thematic material.

Debussy's harmonic concepts have already been mentioned. To the listener today who is familiar with the same composer's well-known orchestral works (*Prelude to the Afternoon of a Faun*, 1894; *La Mer*, 1905) the harmonic vocabulary of the opera will offer no difficulties of understanding, but to many of his contemporaries it seemed revolutionary and startling. Debussy's harmonic usage reflects his interest in music of other, especially Eastern, civilizations. The score of *Boris* impressed him particularly because of the fresh, unorthodox harmonic style. Whole-tone and other scales, not indigenous to Western European music, affected his harmonic language, resulting in ambiguity with regard to key and tonality. Ambiguity also results from his characteristic use of consecutive dissonances, especially seventh, ninth, and eleventh chords, as in the following passage (ninth chords, descending by whole tones):

EXAMPLE 4

As Melisande's hair falls down, the orchestra plays a series of

<hr />

[9] *Debussy's "Pelléas et Mélisande"* (New York, 1907), p. 58.

descending seventh chords. Act I ends on an unresolved chord, dissonant by nineteenth-century standards, which vanishes into nothing. Parallel motion, normally avoided in traditional harmony, occurs continually. It is not restricted to these chords but may involve triads in unrelated keys.

EXAMPLE 5

Harmonic vagueness is often the result of chromatic shifting, of wavering between major and minor

EXAMPLE 6

or of fluctuating motion in the inner voices.

EXAMPLE 7

Elsewhere incomplete harmonies (chords without thirds) provide unusual coloristic effects. After such vague or complex passages a return to traditional harmony may be effective. In IV/2 Arkel speaks of the new era, full of joy, that he foresees. The accompaniment works its way, through an involved passage, to a bright D sharp major chord, forte—an unusually clear harmonic outburst. Elsewhere widely spaced chords provide a specially warm, sonorous effect.

In their search for new harmonic resources Debussy and other composers of the early twentieth century turned to the modality of medieval and Renaissance music. Modality, rather than major–minor tonality, occurs often in *Pelléas and Mélisande*. It is used freely, i.e., without remaining consistently within a mode. The following passage is basically modal, but with an admixture of foreign tones:

EXAMPLE 8

[*Is it you, Golaud? I hardly recognized you.*]

Mélisande's song at the opening of the Tower Scene is an especially beautiful instance of modality, simple and touching, completely unaccompanied.

A large, diversified orchestra provides an accompaniment of many hues. We seldom hear all instruments at once, in a general, massive sound. Instead Debussy shows himself to be the master of coloristic effects, working with subtle, ever changing nuances of color. Certain instruments and instrumental combinations are favored, among them muted strings. Each string part may be divided several ways, and may carry special bowing instructions such as *sur la touche* ("on the fingerboard"). The gentle, rippling sound of two harps and the nostalgic quality of the English horn are often heard. French horns and trumpets are apt to be muted. The expressive low registers of flute and oboe are not neglected; among the strings the mellow sound of the viola is given prominence, including brief solo passages. Such an "accompanying" passage may have greater melodic interest than the voice line:

EXAMPLE 9

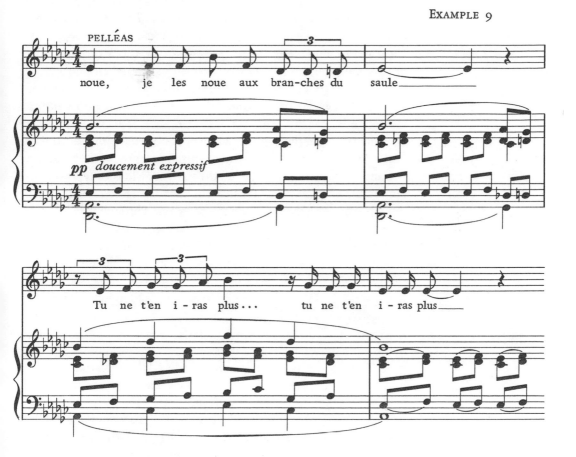

[I tie them to the willow branches . . . I won't let you go.]

When Genevieve reads Pelléas' letter (I/2), the accompaniment consists of very few instruments, in unorthodox groupings such as divided cellos and violas and one solo bassoon. There are long phrases with no accompaniment save an occasional punctuating chord. In general the opera's full orchestral score presents a characteristically "open" appearance, due to the many rests on virtually every page. Such selective, restrained scoring shows Debussy's supreme command of the orchestral palette. Many orchestral effects, novel at the time, were borrowed by later composers. The harp glissandos and woodwind broken chords "painting" water (II/1) are but one of these.

Essentially the orchestra is that used for Wagner's *Tristan,* yet the manner in which it is used shows well the different aesthetic, the sound ideal of the impressionists. *Pelléas* was a musical answer, along with many of Debussy's verbal comments (often caustic and bitter), to the preponderance of German music in the Paris concert life. Wagner figured largely in this repertory. To a public that delighted in the "Ride of the Valkyries" Debussy's restrained score may have seemed incomprehensible and, to some, dull. His orchestra produces murmurs rather than clarion calls. In the words of the composer–critic Lalo, Debussy's instrumentation is "the most discreet in the world: it is afraid of noise, it does not suffocate the voice, and one does not miss either a word or a note."[10] The orchestra is seldom in the foreground—at times it is completely silent—yet it is dramatically and musically as important as the singing. It establishes the mood of a scene effectively, though the means need not always be novel. Throughout III/2 the atmosphere is ominous. Sounds in a low register prevail: muted brass, pulsating timpani. Elsewhere, too, a turn of events, a change of mood is indicated in the orchestra before it is made explicit by the dialogue. Or the orchestra may inform us of a person's emotional state. In IV/2 Golaud's jealousy and rage mount. "Her eyes might give lessons in innocence to God!" A crescendo leads up to a pizzicato chord, fortissimo—a wonderful way to represent tension that is about to reach the bursting point.

Though the orchestral interludes have the practical purpose of allowing time for scene changes (their necessity having become evident during rehearsals), they fulfill a dramatic purpose as well, providing a transition from the atmosphere of one scene to the next. Following the scene by the fountain (II/1) the orchestra for some time continues the rippling-water patterns but gradually prepares the serious mood of the following scene, which is established with the change in meter and tempo (lent, $\frac{6}{4}$ time). After the curtain comes down on the gloomy scene in the subterranean vaults (III/2) the orchestra, within about a dozen measures, establishes the atmosphere of the terrace scene, with a fresh sea breeze. The length of the interludes varies greatly. That which

[10] Seroff, *Debussy,* p. 206.

connects Scenes 3 and 4 of Act IV is very short; possibly the great length of Scene 4 is responsible for this. At least one interlude is longer than the scene which it follows. Regardless of their duration these interludes are dramatically important, containing the most extensive development of thematic material.

Octavian and the Marschallin in Act I of "Der Rosenkavalier" in San Francisco.

11

TWO OPERAS BY RICHARD STRAUSS

STRANGE AS IT MAY SEEM, THE OPERAS OF Richard Strauss (1864–1949) are the most recent ones to have found a permanent place in the repertory. His long, active life as a composer began in the era of Wagner and Verdi. When he passed away, Bartók had been dead for four years; Schoenberg (d. 1951) had written most of his major works, having outlived *his* principal disciples Alban Berg (1885–1935) and Anton Webern (1883–1945). Strauss's last opera, *Capriccio,* appeared in 1942, but his operatic reputation is largely based on works written before World War I, above all on the two operas discussed in this chapter. We thus have the curious situation that a major composer, who wrote operas during most of his life, is represented on the stage chiefly (though by no means exclusively) by works written thirty to forty years before his death.

(A comparison to Sibelius may come to mind, although unlike Strauss the Finnish composer wrote little and published even less during his last thirty years.)

Before Strauss turned to opera he had earned substantial successes, along with vehement criticism, with a series of orchestral works: the tone poems, beginning with *Don Juan* (1889) that soon became, and remain, pillars of the symphonic repertory. Pictorial realism abounds, especially in *Till Eulenspiegel* and *Don Quixote,* regardless of the extent to which the composer wished them to "tell a story." The step from tone poems of this kind to opera was not a big or unexpected one.[1] Later in life the composer regarded these orchestral works as a preparatory phase for his extensive activity in the field of opera. In these early works he shows himself to be an undisputed master of orchestral writing—a mastery that also led him to write a treatise on instrumentation, still one of the most valuable works in that field.[2] All his operas, from the earliest *Guntram* (1894) on, are characterized by imaginative, unorthodox, frequently stunning, and generally masterful handling of the orchestra. That the orchestra should carry such an important share of the musical drama was part of the composer's operatic credo, expressed in conversations and letters. "Only with the invention and greatest diversification of the modern orchestra could [opera] rise to highest perfection." Wagner's life work lies behind this view, and young Strauss had the best opportunities to absorb the Wagnerian idiom while employed as court conductor in Weimar, 1889–1894. In the latter year he also conducted *Tannhäuser* at Bayreuth and gave lecture recitals on Wagner's work. *Guntram,* not surprisingly, was rejected by the public as "imitation Wagner"; in a number of ways it does lean heavily on that composer's style. What may seem surprising is its dedication to Verdi, of whose *Falstaff* Strauss was particularly fond. But this affinity, and the dedication resulting from it, becomes understandable when we think of the Strauss of *Rosenkavalier.* The warmth and humor of that work reveal a kinship to *Falstaff* as well as to *Die Meistersinger.*

Versatility of approach to librettos of greatly varying subject matter and literary style distinguishes Strauss from Wagner, whose custom of writing his own texts Strauss no longer followed after *Guntram.* The operas to which we turn now, while only two out of fifteen, are good examples of this great literary and musical diversity.

[1] Norman Del Mar, in his chapter headings, refers to *Salome* and *Elektra* as "stage tone poems." (*Richard Strauss,* London, 1962).

[2] Strauss's *Instrumentationslehre,* 1904, is based on Berlioz's *Traité d'Instrumentation et d'Orchestration,* 1844, but is far more than a new edition of that work.

***Salome* (Dresden, 1905)**

The biblical story in which Herod, Herodias, and John the Baptist
(rather than Salome) are the principal figures had received a
variety of artistic treatments before Oscar Wilde became attracted
to it. Among his sources of inspiration was a series of paintings on
the Salome theme by Gustave Moreau, done in the 1870's. Strauss
also familiarized himself with earlier Salome paintings, including
some by Dürer and Leonardo da Vinci.

Salome and Herod.

That the subject should have appealed to Wilde is understandable in view of his personality and literary orientation. The exotic milieu and the sensuous, heavily perfumed qualities that were contained in the subject or could be read into it; the general atmosphere of decadence and depravity; the mixture of religious and erotic elements—these had attracted other artists of this *fin de siècle* period, though Wilde's treatment, in French, was the most outspoken (it scandalized the public for some time to come). It goes far beyond the interpretations of Flaubert's short story *Herodias* or Massenet's opera *Hérodiade*.

In the Gospel accounts Salome (she is not mentioned by name but merely referred to as Herodias' daughter) asks for the head of Jochanaan (John) at the instigation of her mother. Herodias' hatred of the holy man stems from his public disapproval of her marriage to the Tetrarch, Herod Antipas, her own husband's half-brother. Just what happened to her first husband is not altogether clear in the historical accounts.[3] The implication in Wilde's drama is that she had him murdered in order to be able to marry the Tetrarch, while Herod's first wife, anticipating a similar fate for herself, had left the country. Certainly there is nothing in the historical sources to indicate the motive from which Salome acts in Wilde's play: the wounded pride of a spurned woman. The young princess' intense physical desire for the incarcerated prophet is the product of Wilde's own imagination. But he has her act not merely out of a desire for revenge: the climax of Wilde's drama is reached when Salome, having obtained her wish, proceeds to make love to the severed head of Jochanaan. That she should then be killed at Herod's command also is the playwright's invention.

Wilde's reputation as *enfant terrible* of the literary world had been established before *Salome*. The play failed in Paris and predictably ran into trouble with censors in many places, but became a success in the German translation by Hedwig Lachmann. This is the version Strauss came to know in Berlin; in spite of its notoriety the play appealed to him as an opera subject. A Viennese poet had begun to prepare a libretto for Strauss, but he soon discarded it and decided to compose the text of the play itself—a rare procedure in opera. Substantial cuts including the omission of several characters were made in order to preserve the dramatic pace and impact of the spoken play. This objective was fully accomplished: the opera is short, in one act, and contains few if any static moments.

Strauss's opera, even more than Wilde's play, was a *succès de scandale*. Some of the members of the cast resented the "un-

[3] For further historical background see Ann Lingg, "Meet Herodias," *ON*, March 13, 1965. She does not indicate her sources.

singable" parts as well as the subject itself. The singer who was to have the title role refused it, saying that she was "a decent woman." Perhaps she realized that her figure would not render her very convincing in the role of a fifteen-year-old seductress. Only by various threats to the management did Strauss succeed in getting the work ready for the Dresden premiere.

Censorship troubles followed in other cities. In Berlin *Salome* was banned by the emperor, while in New York the owners of the Metropolitan Opera House threatened to cancel the lease after one performance. Among the New York critics William Randolph Hearst, while admitting Strauss's musical genius, referred to *Salome* as a "so-called work of art . . . a crime committed in the name of music. . . . In a public performance, a woman is made to declare a desire to bite the swollen lips of a severed head, 'as one would bite a ripe fruit.' If that is art, will somebody set to music that department of Armour's packing house in which they make the sausages." *Salome* was not again performed there for twenty-seven years.

For some of the public Strauss had already acquired some notoriety through his tone poems, especially through some of the unconventional orchestral effects. *Salome* contains numerous further instances of startling instrumental sounds, to say nothing of the novel tasks assigned to the human voice. In *Elektra* (1909) Strauss progressed further in these directions.

The storms that accompanied rehearsals and early performances of *Salome* do not account for its lasting appeal. For that there are dramatic and musical reasons besides the purely sensational, shocking qualities of the piece. It appeals, today as then, through the directness of its musical language in both lyrical and violent passages. The strong psychological and symbolic undertones in the drawing of individual characters and scenes fascinate today as they did in the first decade of this century, when the writings of Freud began to appear.

This kind of musical drama dispenses with the traditional formal frame. There is no overture, not even a short instrumental introduction. The curtain rises at once, and the drama unfolds without any preliminaries—the "slice of life" technique already encountered in operas of the verismo school. Equally abrupt is the opera's ending. Salome's long, ardent monologue, culminating in her "I have kissed thy mouth, Jochanaan," is followed only by Herod's brief command, "Kill that woman!" In but nine measures, molto allegro, his order is carried out and the final curtain falls.

From the opening lines on, Wilde's language, through its rich imagery, conveys the flavor of biblical poetry—the Psalms, or

"I have kissed thy mouth, Jochanaan!"

the Song of Songs. But it is not merely picturesque: through references to symbols such as the moon it establishes moods in typically Expressionistic fashion. The full moon illuminates the opening scene and, with few interruptions, remains in sight to the end of the opera. Its effect on the principals of the drama differs; what they see in it and what they say about it is intended to reveal something about each of them, like an interpretation of a dream. The young page refers to it first, comparing its strange appearance to "a woman rising from the tomb," a comparison that helps to establish the ominous, foreboding mood felt through the entire work. To Narraboth, enamored as he is of Salome, the moon appears "like a little princess; . . . one might fancy that she was dancing." Later on Salome herself compares it to a chaste woman, while to Herod the moon is "a mad, drunken woman, looking everywhere for lovers." Characteristically it is Herodias, the calm, determined one, who replies "the moon is like the moon."

The structure of Wilde's drama results in a gradual buildup of tension. With Narraboth's opening exclamation "How beautiful is the Princess Salome tonight!" a lyrical mood is suggested, but it is soon dispelled. The young page is concerned because Narraboth watches the princess so much. This is dangerous: "terrible things may happen." From then on the feeling of impending doom never quite leaves us; rather it is strengthened by a variety of omens and revelations. The depraved nature of Salome's lust for Jochanaan reveals itself gradually. That she should enjoy listening to his accusations of her and her mother seems strange until we realize that she derives sensuous pleasure from the very sound of his voice. She begs him to continue. This excited passage then leads into her song in praise of the prophet's beauty. Salome's passion is ardent and unrestrained from the beginning of this scene, but while at first she exclaims about the beauty of his body it becomes increasingly clear that it is his ugliness that both attracts and repels her. "Thy body is hideous . . . like a tomb, full of loathsome things." The frenzy of this scene increases as Salome exclaims, three times, "I want to kiss thy mouth, Jochanaan," each exclamation a half-tone higher than the preceding one. The frenzy subsides, temporarily, when the prophet, having cursed her, returns to the cistern. During the next scene Salome remains in the background. When Herod promises her anything she wants, her plan is made; now the tension again mounts steadily. Herod desperately tries to have Salome change her mind. His language and music reflects his mounting anxiety, caused by her relentless and ever more insistent "Give me the head of Jochanaan." At last he sinks back in his seat, weak and despairing. From then on to the end of the opera Salome's thoughts and actions are in the foreground.

Though childlike, petulant, and impulsive, Salome, through intuition and cleverness, knows how to use others for her own goals. In this way she is strong, while Narraboth, the young captain, is weak. His infatuation with Salome has made him helpless—a plaything and a tool she uses cleverly and cruelly. Weakness of another kind characterizes her stepfather, a "neurotic tyrant" (Del Mar). He vainly attempts to assert himself against his domineering wife. He is completely wrapped up in himself: it is not Narraboth's death that concerns him, but the unpleasantness of having stepped in a puddle of blood. He fears many things, both real and imaginary: the noise of wind and flapping wings, the light of moon and stars. Though he fears Jochanaan he also admires him—"He has seen God"—but he is terrified by the possibility that the dead might return to life. His weakness is symbolized by the death ring, taken from his finger and conveyed to the executioner before Herod realizes what has been done.

In a different way from Salome, Herod contributes to the fragrance of decadence that pervades the opera. His unfatherly interest in Salome constantly annoys Herodias, who is cold, rational, and determined. She really despises Herod, whom she presumably married for the prestige of his present position, though she also reminds him cynically of his low origin. Her matter-of-factness is reflected in her music: the ominous storm which he imagines hearing and which we hear in the orchestra subsides each time Herodias firmly says "No, there is no wind."

Strauss has been accused of giving weak music to Jochanaan, a charge that he denied though he admitted that his original plan had been to have the prophet appear "somewhat grotesque." As the opera stands, Jochanaan and his music represent effectively the different world to which he belongs, and this contrast produces much of the dramatic tension. It extends to some of the opera's themes. Salome's principal theme, heard at the very beginning of the opera and countless times thereafter, has a sensuous, feminine (or feline) quality, expressed through its curving line, rhythmic subtlety, and colorful harmonic implications. It is chiefly given to the clarinet. This is quite different from the hymnlike theme that represents John the Baptist: solid and confident, with its simple, triadic outline and clearly defined rhythm, predominantly played by brass instruments:

EXAMPLE 1   Salome's Theme

EXAMPLE 2   Jochanaan's Theme

Jochanaan shudders at Salome's unashamed, lustful demands, sternly censures and finally curses her. But his music never reaches the degree of intensity and violence found elsewhere in the opera. At times the prophecies of the holy man result in an abrupt change of mood, particularly effective when his voice is heard from a distance, offstage—lyrical, dignified, clear, and certain.

Salome contains no ensemble scenes. This may be rare in an opera but is the logical result of composing a stage play where several people do not normally speak at the same time. Nor is there a chorus, but several times the excited disputing among the

Jews (four tenors and one bass) produces lively, contrapuntal writing. They argue about questions of dogma and scriptural interpretation, among themselves and with the two Nazarenes. There is something grotesque about this group, and the musical treatment of the scene is somewhat reminiscent of a contrapuntal passage in *Till Eulenspiegel,* said to represent disputing among the university professors.

The Oriental atmosphere, rich and glowing, the brutal, passionate, and mysterious moods—all these are masterfully established by the music. Strauss once remarked that previous operas on Jewish or Oriental subjects had failed to convey this atmosphere— something he accomplished, without recourse to actual Jewish melodies, primarily through his harmonic language and colorful orchestration. In moments of violence especially, his use of dissonance still appears striking today, with clashes that are difficult to explain within the framework of traditional harmony. Here Strauss creates Expressionistic effects that point ahead to Schoenberg. Many passages show remarkable harmonic usage: Herod's frenzied pleading with Salome not to hold him to his oath, and his eventual giving in (No. 298 in the score); or the ominous interval between Herod's consent and the appearance of the "large, black arm of the executioner," a passage also noteworthy for details of its orchestration. In Strauss's own words, "the needs of the moment inspired me with truly exotic harmonies. . . . The wish to characterize the *dramatis personae* as clearly as possible led me to bitonality."[4]

[4] *Recollections and Reflections,* trans. L. J. Lawrence (London, 1953), p. 150. Bitonality—the simultaneous use of two keys—can be found in the opera's last scene. (*Recollections and Reflections* copyright 1949 at Atlantis-Verlag, Zurich. English translation copyright 1953 by Boosey & Hawkes Ltd. Reprinted by permission of Boosey & Hawkes, Inc.)

309

Naturally, Strauss's advanced harmonic style also is evident in his melodic writing. An abundance of awkward chromatic intervals resulted in the verdict "Unsingable," just as many instrumental passages in the earlier tone poems had been declared unplayable. In time, both verdicts turned out to be wrong. Again, we often are on the border of tonality. Salome's lines, while she anxiously waits for the blow of the executioner's sword, are savage and menacing:

EXAMPLE 3

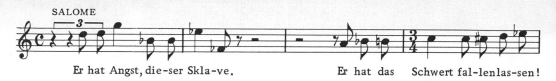

[*He is afraid, the slave! He dropped his sword!*]

Passages of this kind, chromatic and complex, also foreshadow the agitated, speechlike effects, the *Sprechstimme* of Schoenberg and Berg (see below, Chapter 12).

Strauss associates themes with the principal characters; their treatment in some ways resembles Wagner's *Leitmotiv* technique. A theme may be subtly modified, and it may recur, almost hidden, but for a good psychological reason. An example of this procedure is provided by the theme, so central to the dramatic outcome, with which Salome so insistently demands the head of the prophet:

EXAMPLE 4

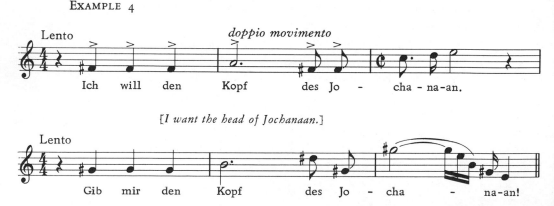

[*I want the head of Jochanaan.*]

[*Give me the head of Jochanaan!*]

This theme is closely, yet rather subtly, related to her earlier expression of longing and desire:

EXAMPLE 5

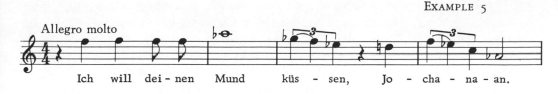

Allegro molto

Ich will dei - nen Mund küs - sen, Jo - cha - na - an.

[*I want to kiss thy mouth, Jochanaan.*]

After she is spurned and cursed by the prophet, her feelings contain the new element of revenge—a transformation well expressed in the new theme. A study of the orchestral score reveals some subtle details of Strauss's characterization of the princess: we can practically point to the moment when the thought of asking for Jochanaan's head first occurs to her. Following his curse, there is a long orchestral interlude, the beginning of which is marked "mit äusserster Leidenschaft." During this interlude Salome remains on stage, sitting on the edge of the cistern, brooding. Herod then enters and, in time, Salome agrees to dance for him. Again the orchestra reveals her real motive in complying with the Tetrarch's wish, immediately before she begins to dance:

EXAMPLE 6

Engl. Horn, Heckelphon, Viola

Trumpets, Trombones

There are other instances in which the orchestra, through specific themes, illuminates a situation or subtly reveals some psychological development.

The variety and ingenuity of Strauss's orchestration is evident on every page of the score. To obtain the effects he wanted the composer frequently had recourse to unorthodox instrumental devices. A phrase in the contrabasses is marked "howling"; it precedes the soldiers' question "Who are those howling wild animals?" (meaning the Jews who are disputing excitedly). During the interlude of the prophet's execution the lowest string of some of the basses is tuned down; another bass player is to produce a special effect (according to instructions in the score) "resembling the subdued moans and groans of a woman." When the arm of the executioner at last becomes visible, Strauss's mammoth orchestra is silent, except for a swelling roll on the bass drum. In another place a passage in the violins is marked "verschmiert" (blurred), while both the first and second violins play *col legno* (with the stick, rather than the hair, of the bow).

Such a large, active orchestra and such a complex score impose special requirements on the singers.

Generally speaking, the acting of the singers should contrast with the excessive turmoil of the music [and] be limited to the utmost simplicity. . . . Turmoil on *and* in front of the stage—that would be too much. The orchestra alone is quite adequate.[5]

By the same token, Strauss was famous as a restrained, unassuming conductor of his own operas. With every detail of interpretation indicated in the score he saw no need to indulge or exert himself in conductorial antics.

Der Rosenkavalier (Dresden, 1911)

Having shocked the world with *Salome* and the later *Elektra* (1909), Strauss, to the surprise of many, turned to a *Komödie für Musik*—a comedy of manners and morals, delightful and charming. Hugo von Hofmannsthal, who had furnished the libretto for *Elektra,* gave him a fairly detailed outline of the plot, and the composer realized at once the subject's great dramatic and musical possibilities. The progress of their collaboration can be traced in the extensive correspondence between poet and musician, fascinating because one gains an understanding of the difficulties with which such a complex work of art comes into being. As soon as Strauss had read the text for Act I he wrote an enthusiastic letter to Hofmannsthal. Impressed by the clarity with which the characters were drawn, Strauss immediately composed whatever parts of the text were supplied. As the score grew, numerous changes were made in both text and music, some of them affecting the nature of the work as a whole. The original plan had been for a *Spieloper,* pure comedy; eventually, *Rosenkavalier* included much that was serious and thoughtful. This is due, in the first place, to the way in which the part of the Marschallin was modified, turning her into a complex, noble human being.[6] Hofmannsthal was chiefly responsible for this change, but in other instances Strauss—the stronger, domineering personality—demanded changes in the text to conform with his dramatic and musical ideas. Only one and a half

---

[5] *Recollections and Reflections,* p. 151.
[6] This transformation is not unlike Wagner's developing the part of Hans Sachs in *Die Meistersinger* (see above, p. 203).

years elapsed from the time of Hofmannsthal's original scenario to the completion of the opera—a remarkably short time in view of the length and complexity of the score and the many revisions of text and music. The speed with which they both worked can be inferred from a letter by Strauss saying that while the score of Act II was already being engraved he was "still waiting anxiously for [the concluding text of] Act III."

From the beginning Strauss had realized that excellent acting and staging would be needed to put this comedy across—acting of which the opera singers in Dresden would not be capable without some special coaching. He therefore called on Max Reinhardt, then the most distinguished director for the legitimate stage, to help— an unorthodox step that caused some ruffled feelings but contributed materially to the success of the premiere.

Though public and critics had some reservations, mostly about the moral aspects of the plot and about the waltzes discussed below, *Der Rosenkavalier* has held a place of special affection in the hearts of opera lovers ever since its first performance. The reasons are many, including the literary quality of the text, written with a care often lacking in librettos. The language is beautiful; few if any other opera texts read so well.[7] Hofmannsthal was a writer of the first rank, not a manufacturer of librettos. He used both poetry and prose, with fine insight, according to each dramatic situation, and without falling into rigid rhyme schemes.[8] Some poetic passages, warm and simple, have the flavor of Austrian folk song, e.g., the duet "Ist ein Traum" in Act III. Throughout the opera Hofmannsthal gives us an abundance of genre painting, a lively, convincing, and amusing picture of Viennese life during the reign of Maria Theresa, even though some of the details are not authentic. We meet three levels of nobility: the true aristocracy represented by the Marschallin; the impoverished but all the more class-conscious country aristocracy (Baron Ochs); the recently titled, wealthy, and socially ambitious merchant (Faninal). We learn a good deal about moral standards, not only from Ochs's Leporello-like account of country maidens and warm summer nights; about the place and behavior of servants; and about ceremonial such as the Marschallin's *lever* scene, said to have been inspired by two paintings by Hogarth. Many turns of phrase —the forms of addressing people of varying social standing—help to convey a picture of the time, while the dialect spoken by Ochs, "Mariandl," and others contributes local flavor. Humor pervades the entire opera, though only rarely of the slapstick variety:

[7] There even exists a recording of Hofmannsthal's text—read by actors, not sung.

[8] The duet in Act II, "Mit ihren Augen voller Tränen," score Nos. 116 ff., may be studied with this in mind.

I feel that an atmosphere of prevailing gaiety . . . is more likely to
meet with lasting favor, even from the general public, than any approach
to the coarser style of operetta. Look at *Die Meistersinger* or *Figaro*—in
each of these you will find little to excite laughter, but much to smile at.[9]

Humor dominates entire scenes, or it appears in little touches: the
three orphan girls blurt out their thinly veiled but well-rehearsed
appeal for money, only to be directed to start again, softly, by their
mother. The desperate Faninal embraces Ochs, who winces because
of his wounded arm; the tenor's Italian aria is interrupted by
Ochs's table pounding.

Written with loving care, Hofmannsthal's text contains much
detail that may go unnoticed in listening to a performance; its
careful reading (even *after* attending a performance!) will be all
the more rewarding.

Hofmannsthal's intention had been to entitle the opera *Ochs
von Lerchenau*. Strauss's wish to have Octavian be the title role
prevailed, yet most people who know the opera will agree that the
central figure in the drama is the Marschallin. The interpretation
of this difficult but rewarding role has been a challenge to some of
the greatest sopranos. Too often the author's intentions are disregarded, and the entire play receives a twisted interpretation.

[9] Letter of July 3, 1909.

The Marschallin must be a young and beautiful woman of thirty-two at the most who, in a bad mood, thinks herself an "old woman" as compared with the seventeen-year-old Octavian. . . . Octavian is neither the first nor the last lover of the beautiful Marschallin, nor must the latter play the end of the first act sentimentally as a tragic farewell to life, but with Viennese grace and lightness, half weeping, half smiling.[10]

She realizes, even at thirty-two, that "time is a strange thing" that will rob her "sooner or later" of what makes her desirable in Octavian's eyes. But this reflection about age is not a rebellion; too often it is overacted. Her soliloquy in Act I ("Da geht er hin") is telling. She does rebel, at first, against the injustice of the world that allows a good-for-nothing like Ochs to marry Sophie. But "Man ist dazu da, dass man's erträgt" ("We are here to bear it all"), and this philosophy she applies to her own inevitable aging as well. To Octavian she shrugs off her sadness as a passing mood, but it remains with her through the rest of the opera. She also shows vivaciousness, even a sense of daring, of playing the comedy to the full, as when she decides to show to Ochs the medallion with Octavian's picture. Nevertheless, an aura of gentle melancholy surrounds her much of the time, giving a bittersweet flavor to the important finales of Acts I and III. To have the little Moor reappear at the very end of the opera does more than provide a light touch before the final curtain. It symbolizes her generosity: she has sent *her* servant to retrieve a handkerchief belonging to Sophie—the young girl who has replaced her in Octavian's affections so very soon.

Many a listener today finds it difficult to understand that in an opera with so much realistic detail a principal male role should be sung by a soprano—a "trouser role" in the tradition of Mozart's Cherubino, who may indeed have been the model for Octavian. Whatever reasons Strauss may have had, he created a part that is difficult to make credible. Octavian's high voice implies physical youth. At seventeen he is supposed to be boyish and impulsive, but also an impetuous and ardent lover.[11] During the crisis of Act II he is resolute and daring, so much so that even Ochs, though annoyed, is impressed and reminded of his younger years. Octavian must be just as convincing here as in the first act, when, in his childlike desire to ignore the reality of daylight, he closes the curtains. Not enough: he must also play well the part of Mariandl; play it well enough, at any rate, so that Ochs, who is not a complete fool, does not discover the hoax, puzzled as he is by the resemblance. Both Octavian and especially the fifteen-year-old Sophie must appear young, rather unsure of themselves, and shy.

[10] *Recollections and Reflections,* p. 160 f.
[11] A passionate love scene wisely was left to be imagined before the curtain goes up on Act I; it is musically suggested by the orchestral introduction.

Hofmannsthal insisted on this interpretation of both roles; particularly in their duets he wanted the general mood to be naïve and tender, with "no Wagnerian screaming at each other."

Baron Ochs von Lerchenau is a less complicated character, though here, too, the librettist warned of overacting and oversimplification. Ochs is a country squire, in daily contact with the common people who work his land, but he has had the customary education of a nobleman "whose manners in the Marschallin's living room are good enough, at least, to avoid his being thrown out after five minutes" (Hofmannsthal). Ochs freely expounds his views on a variety of subjects. We are well informed about his moral principles (or their lack), not only through the famous and often drastically cut account in Act I but also through more casual remarks. When Octavian and Sophie have been surprised together, Ochs is mostly annoyed because of the resulting delay in signing the contract, not by any impropriety: "Gratulier' Sie sich nur, dass ich ein Aug' zudruck'! Daran mag Sie erkennen, was ein Kavalier ist!" ("Thank your lucky star that I am willing to ignore the whole thing! That ought to show you what the word 'gentleman' means!"). In spite of his masculinity and virility, of which he boasts a good deal, he practically faints when his skin has been scratched by Octavian's sword. The dueling scene and ensuing commotion, incidentally, were suggested by the composer, who

Ochs after the dueling scene, Act II.

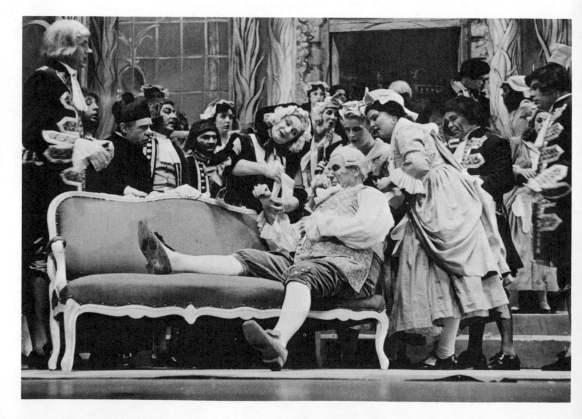

saw a need for some dramatic high point that was lacking in the original plan for Act II. In the tavern scene Strauss also contributed to the portrayal of Ochs. He suggested that an extremely comical effect could be created by having the Baron's feelings of tenderness suddenly give way to rage, because of Mariandl's resemblance to the rascally Octavian. The librettist, on the other hand, took issue with some musical matters:

A certain detail in your setting of Ochs' air has quite upset me—I refer to the line "Muss halt ein Heu hier in der Nähe dabei sein." . . . This is conceivable only in a quiet tone, as a stupid piece of coarse familiarity. . . . It must be whispered. . . . It gave me quite a shock to find the word "Heu" shouted fortissimo![12]

Herr von Faninal, less important than the characters discussed so far, is nevertheless drawn with loving care. He is greatly elated to have arrived socially by marrying off Sophie to a member of the real aristocracy. One chuckles at some of the details through which his true nature—that of a merchant—is revealed, as when he urges his servants to get help for the wounded Ochs: "Gelaufen um den Medikus! Geflogen! Meine zehn teuren Pferd' zu Tod' gehetzt!" ("Get a doctor! Run! Fly! Don't care if you ruin my ten expensive horses!"). The humiliated man constantly changes from towering rage against Sophie and Octavian to obsequious courtesy to Ochs, who, he hopes, will still condescend to become his son-in-law. In his predicament he appears both pathetic and comical.

Hofmannsthal's libretto was bound to be successful in the hands of a composer of Strauss's calibre, for it has everything: lively action, broad and subtle humor, quiet, lyrical scenes with some sentimentality; beautiful sets and costumes. The *lever* scene and the presentation of the rose offer much to the eye and make up for the absence of a ballet, which Hofmannsthal at first had intended to include. The mood of certain scenes, and some of the character drawing, remind one of Wagner's *Meistersinger*—a resemblance of which Strauss was quite aware. Having considered a more lively finale for Act II—he thought about a brawl involving the servants—he decided against this in order not to "give competition" to the second-act finale of *Die Meistersinger*.

Rosenkavalier is a period piece, a portrait of mid-eighteenth-century Vienna. To evoke its atmosphere Strauss wrote a group of delightful Viennese waltzes, although he knew as well as his critics that the waltz was not known then. He did so because the waltz is characteristically Viennese and because of the associations with gaiety, carefree festivity, and exuberance which the dance still has

[12] Letter of June 12, 1909.

The presentation of the rose, Act II.

today. Minuets, gavottes, and other authentic dances of Maria Theresa's age would hardly have served that purpose.[13] Waltzes enliven many scenes of this opera, always establishing a mood of gaiety and *joie de vivre*. A waltz accompanies the tender breakfast scene early in Act I (No. 49); it subsides when Octavian's mention of the field marshal dispels the happy mood. Another waltz begins (No. 88) when the Marschallin realizes, to her relief, that the intruder whose voice she hears in the anteroom is not her husband. To the accompaniment of a waltz (No. 143) Ochs furtively tries to arrange a supper date with Mariandl; the melody reappears at the appropriate time in Act III. With still another waltz tune (No. 90) he brashly tells the embarrassed Sophie that in his company "no night will be too long." This melody returns at the end of the same act while Annina delivers a letter from Mariandl—a letter that puts Ochs back in a jovial, contented mood (No. 236). We also hear it during the tête-à-tête in Act III (No. 101). Most of the dinner music played backstage in Act III

[13] Strangely enough, while the anachronism of the *Rosenkavalier* waltzes was the target of much criticism, the waltzes in Gounod's *Faust* seem to have escaped it. One might raise the question whether an opera should employ music only in the style of the period in which it takes place—medieval for *Faust*, Rococo for *Rosenkavalier*. Even Strauss's critics probably would answer that general question in the negative.

318

consists of waltzes (Nos. 51, 61, 66); others are heard from the pit orchestra (Nos. 74, 82). Subtly waltzlike strains, at a slower tempo, can be detected even in the great trio later in this act (No. 285, "Hab mir's gelobt").

The Viennese flavor that permeates the score does not come from the waltzes alone; it also characterizes the orchestral writing in passages such as

EXAMPLE 7

[*I shall send you a messenger, Quinquin, to let you know whether I shall take a drive in the Prater.*]

where the Marschallin speaks of taking a drive in the Prater.

Both vocal and orchestral writing in this gay opera lack the harsh, angular quality of *Salome,* the sudden leaps, the forced-sounding notes in extreme registers. Instead melodic lines are warm and ingratiating, whether sung or played. Most of the vocal writing is in continuous dialogue, though there are some solo passages that are fairly well set off from what precedes and follows—in mood if not by an actual pause. In the first act these are the tenor's Italian aria, Ochs's long description of his amorous activities, and the Marschallin's soliloquy, "Da geht er hin." Several ensemble scenes are more easily extracted from the opera and are at times heard on the concert stage. Since Octavian is a mezzo soprano, there is a preponderance of high voices, which Strauss combines in several beautiful and moving duets and trios, especially in Act II ("Mit ihren Augen voller Tränen," No. 116) and at the end of Act III (the trio "Hab mir's gelobt," No. 285, followed by the brief duet "Ist ein Traum," No. 297). The confusion of the *lever* scene, containing so much simultaneous activity, gave Strauss an opportunity for ensemble writing on a large scale, as did the scene following the duel, and the imbroglio of the last act.

Skillful orchestral writing enhances the opera's dramatic effectiveness throughout. Strauss rarely makes use of a general orchestral sound, unless a massive, tutti effect is needed. Even then one or several instruments may stand out, for an effect of special intensity. Thus the high trumpet tone at the emotional climax, following the Marschallin's final leave-taking. Strauss's orchestration is always imaginative and to the point, and in its timbre captures the mood of the situation. At times the large orchestra is reduced to a few instruments, producing the texture of chamber music (string quintet and woodwind quartet in the Marschallin's soliloquy, No. 271). Elsewhere ingenious combinations of instruments provide striking color effects which may be combined with equally striking harmonies:

EXAMPLE 8

As in *Salome,* the orchestra takes part in the presentation of themes. Since they function as leading motives, the attentive listener will find frequent hints and explanations of the action in the accompaniment. The Octavian theme, youthful and vigorous, is transformed into a waltz when he appears disguised as Mariandl.

*Act III in a San Fran-
cisco production.*

EXAMPLE 9

EXAMPLE 10

When the Marschallin explains that because of her migraine she
has given orders not to be disturbed, the orchestra reveals the real
reason, with a theme from the love music of the opening scene
(No. 14, "Wie Du warst"). Later in the act she predicts that
Octavian will leave her in favor of someone younger—and the
orchestra suggests, subtly, Sophie's theme (No. 316).

    Der Rosenkavalier has remained Strauss's most successful
opera. When the composer's eightieth birthday was celebrated in
Vienna by a festival of his operas, *Rosenkavalier* received its 330th
performance there. In all there had been 1,112 performances of
Strauss operas there up to that time: the equivalent of four complete seasons of "nothing but Strauss."[14]

[14] Alexander Witeschnik, *Wiener Opernkunst* (Vienna, 1959), p. 226.

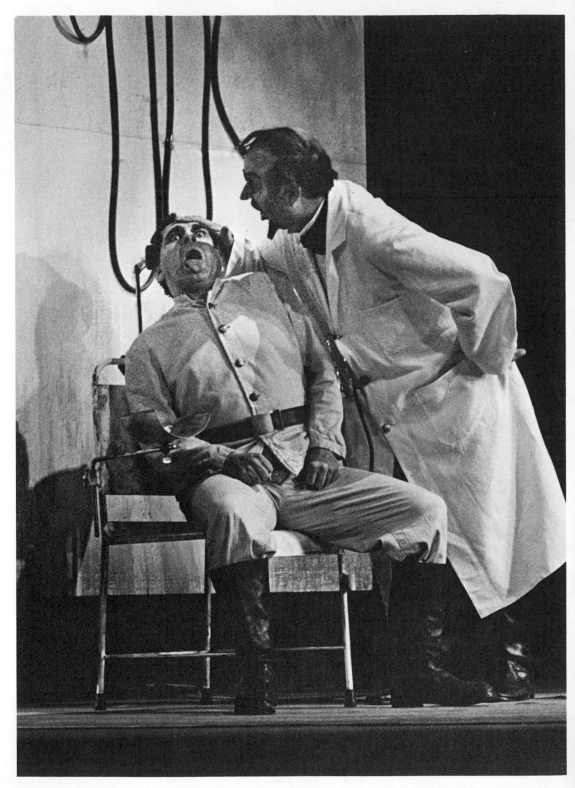

"Wozzeck, show me your tongue." Scene from a San Francisco production.

12

EXPRESSIONISM AND THE LITERARY CLIMATE OF THE TWENTIES

As an artistic movement expressionism emerged at the time when Freud and others were beginning the serious and scientific study of the workings of the human mind, especially its hidden aspects, which they tried to explain and explore by probing into the subconscious. Expressionism in all the arts was an essentially introspective movement. In the visual arts this showed itself through a lack of concern with realistic portrayal of the outside world. Instead the artist tried to reveal, through choice of subject and through his technique, something about his (or someone else's) inner self. Expressionistic art emphasized the serious and problematic—man's fears, phobias, obsessions, and frustrations—areas that were also being studied in the relatively new fields of psychology and psychiatry.

The First World War and the events

An example of expressionism in painting: "Night," by Max Beckmann (1918–19).

that followed it gave much impetus to the movement, especially in painting and literature. Expressionism was much in evidence in Germany during the 1920's, a period characterized by great political and economic upheavals, by disillusionment, skepticism, and cynicism. Germany had lost a war; instead of fervent patriotic sentiment and the fulfillment of political promises there was revolution, inflation, and hunger. Bitterness was widespread about the plight of veterans—many of them maimed and penniless— who a few years earlier had marched away to war as heroes, amid garlands, banners, and brass bands. The high life of war profiteers stood in glaring contrast to the plight of soldiers, widows, orphans, and other victims. Under these circumstances artists quite understandably became bitter critics of society. Established political, moral, and religious principles were widely questioned and satirized through various media, including the legitimate theater, cabaret, and various types of musical theater.

Several operas written during the 1920's reflect this political and artistic climate, especially in Germany and Austria. American jazz had a marked influence on the musical theater, as it generally did on European composers after World War I. Of these lighter theatrical works with a social, political message, few have survived. Kurt Weill's *Dreigroschenoper* (*Threepenny Opera*, 1928), with text by Bertolt Brecht, has had long runs in recent years. *The Rise and Fall of the City of Mahagonny*, 1927, by the same authors, has fared less well. *Dreigroschenoper* is a free adaptation of John Gay's *Beggar's Opera*, drawing parallels between the corruption of London society in the 1720's and the Germany of Weill's day. Brecht's text is not merely witty but bitter, cynical, and at times sad. Philosophical observations are cruel and to the point: "Erst kommt das Fressen, dann kommt die Moral" ("First, a full stomach; then we'll talk about morals"). Operas by Ernst Krenek (*Jonny spielt auf*, 1927; there have been some recent revivals) and Paul Hindemith (*Neues vom Tage*, 1929) belong here. Hindemith's "merry opera" is a satire on contemporary morals and manners, poking fun at the marital tiffs of modern couples (in this respect it is comparable to Schoenberg's *Von Heute auf Morgen*, 1930), at German officialese and bureaucratic language, sensational newspaper headlines, and the advantages of modern hot-water boilers.

Qualities of expressionism can be found in later operas as well. Benjamin Britten's *The Turn of the Screw* (Venice, 1954), to name but one, is not the most successful work by today's most successful English composer of operas, but it contains characters that fascinate because of their psychological complexity. A number of scenes are dark, brooding, and ominous, at times leaving us to doubt whether certain incidents of the plot are real or imagined by the protagonists.

Another type of musical drama in vogue during the Twenties (though with less relation to expressionism) is the *Lehrstück* ("teaching play") : theater intended to be more than passive entertainment for young audiences. Works of this kind—the term "opera" is hardly appropriate for some of them—may involve audience participation and be intended for young performers as well. Hindemith's *Lindbergh Flight* and *Wir bauen eine Stadt* are examples; later ones include Benjamin Britten's *The Little Sweep*, 1949, and *Noye's Fludde*, 1958.

Alban Berg, *Wozzeck* (Berlin, 1925)

Among more substantial, serious, and typically Expressionistic operas, works by the Viennese composers Arnold Schoenberg (1874–1951) and Alban Berg (1885–1935) stand out. Schoenberg's *Erwartung* (*Expectation,* 1909) and *Die glückliche Hand* (*The Lucky Touch,* 1913) both dramatically and musically display qualities of expressionism: the ominous, nightmarish moods and words; symbolism of language, action, and staging, occasionally bordering on the surrealistic. At many points jagged melodic lines, harshly dissonant harmony, and thick orchestral texture reveal kinship to Strauss's *Salome.* Neither of these short operas, however, has succeeded in gaining a place in the repertory comparable to that held by Berg's opera *Wozzeck.*

Berg's source of inspiration for *Wozzeck* was a play written almost a hundred years earlier by Georg Büchner (1813–1837). Quite early in his short life Büchner had become deeply concerned with the political upheavals of the post-Napoleonic era. He took part in the Hessian revolt, his sympathies, as always, being with the underdog. In an appeal published secretly as a pamphlet he urged the peasants to revolt, to reject the idea that their lords were entitled to their privileges by divine right. "This government is by the grace, not of God, but [the devil]." By 1835 it was no longer safe for Büchner to remain at home. Soon after he had fled, first to Strasbourg, then to Switzerland, a warrant for his arrest was published.

Büchner's play *Woyzeck,* a fragment, was found posthumously among his papers. It is based on an incident that had taken place in 1821: a wigmaker, Johann Woyzeck, had stabbed and killed a woman out of jealousy. An extended trial followed during which Woyzeck's lawyers entered a plea of not guilty, claiming insanity for their client. Woyzeck had had visions and hallucinations—a persecution complex. A knife, so important in the play and opera, had figured in these visions. The argument, and the consulting of doctors, were unusual for the time. In 1824 Woyzeck was executed, but there was further discussion of the case in medical journals. Büchner, whose father was a doctor, may have come across it there. His play was first assembled and published in 1879 by K. E. Franzos. This version contains twenty-three scenes, though several other scenes were found among Büchner's papers.

In retrospect it does not seem surprising that this strange, powerful drama, with its grotesque qualities, should have been staged repeatedly during the era when expressionism was establishing itself. Berg attended several performances of the play in 1914, was profoundly impressed, and resolved to write an opera on the subject.[1] In arranging the libretto Berg made few changes; no doubt he realized that the rhapsodic quality of the original, the rapid succession of many short scenes, had the makings of an

---

[1] Another drama by Büchner, *Danton's Death,* has also been made into an opera, by Gottfried von Einem (1947).

unusual but powerful musical drama. Generally speaking, short scenes are more successfully set to music than wordy dialogue, though their rapid succession may create problems for the stage director. Some condensation was deemed necessary. Berg's libretto has three acts of five scenes each. With few exceptions it uses Büchner's lines. In one version of the play the final scene takes place in the hospital's dissecting room. This scene Berg omitted— wisely so, most admirers of the opera would say, for the scene with the children, gruesome though in a different way, makes a most moving end.[2] Certain scenes had special meaning for the young composer, who (by the time the libretto was finished) had had some traumatic experiences of his own as a recruit in the Austrian army. (He once reminisced about the strange sound of a whole barracksful of soldiers snoring—a recollection responsible for a similar scene in the opera.)

Berg had finished the *Wozzeck* score early in 1922. Singers, orchestra, musicians, and others found the music extremely diffi- cult, and no complete performance took place until Kleiber pro- duced *Wozzeck* in 1925. The premiere in Berlin was preceded by 137 rehearsals. Its reception was mixed: critics' attitudes ranged from enthusiasm for something new, powerful, and even beautiful to (more typically) devastating condemnation. At the dress re- hearsal already there had been demonstrations and violence of the kind known from many Schoenberg premieres in Vienna ten or twenty years earlier. The first performance was just as lively, though applause eventually won out over hissing and catcalls. One perceptive critic noted not only that Büchner's text was eminently suitable for musical setting but that the music succeeded in bring- ing hidden psychological meanings to the surface.

Wozzeck has remained a most successful example of ex- pressionism in opera. By 1936 it had been performed 166 times in 26 cities and translated into four languages. Until the Nazi regime banned it as degenerate art, it had even been financially successful. Berg had at times been bitter about the lack of recognition given his music in his native Austria. Official recognition of a special kind came belatedly, twenty years after his death, when *Wozzeck* was one of the operas chosen by the Austrian government for the week of gala performances celebrating the opening of the rebuilt Vienna State Opera. Since then *Wozzeck,* Berg's only complete opera, has been acclaimed the world over—a rare achievement for a "modern" opera.

As a play and as an opera *Wozzeck* incorporates qualities of realism and naturalism as well as expressionism. The depressing

[2] For a collation of the play and libretto, see H. F. Redlich, *Alban Berg: The Man and His Music* (London, 1957), pp. 80 ff.

atmosphere of nineteenth-century army life pervades much of the work. A great gap between the officer class and the ordinary soldier had existed in Büchner's day; it was still painfully evident in the Austrian "Imperial and Royal" army which Berg knew well. Both the Captain and the Doctor represent this upper social stratum. Wozzeck and his world are so far removed from their own world that real understanding or compassion is unthinkable, in spite of the Captain's occasional joviality and condescending advice. In their eyes Wozzeck, as a lowly private and orderly, hardly is a human being. He is there to serve the Captain, to take orders, and not to think too much. Experiments and cruel teasing are the order of the day—a creature such as Wozzeck surely can have no feelings worth considering. This strange, frightening world is depicted in a realistic manner. Many dramatic details show a naturalistic, analytical, almost clinical approach: the snoring chorus, the out-of-tune piano in the tavern scene, the dispassionate observations of the Doctor and Captain as they hear Wozzeck drown, and, particularly, the matter-of-fact conversation of the children in the opera's last scene.

Wozzeck, then, is an essentially naturalistic piece, a cruel, unretouched picture of society. At the same time the dreamlike, nightmarish atmosphere, the grotesque and exaggerated qualities of some scenes make the impact of the whole even stronger. I/2 is a scene of this kind, with the strange things Wozzeck sees and hears ("This place is cursed"). The fiery setting sun figures prominently, as does, later on, a large red moon—a favorite Expressionistic symbol reminding one of *Salome* or Schoenberg's *Pierrot Lunaire*. Scenes III/2 and III/4, by the pond, are similar in mood. They are typical for Expressionistic art of the time. As Kerman has pointed out, one can interpret Wozzeck, the Doctor, and the Captain as "ordinary denizens of a distorted world" rather than as "aberrations in the world we know."[3] According to either view the opera takes place in the world of reality; it is not a fantasy, acted out in the realm of the subconscious, like the out-and-out Expressionistic *Erwartung*.

With this basically realistic setting, *Wozzeck* is an especially demanding opera to produce. Acting must be realistic, and many scenes (e.g., the tavern scenes) contain much action, to be synchronized with music of extreme complexity. The quick succession of many scenes also imposes special requirements of staging, with the length of the orchestral interludes determining the time available for changing the sets. For purely artistic but perhaps also for technical reasons Berg had considered film as a possible, if not the best, medium for his opera.

[3] *Opera as Drama*, p. 228.

All the principal characters are carefully drawn: Wozzeck, Marie, the Captain, and the Doctor. With Andres and the Drum-Major there was less need for subtle characterization. In the five scenes of the first act all of these are introduced, one by one, in their relation to Wozzeck:

Scene 1—The Captain
2—Andres
3—Marie
4—The Doctor
5—The Drum-Major

Wozzeck appears here as quiet and repressed. He "takes" injustice without fighting back—too much so. Therefore the explosion, when it comes, is all the more violent. Kicked around by all, he certainly is no conventional hero. In the opening scene his outburst "Wir arme Leut!" ("We poor folk!") is not yet too violent, and his remarks generally make sense. But from I/2 on it is evident that all is not well with him. Throughout the opera events weigh on him increasingly and his mental equilibrium deteriorates accordingly. In the play his abnormality is dwelt on somewhat more: his rambling, incoherent remarks are more numerous, and there are more corroborating statements by others. Thus Andres: "Franz, du kommst ins Lazarett. Du musst Schnaps trinken, das töt' das Fieber." ("Franz, you'll end up in the hospital. You ought to drink Schnapps; that'll kill the fever.")

The opera's second act shows Wozzeck's progressive deterioration. In the first scene Marie's obviously guilty conscience about the earrings arouses his suspicion, while in the following scene the Captain and the Doctor tease him about the Drum-Major. Scene 3 shows his growing certainty of Marie's unfaithfulness. He repeats Marie's "Better a knife . . ." as if hypnotized by the idea: "My head is swimming." In the following tavern scene much of his conversation is incoherent. As he stares at the dancers he has strange visions. The Drum-Major's boasting, insults, and blows in the next scene do the rest. The third act catastrophe is the predictable result of what has happened before. Many analysts of this act claim that Wozzeck "atones for the murder of Marie by committing suicide,"[4] yet this is not stated or implied in the text. Berg's own stage directions indicate "he drowns" (see full score p. 457), an end which is more consistent with Wozzeck's portrayal throughout the opera.[5]

[4] E.g., Willi Reich, in *MQ,* January, 1952, p. 6, this portion of the article being based on a lecture by Berg.
[5] In one of Büchner's fragments Wozzeck returns from the pool and embraces his child. See also George Perle, "Woyzeck and Wozzeck," *MQ,* April, 1967.

Wozzeck and Marie.

Marie, though a considerably less complex character, is neither all good nor all bad. As one of the "poor folk" she has few pleasures in her drab existence and is governed by basic emotional impulses. The strutting, virile Drum-Major in his resplendent uniform holds an irresistible physical attraction for her—an attraction which one understands more as one learns more about the downtrodden Wozzeck and his strange visions and remarks. She is not without qualms of conscience. Genuinely moved by the Bible story, she sees herself as the sinner. A strong sense of independence causes her to blow up at Wozzeck, warning him not to strike her: "Better a knife in my body!" This outburst now remains with Wozzeck, and the knife becomes an obsession.

In his own way the Doctor appears almost as mad as Wozzeck. It is frightening that there should have been models for this character in both Büchner's and Berg's experiences with army doctors. In the opera's fourth scene the Doctor's perverted personality is revealed to us: his fantastic theories about diet and muscular control, amounting to fixations, and his rambling, erratic mind. In his conversation he jumps from one subject to another. His excitement mounts, but he suddenly reminds himself that he must control his temper. "To be angry is bad for one's health, is unscientific!" With scientific detachment he checks on his own pulse. He delights in diagnosing Wozzeck's trouble to his uncomprehending face, as he does later with the Captain: "You have a fine aberratio mentalis, partialis, 2d species, a very nice case!" Soon the thought of future glorious scientific achievements once more sends him into ecstasy, and he has visions of immortality. Again quite abruptly he comes back down to earth: "Wozzeck, show me your tongue," and the curtain falls. Wozzeck is a mere object for the schizophrenic Doctor. The grotesqueness of all this is reinforced by the music; thus in II/2 a lilting waltz forms the background for the Doctor's analysis of the Captain's symptoms.

In his manner the Captain seems demented, too, though to a lesser degree than Wozzeck or the Doctor, since he has neither hallucinations nor theories except for an obsession for doing things slowly and deliberately. He is excitable—one might say that he is "cracked," just as his voice frequently cracks under the strain of excitement. Occasionally Berg writes ensembles in which each participant displays his own character traits. In II/2 Wozzeck, having been teased about Marie's unfaithfulness, expresses his despair, the Captain rants as usual about Wozzeck's being "a good human being," while the Doctor, with scientific detachment, observes Wozzeck: "pulse irregular, face muscles stiff, staring eyes."

Berg's score is among the most complex in operatic history— it certainly was in 1925. Not only does he call for a larger

Wozzeck and the Captain.

orchestra than Wagner or Strauss before him, but he includes a tremendous amount of detailed instruction to singers, players, and others. Dynamics and tempo changes are indicated with precision. Principal and secondary musical lines are indicated with symbols borrowed from Schoenberg. Instructions on how to produce certain sounds, arrows indicating the exact moment when something is to happen on stage, directions for stage musicians to assume their stations, these and countless other details were incorporated in the score. Because of the many verbal instructions contained in the printed score an extensive glossary with English translation is provided by the publisher. With this kind of precision Berg follows the tradition of his teacher, Schoenberg, who, in turn, had continued the practice found in the large scores of Gustav Mahler.

There is more organization and planning in *Wozzeck* than meets the eye and ear of the casual observer. The formal plan of the opera has often been discussed—the composer's own remarks having provided the point of departure. An overall symmetrical arrangement exists: there are three acts of five scenes each; the middle act is the longest. The music of each scene employs, with considerable freedom, formal designs familiar from earlier periods, such as passacaglia, fugue, suite, theme and variations (seventeenth-eighteenth century), sonata movement and rondo (eighteenth-nineteenth century), scherzo, military march, and rhapsody (nineteenth century). The following table shows the basic musical organization of each scene.[6]

ACT ONE (Wozzeck in relation to his environment)

1—Wozzeck and the Captain: Suite
2—Wozzeck and Andres: Rhapsody on three chords
3—Wozzeck and Marie: Military march, lullaby
4—Wozzeck and the Doctor: Passacaglia (theme and twenty-one variations)
5—Wozzeck and the Drum-Major: Andante (rondo)

ACT TWO (Dramatic development)

1—Marie and the child (later also Wozzeck): Sonata movement
2—Captain, Doctor, later Wozzeck: Invention (fantasy) and fugue on three themes
3—Wozzeck and Marie: Largo for chamber orchestra
4—Wozzeck and others at inn: Scherzo with 3 trios
5—Wozzeck and others in barracks: Introduction and rondo marziale

[6] For detailed formal analyses of all scenes the reader is referred to the studies of H. Redlich (*Alban Berg: The Man and His Music,* London, 1957, Chapter IV) and Willi Reich (*The Life and Work of Alban Berg,* London, 1963, pp. 117 ff). See also Reich's above-mentioned article in *MQ*.

1—Marie and child: Invention on a theme (seven variations and fugue)
2—Wozzeck and Marie at pond: Invention on a tone
3—Wozzeck and others in tavern: Invention on a rhythm
4—Wozzeck at pond (later Captain and Doctor): Invention on a six-note chord
5—Playing children: Invention on a perpetual motion in eighth-notes

Here we shall restrict ourselves to a look at the internal organization of certain scenes and the way in which musical form is related to dramatic function. The opening scene follows the pattern of a Baroque suite—a succession of dance movements preceded by a prelude. (Berg also provides a postlude, which consists of the prelude played backwards.) The composer's choice of a suite may have been due to the nature of the text, which consists of the Captain's ramblings: he expresses a variety of thoughts, in no coherent pattern, and there is no dramatic development. A passacaglia serves as formal pattern for the scene in the Doctor's study. Here the "obstinate" repetition of a melody symbolizes the Doctor's morbid preoccupation with his scientific theories. In the scene of Marie's murder ("Invention on one tone") the tone, B, is present throughout, having been anticipated in the preceding orchestral interlude. It moves from the lowest register to high harmonics, played on a solo violin; from there it moves to the harp, to the contrabass, to the violin (tremolo, sul ponticello), and so on. At the end it reaches us with extreme intensity, as a tremendous rhythmic canon presented by strings and winds.

EXAMPLE I

As the murder takes place the tone is mercilessly reiterated on the timpani. In a score of such harmonic complexity Berg's selection of a single tone as basis for the climax shows great dramatic insight. In other scenes the choice of musical form may have been made in accord with purely musical considerations.

There are many subtleties of formal organization. The basic rhythm of III/3 is anticipated at the end of the preceding scene, both in the "canon" quoted above and in the bass drum, bars

Wozzeck after the murder.

114–115. Formal correspondences exist between the act endings, which (according to the composer) are based on identical harmonic progressions. Furthermore, the last bars of Act II (silence, then curtain) correspond to the first bars of Act III (curtain rises, then silence). The question has often been asked to what degree these subtle details of formal organization are of importance to the audience.[7] Berg on several occasions made it quite clear that in this opera the music at all times serves the drama, that he wanted to give to the theater what belongs to the theater. The audience was not to be aware of these suites and inventions but was to be absorbed by the drama, which "extends far beyond the fate of Wozzeck, the individual." In a sense this is no different from the meaning and function of form in much other music, whether in a Beethoven symphony or a fourteenth-century motet. The listener, depending on how much he is at home in a particular musical style, may be vaguely aware of the formal structure of such works—yet his enjoyment is not predicated on this awareness.

Wozzeck is aesthetically neither better nor worse for its "forms." . . . At home one goes with pleasure through the intellectual exercise of tracing all the threads of the various patterns; but when listening to *Wozzeck* one forgets or puts aside most of what one has learned in this way and simply surrenders oneself to the broad musical impression. The non-technical listener, indeed, can do nothing but this.[8]

[7] Thus Kerman, pp. 225 ff.; he calls the opera "over-composed and over-analyzed," pointing out that these details are lost on anyone except the analyst who spends long hours with the score.

[8] Ernest Newman, *From the World of Music*, p. 152. Copyright 1956 by John Calder. Used by permission.

In a way of his own Berg adopted the nineteenth-century technique of associating characters with musical motives or themes. Wozzeck, Marie, the Captain, the Doctor all have themes of their own. But because of Berg's melodic style, so different from that of the operas discussed so far, these motives do not readily impress themselves on the listener. Wozzeck's exclamation "Wir arme Leut!", a sentence crucial to the drama's meaning, is also one of the chief musical themes:

EXAMPLE 2

Wir ar - me Leut !

At times a theme, slightly modified, may be given to different characters who express similar sentiments. Marie's "sigh" or "lament" theme:

The Doctor and the Captain.

EXAMPLE 3

is later voiced by Wozzeck, who has stopped listening to the Doctor's raving

EXAMPLE 4

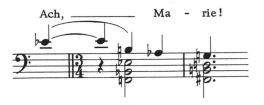

Marie's cry, first to the Drum-Major, later to Wozzeck—"Rühr' mich nicht an!" ("Don't you dare touch me!")—is made to near-identical music. At her death numerous previously heard themes pass in quick review, as many incidents in life are supposed to do at such a moment.

An important characteristic of melodic style in this opera is *Sprechstimme* or *Sprechgesang*—a manner of using the voice that is neither ordinary speech nor singing. Berg explains *Sprechstimme* in the preface to the score of *Wozzeck,* calling it "a kind of rhythmical declamation" that had been previously employed in several Schoenberg scores. Special notational symbols indicate where the pitch of the written note is to be approximated only, by the general rise and fall of the speaking voice. Melodic passages written in conventional notation presumably are to be sung, at the indicated pitches, yet in performance they frequently also are only approximated, though with a singing, not speaking voice. In either case rhythmic values are to be observed minutely.[9] To the listener who hears it for the first time, *Sprechstimme* may seem startling, unnerving, hysterical. Eventually he may find that, because of its intensity, it offers a new but appropriate vehicle for Expressionistic musical drama. In addition to normal singing and *Sprechstimme,* regular speaking with orchestral accompaniment—melodrama—is used. In general, Berg's melodic style shows how far he had abandoned conventional tonality and harmony based on the interval of the third. Skips of a fourth are frequent

[9] See Hamm, *Opera,* p. 39.

EXAMPLE 5

Schies - sen steht je - dem frei !

[Everyone is free to shoot.]

along with the intervals of seventh and ninth.

In his use of melodic dissonance Berg went considerably beyond the style of Strauss's *Salome.* Yet this is not to say that warmly lyrical lines, with suitable accompaniment, are absent from the opera. The opening scene furnishes an example, in bars 146 ff.: "Es muss was Schönes sein um die Tugend . . ." ("It must be a wonderful thing, virtue . . ."), with the "Wir arme Leut" theme wandering through the orchestra.

Several folk songs are heard in *Wozzeck.* Berg was fond of quoting extraneous material (e.g., the folk song, dance, and Bach chorale in his violin concerto), adapting it to his own melodic and harmonic idiom. His folk songs are recognizable as such, for the traditional rhythm patterns, using symmetrical, regular periods, are preserved. This is true of Andres' song, quoted earlier, and of Marie's lullaby with its steady rhythm in $\frac{6}{8}$ time, or of Wozzeck's song in III/3.[10]

The term "atonality," for better or for worse, is generally used in describing the harmonic style of Schoenberg and his school. Neither Schoenberg nor Berg liked the term. What it is intended to convey is the absence of a tonal center or key in this music—again a development the early stages of which can be traced in the music of Wagner, Mahler, and Strauss. A feeling of key is lacking in most of Berg's score, and dissonance no longer functions in the traditional manner of resolving to consonance. For a drama that is consistently tense, with few letups, such a complex harmonic idiom seems appropriate. Certainly today it offers fewer obstacles to the listener than it did in 1925. The interval of the fourth is prominent, harmonically as well as melodically. At times intervals are used for special effects. The feeling of Marie's loneliness—wrapped in thought, waiting—is conveyed by sustained perfect fifths, pianissimo (e.g., I/3, bars 415 ff.). Elsewhere the general harmonic idiom is adapted to specific dramatic purposes.

[10] There the abrupt ending is understandable to German-speaking audiences who know the text of the folk song. It ends with the words "Mein Töchterlein liegt auf der Totenbahr" ("My daughter is laid out on her deathbed"), and Wozzeck catches himself, before singing the last word, cursing. This is the very thought he wanted to forget at the tavern.

To characterize, in a stylized manner, the sound of a military band, there is much playing in parallel thirds, suggesting tonal harmony and traditional band scoring. To evoke a fairy-tale mood, the fifth of the seven variations in III/1 is in f minor, with a key signature—at the precise moment when Marie begins her "once upon a time" story for her child.

Polytonality (simultaneous use of two or more keys) makes its appearance in II/4, the tavern scene—e.g., in bars 425 ff., where the waltz melody is in E flat major but the bass progressions of the accompaniment are in G major. Dramatically this serves to characterize the general drunkenness of the scene: the musicians and everyone else hardly know what they are doing.

Berg's rhythm is as complex as his melody or harmony. Some of his motives are more rhythmical than melodic, such as the "Ja-wohl, Herr Hauptmann" ("Yes, Sir"), uttered on a monotone. While the rhythmic flow of the voice parts generally observes the prosody of speech, orchestral rhythms are apt to be complex and difficult, with different patterns going on at the same time. The coordination of these two presents substantial difficulties, especially when coordination of stage and pit are involved, as in the following example from I/1:

EXAMPLE 6

[*Wozzeck, you always look so out of breath! A good man's not like that.*]

Rhythmic independence is carried even further in I/3, where four bars of the earlier march music are inserted in the lullaby. A footnote in the score indicates that this passage should be in the earlier march tempo, independent of the context at this point.

Throughout the opera Berg's large orchestra provides a rich tapestry of sound, always expressing the dramatic situation and evoking a great variety of moods. It represents equally well the atmosphere of impending doom and of devil-may-care gaiety; it paints and transforms the sounds of nature (e.g., the wind in I/1); it represents the supernatural sounds and sights, figments of Wozzeck's feverish imagination; it practically makes us see Wozzeck stagger into the pond and drown (note the glissandos at the interval of a minor ninth). The full orchestra is heard rarely, for special purposes only. Smaller instrumental combinations of ever changing composition are usually employed, including a chamber orchestra with the instrumentation of Schoenberg's *Kammersinfonie* in II/3. Here the orchestral forces are divided into self-contained groups. Stage music is heard in each act: the military band in I/3, a dance band in the tavern scene, II/4 (including guitars, accordion, and "fiddles" with a tuning different from normal violin tuning), and the out-of-tune upright piano in III/3.

The orchestral interludes have already been mentioned. Here more often than during the scenes the full orchestra is heard. The interludes literally are connecting pieces; they may be based on material from the preceding or following scene and they often provide a gradual transition from one to the other. The music connecting Scenes 2 and 3 in Act I contains a beautiful characterization of nightfall, with distant bugle sounds and various more or less stylized sounds of nature. The interlude between Scenes 4 and 5 of Act III is the longest one and of special weight. It brings back many motives that had been important to the action up to that point.

Early *Wozzeck* audiences were frequently helpless when confronted with the new and violently dissonant music. Today the opera has become a classic. Its wide appeal rests not on its skillful musical construction but on the singularly successful dramatic treatment, the psychological characterization, and the emotional expressiveness of the music.

A recent Vienna production of Wagner's "Das Rheingold," with simple sets and projected backgrounds.

13

NEW CONCEPTS
OF STAGING

IN THE PRECEDING CHAPTERS WE HAVE noted many changes in both the dramatic and musical style of opera, from its beginnings in the Baroque era to the Expressionistic works of the 1920's. As we approach the contemporary scene it may be well to dwell briefly on operatic staging, important in any discussion of opera as something to be seen, not merely to be listened to. New approaches to staging, acting, and directing were made in many dramatic genres after the First World War, not only on the legitimate stage but also in opera and in the emerging art of the motion picture. As new techniques and styles developed, these were not only applied to new works—in our case, operas—but to the established repertory as well.

We have seen that late nineteenth-century opera generally reflected the movement of realism, not only in the choice of subject matter and its dramatic treatment but also through stage sets, costuming, and decor in general. Much attention was paid, especially in the case of historical subject matter, to accuracy, down to minor details of stage props. As electric stage lighting was introduced and improved, the traditional painted backdrops of the candle and gaslight era no longer were acceptable, nor were furniture and other props that were merely painted on canvas. Electric light at first tended to destroy illusion, and bright illumination required greater realism of sets. Acting, especially facial expression, and makeup also were affected. Aside from providing illumination, electricity became increasingly important after 1900 as a source of power, to work elevator and revolving stages and other machinery. In general, many improvements in technology worked at first in the direction of greater realism on the stage.[1] But this development was affected by counter-currents. Many directors, and a growing portion of the public, felt that extreme realism of staging tended to obscure what good theater really was about, leaving too little to the imagination and steering stage designers and directors away from creating an atmosphere of the fantastic, the fairy tale, the mysterious so much more appropriate for a good deal of theater, especially opera. After 1900, as directors and technicians gained experience in handling the new tool of electricity, many of them realized its inherent potential of enhancing and visibly expressing the level of intensity created by poetry and music. By constructing sets that were uncluttered and by suitably poetic, evocative lighting, the visual impression could be immeasurably enhanced.

One of the early proponents of this kind of staging was Adolphe Appia (1862–1928), a Swiss designer with a strong interest in opera, especially Wagner's music dramas. Appia felt that Wagner, as a stage director and designer, had handicapped himself, never allowing his staging to reach the level of eloquence of his poetry and music. Appia brought a new, creative approach to the use of light. Stage lighting does not merely illuminate: it creates mood and atmosphere; it also helps in establishing a feeling of depth, of third dimension. Appia also gave a new quality to his sets through the use of simple platforms, stairs, curtains, and cyclorama. His views on the relation between scenery, acting, and music in opera were set down in a thoughtful book, first published in 1899.[2] In many ways Appia was applying symbolism to the staging of musical drama; his views may be related to

---

[1] Herbert Graf's very informative book *Producing Opera for America* (New York, 1961), pp. 25 ff., contains a good summary of these changes; it includes diagrams, cross-sections of stages, and other illustrations.

[2] *La musique et la mise en scène;* English translation, *Music and the Art of the Theater* (Coral Gables, 1962).

Opposite: Wagner's "Das Rheingold," Scene 4. Top: The original (1876) set, at the same time Romantic and realistic. Bottom: The same scene in a 1962 Bayreuth production by Wolfgang Wagner.

those of Gordon Craig and others in the field of the legitimate stage.[3] Alfred Roller's famous Wagner productions in Vienna reflected some of Appia's suggestions, as did, to a lesser extent, the sets which Josef Urban, who knew Craig's and Appia's theories, designed for the Metropolitan Opera and other stages in the United States.[4] Others, too, were at work during this period: two young Americans, Norman Bel Geddes and Robert Edmond Jones, made important contributions to stage design at the Met after World War I.

Twentieth-century stage design in these and other ways has been related to stylistic trends in the visual arts. The influence of cubism, with its tendency to simplification and abstraction, its concentration on simple, basic shapes, is evident in stage sets of the kind just discussed. The general trend toward simplicity and functionalism in contemporary design extends to architecture, interior decorating, and even to machinery as well as to staging: a getting away from the cluttered stage in favor of simplicity of lines and shapes. Simplification of the set also tends to concentrate attention on the singer-actor. Much scene design today shows an affinity to abstract painting, to the use of color, including lighting, for nonrealistic, Expressionistic effects. Sets may convey the atmosphere of a dream world, nightmarish or fantastic and nostalgic, reminiscent of canvases by Dali, Di Chirico, or other surrealistic painters. Special lighting effects can be created with the help of projection, whether still or animated, whether abstract or realistic. Photographic projection for some time has been successfully used (in Europe more than in America) in lieu of cumbersome realistic scenery or props. Unusual experiments involving simultaneous projection of several filmed backgrounds with live action in front of the screens and with singing that is partly live, partly recorded, have recently been carried on with success by Vaclav Kaslik of the Prague National Opera. In a 1968 production of Offenbach's *Tales of Hoffmann,* the action (partly realistic, partly surrealistic) was carried on simultaneously on two stages—a main stage in front and a raised second stage.

Symbolism in stage design has maintained its importance from Appia's days to the present. A minimum of props and an emphasis on more-than-lifesize, massive walls and iron bars characterized a *Fidelio* production by Karajan in Vienna, suggesting the atmosphere of violence and oppression that permeates the opera. Very dim lighting, typical of Karajan's productions in

[3] The subject is well discussed by Graf, *The Opera and Its Future in America,* Chapter 7. See also Geoffrey Skelton, *Wagner at Bayreuth* (New York, 1965).

[4] Late in his career Wagner himself is said to have turned against too realistic costuming and makeup. Having made the orchestra invisible, he now almost wished to have done the same for the stage. See also Roller's remarks (1909) as quoted by Graf, *Producing Opera for America,* p. 40.

Offenbach's "Tales of Hoffmann" at the Deutsche Oper, Berlin: The 1968 production (staged by Vaclav Kaslik, with sets by Josef Svoboda) with simultaneous action on two stages.

general, reinforces this; even for the finale, happy and triumphant, the lighting is not brilliant. In another recent *Fidelio* production in Germany the basic set represented the Berlin Wall, a symbol with strong emotional implications for most Germans during the 1960's. Walls certainly are important in *Fidelio,* though the introduction into Beethoven's opera of this symbol has been criticized by some as mere sensationalism—a way of making artistic capital out of a burning contemporary political issue. One reviewer has referred to the "disease" of relating everything to ourselves and of arranging works of art according to the needs of the day. A 1957 Cleveland production of *Tosca* was done in modern dress, arena style. The locale was given as an unnamed Iron Curtain country, the time "tomorrow." Such practices are objectionable in the eyes of many if they involve liberties with text and music. Herbert Weinstock has deplored the great liberties which some stage directors, editors, and producers take today with older operas, especially with early nineteenth-century opera buffa. Their eagerness to make works palatable and appealing to twentieth-century audiences results not only in distortions of plot, text, and music but also in the introduction of "gimmicks" in the stage business.

For example, Doctor Dulcamara, in a Metropolitan production of Donizetti's *L'elisir d'amore,* instead of making his entrance standing up in a cart, descends on the stage with a balloon. Few conductors, in our age of style consciousness and respect for musical scholarship, would take similar liberties with an orchestral score of the same period.[5] To this the defenders of such practices may answer that they are stressing the timeless qualities of a work by relating it to settings or events of our own day. Certainly attempts of this kind are more frequent in our century than in times past, and they are found in spoken plays as well (e.g., a production of Shakespeare's *Julius Caesar* in the milieu of Mussolini's Italy).

Since the mid-1950's, many Wagner productions at Bayreuth, under the direction of Wieland (d. 1966) and Wolfgang Wagner, have reflected some of these new trends. Because of the strong tradition established on that stage by Richard Wagner himself, avant-garde approaches to scenery design and lighting have met with strong criticism. Nevertheless, the new Bayreuth ideas have been transplanted to many other European houses. Many sets feature an almost totally bare stage and very subdued lighting. The tendency is toward simplification in other ways also: in crowd scenes there is a minimum of motion and acting, people being deployed in static groups. In *Lohengrin,* for example, the chorus is arranged in a geometric pattern and the singers remain motionless through an entire scene. They represent a collective force or shape in the total visual picture, rather than a number of individuals.

One of the most influential and successful contemporary stage directors is Walter Felsenstein of the Komische Oper in East Berlin. Characteristically for our age Felsenstein is chiefly motivated by a belief that opera must be good theater, dramatically and visually convincing. The term *"Musiktheater,"* rather than "opera," is widely used with this meaning.

Felsenstein came to opera from the theater: he was an actor, and he plays no musical instrument. In his formative years he was disappointed with opera performances he attended because of the routine acting, lacking in dramatic conviction. He has consistently opposed "theatrical" acting, whether on the legitimate stage or in opera, and he works for integrated productions that are convincing in every visual detail. He has objected to most singers' persistent desire to shout. "Forte," he has remarked on occasion, means "strong," not "loud." He insists on adequate stage rehearsal time, believing that the director must do more than tell the singer what positions to assume and what gestures to make at a given time.

[5] Herbert Weinstock, "The Germ and the Virus," *Saturday Review,* December 25, 1965.

Rather, he sees the director's job as that of explaining all details and implications of a dramatic situation to the singer, who then must create his own interpretation and communicate it to the audience. Unlike many of his colleagues, Felsenstein has shown a preference for staging contemporary operas, since these always are allotted more rehearsal time.[6]

In Felsenstein's view the stage set assumes an important function: it must not be mere "Dekoration"—the German term for "stage set" used during the nineteenth century—but it must "play along"—it has to be an organic part of the performance. The action takes place in it rather than in front of it. Felsenstein is skeptical about the French custom and current vogue of asking famous painters to design sets. Too often they are not men of the theater, and what they contribute is apt to look more like a picture gallery than an organic part of the drama. Felsenstein's sets are apt to be traditional; he does not advocate any particular ism. Not only set design, but acting and all other aspects of a performance, including the translation of foreign-language operas, receive careful attention. Felsenstein and other leading directors (both artistic and administrative) today are hopeful that the *Musiktheater* concept will establish itself with the general public, which for too long has been satisfied with mere beautiful singing by famous stars. Excellent staging, it is also felt, can make palatable and attractive an opera that might be musically avant-garde or difficult for other reasons. This is comparable to what happens in some motion pictures: the attention of the viewers is focused on what they see on the screen, though at the same time, via the sound track, they are exposed (and thus "conditioned") to music they might consider difficult or even unenjoyable if heard by itself.

Experiments with other than the traditional proscenium stage have included the field of opera, though this is true more of Europe than of the United States, where architectural experimentation has lagged and few modern houses have been built. Tent and arena theaters have served for productions of "opera in the round," but opera presents special problems for that kind of staging, the position of orchestra and conductor necessarily being fixed.[7]

In the total picture of opera today, these and other experiments with new concepts of staging are rarer than traditional productions, offering great realism in every detail of staging. Act II of *La Bohème,* as given in Vienna during several recent seasons, is a particularly successful example of the latter. The set, represent-

[6] W. Felsenstein and S. Melchinger, *Musiktheater* (Bremen, 1961).
[7] *Producing Opera for America,* pp. 104 ff.

ing a street in front of a Paris cafe, is constructed on several levels and conveys very convincingly the atmosphere of a bustling holiday crowd. Realism of this kind, approaching that of a movie set, lavishly executed, often brings audience applause as soon as the curtain rises.

Yet even with generally realistic staging, the late nineteenth-century manner cannot simply be transplanted into our own age. The various movements in the fine arts just mentioned have affected tastes even of those who prefer traditional staging. As Herbert Graf observes, Wagner's first Bayreuth productions would not please today's audiences—they would look old-fashioned, like magazine illustrations from the period. Tastes in costuming also have changed, as have our ideas of beauty. "Lohengrin with a beard would not so readily win the interest of modern women as in Wagner's time when a beard was the symbol of manhood."[8]

Steadily rising costs have led to some ingenious practices in stage design. A number of productions in recent years have been moved in their entirety from one opera house to another, transportation costs being less than the cost of a new production. Such arrangements may even span two continents. The sets for one

Act II of "La Bohème" in Vienna: An unusually elaborate realistic set by Franco Zeffirelli.

[8] Herbert Graf, *Opera for the People*, pp. 97 ff.

production—Donizetti's *Daughter of the Regiment*—were used in Palermo, Sicily, and then shipped to Dallas, Texas. Large houses in different parts of the world may effect exchanges of this kind, the result being a greater number of new productions at both places than would otherwise be financially feasible. A new *Ring* production by Karajan for Salzburg was begun in 1967, to be completed in the 1970/71 season. Each production was being brought to the Metropolitan, and performed with essentially the same cast. Savings of an additional kind were expected from this procedure: with the same sets and singers more of the available rehearsal time can be used for lighting rehearsals, something of special concern to Karajan.

Concern with greater dramatic credibility in opera has increasingly led to the employment of stage directors from the legitimate theater and motion pictures. The opening season of the Metropolitan Opera National Company, 1965/66, brought to that institution experienced directors with a variety of backgrounds, including José Quintero, a New York theatrical director, and Toshio Aoyama, who had come to operatic fame with the *Butterfly* production at the Metropolitan in 1957. Jean-Louis Barrault, actor and director of French stage plays and films, has directed *Wozzeck* (Paris, 1964) and *Faust* (New York, 1965), bringing new ideas of staging to both operas. Likewise the Italian director Luchino Visconti has done operas in London, Milan, Vienna, and elsewhere, having achieved equal or greater fame with motion pictures (*Boccaccio 70; The Leopard*) and stage plays by Chekhov, Cocteau, and Tennessee Williams. Ingmar Bergman, Sweden's most successful film director today, also has directed opera (*The Rake's Progress*, Stockholm, 1961;[9] *The Magic Flute*, Hamburg, 1963), as has Margherita Wallmann, who came to opera from a background of modern dance.

The staging of opera, then, has changed a great deal during the twentieth century, incorporating some of the experiments carried on in other dramatic media. Though it has been claimed that operatic staging tends toward conservatism, new approaches are being tried today. Those mentioned in the preceding pages are but a few of them. Indeed, such changes and experimentation are indispensable if opera is to retain its appeal today, especially for the younger segment of the public.

[9] For some details about this *Rake* production see Stravinsky and Craft, *Dialogues and a Diary* (New York, 1963), pp. 165 ff.

Tom Rakewell in the brothel scene of "The Rake's Progress" in San Francisco.

14

NEOCLASSIC OPERA

AFTER THE INTENSE EMOTIONALISM OF late Romantic music, and after the equally intense concern with the dark and problematic that characterized Expressionistic art, the inevitable reaction set in between the two World Wars. Twentieth-century neoclassicism represents a return to some of the aesthetic and artistic values of earlier periods, a favoring of objectivity rather than soul-searching individualism, clarity of expression in place of impressionistic vagueness.

The term "neoclassicism," like "classicism," has a variety of musical connotations. Composers again were seeking the simplicity, grace, and serenity admired in so much Greek and Roman art as well as in music from the late eighteenth century. Gracefulness meant a turn from overwhelming masses of sound to the restraint of smaller vocal and instrumental combinations, while the desire for clarity was reflected in shorter and simpler musical structures. Transparent contrapuntal writing was favored over thick, complex harmonic texture, and composers of instrumental music in particular favored the simpler forms of pre-Romantic music. Since this often meant a return to *early* eighteenth-century musical practices, the term "neo-Baroque" at times would seem more applicable, but it has not come into general use.

An antisentimental outlook had characterized the theater after World War I, especially in Germany. While this is reflected in drama on political subjects—hard, satirical, matter-of-fact— such an outlook also pervaded other types of drama. Emotional restraint rather than effusiveness, stylized language and acting, universal meanings—these are some of the characteristics that caused the term "classic" to be applied.

Ever since its inception opera had shown an affinity for classical subjects. Early opera dealt with these almost exclusively; in the eighteenth and nineteenth centuries, as we have seen, a wealth of other dramatic resources were tapped. It comes as no surprise that the rekindled interest in the aesthetic values of classicism should, in our own century, have brought with it a favoring of opera subjects from antiquity. Neoclassicism is not a mere imitation of earlier art, and in the case of Neoclassic opera in particular the ways in which these subjects have been treated vary a good deal. Even the most casual study of both text and music of the following works (not all of them operas, but all involving both drama and music) will reveal this. Some are faithful to the classical myth, while others treat it in a free, fantastic, parodistic, or anachronistic manner, mixing legend with modern history, and using modern language or contemporary dramatic devices.

Arthur Honegger, *Antigone* (1927; text by Jean Cocteau, after Sophocles)

Carl Orff, *Antigone* (1949); *Oedipus der Tyrann* (1959; texts for both by Hölderlin, based on Sophocles); *Prometheus* (1968; based on Aeschylus)

Egon Wellesz, *Alkestis* (1924; text by Hugo von Hofmannsthal, after Euripides)

Ernst Křenek, *Orpheus und Eurydike* (1926; text by Oskar Kokoschka); *Das Leben des Orest* (1930; text by the composer)

Darius Milhaud, *Orestie* (a trilogy based on Aeschylus, translated by Paul Claudel, composed 1913–1924)

Benjamin Britten, *The Rape of Lucretia* (1946; based on several sources including Livy and Ovid)

Hans Werner Henze, *The Bassarids* (1966; based on Euripides' *The Bacchae*)[1]

[1] See also Grout, *SHO,* Part 5, "The Twentieth Century."

After his ballet scores (still his most frequently performed works today) for *The Firebird* (1910), *Petrushka* (1911), and *The Rite of Spring* (1913), Igor Stravinsky (born 1882) wrote works on a significantly smaller scale—simple, even austere by comparison. His *Soldier's Tale* (*L'Histoire du soldat,* 1918) stands in marked contrast to the earlier works, requiring a small number of dancers, instrumentalists, and a narrator—all on the stage. American popular music of the time, particularly its rhythms and instrumentation, appear as a major source of inspiration for this work. Numerous later Stravinsky scores reflect both his interest in subjects from antiquity and his attraction to eighteenth- and early nineteenth-century music, leading him to rework music of other composers. *Pulcinella,* 1919, is largely based on melodies by Pergolesi. With the *Symphony of Psalms* Stravinsky turned to a liturgical text. The impersonal, ritualistic quality of a text from the Vulgate, in a "dead" language, appealed to him. Several years earlier he had written the opera–oratorio *Oedipus Rex.* This work

**STRAVINSKY
AND NEOCLASSICISM**

is based on the Greek drama by Sophocles, in Cocteau's French adaptation, but here again Stravinsky believed that a monumental, less personal effect could be achieved by having the text translated into Latin. A speaker, in white tie, narrates the action in an unemotional manner. The singers stand like statues; they do not act. This quality is emphasized by the music, especially in the choruses.

Several ballet scores on classical subjects followed. Having finished the score for the ballet *Orpheus* (1947), Stravinsky, who had composed several shorter operas earlier in his career, made plans for a full-length opera.

Igor Stravinsky, *The Rake's Progress* (Venice, 1951)

During a visit to Chicago in 1947 Stravinsky had seen a series of eight paintings by William Hogarth entitled "The Rake's Progress." They impressed the composer from the beginning as a succession of operatic scenes, and the milieu of eighteenth-century England evoked by Hogarth suggested a work with some of the qualities of opera from that era—a small-scale work, with few roles, and with small chorus and orchestra.[2] A friend suggested W. H. Auden as librettist—a poet well acquainted with English literature from that period and with experience in writing lyrics for music. Stravinsky's enthusiasm grew as the collaboration progressed and a scenario was developed. Both librettist and composer knew that *The Rake's Progress* was to be the kind of "Mozart-Italian opera we both most desired." In writing the text, Auden drew on the further collaboration of Chester Kallman. The libretto was finished in 1948; Stravinsky spent three years on its composition. The premiere of the first full-length opera by the distinguished composer was a major musical event—and a successful one. Within a short time the opera was produced all over Europe; it reached the Met in 1953 and has been in the world repertory since then. A Stockholm production by Ingmar Bergman, the well-known motion-picture director, was especially successful.

William Hogarth (1697–1764) is best known as a painter–commentator on life in English eighteenth-century society. He is said to have conceived of series such as "The Rake's Progress," "The Harlot's Progress," and "Marriage à la Mode" as close to stage sets, treating a subject in painting as a dramatist would in a play. "The painting is the stage; the men and women in it are the actors." To tell a story through pictures and thereby to point a moral was not unusual during Hogarth's time and for some time to come. His paintings contain a wealth of detail, much of it

[2] Igor Stravinsky, "Reflections on the Rake," *ON*, February 9, 1953.

apparent on close inspection only, and of symbolic significance for the moral story. The series soon achieved great popularity as engravings; "The Rake's Progress" appeared in that form in 1735.[3]

Stravinsky has said that in Hogarth he found the quintessence of eighteenth-century England, with its characteristic color, manners, and morals, and that this as well as the theatrical quality of the paintings attracted him. Librettist and composer succeeded well in transplanting the spirit of the paintings into their opera. Originally they had planned to stay close to Hogarth, but eventually the story developed according to their own plans. These included the invention of two major characters not seen in the paintings: Nick Shadow and Baba the Turk. The former fulfills a number of dramatic functions: in particular he personifies the element of evil (which Tom Rakewell does not personify), providing a foil to the part of Anne. Tom's marriage to Baba, suggested by Nick, becomes an important part of the drama, with implications that could not have been suggested by a painting. In Hogarth, the Rake marries an ancient hag. To have Tom marry Baba is the most ingenious departure from Hogarth's moral tale, based on reasoning that is considerably more sophisticated than one would expect to find there. People, Nick's argument runs, are slaves either to pleasure or duty, and the only person who is free is the one "who chooses what to will . . . whom neither Passion may compel nor Reason can constrain." As Nick puts it,

> What deed could be as great
> As with this gorgon to mate?

Nick's "devilish" suggestion, greeted at first by skepticism and then by roaring laughter, leads to the more fantastic complications of the opera.

The episodes with Baba gave the librettists the opportunity to expand the tale beyond the eighteenth-century framework by adding fantastic, even surrealistic touches, such as having her sit motionless from II/3 (winter morning) to III/1 (spring afternoon), and then complete the sentence which she had begun in the earlier scene. Nor is the episode of the bread machine found in Hogarth. Other modifications were made for dramatic purposes. In Hogarth's first tableau the father (rather than a distant uncle) is presumed to have died, an event suggested by the women's tears. In the opera the father has a fairly important role. In the painting of the marriage ceremony, the young girl (whom the Rake pre-

---

[3] A reprint of several of Hogarth's series, with eighteenth-century commentary, was published by Lear Publishers (New York, 1947).

Four engravings from Hogarth's "The Rake's Progress." Above: As soon as the father (in the opera a rich uncle) dies, the house is ransacked for hidden treasures.

Below: The Rake, having come into money, is surrounded by purveyors of luxuries.

Above: The Rake squanders his wealth and health.

Below: Bedlam.

Tom Rakewell learns from Nick Shadow of his inheritance.

sumably had seduced earlier) and her mother are seen in the background, arriving in order to protest the marriage. Other scenes show the Rake in the gambling house bewailing his losses, and then in prison. Hogarth's last picture must have made a special impression on Auden and Stravinsky, for the stage directions in the score mention several of the figures shown by the painter. The scene is London's hospital of Bethlehem (Bedlam; the lunatic asylum in Hogarth's time); the Rake lies on the ground, chained, surrounded by his fellow inmates, while his still-devoted girl appears in the background.

In all, Stravinsky's opera not only preserves but accentuates the eighteenth-century moral flavor of the tale. It is in the spirit of the period to have the characters' names symbolize their outstanding character traits. Thus we have Anne Trulove, Tom Rakewell, and Sellem, the auctioneer; also, more subtly named, Nick Shadow. The opera's basic moral theme is accentuated in various lines. In the brothel scene Tom is able to define beauty and pleasure. He even realizes beauty's basic flaw: it dies. But significantly he fails when asked to define love. At the end of this scene Nick raises his glass:

> Sweet dreams, my master. Dreams may lie,
> But dream. For when you wake, you die.

Later he similarly counsels his protégé: "Enjoy. You may repent at leisure." And in the epilogue the moral of the play is neatly summed up. Such epilogues, addressed to the audience, are in the eighteenth-century tradition—*Don Giovanni* comes to mind, here and elsewhere in the opera—but occur only rarely in the following century and a half.[4]

The Rake's Progress in many ways follows the conventions of eighteenth-century opera and spoken drama. There are asides addressed to the audience, and there are arias that are commentary and reflection on what has happened, in the earlier tradition. In III/1, even the chorus addresses the audience. In the Stockholm production of the opera the singers delivered their arias to the audience, from the footlights, in a manner said to have pleased the composer greatly. Stravinsky has said on many occasions that he believes in "opera," i.e., the traditional number opera of the eighteenth and nineteenth centuries, rather than in "music drama," in the continuous, Wagnerian manner.

Auden has stated his own reasons for preferring this kind of opera.[5] According to Stravinsky himself, Auden performed "miracles of versification," creating a text that persuasively suggests the flavor of the period. Arias and ensembles had to be written with the dramatic requirements in mind, dividing the text into self-contained units in the Classic manner. Many of these units turned out to be shorter than they are in Mozart's operas and eighteenth-century convention is departed from as well when Stravinsky has one character sing two arias in succession.[6]

As in eighteenth-century English literature, there are numer-

4 Colin Mason points out other similarities and differences between *The Rake's Progress* and *Don Giovanni*. ("Stravinsky's Opera," *Music & Letters,* January, 1952.)

5 E.g., in his article "Some Reflections on Music and Opera," *The Partisan Review,* XIX, No. 1 (January–February, 1952), pp. 10–18.

6 Anne in I/3; Baba in II/3. In both instances so little action or dialogue intervenes that one might look at them as essentially one aria or scene with contrasting sections.

ous allusions to classical mythology. Kerman points to the opera's opening duet, with its reference to the Cyprian Queen (Venus), as indicating the theme of the opera as a whole: the story of Venus and Adonis, in the librettist's own version. The myth is alluded to in several places, not merely at the opera's end, when Tom, insane, believes himself to be Adonis.[7]

Sellem's wonderful address to the prospective buyers also captures the spirit of the age of rationalism, in which nature was seen to hold everything in divine balance. "A thousand lose that a thousand may gain, and you who are the fortunate are . . . also . . . Nature's very missionaries." Tom's monologue at the opening of Act II also brings language evocative of the period. Epilogues customarily were written in a lighter vein, and the *Rake's* librettists conform by providing stanzas in simple verse with naïve rhymes ("Soon or later . . . theater"; "Julius Caesar . . . agree, sir!").

In a more profound way than is suggested by Hogarth, the opera traces Tom Rakewell's "progress." He is not merely a young man who follows the road to perdition because money provides him easy access to vice. The nature of the drama, especially the pact with the devil, may suggest the Faust story, but the comparison does not hold: Tom is no Faustian character. Baba's description of him, to Anne, is to the point:

> He's but a shuttle-headed lad:
> Not quite a gentleman, nor quite
> Completely vanquished by the bad.

Essentially he is weak and lazy—not even a rake at heart. Arrogance and excessive self-confidence characterize him in the opening scene. We note how he interrupts Father Trulove, "the old fool," as though Tom were tired of such parental qualms (p. 10 of the vocal score). That laziness is the cause of his downfall is evidenced by his first aria, ending with his first wish, for money. This ties in with the moral of the epilogue. But money does not bring happiness, and in the brothel Tom weeps. When Nick asks him to define love the question reminds him of Anne, and he wants to leave "before it is too late." Consequently his song of initiation into the Temple of Delight turns out to be a sad song, addressed to the Goddess of Love (again Venus), that she may not forget him. His desires are limited; unlike Faust he does not wish for *all* pleasures, let alone all experiences. Thus in Act II Tom wishes he were happy—and the devil appears again, to further his "progress." Eventually Tom believes that happiness might be achieved

---

[7] *Opera as Drama*, p. 236.

by doing good; quite an un-rakish sentiment. His dream about the bread machine excites him; "I wish it were true"—and once more Nick, his veritable shadow, is present. One gains the impression that the opera's rake has some redeeming qualities, and before the fable ends as it must there is the cemetery scene, not based on

Hogarth. Here Tom's life is at stake, and we might expect retribution to take its course at once. Instead, Tom receives help with the guessing of each of the three cards. The first time, Nick himself suggests Anne, Tom's "Queen of Hearts." With Card Two the assistance seems to come from higher quarters: the "spade" falls, startling Tom and causing him to curse: "the deuce!" Finally, Anne's voice, offstage, gives him the needed courage and clue to guess the third card, and one might expect another opera to end with the salvation-by-woman theme. Just why love seemingly redeems Tom Rakewell only to let him die of a broken heart is an unanswered question, though we may assume that Hogarth's ending of the story had to be respected. Tom does not make crucial decisions but merely utters wishes. Like Faust he soon becomes disappointed with what the devil can provide, but this is not enough to save him.

Tom's "progress," aided and abetted by the devil, stands in contrast to Anne Trulove, his country sweetheart, who is all her name implies. She is not only steadfast but also level-headed. Unlike Tom, Anne does make decisions. At the end of I/3, her great scene, her decision is based on the needs of others: she will leave her father, who "has strength of purpose, while Tom is weak and needs the comfort of a helping hand . . . [Aria:] I go to him." As she arrives before Tom's London house (II/2) she is frightened at first but remembers Tom's and her vows: "A love that is sworn before Thee can plunder Hell of its prey." These words, and the music, are heard again in the graveyard scene, helping Tom to beat the devil at his own game.

Anne's devotion leads her to visit Tom in Bedlam, but level-headed as she is she once more obeys her father and leaves Tom, after having put him to sleep with her Lullaby. "It is no longer I you need."

Father Trulove's remarks about honesty and laziness in the opening scene set the moral tone of the story. He is an upright citizen and at once voices his hope: "May a father's prudent fears unfounded prove," thus adding a dampening third voice to the opening duet. The difference between Trulove and Tom is accentuated in the ensuing conversation in recitative and by Tom's aria "Since it is not by merit we rise or we fall." When hearing of Tom's unexpected inheritance Trulove once more is concerned that it "may only encourage his sins." In the opera's last scene Trulove still reflects piously that "God is merciful and just, God ordains what ought to be."

Nick Shadow, it has been pointed out, is not seen in Hogarth's paintings but was invented by the librettists. As devils go he is not very sly or subtle—but he does not have to be for a weak and not very astute "master" like Tom. He does appear affable and gentlemanlike, in the best Mephistophelean tradition. Until he pronounces the curse on Tom he is, in fact, a likable character. He is terrifying only during these last moments, before he sinks into the grave, and his music changes appropriately during this scene.

Baba the Turk, also an ingenious invention of the authors, forms the center of attention whenever she appears. Her stature would not be the same if she merely were a freak—the bearded lady, the circus attraction. In Stravinsky's words "She enters the drama [though not until it is almost half over] as a monstrosity from nowhere, she leaves it as a sympathetic personality." Certainly she is a puzzling character; Stravinsky admits that it was hard to make her believable. This is accomplished by having her undergo the change from circus attraction, hailed by the waiting crowd, to the utterly commonplace, homey type, chattering away at the breakfast table. Neither she nor Tom is suited for this atmosphere of inconsequential marital bliss (her song is wonderfully commonplace), and the episode is doomed to failure. Soon Baba regains her artistic temper—perhaps to everyone's relief—and smashes objects from her valuable collection. After being awakened from her enforced hibernation she steadily gains in

The auction scene.

stature—a further change that makes her an absorbing character.

In Sellem, the auctioneer, the authors have created a well-drawn minor role. The exaggerated pathos of his introductory speech (in recitative, p. 150) is accentuated musically by the many large intervals, especially descending skips, giving the impression of the well-rehearsed, often-repeated, almost automatic delivery. The ensuing aria and "Bidding Scene," rapidly paced, give a believable portrait of the professional auctioneer who must keep things lively and moving in order to succeed.

Stravinsky has said that while composing *The Rake's Progress* he played and listened to Mozart's *Così fan tutte,* almost to the exclusion of other music, steeping himself in this kind of eighteenth-century opera. His score, standing at the end of his Neoclassic period, does embody much of the general spirit and some specific features of Mozart's late Italian operas. Some features of form and organization suggest Classic models. Chiefly these are the individual closed-form numbers: arias and larger structures, and the harmonic schemes governing key relationships.[8] But there are other structural links between parts of the opera, more commonly found in nineteenth-century music. Robert Craft, in his commentary for the opera's first recording, has pointed out some of these. The music of Anne's prayer in Act I ("O God, protect dear Tom," p. 65) returns in the next act when Tom prays that he may "deserve dear Anne at last" (p. 129). The chorus at the beginning of I/2 is repeated later in the scene. Baba's interrupted aria in II/3 is resumed and finished in the third act, based on the same musical material. In the graveyard scene (III/2) Anne's voice is heard in the melody of her second act aria (p. 97). The street song ("Ballad Tune") is heard several times, with various modifications until, at the end of the graveyard scene, Tom sings it once more, "in a child-like voice." The formal cohesion of an extended scene (III/1) is aided by opening and closing it with identical music.

Recitative and aria structures and some other formal devices (e.g., the use of an ostinato in the graveyard scene, a device as old as the conjuring scenes of early Baroque operas) are the major links between Stravinsky's opera and Classic tradition. The very existence, in a twentieth-century opera, of secco recitative with harpsichord accompaniment is a strong reminder of that tradition. Often the harpsichord begins with the customary sixth-chord (triad in first inversion) and continues to supply a minimal chordal skeleton for the singer, though the harmonies may remind

[8] Discussed in Colin Mason's article.

us of Stravinsky's own practices. Well adapted to the English language, his recitative subtly follows the text meaning. There is no rigid separation of secco and accompagnato—less than in a Mozart opera, where the two are mingled occasionally. Nick's advice (II/1, p. 83) is given in arioso–accompagnato style, with secco chords here and there ("Consider her picture once more"). Earlier in this scene Tom's recitative uses in the accompaniment a bit of the preceding aria accompaniment ("Vary the song"). There is frequent alternation between harpsichord and orchestra during the following conversation between Tom and Nick. The recitative at the end of I/1 starts as conventional secco. When, in response to Tom's question, Nick alludes to the condition of his service, an ominous bass line in the (now instrumental) accompaniment alludes to what will happen, though Nick's words sound harmless enough. Occasionally Stravinsky's accompagnato contains a regular metrical accompaniment while the voice part has the free inflection expected in recitative.

EXAMPLE 1

Arias show variety of formal design. The harmonic layout is often clear, in line with Classical principles. Important motives may be stressed through repetition, as in the opening duet (Anne: "The woods are green" and "With fragrant odors"; then Tom: "Now is the season"; again Anne: "How sweet, how sweet" and "Love tells no lies."). A number of arias are in ternary form, with faster middle section and varied reprise (Tom's "Vary the song," II/1). Others, somewhat simpler, have two basically similar parts (Anne's "Quietly, night," p. 61, with its repeat on p. 63). To indicate the general character of certain arias Stravinsky uses the terms of early nineteenth-century opera. Tom's "Love, too frequently betrayed" is a cavatina, a simple, fairly short, nonsectional aria. Anne's "I go to him" is called cabaletta—the lively, determined continuation of "Quietly, night." Here the composer has provided the traditional brilliant exit aria and act finale, complete with da capo and ending on a high C. Anne's lullaby (III/3) is a simple strophic song with choral interjections.

Tom has been provided with a number of arias that musically show his "progress." He begins with the strong, confident "Since it is not by merit," but his disillusionment already speaks from his aria in the next scene, "Love, too frequently betrayed." The second act opening is in a dejected mood: "Vary the song," a long and expressive aria, leading into a recitative followed by a reprise. The next scene provides no occasion for an aria, though Tom is involved in an impassioned, pleading conversation with Anne and, peripherally, Baba. The latter also dominates, loquaciously, the first part of II/3; Tom does not have a chance. Neither the remainder of this scene nor the following auction does much to further Tom's "progress," and musically he remains in the background. The graveyard scene is all action, given over mostly to expressive recitative and arioso, beginning with the quavering lines that express Tom's terror. He is now changed; his sing-song at the end of the scene and his remaining lines (in the duet "In a foolish dream" and in the finale) are eloquent musical expressions of his troubled and clouded mind.

Only in a few places does Stravinsky's vocal style more than suggest the Mozart era or the early nineteenth century. Anne's cabaletta comes closest to it. The "Ballad Tune" of III/1 suggests English popular music of the time.

EXAMPLE 2

If   boys   had wings__ and   girls__ had   stings

And   gold___ fell from   the   sky, _____

When it returns in the graveyard scene the gaiety seems ironic. Elsewhere the many large skips, including minor and major sevenths and ninths, distinguish Stravinsky's melodies from those of the earlier age. Baba's part has an extensive range, especially in II/3,

EXAMPLE 3

am   ha -   ted, am_____   ha - ted,

the outburst that leads Tom, who no longer can stand it, to shut her off. Here and elsewhere in the opera coloratura occurs, for affective rather than display purposes, with the composer's own characteristic patterns. Tom's melody is especially elaborate in the final scene: it conveys great anguish and agitation, intensified by his insanity. Stravinsky's rhythm also assigns his melodies to our own age, for phrases are irregular, asymmetrical, with his characteristic sudden shifts of accent:

EXAMPLE 4

To hear _____ the cra-shing of fur - ni - ture sma-shing   Or heads

be-ing bashed   in a ta - vern brawl,   in   a ta - vern brawl?

"To hear the crashing . . ." would normally suggest $\frac{3}{8}$ time, but that would be too staid for this scene, which, through its syncopated rhythms, achieves a gay ragtime mood. There are few if any passages with predictable four-bar periods. Accents often occur on a weak beat:

367

EXAMPLE 5

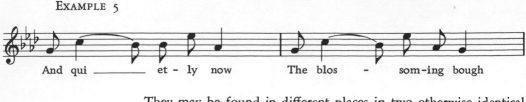

And qui ———— et - ly now   The blos -   som –ing bough

They may be found in different places in two otherwise identical passages:

EXAMPLE 6

For ——— he a - lone, —— for he — a - lone is free Who chooses what to will,

By contrast the duet–finale of II/1, in regular, driving $\frac{6}{8}$ time, strongly suggests the spirit of Mozart's *Così*.

Stravinsky's harmonic idiom, though clearly his own, does show greater affinity to essentially diatonic eighteenth-century usage than to nineteenth-century chromaticism. But primary triads are less favored than they were in the earlier period, while harmonic tension often is the result of dissonant counterpoint within an essentially tonal framework.

EXAMPLE 7

There are numerous passages of this kind in which the inner and bass voices have a strong life of their own. Polytonal effects appear occasionally, as at the beginning of the cabaletta, where the melody outlines a tonic chord (C), the inner voices continue the dominant harmony of the preceding bar (G[7]), while the bass outlines a subdominant (F) chord.

EXAMPLE 8

Most ensembles in *The Rake's Progress* belong to the action-advancing rather than reflective type. The first part of the quartet in I/1 neatly presents the point of view of the drama's principals up to that point, but Nick then reminds Tom of things that must be done (p. 25), to which Anne and Trulove agree. The trio in II/2 is the classic example of the ensemble in which each character comments on what action has taken place. At the end of this trio, in spite of the three independent texts, all three parts end on the word "forever," the meaning being different in each context. The librettists employed this technique in a number of other ensemble scenes. Other ensembles, especially duets, are closer to the earlier, Baroque type: characters sing consecutively, expressing similar sentiments, then join in true ensemble at the end (Tom and Nick, duet–finale of II/1).[9] As he wrote the libretto, Auden tried to distinguish the principals by the pace of their speech. In a letter to Stravinsky Auden stated that

---

[9] Stravinsky, in this opera in particular, was concerned that the text could be clearly understood. This may be one reason why so many of the ensembles contain alternating rather than simultaneous singing.

in order to distinguish Baba in character and emotion from the two lovers [trio, II/2], it seems to me that her rhythm should be more irregular and her tempo of utterance faster. In writing her part I have therefore given any line of Baba's twice the number of accents as compared with the equivalent line of Anne's or Tom's.[10]

The result of this distinction is easily observed in the music (p. 107).

Baba's duet with Anne (III/1) does a great deal to clarify the situation and to advance the drama. This is where Baba rises considerably in stature, giving unselfish advice to Anne while Sellem and the chorus enter into the ensemble with brief interjections. The epilogue, a special kind of ensemble, has already been mentioned. Its formal arrangement is comparable to the eighteenth-century vaudeville finale. Each of the participants sings a different stanza, followed by the quintet ending, also musically different.

Choruses are important in several scenes. The brothel scene opens chorally and ends with the folklike "Lanterloo, my lady." In the auction scene a "Crowd of Respectable Citizens" and other groups participate, sometimes actively as bidders, at other times as bystanders, to the very end when Baba's grand exit is followed by their hushed comment: "We've never been through such a hectic day." The opera's finale, with Anne's Lullaby, enlists the chorus in a manner suggestive of Gluck's *Orpheus*. In both operas the effect is moving. Gluck's chorus of spectres and monsters comments on the effect that Orpheus' singing has on them; Stravinsky's chorus of inmates—invisible in their cells—sings "What voice is this? What heavenly strains Bring solace to tormented brains?" Their final "Mourn for Adonis" in its simplicity suggests a chanted prayer, on repeated notes, mostly in unison.

A small orchestra of Mozartean proportions provides the accompaniment and some independent music. That the wind section lacks trombones makes for a light texture in the bass register. Much of the time the scoring is transparent, giving the impression of chamber music. Pastoral effects are created by lyrical woodwind passages. In the brothel scene Tom's mournfulness, in contrast to the boisterous environment, is expressed by two clarinets. The harpsichord is a prominent member of the orchestra, not only to accompany the secco recitative but especially in the graveyard scene, where the other instruments are often silent. A harpsichord flourish introduces each appearance of Nick Shadow, and a distinc-

[10] Stravinsky and Robert Craft, *Memories and Commentaries* (New York, 1960), p. 152. By permission of Curtis Brown, Ltd.

tive harpsichord passage accompanies the card routine each time. Throughout the opera there are accompaniment passages in which regular rhythm patterns are established and accentuated by the basses, with short notes and afterbeats, in the manner of nineteenth-century Italian opera (I/1, "I wished but once"; III/1, "He loves me still"; "I shall go back"). Persistent accompaniment figures are used to good effect at the opening of II/3, where they characterize Baba's ceaseless chatter at breakfast. Waltzlike music accompanies the wheeling-in of Nick's bread machine. Stravinsky said that he intended this music to be "completely indifferent."[11] The waltz continues in the orchestra, making light of Nick's demonstration of the fabulous gadget to which Tom attaches such profound hopes. A powerful ostinato, largely rhythmical, pervades the graveyard scene, becoming more and more intense until Nick is defeated. Here again a similarly tense scene is evoked: the arrival of the marble guest at Don Giovanni's dinner.

A very short prelude stands at the opera's beginning. Emotionally neutral and thematically unrelated to the opera itself, it is a "curtain raiser" in the manner of Baroque opera from Monteverdi's age. The opening duet is preceded by a brief introduction for woodwind quartet, and the graveyard scene similarly opens with a prelude for string quartet.

[11] Stravinsky and Robert Craft, *Dialogues and a Diary* (New York, 1963), p. 168.

"All the documents must be signed." Magda and the Secretary in a San Francisco production of "The Consul."

15

TWO AMERICAN

OPERAS

Opera in nineteenth-century america for the most part reflected European traditions and styles, through the repertory performed here and through the place opera occupied in the social and artistic life of the country. What had been true of other branches of music also was true of musical drama: American composers not only looked to the Old World for models but frequently obtained their training at the conservatories of Europe's leading musical cities. Understandably, then, the music of these German, or French, or Italian-trained Americans often reflected the style of their masters—a state of affairs that can be compared to the eighteenth century, when Italian composers, especially of opera, were to be found everywhere, providing models for composers of other nationalities.

This is not to say that some American

AMERICAN OPERA COMPOSERS

composers of the late nineteenth and early twentieth centuries did not achieve some originality in their operas. Some of them produced works on American subjects (George Frederick Bristow, *Rip Van Winkle*, 1855; Charles Wakefield Cadman, *Shanewis*, 1918; *A Witch of Salem*, 1926), but most composers showed themselves to be Europe-oriented, both in their choices of subjects and in musical style (John Knowles Paine; Frederick S. Converse, Horatio Parker).

More widespread attempts to produce music, including opera, that was distinctly American were made in the 1930's. This development was paralleled in the other arts. Wider circles became aware and appreciative of Americana—of our indigenous cultural heritage. American folk art—including that of the Indian and Negro—was studied, discussed, and collected. "Early American" became acceptable and even fashionable in the decorative arts. The colorful history of the American West served to inspire artists in many fields: drama, novel, painting, ballet, music. In the history, folklore, landscape, language, and daily life of the Wide Open Spaces artists saw qualities that seemed more distinctly American than those of the East, traditionally considered a melting pot of European cultures.

The interest in Americana received a boost and official encouragement through various government-sponsored projects during the Depression. Artists were commissioned to paint murals in post offices and other federal buildings; the subjects understandably were usually taken from national or regional history. A writers' project produced guidebooks for the then forty-eight states. A major project was the recording of folk music from many parts of the country. To some extent this kind of American nationalism in music is still with us today, though its heyday occurred in the Thirties and Forties. Deems Taylor, George Gershwin, Aaron Copland, Louis Gruenberg, and Ernst Bacon are a few of the many composers who contributed operas with an American flavor.[1] Gershwin's *Porgy and Bess,* first produced in 1935, still is the most successful American opera in a folk idiom—one of the very few to have achieved the status of a classic. Among the operas of Douglas Moore, who was consistently attracted to specifically American subjects, *The Ballad of Baby Doe* has been especially successful.

[1] More recent operas on American themes include Copland's *The Tender Land* (1954), Marc Blitzstein's *Regina* (1949, based on Lillian Hellman's play *The Little Foxes*), and Robert Ward's *The Crucible* (1961).

Douglas Moore, *The Ballad of Baby Doe*
(Central City, Colorado, 1956)

Douglas Moore, a New Yorker, graduated from Yale College
(1915) and the Yale School of Music (1917). Like so many
American composers of his generation he undertook further study
in France, with Nadia Boulanger and with Vincent d'Indy. Ernest
Bloch, too, had a strong influence on Moore's development. Well-
versed in many genres of music, Moore always had a fondness
for dramatic music. Earlier operas, all based on American subjects,
include *The Devil and Daniel Webster* (1938, libretto by Stephen
Vincent Benét) and *Giants in the Earth* (Pulitzer Prize, 1951).
Baby Doe was followed by *Gallantry,* a "soap opera" (1958), *The
Wings of the Dove* (1961), and *Carry Nation* (1966).

Baby Doe, according to Moore's own account, was his

first experience with history. . . . In 1935 I read in the morning paper
of the death of an old woman who was found frozen in a miner's shack
outside Leadville, Colorado. . . . This certainly seemed like opera
material, and the further I got into the story the more fascinating it
was. . . . For some reason this opera never got written in 1935, but I
was overjoyed when in 1953 the Central City Opera invited me to write
it for them to produce. Baby Doe, before her marriage to Tabor, had
actually lived in Central City, so there was great local interest in her
story.[2]

It is difficult to turn historical figures into believable human
beings in an opera, Moore believed: "Once they get into the history
books they seem to want to stay there." But in planning *Baby Doe,*
in collaboration with the writer John Latouche, these difficulties
were solved to the composer's satisfaction. The idea of producing
such a work at Central City, in the territory where much of the
action takes place, was a felicitous one. The first run was a decided success which has led to a number of revivals there.

Some revisions and additions (the gambling scene in II)
were made after the premiere, shortly before Latouche's death. The
first New York performance, by the New York City Center Opera
Company, took place in 1958. The work has since had a healthy
number of productions, including both professional and college
workshop performances.

[2] *ON,* September 30, 1961, pp. 10 ff. Further historical detail is provided in
Caroline Bancroft, *Augusta Tabor* (Boulder, Col., 1961), and in the same author's
Tabor's Matchless Mine (Boulder, Col., 1964).

The story of Horace Tabor, his wife Augusta, and Baby Doe is not only colorful but based on actual happenings. Its general outline, and many details of the plot (e.g., President Arthur attending the wedding) are authentic. A tale of this kind strikes us as typically if not uniquely American: the story of a simple stone-cutter from Vermont who went West, hoping to strike it rich. For twenty years Tabor and his strong-willed, practical wife lived in abject poverty; her frugal managing of the household averted the worst. Eventually perseverance and luck brought a turn in Tabor's fortunes. One silver mine paid off handsomely, others followed, and he quickly became the richest man in Colorado. Such sudden

The wedding.

wealth was distasteful and suspect to Augusta. Her lack of enthusiasm for the high life, her constant reservations about further
speculation, and her distrust of Tabor's judgment inevitably led to
their estrangement. He found warmth and affection elsewhere,
along with enthusiasm for his enterprises. Elizabeth McCourt
("Baby") Doe arrived on the scene at the psychologically right
moment—a colorful character in her own right, not just a "dame."

Having arrived financially, the historical Tabor sought after
political fortunes as well. He did not succeed in being elected to
the Senate, though he obtained an appointment to an interim term
(1883). His support of William Jennings Bryan, who cam-
paigned on a "free silver" platform, is historical, though Bryan's
campaign speech, as delivered in II/3, may not be authentic in
those surroundings. With Bryan's defeat and the abolition of the
silver standard Tabor was ruined. He died in 1899, as he does in
the opera,[3] though its last scene is, of course, a free dramatic
treatment.

History thus provided the authors with a time-tested theatrical formula. The dramatic triangle, an age-old device, is not given
any significantly new slant. After Augusta finds out about "the
other woman" there is a confrontation in which the dialogue
progresses along traditional lines. *Now* Baby Doe will *not* give up
Horace Tabor. Augusta is divorced and Tabor's second marriage is
happy, but his stubborn belief in silver and in the Matchless Mine
leads to his ruin. Augusta shows that she still harbors some affection for Horace: she overcomes her pride sufficiently to attend the
governor's ball (II/1) but not enough to respond to Mama Mc-
Court's entreaties (II/4). Details of the plot are also managed in
traditional ways. Tabor, having finished his "Warm as the Autumn Night" (I/2), passionately kisses Baby Doe's hand. At that
moment "a light goes on in one of the upstairs windows and
Augusta peers out." In a way, and perhaps intentionally, these
conventional touches suggest dramas and novels of the Victorian
age—making the opera a "period piece" in more ways than one.
Since much of the drama, and some of the music, employs time-
tested, conventional formulas, the opera, though Moore's most
successful, has come in for its share of criticism.

Many scenes successfully capture the spirit of the American
West, colorful and exuberant. All the trimmings are there: gun-
toting and yippee-shouting miners, saloons with bouncers, piano-
playing "perfessors," and loose women. Remarks by Augusta's
friends and Tabor's cronies (I/2) show the somewhat strained
efforts of both groups to be "refined." The veneer of culture—

---

[3] All dates given in the printed vocal score are accurate.

operas and string quartets in an 1880 mining town—was indeed thin. The scene with Bryan (II/3) has all the trappings of a political rally. Slogans and jingles sound authentic—the clichés of Bryan's speech, the chorus "We are marching to glory." These and other scenes (opening and wedding scenes) are colorful and effective. They require a fairly large cast, including chorus and dancers —requirements which have made the opera attractive for college and other opera workshops that seek to involve many participants.

In the opera's last scene the authors attempt to give some kind of dramatic cohesion to a story which, in history, extended over half a century. After her divorce Augusta actually had soon lost contact with Tabor and his new wife. But the opera's authors were reluctant to "give her up" after the first act, and she reappears in three of the five scenes of Act II. Some way of at least suggesting Baby Doe's later fate was also considered desirable. Both purposes are accomplished in the last scene, with its glances into the past and future. The idea of a flashback technique seems sound enough for this purpose, especially in view of the possibilities of modern stage lighting. Here again, however, the dramatic devices do not completely succeed. Psychological meanings and implications are a little too pat at times: the "figure" whom Horace addresses as Ma, lovingly, then "suddenly slaps him with

The chorus from Act I.

angry force. He cringes. . . . He tries to embrace her but she suddenly throws her bonnet back and turns: it is Augusta."

Flashbacks in this scene refer to incidents in Tabor's life before the action of the opera itself, though at one point text and music recall the opera's opening scene ("Tabor owns the big hotel"). In performance the end of this scene can be quite moving, with its allusion to Baby Doe's death, many years later. "As a white drift of snow begins to fall, Baby Doe sits by the mineshaft, waiting."[4] With this brief glimpse Baby Doe's continued devotion to Tabor and to the Matchless Mine, after his death, is brought into the drama—a scene which, out of context, would hardly be clear or strong enough for an ending. But here as in other operas (*Tosca* comes to mind) the audience is expected to know the basic historical background—in this case the newspaper account which initially caused Moore to become interested in the subject.

Latouche's language is imaginative and varies according to the dramatic requirements of each situation. In the appropriate moments it is poetic, though rhythmically free and, most of the time, without rhyme. In the lively scenes (opening; wedding; Bryan's speech) it captures the flavor of the period and setting. Elsewhere, occasionally, a line doesn't come off. (Tabor, last scene: "You were always the real thing, Baby.") Each of the major and many of the minor characters come to life as a result of the well-written dialogue.

Augusta stands out as the most absorbing character, because of the conflicts within herself and because she is the one who changes most. Her typical New England frugality was bound to clash with Tabor and his dreams of glory and riches. Both Augusta and Tabor are up against their natural dispositions: once success came to Tabor the conflict was unavoidable. Augusta is domineering by nature. Horace, she feels, is a dreamer. "The man's a child. . . . He knows without me he'd be lost" (I/4). This, of course, represents her own unwillingness to give him up. She feels that she must manage him. Out of such concern she had taken matters in her own hands. Rummaging through his papers—"Men are messy"—she first finds and pockets the check and then comes across the gloves. She is surprised, but not crushed. Though sorry for herself and bitter, she soon regains composure. When Tabor enters she is cold and acid. In the scene with Baby Doe, after the letter writing, she is harsh and adamant—expectedly so, though her manner and her remarks cause Baby Doe to change her mind about giving up Horace. When her "friends" goad her, she nevertheless intends "to do nothing at all"—until she hears that Tabor

---

[4] Directions in the vocal score: "She is standing in front of the shaft."

plans to divorce her. That, the ultimate disgrace, puts her beside herself and rouses her fighting instinct. When Augusta returns in the second act, she has changed. It is ten years later, and she sees things in a different light. "The wrong was done long before you came," she tells Baby Doe, realizing, presumably, that her own manner had turned Horace away from her. She now has come back out of real concern for Tabor—a motherly–wifely protective instinct. Now she asks nothing for herself. And yet, after Bryan's defeat and Tabor's ruin, she cannot bring herself to help, for her pride has been hurt too much during the previous encounter, which, she was determined, was to be the last one.

Augusta's conflicting emotions are well drawn. In comparison, Tabor is quite uncomplicated. The situation in which he finds himself at the opera's beginning is easily understood: after long years of marriage to Augusta, who always belittles, always disapproves, Tabor is "due" for the arrival of a Baby Doe; his reactions and behavior are not surprising. His fanaticism about the Matchless Mine, and about silver in general, becomes his undoing. It causes him to speak harshly to Augusta, though "truly, she came in kindness" (II/1). Instead of heeding her advice he makes Baby Doe swear always to "hold on to the Matchless Mine. . . . You'll keep it always." Two years later he still closes his eyes to the inevitable, though his card-playing cronies try to convince him that silver is done for. They finally give up. "You're cracked. You must be crazy!" Tabor remains the same, from the beginning of the opera to his death.

Baby Doe does change somewhat in the course of the opera. When we first meet her she is the designing female all right; her actions rather than her words betray this in the opening scenes. This is the historical Liz who made a play for rich Tabor, after her own husband had failed to make good in the scramble for silver and had turned from bad to worse. Baby Doe sings and plays the piano, "with a cross-handed elegance," obviously for Tabor's benefit, though at the end of her song she pretends she didn't know he was listening. Her scheme of ensnaring Tabor pays off, but in time the liaison develops into something more substantial: deep affection and real devotion on both sides. Moore's Baby Doe remains faithful to Tabor and to his belief in the Matchless Mine, as did the historical Baby Doe.

A number of minor characters lend color and humor to the plot: Mama McCourt, delighted with her daughter's newly found wealth and happiness, given to malapropisms, is a rewarding though easily overplayed comic role. Ingenious touches are provided by the four "friends" who are "hovering around Augusta like Victorian Eumenides" (I/5), or the State Department "Dandies" (I/6).

Augusta and her "friends."

Moore's music likewise provides the color and flavor of place and period. In the composer's eyes this "use of local color does not make it a folk opera any more than Verdi's *Aida* is an Egyptian folk opera"—a statement[5] that might be disputed by those who detect only a negligible Egyptian flavor in Verdi's score. At any rate, Moore uses no folk tunes as such. The music is all original, though the flavor of the American West pervades a good portion of the score. Simple melodies, with easy-going, frequently syncopated rhythms in the American folk tradition, are plentiful. This idiom (including a "blues" note) pervades the opening scene, as the girls are "carolling shrilly":

Poco meno

THE GIRLS: (*Carolling shrilly*)   EXAMPLE I

Ta - bor owns the op - 'ry house,   Ta - bor owns the big ho - tel,

[5] Quoted by Paul Jackson, *ON,* November 5, 1956.

EXAMPLE 1   (*cont.*)

Ta - bor owns this hon - ky - tonk,

Ta - bor owns _____ the whole damn town. _____

It is again suggested later in the same scene, not only in the tune itself

EXAMPLE 2

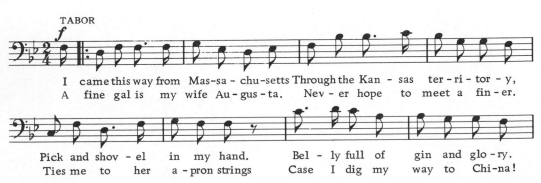

TABOR

I came this way from Mas-sa - chu-setts Through the Kan - sas ter - ri - tor - y,
A fine gal is my wife Au-gus-ta. Nev - er hope to meet a fin - er.

Pick and shov - el in my hand. Bel - ly full of gin and glo - ry.
Ties me to her a - pron strings Case I dig my way to Chi - na!

but also in the arrangement: each of Tabor's verses is followed by the refrain, sung by the chorus:

EXAMPLE 3

CRONIES & CHORUS

Dig, Dig, you go-phers, Dig them holes. Dig a -

way to save your souls. _____ There's _ moun-tains ga - lore of

sil - ver ore. It's cheap in Col - o - ra-do.

Elsewhere, too, there are tunes that sound as though one had heard them before—which must have been the composer's intention. Patriotic airs of the nineteenth century are brought to mind by the women's chorus in the scene with Bryan:

EXAMPLE 4

La, la, la, la, la, la, la, la, la, etc....

Waltzes and waltzlike rhythms are numerous, again suggesting the period. A waltz is heard in the opening scene, accompanying Baby Doe's entrance:

EXAMPLE 5

I beg your par - don.

Can you di - rect me to the Clar - en - don Ho - tel?

The sound of the honky-tonk piano that plays it at this point seems to be part of her characterization. This waltz is heard again as the curtain goes up on Act II, the governor's ball.

The normal prosody of American speech presents no obstacles to Moore's melodic style: it is consistently observed, sometimes within the regular patterns of $\frac{4}{4}$ time in the accompaniment,

EXAMPLE 6

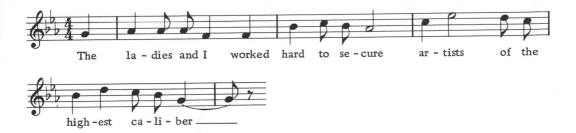

The la - dies and I worked hard to se - cure ar - tists of the

high -est ca - li - ber ____

elsewhere with the help of frequent changes in meter. Much of the time melodies display an expressive declamatory style—a kind of "endless melody" that is neither recitative nor aria, in which the line changes freely according to the nature of the dialogue. Augusta's soliloquy (II/4) shows this manner. Where a sentimental dramatic situation suggests it, Moore does not hesitate to provide melodic lines, and accompaniment, strongly reminiscent of sentimental operettas of the late nineteenth or early twentieth centuries, in this way again providing the flavor of the period. This applies to most of I/2, especially the Willow Song and the love duet.

Except for some of the set numbers (waltzes, arias) Moore's rhythm is free and flexible. Occasionally accompaniment patterns are set up, in ostinato fashion. I/1 contains several: one for Augusta's pleading with Baby Doe,

EXAMPLE 7

Allegro risoluto

Sil - ver is done for, done for, done for.

385

EXAMPLE 7   (*cont.*)

I have news to-day,   from   Wash-ing-ton,   that the

another accompanying Tabor's entrance and repartee.

EXAMPLE 8

Au-gus - ta,   what are   you   do-ing here?

Much of I/6, the wedding reception, is in ⅞ time, which imparts a slightly unstable quality to this scene—intended, presumably, to convey the atmosphere of this gay party, posh and *nouveau riche*.

Moore's harmonic usage has been called traditional and conservative. It shows, at any rate, that he was not the proponent of any one style or school of the twentieth century. In the folklike scenes his harmony is simple and largely diatonic; in the lyrical scenes it becomes fuller and more chromatic. Tensely emotional moments (several occur in I/3) bring a good deal of accented dissonance, though tonalities are always defined. As Augusta discovers the gloves and reads the card we hear a melody that is traditionally and sentimentally accompanied (solo violin and harp), in A flat major, with added sixths. Then, as she reads Baby Doe's name, harmony and rhythm change abruptly. Tonality is seldom lost sight of. At the opening of II/4, as newsboys shout offstage, bitonality is suggested, as a momentary, coloristic effect:

EXAMPLE 9

Baby Doe contains continuous music, but there are self-contained songs or arias. Some have been published separately: Tabor's "Warm as the Autumn Night" (I/2), the Willow Song (I/2), and the Silver Song (I/6) among them. Arias are well prepared dramatically. In I/6 the Dandies declare that "gold is going sky-high, but silver is doomed." Tabor replies heatedly; Baby Doe, to calm everyone down, begins her song by admitting that "Gold is a fine thing. . . . But I am a child of the moon and silver." The aria has good melodic lines, backed up by an effective, traditional accompaniment: little obbligato figures, echolike in places, for solo violin, trilling flutes, harp, and other instruments.

Ensembles frequently are short. Some make their point in a kind of surrealistic manner. The ensemble of Augusta's "friends," with their acid exclamations (I/5), amounts to a caricature ("Shout it from the housetops"). One recent production accentuated this grotesque quality by having only their heads visible. These friends have their counterpart in Tabor's cronies, somewhat more humanly drawn, and in the wonderful "State Department Dandies" who also parrot each other constantly. Moore is at his best in scenes like I/6, the wedding reception, well paced, with constant alternation between solo passages, ensembles, and choral exclamations.

At the time of Douglas Moore's death (July 26, 1969), *Baby Doe* was indeed "on the way to becoming part of our culture" (Julius Rudel), after 171 performances by 34 companies; and it was being continued in the New York City Opera repertory during the 1969–70 season.

MENOTTI'S OPERAS

More than any other mid-twentieth-century American composer, Gian-Carlo Menotti has succeeded in making a place for opera in America as an indigenous, widely accepted form of drama rather than an esoteric, foreign art form intended for a social elite. Though Italian by birth (1911) and citizenship, Menotti not only had his professional training in this country (Curtis Institute, Philadelphia) but has written his most successful works to librettos in the English language. His success as an opera composer began in the United States, was solidly established here (especially on Broadway), and then became worldwide.

After a number of earlier works, *The Medium* (1946), a chamber opera commissioned by Columbia University, was the first to be produced on Broadway—a fascinating psychological drama which won acclaim as a motion picture as well. Menotti earned similar and even greater success with *The Consul*. This "musical drama" was written for Broadway, where it had a long run. It won the Pulitzer Prize for Music and the New York Drama Critics Award for the best musical play. *The Consul* has been translated into at least nineteen languages and has been performed in at least twenty-seven countries, sometimes at large houses such as the Vienna State Opera (1951). It was the first opera to be shown on pay television (see Chapter 16). *The Saint of Bleecker Street* won similar awards a few years later, and Menotti's television opera *Amahl and the Night Visitors* (1951) has achieved the status of a classic. Its showing at Christmas time soon became an American ritual. Menotti's *Help! Help! The Globolinks!* was enthusiastically received at its Santa Fe premiere (1969).

What are the reasons for Menotti's spectacular success, in a country in which opera has had only limited acceptance from the general public? Menotti has shown good judgment in his choice of subjects, and he has repeatedly demonstrated a flair for effective dramatic treatment. While many critics have pointed to his musical eclecticism—the term often implying criticism—there is general agreement that his librettos are absorbing, well constructed, and well paced. Menotti writes his own librettos; he considers the union of poetry and music so essential that for some time he refused to have his librettos published separately. At that they make considerably better reading than many others. For *The Consul* and other operas (*The Last Savage,* 1963) Menotti has been his own stage director as well.

Gian-Carlo Menotti, *The Consul* (New York, 1950)

A measure of the success of *The Consul* is due to the topical nature of the story, especially among European audiences for whom the plight and tragic fate of John and Magda Sorel were all too close to their own experiences. The turbulent era during and after World War II found countless Europeans desperately trying to obtain visas that would enable them to start a new life in a free world.

The subject certainly is political. Many details of text and action are fervent accusations of the practices of totalitarian regimes—the rule by force and terror, the secret police, the resulting clandestine resistance groups. Few opera composers of the present have provided this kind of indictment. But *The Consul* does not take place in any specified country—not Nazi Germany, nor Mussolini's Italy, nor a particular Iron Curtain country. Menotti's indication of locale is merely "somewhere in Europe," and the time is "the present." In this way the opera acquires a larger meaning, as a protest against man's inhumanity to men, against man's loss of identity and dignity in a world of filing cabinets, questionnaires, and regulations. Red tape and bureaucratic procedures—the "machine"—govern the lives of men. Frontiers are closed, and death becomes certain for the desperate one who lacks the all-important document. The opera thus is an impassioned outcry against political nationalism ("Oh let all flags be burned") but also a plea for humaneness and compassion. Many sensitive listeners will be moved by both implications.[6]

---

[6] W. H. Auden, on the other hand, believes that the tragedy of *The Consul* is "Too clearly a situation some people are in and others, including the audience, are not in, for the latter to forget this and see it as a symbol, say, of man's existential estrangement. Consequently the pleasure we and the singers are obviously enjoying strikes the conscience as frivolous." (Quoted by Ulrich Weisstein, *The Essence of Opera,* New York, 1964, p. 355.)

Menotti's musical style has so often been compared to that of Puccini that the observation must be tiresome if not painful to him; yet the similarity extends to the drama as well. The general subject and some details of dramatic treatment in *The Consul* strongly suggest the verismo of *Tosca*. Certain parallels of the action are evident: a brutal police agent suavely working on a defenseless woman to obtain the desired information involving her politically suspect lover or husband, leading to her suicide at the end of the opera; the very opening scene with the fugitive staggering in, looking for a place to hide; the letter-writing scene. But Puccini's opera is true verismo, without the implied larger meanings. Furthermore, Menotti's language frequently rises to a higher poetic level, symbolic in meaning. *The Consul* requires small rather than grand or elaborate stage sets: the shabby apartment and the dreary anteroom. In the dream sequences this is somewhat extended, but though (in the final scene) one wall "dissolves," the dream action is confined to the same set.

This is fast-moving drama, relying for its strong effects on techniques and devices that had been well tested in earlier twentieth-century stage plays and films. Dream sequences, especially nightmares, are favorite vehicles for characterization in our psychology-conscious age. Two such scenes occur in *The Consul,* with the not unusual Freudian implications. In II/1 John appears to Magda, accompanied by the Secretary ("voluptuous and evil"). John turns to her repeatedly, calling her his "dear little sister. . . . She must eat with us and share our bed. . . . You must love her." Magda's vision in the last scene, as the gas takes effect, also contains some familiar nightmarish effects: the disembodied voices, coming from nowhere and everywhere; the sensation of wanting to run but being able only to walk in an agonizing, paralyzed fashion; the dream waltz. All along Magda *knows* it is a nightmare and tries to wake up—also a familiar experience. Scenes of this nature owe some of their popularity today to modern staging techniques, especially to the use of projection and other special lighting effects.

Dramatic contrast lends special emphasis to many scenes. At the very beginning the sentimental French popular song drifting in through the open window stands in vivid contrast to the drama on stage.[7] The clever hypnotization scene leads into the deadly serious finale of Act II. Elsewhere, too, the role of the Magician provides the only light touch—badly needed contrast for the tragedy. The hopelessness of Magda's plight is accentuated in III/1. As she

---

[7] Such a technique also has often proven to be effective: the gay chorus of revelers in the last act of *La Traviata,* the Duke's "La donna e mobile" in *Rigoletto,* the cantata in Act II of *Tosca.*

makes her fatal decision, seeing no other way out, the Secretary, at last, hands the visa to the happy Vera. "This is the end," the Secretary says, sounding almost human for the first time, and the listener is moved by the irony, knowing that Magda has just resolved to end her own life.

Numerous other effective dramatic devices should be noted. Special importance and distinction is given to the Consul himself—the awesome, Godlike figure whose signature on a visa can mean life or death—by never having him appear at all. The closest we come to meeting him is to see his shadow on the door to his inner sanctum. At the end of this scene a climax is carefully prepared. Everyone in the waiting room, but especially Magda, is holding his breath. The door opens; we almost see the Consul— and the visitor whom he bows out turns out to be Magda's greatest enemy, the secret-police agent. There are lesser touches, familiar in this kind of drama but still effective: the phone that rings unanswered; the blood stains, quickly wiped away before the police enter; the telltale raincoat that Magda forgot to hide.

In *The Consul* the traditional pathos and elevated language of opera serve Menotti to create a strong, even grotesque effect: the apotheosis of bureaucracy, something essentially unpoetic. Through repetition of words and music the Secretary's instructions acquire an almost ecstatic flavor as she and others sing: "All the documents must be signed. Seas go dry and suns grow cold, but all the documents must be signed" etc. Poetic language stands in stark contrast to the cruelly realistic meaning. Phrases of this kind are repeated, as in a litany: "Your name is a number . . . your hopes will be filed. Come back next week." This unending quality of the bureaucratic process is emphasized by music that grinds on, barrel-organ style, in monotonous rhythm patterns (Mr. Kofner's refrain "Oh yes, tomorrow and the day after tomorrow. . . ."—p. 55 of the vocal score. Three months later it is still the same sad "tomorrow"—p. 154.) At times Menotti's language is too poetic for the dramatic situation and hence awkward. Magda's explanation to the Secretary begins with rather everyday language, as she says that her house has become a trap for her husband, but then she continues: "The hidden hunter waits for the heart-sick panther to return." But elsewhere the imagery seems right. ("The hands of the clock glitter like knives"; i.e., the time to save John's life is running out.)

In the absence of the Consul himself, the Secretary is one of the most important figures in the drama. She is a type, but only too real: the insignificant human being whose importance is solely a reflection of someone else's authority. This second-hand power makes her an "official," with an air of superiority. The routine of

Magda's impassioned outburst about "papers" and the walls erected between people by government red tape.

her daily work has made her insensitive to the plight of the unfortunates with whom she is in constant contact, and her manner is defensive and haughty. "No one is allowed to speak to the Consul." Her forbidding, official personality is accentuated by the coy phone conversation with a personal friend. It takes Magda's superhuman emotional outburst, bordering on madness, to get her to admit that it "might be possible" for someone to see the Consul—if an appointment is made in advance. Only at the very end, when it is too late, does she make a feeble effort to help, but even then her first thought is that allowing John the extraterritorial protection of the consulate might get her in trouble. When all is said and done our feelings for her are cold. She complies with the rules of the system, only mildly bothered by the cruelties it works on troubled people. At times she resents their very presence ("Oh, those faces!"), but never the system. The best thing to do, she finds, is to go to the pictures and not to think—a very realistic portrait of most of us.

Both Magda and John appear as victims, but though John is more actively involved in events, Magda's fate evokes our strongest compassion. Her predicament—circumstances over which she has no control—becomes greater and greater and, her appearances at the consulate showing no signs of success, all the more agonizing.

Utterly helpless in the face of the net of red tape around her, her words and actions become desperate; in some of her exchanges with the Secretary she is hardly coherent. The drama's tragic aspects are most strongly reflected in her words and actions. By comparison, her husband remains a background figure. A third person, Assan, communicates John's intention to return, against the better judgment of all, leading Magda to suicide as the only way to convince him that there is no longer anything for him to come home to. At the end there is nothing left for him but to give himself up, thinking of the consequences for Magda if he did not.

By and large, Menotti's music fulfills the avowed purpose of underscoring the drama, furthering it rather than interrupting or arresting it. The general pace, as a result, is rapid. All manners of text treatment occur, from spoken dialogue to warm and expansive melody. All of these become part of the action. Part of what Menotti admires in Mussorgsky and Puccini is the skill with which they wrote arias that advance the action. Several arias or other set pieces (ensembles) occur in *The Consul,* with expressive, at times impassioned melodies.[8] In lyrical scenes Menotti is closest to the Italian tradition. It is curious that the melody sung, in Italian, by the Foreign Woman, shows this best (pp. 63 ff.). Magda's "To this we've come" (II/2, p. 198) likewise has a melodic line of great intensity, but it soon leads back to recitative, as though such an emotional outburst should never have occurred. As a result of the Secretary's instructions to fill out even more forms she loses control completely (p. 206), and bursts into another aria-like passage that culminates in her line "That day will come!" Yet even the most emotional melodies lack vocal display for its own sake. Coloratura occurs only once, significantly with an absurd connotation: when the megalomaniac magician sings about himself. Since the action is continuous, musical numbers (with the exception of the Lullaby) are difficult to extract for concert performance.

In Menotti's view opera, like most modern drama, should essentially be a "dialogue of action." Recitative of many descriptions, rather than a succession of arias, therefore is at the opera's core. He changes freely between aria and arioso, regular spoken dialogue, melodrama, and recitative. The latter may be completely unaccompanied (pp. 140 f., 225 f.), barely accompanied (e.g., by a piano tremolo, p. 129), or harmonically and rhythmically more clearly defined. During Magda's and John's breathless conversa-

---

[8] Menotti feels that other contemporary opera writers have shown "a certain indolence toward the use of the voice . . . a tendency to treat [it] instrumentally, as if [they] feared that its texture is too expressive, too *human.*" (*ON,* February 8, 1964, p. 12.)

tion in I/1 the accompaniment has a regular rhythm pattern and some melodic lines. For some quasi-spoken lines Menotti uses the special notational symbols of Schoenberg's *Sprechstimme*. Elsewhere in the score the singers also may merely approximate the indicated tones, though the notation calls for precise pitches.

Ensemble scenes, always effective, vary a good deal in style. The farewell trio in I/1 begins as a canon. Its pitch level rises as the emotional intensity increases. A strong emotional climax is reached, after which there is a tapering off ("Hope be the heaven that words cannot reach") to the end of the scene. A duet between Magda and the Secretary (I/2, pp. 74 ff.) is a good example of the ensemble that advances the action. The Secretary persistently shows a lack of comprehension, and Magda's impassioned plea only increases her rising hostility. The music conveys this well. A quintet follows, providing a good finale. Menotti refrains from handling its central theme—the plea "let all flags be burned"—as a great apotheosis; instead the scene ends *ppp*. The composer's talent for achieving dramatic contrast, mentioned above, is also displayed in *The Consul*'s ensemble scenes. In II/2 the hypnotized people sing their own music, most of it in a steady, dancelike rhythm which is curiously contrasted with the argument between the Secretary and the Magician. Earlier in the same scene we encounter a similar deploying of voices. Vera and the Secretary have their repetitious sing-song about the importance of having questionnaires answered properly. At the same time Magda and Assan carry on a furtive, excited discussion in free, irregular recitative. In the opera's last scene a large group of soloists sings in a simple chordal style while the spoken words of the police agent boom out and Magda's replies are spoken or shrieked. In this scene the large ensemble functions as chorus. There is no chorus as such in *The Consul* or in several other Menotti operas—a fact that may be due to the intimate nature of the drama but also to considerations of budget. Menotti generally writes for small forces. His orchestra is closer in size to a theater-pit orchestra than to that of the conventional opera house. In *The Consul* and other works a piano is included among the instruments, of prime importance in dramatic recitative but seldom heard by itself.

Orchestral interludes connect the first and second scenes of each act, leading from the basic mood of one to the other. Following John's arrest (III/1) the interlude with its sinister march rhythm ($\frac{5}{4}$, then $\frac{4}{4}$ time) continues the tone of that episode for some time, perhaps suggesting military force or police brutality. Generally speaking the orchestra functions in a way that is close to that of motion-picture and radio drama—surging up after the intense, dramatic dialogue is finished. The ends of III/1 and III/2 show this best. Elsewhere the orchestra mostly remains in the background. A two-bar figure in the strings, heard several times at the opening of Act III, represents Magda's hopeless, lonely situation as she sits on the consulate bench, waiting. At the beginning of III/2 the repeated-note pulse softly but persistently expresses Magda's "terrible sureness and determination." In the two dream scenes appropriate instrumental color sets the eerie, unreal mood— again with devices familiar from the sound tracks of such scenes in motion pictures. Gliding into and out of high string chords the orchestra establishes a suitably unsteady, wobbly feeling as Magda opens the jets of the gas stove.

Menotti's harmonies are basically tonal, ranging from the simplest triads to strong dissonance, its extent determined by the degree of dramatic intensity prevailing at the moment. In the last scene the unreal, dream quality of the macabre waltz is suggested by touches (only) of bitonality.

It has been said that Menotti's score for *The Consul* resembles "movie music." There is some justification for the statement if it implies that certain clichés are used. There are passages that sound derivative, all too familiar, such as the orchestral closing bars, after the phone stops ringing. Whether or not one finds Menotti's music original, one must realize that it does not get into the way of the drama but, on the contrary, sustains and increases its impact. And no matter how well-knit the opera is as drama, it owes much of its impact and success to its music. As for Menotti, he does not believe that good opera can result from a good libretto and mediocre music. "If [my] libretti seems alive or powerful in performance, then the music must share that distinction. . . . We have . . . no single example of a successful opera whose main strength is in the libretto."[9]

---

[9] Menotti, "Notes on Opera as Basic Theater," *Perspectives U.S.A.*, Vol. 12 (Summer, 1955), pp. 7 f.

Scene from an NBC Opera Theater production of "Amahl and the Night Visitors." Closeups of this kind are particularly effective on the television screen.

16

MOTION PICTURES AND TELEVISION

As far as the size of its public goes, the film has become the most important kind of theater of the twentieth century, bringing drama to every inhabited part of the earth, to ships at sea and to jet airliners. From the very first public showing of silent films to the latest wide-screen, full-color, stereophonic-sound productions music has been considered a desirable if not indispensable part of the show. How music contributes to this form of theater, and how its place differs from that in conventional musical drama, are the principal questions to be considered in this chapter. A detailed discussion of the complicated technical processes involved in writing music for film and in transferring it from the composer's manuscript to the sound track cannot be undertaken in this book. (Readers who are interested in the subject may consult any of several special studies.[1]) We shall be concerned in this chapter with motion pictures in general, for almost every film today includes music on its sound track. Aside from these general films, a special type needs special consideration for our purposes: the opera film, or filmed opera.

Some of the earliest film showings took place in cafes and other public places in Paris during the last years of the nineteenth century. Musical accompaniment was considered essential[2] and was usually furnished by a piano. Recordings were also used—they were as primitive as the films themselves!—and small orchestras participated in some cases. In 1907 Saint-Saëns wrote music for a film, each selection timed to go with the action. By the time of the First World War, movies had become popular entertainment and the piano player had become an established part of the show. Publishers soon took advantage of a growing market and supplied collections of music suitable for most situations seen and moods suggested by the drama on the screen. Both traditional and original tunes were pressed into service. Some of them—like some of those customarily associated with hero, heroine, and villain—still are remembered today. In collections of "Moving Picture Music" each tune was neatly labeled ("Love Scene," "Explosion or Fire Scene") and numbered for quick reference. Professional movie piano players maintained libraries of this kind. The ability to improvise was highly desirable: the experienced player watched the screen, changing the character of the music with the abrupt changes of action. With this kind of skill at improvisation and modulation a player might well "accompany" a film he had never seen before. For the more important films producers provided specially composed music, carefully timed and cued to the action, sending it out with the film itself. Orchestras played in many of the larger "movie palaces," and for an orchestra improvisation was of course impossible. Some producers supplied cue sheets of musical selections suitable for their film, available at an additional rental fee, while some conductors assembled libraries of their own, using selections as they saw fit.[3] Producers sometimes arranged film previews for the conductors of movie-house orchestras.

By the early 1920's some well-known composers of serious

[1] Among valuable basic sources are John Huntley and Roger Manvell, *The Technique of Film Music* (London and New York, 1957), and *Film Music Magazine* (New York, 1944–1958). See also Ernest Gold, "Notes from the Cutting Room," *ON,* December 23, 1961.

[2] Two reasons, pointed out by Huntley and Manvell, were the noise made by the early projection machines and (artistically more important) the incongruity of seeing in complete silence the many scenes of noisy and boisterous action, including much slapstick.

[3] An amusing description of the way in which such an orchestra operated appears in Huntley and Manvell, pp. 19 f.

music had begun to write for this new and potentially important medium. Milhaud and Honegger were among them. With the invention of sound film vast new possibilities appeared for the composer, though an important source of livelihood disappeared for pianists and other musicians. The "talkies" were well established by 1930; music came to be supplied increasingly by specialists, many of whom settled in Hollywood. Scores continued to be contributed by composers of symphonies and operas, both in Europe and America. Aaron Copland and Virgil Thomson are two of many U.S. composers who have written successful film scores; Vaughan Williams, William Walton, and Benjamin Britten are distinguished English contributors.

The place of music in a film is different from its place in any of the other kinds of theater discussed in this book. As the term "motion picture" implies, to all but the exceptional moviegoer the visual element is most important: his attention is focused, in the first place, on what he sees on the screen and in the second place on the spoken dialogue. Probably even the sound effects that accompany action and speech reach his consciousness more strongly than the music. Stage plays occasionally contain music—"incidental music," as defined in the Glossary. But the function of music in a motion picture is perhaps most closely related to its function in melodrama (also discussed in the Glossary): instrumental music supplying a background to stage action with spoken dialogue. The composer who writes for the motion pictures must reconcile himself to this limitation: in all but exceptional situations his music will be in the background. That it can nevertheless contribute greatly to the film's effectiveness and emotional impact is widely acknowledged; nevertheless film composers have justly complained that their contribution too often is slighted—in publicity, in the credits at the beginning of the picture, and especially in the critics' reviews.

Although it is in the nature of film music to be relegated to the background, the situation can be worsened in actual performance by the projectionist, who may change the volume of sound from what it was intended to be. But even before the composer's work reaches the audience it is subject to cuts and other modifications. Other handicaps exist. Most film scores are written under pressure of time. This is in part due to the customs and economics of the motion-picture industry. Films are produced to satisfy the constant demand for the new—a situation that does not now exist in the world of opera, where composers rarely work under similar time pressure to finish a work. A film composer, moreover, who is under contract to a studio may be assigned the film for which he is to write music. He may consider it unwise to turn down the assignment even if the subject or the script does not appeal to him.

These conditions are handicaps in comparison to those prevailing in other areas of music, but they are not unlike the working conditions of many composers in the eighteenth century, a period in which opera flourished.

Granted that most film music is background music, what can and should it accomplish? Ideally it can function much as music does in an opera, underscoring the mood of the action, preparing the mood for a scene before any action takes place, or providing an appropriate conclusion. Its importance thus varies, and in accomplishing these things it will intrude more or less into the spectator's consciousness. As in opera, the accompaniment can say things that are not expressed by words, in a manner that is quite eloquent and that at the same time speeds up the action. A change in mood is often accomplished in the music before the cause of it is observed on the screen. Take the example of a tête-à-tête that will be interrupted by the unexpected arrival of another person. An effective dramatic technique, known to us from opera, is involved here: for a moment the happy mood of what we are seeing is already contrasted with the ominous sound that introduces the next scene.

Music can accompany the action in a more direct sense. Very rhythmical music may accentuate some vigorous activity on the screen—running, riding, machinery moving. Music employed for this purpose can accomplish more than mere sound effects would, by relating the activity emotionally to the dramatic situation in which it takes place. Without music, for instance, the same running motion might express flight in terror or happy anticipation. In scenes of this kind precise synchronization of music with motion on the screen is necessary. Generally speaking, film music requires even more precise timing than stage action does in an opera. In cartoons, especially, with an abundance of slapstick activity, jerky motion, and sudden halts, split-second timing is a must. Here the animation may be adjusted to the music rather than the opposite, normal procedure. In the early days of sound films, precise synchronization was the rule, perhaps under the influence of the very popular cartoons, but eventually it was found that music could also be effective if it merely matched the prevailing mood of a sequence or entire scene. The other technique normally was employed in scenes with vigorous motion.

The amount of music heard will vary from film to film, depending among other things on the preferences of director and composer. More directors today realize the value of complete silence, even for some extended scenes.

Music of different styles, regions, and periods can enhance the visual effect. Oriental music (a vague term) or cowboy music may immediately confirm through the ear what the screen suggests to the eye. Occasionally an instrument may be representative of the locale: in Orson Welles's famous film *The Third Man* (1949), which takes place in Vienna, a zither provides the musical accompaniment. For a historical film, music of the appropriate period can create the right atmosphere: in Jean Renoir's *The Golden Coach,* a story with an early eighteenth-century setting, music by Vivaldi (ca. 1678–1741) is heard almost exclusively. It is well known that conscientious producers spare no effort to obtain accuracy of historical detail in sets, costumes, and props; occasionally this effort will extend to music, even to reconstructing musical instruments of a bygone age.[4] But just how authentic the music ought to be is a question on which composers and directors disagree, especially in the case of films taking place in remote times or places. Roman Vlad's music for *Romeo and Juliet* (1954) is a case in question. Though the action takes place in the early fifteenth century, Vlad did not attempt to use music from (or write music in the style of) that period, believing that it would

[4] See Jean Renoir in *Film Music Magazine,* September, 1954.

Gino Mattera and Italo Tajo in a scene from the Columbia Pictures film "Faust and the Devil," inspired by Goethe's drama and Gounod's opera "Faust."

sound unfamiliar and "archaic" to the average person, whereas the historical sets, costumes, etc., would be more familiar to the eye. Instead, music in the style of a somewhat later period was employed. When music-making was part of the action, instruments of the fifteenth century were used.

If a film is set in, say, biblical times, different problems are faced by the composer, since our knowledge of music from that period is scanty. Here too composers have sometimes shied away from the most authentic sound possible because they feared that, being unfamiliar, it might be unpleasant and offensive to the audience. Instead they have tried to provide music which, in their opinion, suggests the flavor of the period in a general way. Anachronisms of this kind may be disconcerting to the spectator who is musically knowledgeable and to whom the sound of Bach does not evoke the fifteenth or sixteenth century. And film composers deliberately introduce anachronisms in some scenes: Even in a film with a fifteenth-century setting the music is apt to sound like Rachmaninoff or Tchaikovsky—the sound that many listeners most readily associate with "romantic" situations—when the hero gazes fondly at the heroine.

A film version of "La Bohème" in a production by La Scala, Milan. Adriana Martino sings Musetta's Waltz.

The working relationship between scriptwriter or director and composer is similar to what we have encountered in opera. Normally the composer has the complete script (the equivalent of the libretto) available before he begins composing. There may be extensive consultation before shooting starts, leading to changes in the script. Occasionally this may occur even after production is well under way. Similarly, the composer and director may agree that in a certain sequence the music is important enough (establishing emotional tension; bringing back a melody which through repetition has become familiar) to govern the length of the scene. But these are exceptional cases. The general practice is for the composer to write passages of music to go with sequences and scenes of fixed length—a rather piecemeal procedure if compared to the writing of a symphony or opera.

The stopwatch is an indispensable tool for the film composer, who measures his music by seconds and fractions of seconds. His score contains periodic indications of time elapsed. So that his music will be accurately timed, he works with a "timing sheet" on which the action of each scene is completely described and timed. Mechanical devices such as the movieola also help the composer to synchronize his music with the film.[5] Most composers tend to provide ample music rather than too little, realizing that cutting is easier than adding on and that in the final stages of editing some of the music may have to make room for dialogue or sound effects. As Copland says, this is the time when "the composer sees his music disappear. . . . [It] calls out all a composer's self-control; it is a moment for philosophy."[6]

In orchestrating his score the composer must bear many things in mind, including the ranges and qualities of the actors' speaking voices. When his music accompanies their dialogue, the orchestration will differ according to the high or low, strident or relaxed sound of their speaking voices. If on-screen singing is involved (as in a filmed musical) similar considerations are necessary, and his work is complicated by the practice of having songs pre-recorded or sung by a different person from the one who appears on the screen. Simultaneous filming and recording do not work well, even if the actor is also a singer, because of the acoustics of the shooting stage and because microphones may get in the way of singers and dancers.

---

[5] Aaron Copland's *Our New Music* (New York, 1941) contains an account of how composers worked around 1940. Further information, also about the technical processes involved in recording the music, mixing the recorded sound with speech and sound effects, and transferring it all to the sound track, is contained in Huntley and Manvell, Chapter Four.

[6] Copland, *ibid.*, p. 268.

Composing for the films, then, takes special skills, and the criteria for good film music are different from those for music intended for the concert hall or opera house. In recent years, commercial recordings of film sound tracks have become popular. It has been said that they show who are the good film composers: if the music will "stand up" in a recording, without the film, it is good film music. But since film music, like any other music, should be judged in the context for which it was written, this is hardly a valid standard.

THE OPERA FILM

Soon after the motion picture had grown beyond its infancy, directors began to explore the possibilities of the new medium for opera. In retrospect it seems surprising how many opera films were made in the silent film era. *Carmen* and *Tosca,* both starring Geraldine Farrar, reached the screen in 1915 and 1918 respectively. A film corporation approached Richard Strauss and Hugo von Hofmannsthal as early as 1924 to make a film adaptation of *Der Rosenkavalier.*[7] As sound was added to films, the real possibilities of the medium were discovered. Ever since, there have been opera films of several kinds. Human drama (e.g., the life and loves of an opera singer), in which scenes from an opera were

[7] Paul Beckley, "Divas in Movieland," *ON,* December 19, 1964, gives a comprehensive list of opera films, including Chaplin comedies and the Marx Brothers' *A Night at the Opera.*

Geraldine Farrar in a 1915 film of "Carmen."

incidental to the plot, has proven successful. There also have been "play-within-the-play" opera films. An Italian film of the late 1940's had a plot which largely paralleled that of Puccini's *Tosca,* the principal action being ingeniously interwoven with a performance of the opera itself. Most opera films, however, fall into one of two categories: (1) a stage performance of the opera has been filmed, or (2) the opera has been specially produced in a film studio. Of these the second method obviously offers far greater possibilities since it takes advantage of the many visual effects germane to the camera but impossible to achieve on a theater stage. To photograph a performance that was designed for and is taking place on the stage of an opera house is apt to accentuate the visual shortcomings of such a performance, constantly reminding the viewer of canvas drops and flats, of makeup and of the peculiarities of operatic acting. The camera, with its possibilities of closeups and dissolves, can do so much more than assume the fixed position of a spectator seated in front of the stage. In a film, scene changes can be effected in a moment that would take fifteen minutes or more in the opera house. Realistic location shots, outdoors, are possible, while fantastic, supernatural scenes can be realized in a

Mary Garden and Hamilton Revelle in a 1917 film of "Thaïs."

far more exciting manner. The implications of the camera for casting, acting, makeup, and set construction are very different. Imaginative directors and cameramen have taken advantage of these possibilities, even adding visual details and sequences of their own invention.[8]

Ever since the 1930's opera films have flourished in Europe. American producers have been reluctant, pointing with some justification to the public's lack of acceptance of and familiarity with opera. The idiom is neither realistic in the Hollywood sense nor completely imaginary or fantastic. Continuous singing, it is feared, would not appeal to the average film audience, and the operatic public as such is too small to warrant investment in a full-length production. European opera films have a fairly small but steady market in America, mainly in the larger cities. A Russian film version of Shostakovich's *Katerina Ismailova* ran in New York in 1969. In this and other opera films, English subtitles provide an aid to understanding and enjoyment that is unique to the medium.

Though few opera films have been produced in the United States, American musicals have been all the more successful on the screen, especially after they achieved popularity on the stage (*South Pacific, West Side Story, The Sound of Music*). In these the transition from realistic spoken drama to singing apparently is smooth and "natural" enough to be accepted.

Many opera films are made to a pre-existing sound track by professional singers; the film, with actors who simulate the singing, is then synchronized. Films that consist of no more and no less than the complete opera are rare. For educational reasons brief scenes have sometimes been interpolated in which a commentator narrates the story of each act. Yet this procedure smacks too much of the schoolroom. The best opera films get along without it, especially since English titles make it easy to follow the dialogue in foreign-language films.

OPERA AND TELEVISION

If the importance of a performing medium is to be judged by the size of the audience it reaches, then television may even outstrip film in its potential for musical drama. In the quarter of a century of its existence, television has already acquired as large a public as the motion picture in some countries, or an even larger one. When sets became generally available after World War II, television swept the United States. Europe was behind, but not for long. As early as 1957, it has been claimed, "a single television presentation of an opera in Great Britain [was] seen and heard by at least four million adults—enough to fill Covent Garden every

[8] A *Don Giovanni* film released ca. 1955 includes a chase of the villain through the streets of Seville.

night for nearly six years, Sundays included."[9] In the years since, television has found its way into many more homes, in Europe and other parts of the world.

Since the early days operas have been included in programming. It is true that many of the characteristics and problems of opera films also apply to opera on television, whether a live telecast or previously filmed. Yet television opera has its own potential, its own production methods, its own advantages and disadvantages.

A studio performance of Act I of *I Pagliacci* in 1940 marked the beginning of television opera. It was produced, for a still very small public, by NBC, the company that was to remain the most enterprising sponsor of TV opera for years to come. Herbert Graf was appointed Director of Opera Productions for NBC in 1944. Under his leadership studio productions of individual scenes and condensed versions of operas, all in English, were screened. In 1948 the opening performance of the Metropolitan season, Verdi's *Otello,* was telecast in its entirety from that stage, the first event of that kind. Opening nights in the following two years also were transmitted, but the practice then was discontinued, chiefly for financial reasons. Graf estimated that this *Otello* was seen by "at least ten times as many people as had witnessed all of its fifty-three performances since [the Met's] opening in 1883."[10] Nevertheless, it became clear that the greatest potential of the new medium was to be found in studio productions. Menotti's *Medium* was shown in 1948 over NBC-TV; the same composer's *Amahl and the Night Visitors* (1951) was the first opera specially written for television. (It also was the first production to be shown in color, in 1954.) *Carmen* and *La Traviata* were shown by CBS at about this time. The NBC-TV Opera Company, formed in 1949, has commissioned a variety of works, including Menotti's *Labyrinth* (1963) and operas by Lukas Foss, Stanley Hollingsworth, and Bohuslav Martinu. Aside from special commissions, operas were given that had been infrequently seen in the United States. Prokofiev's *War and Peace* was telecast in 1957 in a version revised by the composer—the first showing of this version outside Russia. New Yorkers saw Poulenc's *Dialogues of the Carmelites* on NBC-TV before its first stage performance in that city. In addition, works from the standard repertory have been given.

Productions at first were limited to an hour, which often necessitated drastic cuts. This policy was relaxed later, but uncut

[9] Kenneth A. Wright, "Television and Opera," *Tempo,* Autumn, 1957—a good survey of the subject.
[10] *Opera for the People,* p. 208. Graf's *Producing Opera for America* also deals with television opera. See also Peter Herman Adler, "A Cruel Medium," *ON,* June 14, 1969.

Poulenc's "Dialogues of the Carmelites" in San Francisco.

performances of full-length operas continued to be rare. NBC's Opera Theater has been the most serious effort in the field, carried on as a sustaining program most of the time since no commercial sponsors could be found. Other stations and networks have produced opera in the United States. Stravinsky's *Flood,* one of the few opera productions financed by a commercial sponsor, received much publicity when presented in 1962.

The often-mentioned high cost of producing opera also affects television. In Europe, we have noted, public funds are used to support opera; they also, to an even larger degree, make possible the work of the government-operated radio and television stations.[11] Under such conditions television opera has made a secure place for itself in Europe. Adequate rehearsal time, and a public already familiar with opera, are further advantages. In countries with only one or two television channels an opera program also has a good chance of being watched on many sets. Through an international organization, *Eurovision,* programs are exchanged and shared by stations in many European countries.

In what ways can opera in the United States benefit from television? That it might reach an audience of practically unlimited

[11] Some revenue is derived from fees paid by owners of radio and television sets.

size is the most obvious advantage. It might—provided the right conditions exist and the right "product" is made available. Assuming that commercial television will continue to be the accepted system, supported by advertising revenue, sponsors will continue to be reluctant to back programs that appeal only to the small public that already appreciates opera. Our general audiences are unfamiliar with its conventions and artificialities. Whatever is to attract them must be direct in its appeal. Once more this means it must be credible as drama, it must be in English, it must appeal visually through good acting and staging. The unsophisticated viewer will not identify with a character in traditional opera if that character has the looks usually (if often unjustly) associated with an opera singer, and if he acts like one. Here lies a challenge, for in television, as in the motion picture, exciting new approaches are possible, even for the staging of operas not written for the medium.

Operas have been telecast in different ways. The showing of a live performance, from the stage of an opera house in which an audience is present, has rarely been satisfactory either to those in the house or to the television audience. Some of the reasons have already been mentioned in connection with opera films: closeups and other camera effects are difficult if not impossible, and there are technical obstacles to the placing of equipment. Even with no audience present, televising a continuous stage performance is difficult, for the medium has its own requirements of acting and staging. To plan the camera work, making good use of several cameras, and to set up sound equipment so as to obtain the right balance may require more rehearsal time than can be spared, during the season, in an opera house. In 1968, as a result of recent camera improvements, a Japanese television company was able to make a color film (videotape) of a Met performance of *The Barber of Seville,* using only the normal stage lighting.

Though telecasts of this kind have been made, better results are obtained in productions specially designed for television. These, too, require special preparations and planning. In the early days of television opera, an hour of rehearsal time often was spent on one minute of show time.

Most studio stages are too small for the needs of an opera. Available space in the main studio is taken up by the set on which soloists and cameras must have room to move. Most operas require more than one set; these must all be constructed and available at the same time, while in the opera house sets can be changed during an intermission. As a result of these crowded conditions the orchestra and conductor are located in another studio and the chorus may be in still another part of the building. All these are connected by closed-circuit television. Soloists on the set will either see the conductor on a monitor screen—an unfamiliar arrangement to which they must adjust—or an assistant conductor, who takes his cues from the monitor, will be in the studio. Earphones help the several conductors to synchronize the work of soloists, silent actors,[12] chorus, and orchestra.

Singing and acting under such conditions evidently poses special problems. A singer may have trouble adjusting to close-by microphones. He cannot give out with his full voice as he would in a large opera house, nor can he simply sing everything *piano*. The microphone may be the best friend of many singers of popular music; for an opera singer gifted with a large voice it can be constraining and inhibiting.

Pre-recording has been found helpful, especially by television opera producers in Italy and Germany. Procedures vary. The entire performance (singers and orchestra) can be recorded first, under musically more comfortable conditions. The opera is then acted out for the cameras while the recording is being played back. Normally the same cast sings and acts; occasionally professional actors appear, especially if this is in the interest of greater realism, as with children's parts normally sung by women. Another procedure has occasionally been tried: the orchestral accompaniment only is pre-recorded and then played back while the singers sing and act in front of the cameras. Musically this is less desirable, since it amounts to having the singers "accompany" the orchestra. No matter which way the opera is presented, well-coordinated teamwork is a must, and liberties in singing or acting taken by the principals, even a few steps taken in the wrong direction, may upset the camera work. If anything should go wrong in a live telecast, little can be done to cover up or to correct. Videotape, therefore, is safer.

We have referred to new approaches available to film and television opera. These include closeups, "panning," and other types of camera motion. Imaginative camera work utilizes the possibilities of photographed or projected backgrounds of buildings or scenery. Instantaneous changes of locale are possible. In one televised *Carmen* the basic set of the finale showed her bedroom, alternating with frequent brief shots of the entrance to the arena or of its interior, one scene showing the arrival of the bull, another Escamillo's entrance. The legitimacy of these techniques may be questioned when applied to earlier, well-known operas, since they were not intended by librettist or composer. What did Verdi want us to "see" during the preludes to *La Traviata?* The TV viewer who knows the work from stage presentations may

---

[12] As in a *Magic Flute* performance where the Three Ladies were represented by ballet dancers while their parts were sung offstage.

prefer to see nothing at these points and to use his own imagination rather than the producer's.[13] But these are clearly possibilities for new operas.

Acting techniques also are affected by television procedures. Singers need not always face front: the conductor will not be there anyway, and monitor screens can be hidden in several places. Microphones and the recording techniques just discussed make facial contortions unnecessary. With pre-recording, an actor may "sing," with his mouth relaxed or even half-closed—especially for sustained notes—which will give a more natural facial expression. Without the need for arm-waving and other grand gestures an entirely different approach to the *writing,* as well as the acting, of musical drama may develop. Complicated thoughts and emotions can be *seen,* reflected on a face, in a closeup. They therefore need not be verbalized, and they may be treated in a musically subtle manner.

The real miracle of television—that we may be eyewitnesses to an event taking place, right then, somewhere else—is of only limited advantage for opera. Television makes it possible to be in on an important premiere in another city or country, the opening of an opera house or of the season, the appearance of a favorite star. To be present, even via television, at a live performance could be exciting and could add to our artistic-emotional experience, aside from the "news value" of the occasion—but this theoretical advantage is nullified by the virtual impossibility of producing a satisfactory telecast of a live performance, in an opera house in which an audience is present. As a rule, bright lights are required for television—a dilemma in opera scenes that take place at night. For the audience in the opera house all illusion will be destroyed, if this has not already been accomplished by cameras, cables, microphones, and personnel in full sight.

Further obstacles exist for the home viewer of televised opera. The image on his set is measured in inches—minute in comparison to what we see on a motion picture screen or in a live performance. (Many commercial TV sets also have inferior sound equipment.) Even if a clear picture is received, its small size makes crowd scenes ineffectual. The triumphal march from *Aida,* the last scene of *Fidelio* or *Die Meistersinger,* are virtually impossible on television. Such scenes are meant to be imposing; instead, individuals appear as large as pinpoints or match sticks, and the overall effect will be confusing rather than grand. The looming ship of the Flying Dutchman, combined with Wagner's massive sound and with effective lighting, can make a powerful impression, one

[13] In a film version of *La Traviata* released in 1968, the Act I prelude serves as background music for the showing of the customary credits.

Scene from a film of "Aida" in which the title role was acted by Sophia Loren, sung by Renata Tebaldi. Aida is shown here with Amonasro, acted by Afro Poli, sung by Gino Bechi.

that cannot be duplicated by a 20-inch screen and a 4-inch speaker. Producers are aware of these limitations, and for this and other reasons increasingly favor intimate or chamber opera, with small casts and sets.

The small screen and familiar surroundings of our own living room can affect our total impression in other ways. Some opera enthusiasts feel that the festive atmosphere of the theater or opera house is an essential ingredient of the total aesthetic experience. This atmosphere—including the presence of many others who have come for a special occasion—creates a receptive frame of mind. For people who are sensitive to these values a live performance will always be preferable.

Realism is the prevailing standard in motion pictures and television, some exceptions notwithstanding. But opera as an art form is imaginative and poetic rather than realistic. This special quality, imparted by the music, may escape the television director who does not know opera. "The rules of opera are not those of the stage play . . . and the television camera can easily function merely as a photographic lens instead of a poetic eye."[14] Many of the operas studied in earlier chapters contain unrealistic elements that will be even more difficult to accept on the television screen than in the opera house. Trouser roles like Fidelio or Octavian are examples.

Traditional operas suffer further on television because producers often are tempted or urged to cut scenes that are visually static, even though they are necessary to the drama and musically beautiful. Television time is expensive, and to the producer who is unacquainted with opera these scenes, since "nothing happens," may seem superfluous. Indeed he may fear with some justification that at such moments some viewers will switch to another program. Even to an operagoer the quartet from Act I of *Fidelio* will seem more static on television than in the opera house.

Production expenses for opera are high. NBC's budget for Prokofiev's *War and Peace* was $160,000. Such figures are even higher when we consider that they apply to a single performance, with perhaps a rerun some months later, whereas at the Metropolitan a new production will stay in the repertory for many years. There have been attempts to cope with costs by showing full-length operas on closed-circuit television. In 1952 the Metropolitan production of *Carmen* was shown to admission-paying audiences in thirty-one theaters in various parts of the country. The experiment was only mildly successful, and since then the earlier hopes pinned on closed-circuit "pay-as-you-see" television have not been fulfilled. Sitting in a motion picture theater, audiences may have expected the techniques and standards of a film instead of the enlarged image from a television screen.[15]

All these considerations lead to the conclusion that the greatest future for television opera lies in musical drama specially written for the medium, respecting the limitations of the small screen and of studio production, and combining music and drama in ways that will appeal to contemporary audiences, whether or not they are acquainted with traditional opera. Past experience has shown that a work written for television can be successfully transferred to the stage, Menotti's *Amahl* being a case in point. Writers who otherwise might be reluctant to undertake an opera for a single television performance should be encouraged by this.

[14] Graf, *Opera for the People*, p. 231.
[15] "Nationwide Opening Night," *ON*, November 1, 1954.

View of the interior of the Vienna State Opera showing the standing room section, admission to which costs about sixty cents.

17

THE PLACE OF OPERA
IN MODERN SOCIETY

In previous chapters we have studied representative and successful operas from Monteverdi to Menotti, and we have noted the changing environments in which these works were performed—from private chambers for select, aristocratic audiences, to the nineteenth-century large opera house, privately or publicly supported, where enthusiasts from many walks of life would eagerly stand in line for hours hoping to buy inexpensive seats or standing-room admission. In our own day further changes in operatic life can be noted, both in Europe and in the United States. Indeed it would be strange if the many political, economic, and cultural changes of the mid-twentieth century had not affected opera, this complex and expensive form of art and entertainment.

　　Traditional opera—the standard repertory—re-established itself with surprising speed at the end of World War II. In spite of overwhelming physical handicaps performances were resumed in Naples and other Italian cities, while fighting continued not many miles to the north. Numerous opera houses had been totally destroyed, especially in Germany and Austria, along with stage sets, costumes, and other properties. Yet soon after the war's end, during the difficult winter of 1945–46, both Allied military and local civilian authorities helped to reorganize the companies that had been scattered during the hectic months and years just past. Opera, a way of life to many Europeans, started to function again, no matter how makeshift the physical arrangements, providing spiritual nourishment to thousands of literally starving listeners. During the years since then operatic life in Central Europe has regained if not surpassed its pre-war vigor. Some houses were rebuilt essentially as they had appeared before the destruction; elsewhere completely new, modern structures were erected. In either case the stage and all technical equipment was upgraded. A good many opera houses, including the Vienna State Opera and buildings in several German cities, now boast the most up-to-date stage installations. Closed-circuit television, complex speaker and intercom systems, versatile lighting equipment, revolving, elevator, and wagon stages, and adequate rehearsal stages are some of these. Exterior and interior design in the new buildings reveals something about the changing place of opera in our society. The auditorium is apt to be simpler than in traditional eighteenth- and nineteenth-century houses. Gone are elaborate royal boxes and ostentatious grand staircases; foyers and lounges are simpler and more functional, while more money is spent on stage, equipment, and dressing rooms—on what is needed on the other side of the curtain. Even within the auditorium tiers of boxes are rare, since architects favor seating arrangements that provide good sight lines from every place in the house. All of which means that today's public comes to see, and hear, rather than to be seen.[1]

　　In Europe today, opera flourishes most vigorously in Germany and Austria; somewhat less in France, Italy, and northern Europe. Several Iron Curtain countries also have active centers of opera. Prague has two opera houses and frequent additional performances in a smaller house—the Tyl Theater, which looks essentially as it did when Mozart's *Don Giovanni* had its first performance there. About a dozen cities in small Czechoslovakia have opera houses. Interest in contemporary opera is strong—more so than in close-by Vienna.

---

[1] Graf, *Producing Opera in America,* pp. 28 ff., describes the architecture and equipment of many recently built houses.

The Staatsoper (Vienna State Opera House) at night. Built between 1861 and 1869, the building was destroyed in 1945, but reopened in 1955.

An observer of the German musical scene recently counted 124 professionally produced operas within one week, many of good quality, even in smaller, provincial theaters. In small towns the individual voices may not be outstanding, but the ensemble often is, showing evidence of careful rehearsing.[2] The typical German municipal theater offers performances six or seven nights a week for ten months, alternating between opera, spoken play, and operetta or musical. Many young American singers, recently graduated from schools of music, have joined these smaller companies in order to gain the experience which is so necessary and still so difficult to obtain at home.

The flourishing of opera in Central Europe is not a miracle. A large public continues to view musical drama as a particularly rewarding kind of theater, as their parents and grandparents did. Opera is established and widely accepted; as a result public funds are normally appropriated to defray a substantial part of the

[2] Ronald Mitchell, "The German Scene," *ON*, February 17, 1962.

expenses, today as in the past.[3] In countries with strong operatic traditions this art form (as well as other kinds of theater and music) is primarily viewed as education rather than entertainment, and tax support is justified by the educational objective. For this purpose a varied repertory is essential, including both the old and the new. Special matinees for students are frequent, and tickets at reduced rates for regular evening performances may be made available through the schools.

Even with its vigorous life European opera today faces problems and undergoes changes. In the past the major houses as well as the provincial ones had prided themselves on the quality of their ensemble. Though singers gave occasional guest performances at other opera houses, the company basically stayed together for the season, and the turnover of personnel from one season to the next was moderate. Under such conditions real teamwork was possible. Principals, supporting performers, chorus, and orchestra could rehearse new productions thoroughly, and refresher rehearsals were possible for works held over from previous seasons. Conductors and directors may rarely have felt that there was "enough" rehearsal time, but by and large the system worked. Artists often were on a salary contract for the season; i.e., they were not paid according to the number of rehearsals and performances in which they appeared. Thus there was less temptation for the management to keep down rehearsals in order to cut expenses. Teamwork also meant that a member of the company might have a leading part in one opera and appear in a lesser role the following night.

Such a situation is rare today, for especially in Europe's most glamorous houses the star system has established a foothold. In this age of jet travel the "local" principals appear at houses all over the world. The successful prima donna (of either sex) may no longer *want* a contract that ties her to Vienna, Milan, Munich, or New York for the major part of the season, feeling that it is professionally more advantageous to divide her time between all these cities and more. Many conductors prefer similar arrangements for themselves.

This state of affairs cannot altogether be blamed on the jet age. It has frequently been pointed out that the opera-minded

[3] Graf, *Producing Opera in America,* pp. 12 ff., gives facts and figures about federal, municipal, and other subsidies in Europe. With the help of substantial subsidies, German opera houses staged sixty new operas during the 1928 season alone. Hans Engel's tabulations of admission prices lead him to the conclusion that opera in Germany today is predominantly for the well-to-do, even though supported out of taxes, i.e., by all. It receives more tax support than other types of music or drama. This is justified officially by the way in which opera provides gala entertainment for occasions of state. (Hans Engel, *Musik und Gesellschaft,* Berlin, 1960, pp. 17 ff.)

public has become familiar with the world's great interpreters through the medium of recordings. Listeners, it is claimed, have become more critical; they now also want to *see* their favorite singers in their favorite roles in their own cities. Box office considerations being important, it follows that the world's leading opera singers today specialize in certain roles which they sing everywhere. A *Rosenkavalier* or *Tristan* cast in London may be basically what one would hear in Berlin, San Francisco, or Buenos Aires. Tight traveling schedules of the stars stand in the way of time-consuming preparations of new, difficult works. Even in Vienna, formerly a bulwark of the repertory concept, critics have raised the question whether the State Opera is becoming a "stop-over place for stars."

If it is true that today's public demands to hear the few singers with supreme qualifications, the demise of the repertory company may be inevitable. It is possible, however, for a company to acquire fame through the overall quality of its productions, though its singers may be less well known. Felsenstein's Komische Oper in East Berlin is a case in point. Other solutions have been suggested and are being tried. The "ensemble-stagione" plan, generally attributed to Herbert von Karajan, has been widely discussed in the European press. Under this plan a new production is prepared with an outstanding cast, is performed for several weeks or months, and is then taken out of the repertory until the same singers are available again, perhaps half a year later. Carried to an extreme the general adoption of this principle could result in an international operatic combine in which leading opera houses would each prepare a few productions and then exchange them. Arrangements of this kind may be in the future for traditional opera. One consequence would be, inevitably, that this standard repertory would be performed in the original language everywhere—a practice that is the norm in the United States and England, but not yet elsewhere. On the other hand, somewhat more careful rehearsing would be possible, whereas under the present system the standard works often are given without any stage rehearsal (once the production has had its premiere), since the famous guest arrives in time only for a quick run-through at the piano.

Today the star system extends even to the stage director. His contractual obligations may extend only to the first performance. After this he leaves, to direct an opera elsewhere, while the local stage director takes over, more or less conscientiously observing his colleague's instructions and intentions. Add to this the appearance of guest stars (who had not been coached by the original stage director in the first place), and it stands to reason that as the months go by a production may depart substantially from the intentions of the director whose name still appears on the program. Guest artists, with only one quick rehearsal, can hardly be expected to change their interpretation of a role to conform with the director's concept. Here again the advantages of the repertory system are obvious.

Numerous opera festivals testify to the health of opera in many parts of Europe today. Following the precedent of the Bayreuth festival, most of them take place in the summer, for when the regular seasons elsewhere have ended, singers are more readily available. Nor is it a secret that a good many festivals are organized, in the first place, to attract the tourist trade which blossoms during the summer months. The number of European festivals is imposing, and their offerings are varied. Bayreuth, Salzburg, and some of the major festivals will serve up music, including opera, specially produced for the occasion, but there have been justified complaints that what is billed as a festival at times is a mere warming over of the past season's attractions—with raised admission prices. Some festivals have special themes. Salzburg stresses works by her most famous son; Glyndebourne's festival likewise is devoted to Mozart, presenting his operas in an intimate setting. Spoleto's Festival of Two Worlds, organized by Menotti, regularly presents major works by young American and European composers. Outdoor performances of operas are an important part of the "Musical May" in Florence, and operettas performed on a floating stage in Lake Constance add a special touch to the Bregenz (Austria) festival. The heat of the Roman summer makes evening open-air performances of opera at the Caracalla Baths doubly attractive.

In cities with regular opera seasons of ten months or more the repertory will of necessity be varied, especially when there are several opera houses. Variety means an extension of the repertory in chronological terms, meaning Baroque and contemporary operas; it also means a cultivation of lesser-known works of the eighteenth and nineteenth centuries. What is particularly gratifying is the experimentation with contemporary operas—experimentation in the sense that these new works, often written in an unconventiontl musical style, have not yet proven themselves. Programming of this sort would be impossible without the substantial government support that characterizes opera in many European countries, including the state-operated radio stations that have resident orchestras and adequate rehearsal time. The Hamburg Opera for many years has promoted the cause of contemporary opera. Between 1946 and 1961, forty-two contemporary operas were produced there. During one week in 1961 a different

Opposite: Hamburg State Opera: The new house (1955).

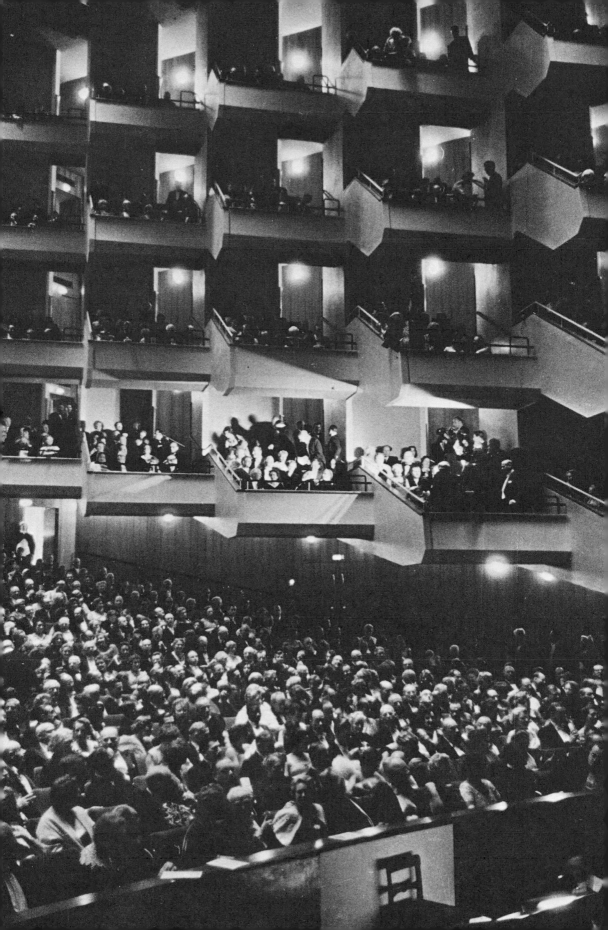

The opera house in Col-ogne.

twentieth-century work was given every night, including Berg's *Wozzeck* and *Lulu,* Blomdahl's *Aniara,* Liebermann's *School for Wives,* Stravinsky's *Oedipus,* and Honegger's *Antigone.* In the summer of 1967 the Hamburg company undertook a North American tour during which it presented contemporary works only. Ensembles in many East and West German cities, including provincial ones, have given new operas, including works in which music, drama, and staging make use of new, experimental techniques. Composers represented, in addition to those just mentioned, include Heinz Werner Henze, Giselher Klebe (*Jacobowsky and the Colonel,* 1965), Luigi Dallapiccola, and Luigi Nono (*Intolleranza,* 1960). Smaller companies, such as the Munich Chamber Opera, have experimented with multi-media presentations of "total music theater."

Just the same, it would be wrong to say that contemporary operas rank higher in popularity than the old standbys. The length of the line of standing-room admission seekers usually is a good barometer. In Vienna, Milan, and elsewhere, *Rigoletto* and *La Bohème* can be counted on to produce longer lines and better box offices than Monteverdi's *Poppea* or Schoenberg's *Moses and Aaron.*

Opera in totalitarian countries is and has been subject to special conditions. In Nazi Germany the repertory had been drastically curtailed, eliminating what was officially branded as "degenerate art" and all works by Jewish composers. It may be a reaction to these restrictions that after the war German opera houses led in the presentation of new works. In Soviet Russia today the government also dictates artistic policy. One difficulty is the absence, so far, of a repertory of operas that preach the message of socialist realism. Gradually these operas are being written, but so far lack public acceptance. For a while the standard repertory was enlisted to achieve the desired ends. This necessitated the taking of considerable liberties with the plots of well-known operas. Such adaptations, according to Honolka and others, were not uncommon in the 1920's, when "Tosca became a heroine of the Communist revolution; Carmen was an agent worthy of the Politbureau who seduces Don José in order to free him from the stranglehold of his reactionary party."[4] This no longer is the practice today, but in discussions of works from the bourgeois repertory writers will preach a moral: how *La Bohème* shows the miserable working conditions of the nineteenth-century artist, so different from those of the socialist state today, or how *Madam Butterfly* amounts to an indictment of American "colonialism." The standard works of Western composers are popular in Russia today, more so than party officials would like to see. A writer in *Pravda* complained that there had been thirty-two sold-out *Traviata*s in one season though many excellent Russian works continued to be neglected.[5]

AMERICA

Many of the characteristics of European opera just described also apply to the current operatic scene in America (meaning, for our purposes, the United States, chiefly, and Canada). There are, however, only a few permanent operatic establishments—repertory companies playing in their own houses, a different opera each night, for several months each year.[6] These companies, especially the Met, the San Francisco Opera Company, and the Chicago Lyric Opera, are on the international circuit and hence experience some of the difficulties discussed above. Chicago's 1967–68 season was cancelled, due to financial difficulties. A special place was held by the Metropolitan Opera National Company, 1965–67—a touring company made up of younger singers. A small number of operas was prepared each season, in original languages and in English,

---

[4] Kurt Honolka, *Der Musik gehorsamste Tochter* (Stuttgart, 1962), p. 217.

[5] John Gutman, "A Singer's Opera," *ON,* March 2, 1963.

[6] Graf, *Producing Opera in America,* pp. 73 ff., lists the major houses and sketches their history and present activities.

and performed on tour throughout the United States, Canada, and Mexico. This company, too, fell into financial difficulties and was unable to continue for the 1968 season.

To plan the repertory has become an extremely complex operation, full of logistics problems. The availability of singers has to be considered, sometimes two or three years ahead, along with other factors: how long an opera has been out of the repertory, how recently it has been broadcast. Rivalries among singers may have to be considered in assigning roles, even to the point of planning what performers will appear in the operas that will be broadcast. A stand-in must be available for every major role in the event of illness. The Met's 1964 production of *Falstaff* was decided on in 1961; director and conductor signed contracts in 1962, and singers were chosen the following year.

For budgetary reasons to be discussed presently, box office considerations are even more important in deciding on the repertory than they are in Europe. As a result (this, at least, is the usual official explanation) the management is loath to gamble on "dark horse" operas, and the repertory leans heavily on the tried and true. To judge by box office receipts at the Met, its public prefers the standard repertory, performed by famous singers, to new works played by well-rehearsed ensembles. Performances of the few contemporary works frequently are not sold out. Even *The Rake's Progress,* the long-awaited full-length opera by a distinguished composer, turned out to be a costly venture, allegedly because of the lack of public response. In its second season several performances had to be cancelled. The trouble with opera, Noel Coward has said, "is not that opera isn't what it used to be, but that it is."

Even with full houses opera is expensive to produce. A work like Menotti's *The Last Savage,* written in a relatively traditional style, required and received many times the amount of rehearsing that would go into the preparation of a repertory work. In 1952 Director Bing stated that a new production cost at least $60,000— designing it, making sets and costumes—and, as we shall see, more recent productions have cost twice that amount. Those in charge of planning the repertory believe that for financial reasons a new work simply cannot be considered unless there is at least some likelihood that it will stay in the repertory for eight to ten years and draw good houses consistently.

In all fairness it must be pointed out that new operas *are* being produced at the Met. For the opening of the 1966–67 season, the first in the new building at Lincoln Center, Samuel Barber's *Anthony and Cleopatra,* commissioned for the occasion, had its world premiere. During the 1920's and early '30's contemporary operas were given, including Korngold's *Die tote Stadt* (1921), Krenek's *Jonny spielt auf* (1929), Deems Taylor's *Peter Ibbetson* (1930), Gruenberg's *Emperor Jones* (1932), and Howard Hanson's *Merry Mount* (1934). They did not achieve lasting success. More recently the New York City Opera has staged a considerable number of new works, including some that are avant-garde and experimental. The 1968 production of Alberto Ginastera's *Bomarzo* attracted much attention, and not only because it had been banned in Buenos Aires "to protect public morality." Though in some ways traditional, the opera makes use of such contemporary devices as tone clusters and aleatory and microtone music.

The standard repertory is changing, then, though not as much in the direction of contemporary opera as one might like to see. When *Wozzeck* was given at the Met it played to full houses—to a public which to a significant extent was not made up of the "regulars" but included many younger people who would not have come for works that had been sure-fire attractions a generation earlier. At the New York City Opera and in San Francisco, twentieth-century works form a somewhat larger part of the repertory. The vogue of Wagner has lessened in America while all of Mozart's mature works are rising in popular esteem. Baroque opera has been rediscovered, and some of Strauss's later operas (i.e., after *Rosenkavalier*) are more frequently given, while nineteenth-century French composers are disappearing—Meyerbeer (German by birth), Auber, Thomas, Massenet.[7]

The reader by now may form his own conclusions as to why the standard repertory is changing. Different methods of voice training and singing, in addition to changing tastes in drama, may account for the disappearance of much of the nineteenth-century repertory. In recent years, however, there has been growing interest in reviving some bel canto works. Bellini's *Norma* has been widely performed. In San Francisco the same composer's *I Puritani* was given in 1966. The following season brought revivals of Donizetti's *L'Elisir d'Amore,* Ponchielli's *La Gioconda,* and Verdi's *Macbeth.*

Opera has always been expensive; opera in twentieth-century America is no exception. Ticket prices reflect this to some extent, with generally unfortunate social implications. Professional opera companies, with wages regulated by union contracts, must budget substantial sums for the orchestra alone, considering that Richard

---

[7] See the tabulations in George Martin's *Opera Companion,* pp. 669 ff. Eric Leinsdorf, a seasoned opera conductor, presents some thoughtful observations about the standard repertory in "What Makes Opera Run," *The Atlantic Monthly,* March, 1966.

Strauss's *Elektra* and Alban Berg's *Wozzeck* require 96 and 113 players respectively.[8] Compared with European conditions, the problems are intensified by the prevailing higher wages and stringent regulations about overtime (evenings, Sundays) for stagehands and other employees governed by union contracts. In spite of the Met's high admission prices[9] and generally full houses, a substantial deficit has been the rule for several decades. In 1950 $750,000 had to be raised by a nationwide appeal to the general public. The undertaking may have been justified by the regular Saturday broadcasts. On the other hand, there are those who feel that traditional opera has no great appeal to the general public, most of whom have never set foot in the Met or any other opera house, and that this public therefore ought not be called on to balance the budget.

How should opera in America be financed? To raise admission prices even higher is out of the question; it would move opera completely into the category of "society" entertainment. For the time being, private contributions continue to be the principal source of income. A new approach has been tried in recent years: raising additional revenue by inviting donors to underwrite a specific new production rather than to make a general contribution. Similar approaches have been successful on Broadway, where backers—"angels"—must be found to finance the costly preparation of a show until (and even after) box office receipts begin to come in. At the Met, the 1962 production of *Die Meistersinger* was supported by a gift from Mrs. John D. Rockefeller, Jr.; the following year a $135,000 gift from American Export Lines made possible a new *Aida*. In 1967, Eastern Airlines pledged $500,000 to support, over a four-year period, a new production of the complete *Ring*. Foundations large and small also have provided funds for specific opera projects, especially the Rockefeller and Ford Foundations. The latter provided $100,000 to the New York City Opera Company to produce eleven operas by American composers; two years later it announced a program to subsidize the production of eighteen new American operas over a decade, setting aside $950,000 for this purpose. This project extended to the Met, Chicago, and San Francisco operas as well.

All this means financing by private individuals or corpora-

---

[8] George Martin gives some statistics about an eight-week season at Covent Garden in London, listing fifteen operas in various orders, according to popularity, expense, and financial success. His figures show that Wagner and Strauss were most expensive, but that *Der Rosenkavalier,* the most expensive, also was the second most popular. Expense, along with musical difficulties, explains why these works seldom are heard away from the large operatic centers. (*The Opera Companion,* New York, 1961, pp. 152 ff.)

[9] Even in the 1929–30 season an orchestra seat, on a subscription basis, cost $8.25. A comparable seat in 1969 cost $15.00.

tions. In addition there have been instances of the allocation of public funds. The pros and cons of government involvement in the arts need not be spread out here, but it is to be noted that support on various governmental levels, especially municipal, is not without precedent in the United States and seems to be growing. San Francisco's War Memorial Opera House, opened in 1932, was the first to be municipally owned; in addition the city of San Francisco contributes to the company's budget. St. Louis, New Orleans, and numerous other cities have supported local opera in a variety of direct and indirect ways. Local opera companies in many cities enjoy at least rent-free use of public auditoriums. Both federal and municipal funds were used to acquire land for New York's Lincoln Center; construction proceeded with the help of foundations and private donors. Some changes in public feeling about government support came about during the Kennedy administration. Yet it is unlikely that the European pattern will be duplicated in the United States for some time to come. Herbert Graf, well acquainted with that pattern, doubts that it would be desirable or justifiable, at least with regard to traditional opera. "Has opera not first to prove its worth to the general citizenry before it can justifiably appeal for public funds?"[10]

The few repertory companies just mentioned do not convey an accurate picture of the increasingly vigorous operatic life in many other American cities. From San Antonio and Houston to Seattle, from Boston and Hartford to Pasadena, from Miami to Portland one could pass through many cities in which civic opera groups mount several productions each season, largely relying on local singers and players but importing internationally known soloists for the leading roles. A new public, and with it an increased appreciation for opera, is developing in the American "provinces."

Today America's audiences for opera are changing. The "society" aspects certainly were more in the foreground at the beginning of this century, when Prince Henry of Prussia, the Kaiser's brother, visited the Met in 1902, causing much excitement and a general lack of audience attention to the performance. Until the old Met permanently closed its doors in 1966, the Golden Horseshoe continued to be society-page news. At opening nights especially, the dress, jewelry, and (occasionally) antics of the boxholders received as much attention in the following morning's paper as did the performance itself. But all along only a small part of the audience considered opera a social event. Real enthusiasm existed among many Americans in the nineteenth and early twentieth centuries, especially among those with family roots in the

[10] *Opera for the People*, p. 239.

operatic countries of Europe. Today's audiences include a large share of younger people who have developed their own taste for opera, and this taste is apt to turn increasingly to works of our own day.

A trend toward informality in dress has resulted in signs at the Met: "The management reserves the right to refuse admittance to any person whose attire is not in keeping with the dignity of the Opera House." Similar signs have been found necessary in European houses. Just the same, the era of formal dress for opera seems to be passing. Here again records and radio have established casual listening patterns: nowadays it is possible to enjoy an opera while stretched out on one's living room floor.

Opera's new public is strongly interested in the dramatic side of opera and therefore wants to understand text and action. It prefers opera in English, and its preference is gradually being taken seriously. The pros and cons of opera in English alone could fill a lengthy chapter. Some of the principal aspects and arguments must be discussed here, since they already have had a bearing on the course opera is taking in America today.[11] With regard to traditional opera, originally composed to texts in languages other than English, there are those who favor performances in the original language because (1) the composer wrote his music with specific words and even syllables in mind. By substituting English words this close association is destroyed. It is further argued (2) that the English language is unmusical and that Italian, especially, is a more melodious tongue, richer in vowels, (3) that most opera singers are foreign-born and that their singing in English would be marred by their accents, (4) that most opera plots and texts are poor anyway and that translations only call attention to these faults, (5) that Wagner in Italian or Verdi in English simply "sound ridiculous" (Auden), (6) that many English translations are awkward, stilted, and prosaic or that they in other ways destroy the mood created by the music, and (7) that most translations are inaccurate because it is virtually impossible to make a literal and correct translation that completely fits the accentuation and phrasing of the composer's vocal line. Other arguments against opera in English exist; those listed are among the most frequently heard objections. They have been met in the following ways by the advocates of opera in English:

(1) That the composer wrote for specific words: This is true—generally speaking, though not always, for some of the greatest operas contain passages in which the music was written first and the text subsequently adapted to it. But granting the basic truth of the statement one must weigh the gains (of this close

[11] *Opera for the People* contains a fine chapter about this.

text–music association) against the loss to the audience who cannot understand the text. More crucial than the subtle association of the specific original word-sound with music-sound is the association of text *meaning* with music. Very often (it should be evident to the reader of this book) what happens in the music, including the accompaniment, makes sense only in relation to what the text is all about. Hence a knowledge of the text—all of it, not only of the plot in general—is essential to full understanding and enjoyment.

(2) That English is unmusical: This argument is particularly weak and most easily demolished. One need only point to the rich past of music originally composed to English lyrics, from Elizabethan songs and madrigals to Handel's *Messiah,* to Gilbert and Sullivan's ever-popular operettas, to the songs and choral works of contemporary English composers, and to today's Broadway musicals, to say nothing of the vast field of popular music. One might counter that any language, spoken or sung, can be expressive and "musical"—to those who understand it—and that therefore it matters little whether it contains many hissing, guttural, or other "unmusical" sounds, as do German, Russian, Czech, and other languages spoken in countries with rich opera traditions.

(3) That opera singers are foreign-born: This argument no longer holds today. At the Met, for instance, the number of American-born (or English, or Australian) singers has increased steadily. By 1950, English was the mother tongue for approximately half the company, and the trend is continuing throughout the United States. It thus seems even stranger to have a Met performance of *The Barber of Seville* in Italian when most of the principals are American-born, or of Wagner's *Rheingold* with an almost entirely American cast, in German. As early as the 1920–21 season it was possible to have *Parsifal* given in English at the Met, with a cast that included no German singers.[12] The argument that foreign-born singers would not be successful singing in English is not in accord with the facts. Ever since the end of World War II American singers have won acclaim at home and on European stages, singing in other than their native tongues. Good coaching will not neglect pronunciation or enunciation. This, incidentally, touches on another argument against opera in English —that singers cannot be understood anyway and that they therefore might as well sing the original text. To which it has been answered, jestingly but with a point, that "if I am not going to understand the words anyway I'd rather miss them in my own language than someone else's."

(4) That opera texts are poor to begin with: There un-

[12] Mary Ellis Peltz, *Behind the Golden Curtain* (New York, 1950), p. 48. English-language performances at that time were still due to anti-German feeling after World War I.

doubtedly are operas that are poor drama, based on librettos of low literary quality but containing beautiful music. If they appeal only as music, the cause of opera would be best served by having them heard in the concert hall rather than on the stage, regardless of the language in which they are sung. If it is musical drama worth presenting on stage, the words should carry out their intended function.

(5) That translated opera sounds ridiculous: If opera is drama (and all composers meant it to be that), the idea of presenting it to a noncomprehending audience is even more ridiculous. Why should Verdi's *Otello* sound ridiculous in English when Shakespeare's *Othello* has become a "classic" on the German stage?

(6) That translations are awkward: This is true, and it means that better translations are needed, not that the original language is preferable. Idiomatic, singable translations are gradually being made available. It is indicative of this trend that beginning with the 1963–64 season new librettos have been sent out by the Met to its Saturday afternoon broadcast audiences— librettos in which new translations of good quality are included and numerous inaccuracies have been removed. Several years earlier the Met production of *Così fan tutte,* in a fine, idiomatic English translation, became very successful and was recorded in its entirety. One of America's leading music publishers is gradually replacing the old, awkward translations in printed librettos and vocal scores by new, greatly improved texts.

(7) That translations are inaccurate: This argument is usually answered along similar lines. It is difficult but not impossible to translate a libretto so skillfully that the original meaning is conveyed without doing violence to the music. Just how literal a translation ought to be depends on one's point of view and on the given text passage. Many recent translations have been far from literal, the translator finding it more important to express the general meaning idiomatically and to preserve the musical line as scrupulously as possible. In a passage of recitative it may be justifiable to modify the music for the text's sake—for instance, by substituting two sixteenth-notes (two syllables) for the original eighth-note (one syllable), since in the original the composer also was guided chiefly by the text's prosody. In an aria the translator will normally avoid any rhythmic or other musical changes, for here musical considerations had been more important to the composer—the beginning, shaping, and rounding-off of a phrase. All of which leads back to argument 1: in a *good* translation the close association between text and music need not be destroyed.

Though the bias of this discussion has been in favor of opera in English, the pitfalls and drawbacks of translations must not be overlooked.[13] Here we have one of the strongest arguments for operas composed to original English texts. Many of today's most informed surveyors of the English and American operatic scene believe that opera, if it is to become a widely accepted and enjoyed art form, must develop its own repertory, in the language of those who are to listen to it, and representing dramatic and musical tastes and techniques of our own day. The views of Oscar Sonneck, a distinguished American music historian who wrote over half a century ago, are still to the point:

Of one thing I am absolutely certain: if opera in America is ever to attain to the distinction of being more than a sensational and exotic, though sincerely enjoyed, luxury . . . it will have to be by the way of good performances of good operas in good English. Esthetically, of course, performances of operas in the original language will always be superior to those in translations . . . but a decrease in esthetic value will be more than offset by the cultural value to the people [listening to] musical dramas in a language they can understand. Even in matters of art, subtle esthetics cannot overrule the demands of commonsense for long without injuring the prospects of art and of native art in particular. . . . Let us wish a long life for the Metropolitan Opera House as an institution, unique and financially able to strive after model performances of foreign operas *au naturel,* but let us also wish that the operatic life of the rest of the country be based in the main on opera in English.[14]

In the process of becoming Americanized, opera in recent decades has started to move out of the opera house. This is not to say that the few established opera houses are losing their public—but as we have seen, their repertory and procedures in general have changed little and are basically those of European establishments. In American cities lacking opera houses traditional opera is at times given in halls entirely unsuitable for the purpose, including civic buildings—armories, convention halls—in which the stage is too small and the auditorium too large. For visual and acoustic reasons such buildings are unsatisfactory, though their seating capacity may be roughly that of the larger opera houses in Europe or the United States. Furthermore, very large halls are seldom filled except for special occasions: the one-night presentation of grand opera by a touring company with a star-studded cast.

By and large, opera today is moving away from the grand

---

[13] If, for instance, several translations of an opera are in general use, singers may be faced with having to learn the same role in different English versions.
[14] *Early Opera in America* (New York, 1915), pp. 218 f.

and spectacular to the more intimate kind of work usually labeled chamber opera. The reasons for this are many. Financial considerations were discussed earlier in this chapter: the virtual impossibility of making ends meet in large-scale productions, and the difficulty of obtaining substantial support from private patrons.

Other segments of American society are cultivating opera today, chiefly educational institutions and civic opera associations. In a sense the American university and music school are assuming a place similar to that of the eighteenth-century princely sponsor of the arts. In neither case was opera expected to be a money-making enterprise, and while a King Louis XIV or a Prince Esterhazy supported opera for his own enjoyment and for prestige, the Opera Department of an American university, naturally, stresses the educational aspects of opera—educational for the performers by providing training for them, and for audiences with little or no other opportunity to see opera. If student and amateur voices are involved, the more taxing works of the repertory, like Strauss and Wagner, normally will not be suitable, though some of the larger universities have not shied away from them. More intimate works which also make smaller demands on chorus and orchestra are apt to have a better chance of being performed creditably. For the requirements of these groups the small theater is more suitable.

Aside from these practical reasons, composers have favored opera on a small scale for artistic reasons. In the intimacy of a small theater acting can acquire a new importance—acting that avoids the grand gestures of nineteenth-century opera and substitutes a more subtle kind of persuasiveness and realism. The singer who does not need to strain his voice will be able to enunciate clearly with less effort; consequently more of the text will be understood. This again favors the dramatic side of opera, the side which the new public does not wish to see slighted. Many of the best-known twentieth-century composers have written successful chamber operas, Benjamin Britten, Paul Hindemith, Darius Milhaud, and Aaron Copland among them. Works of the Baroque and Classic periods, if on an intimate scale, also fit the needs of such groups.

While opera workshops flourish in literally hundreds of colleges and universities, and while civic opera groups (using both amateur and professional talent) have multiplied, opera also has moved into the professional theaters on Broadway. A clear borderline between opera and what is loosely called the "musical" does not exist. Many "musicals" afford sufficient importance to music quantitatively to make the term "opera" equally appropriate. Some contain music that is quite serious, its melodic and harmonic style and its orchestration resembling what is heard in opera or concert hall. Gershwin's *Porgy and Bess* (1935), America's first lastingly successful opera, was written for Broadway. The history of its casting and rehearsing shows how difficult it was at the time to overcome traditions of opera singing and acting.[15] Successful composers whose works have come out on Broadway rather than at the Met include Virgil Thomson, Marc Blitzstein, Kurt Weill, and Gian-Carlo Menotti. One dilemma of this development is that (as a rule, at least) success on Broadway has come to works that are light if not superficial drama. On the other hand, many contemporary operas, though of modest dimensions, are too difficult for college workshops to produce. But in all, opera in America has seen spectacular growth on the college campus and in civic groups. Cooperation between these two is not unusual.[16] Stressing the educational value of opera, the Metropolitan Opera Studio has for some years taken small productions, in English, to schools in New York City and vicinity. Studio performances of this kind serve the additional purpose of giving experience and confidence to young singers, many of whom have eventually joined the Met and other companies.

To put these civic opera groups and newly formed professional organizations on a more substantial and permanent basis, longer seasons are needed. Neither singers nor instrumentalists can make a living from a six-week season, or from four productions spread out over nine months. The same is true of most of America's symphony orchestras. Seasons of twenty weeks inevitably become spare-time activities for most players. To make a living they have to have other, usually full-time, jobs. Combined seasons of symphony and opera may add up to full-time professional work for the orchestra players—a system that has proven successful in some cities.

Summer festivals have become an established part of the American scene, with a favoring of open-air or tent productions. Santa Fe's amphitheater has a roofed stage, originally separated from a partially roofed auditorium by a reflecting pool. Presentations there were so well received that the auditorium had to be enlarged four times between 1957 and 1965. The repertory has been ambitious and off the beaten path, including Henze's *King Stag*, Strauss' *Arabella*, Stravinsky's *Rake's Progress*, and other

---

[15] Numerous northern Negroes tried out who had excellent opera training but had no idea of the dialect of Charleston, S.C. Others appeared at the auditions who could not read a note of music. Gershwin himself said that his choice of a vaudeville performer for the part of Sportin' Life was questioned by many but turned out to be a good one.

[16] *ON*, in one of its fall issues each year, gives data testifying to this growth. See also the chapters "Opera in the Schools" and "Community Opera" in Graf's *Opera for the People*.

Outdoor opera in America: The Santa Fe, New Mexico, Opera House.

contemporary works.[17] Opera under the stars is produced at Denver's Red Rocks Amphitheater and in many other cities. Central City, Colorado boasts a small opera house with a colorful history. Here, too, the size of the house has been kind to young voices. Works from the standard repertory as well as chamber opera are given. Occasionally large universities, taking seriously their role as patrons of the arts, have organized festivals on a large, professional scale. Stanford University's 1965 summer festival had the general theme "The Mozart Era." Included were twenty-seven opera performances by professional companies, among them the New York City Opera Company. Most performances were given outdoors.

[17] Fire destroyed the Santa Fe Opera House on July 27, 1967, just before the scheduled American premiere of Hindemith's *Cardillac.* In spite of seemingly insurmountable handicaps, the season's second premiere, Henze's *Boulevard Solitude,* was given in the local high school gymnasium. The house was rebuilt in 1968.

Concert performances of opera, i.e., with little or no costuming and staging, may merely be substitutes for the real thing; nevertheless their increasing number testifies to a broadening interest. Such performances involve a much smaller financial risk and therefore may be devoted to unusual operas: works that would be difficult and expensive to stage, or long-neglected operas that deserve resurrection largely for musical reasons. The American Opera Society, the Friends of French Opera, and the Concert Opera Association are groups devoted to these purposes. Such productions also sidestep difficult problems of casting since acting ability and physical appearance of a singer are less important.

Thousands of people with an interest in music have had their first contact with opera through recordings. The development of the longplaying record in the late 1940's was of special significance for this. It was in the nature of the earlier recordings to feature short operatic excerpts primarily, though complete recordings (amounting to a heavy stack or several albums of shellac disks) did exist. With the coming of longplaying, high fidelity disks the record industry in general saw tremendous expansion. The list of complete opera recordings now includes all the standard repertory, often in half a dozen different recordings, and much opera that would hardly ever be seen today. There can be no question that this has been a boon to the cause of opera, though here, again, opera's visual impact is lacking.

To be exposed only to the music of an opera can be viewed as an advantage, under certain circumstances. Our imagination can supply a "better" scenic and dramatic realization than that of an imperfect, routine performance. Since singers do not always look their parts, and since scenery may be makeshift and shabby, some opera fans gladly forgo the spectacle and settle for the sound alone as provided by today's high fidelity records. Stereophonic sound has special advantages for opera, making it easier for the listener to imagine singers placed in various locations on stage, creating a feeling of space and third dimension. For the connoisseur a recording conjures up memories of performances seen; for the person who has never seen the opera it will be more difficult to supply mentally what is missing. Many an opera devotee enjoys listening at home in his shirtsleeves, but it is doubtful that he would want to restrict his contact with opera to this, never wishing for the excitement and total impression of a well-staged and -acted performance.

Most opera recordings include the printed libretto, with English translation if sung in another language. This makes it possible for the listener to follow *all* the dialogue, highly desirable for full understanding and enjoyment. In the darkened auditorium this is more difficult to accomplish, though audiences in the early days of opera followed the libretto by the light of a candle.

In a sense, modern recordings are "more perfect" than the best live performance. Engineers, rather than conductor and performers, control the balance of sound. With the turn of a dial a voice may be brought out, dominating the accompaniment in a way that would hardly be possible in actual performance—and in a way that may not have been intended by the composer. Furthermore, with modern recording and tape-splicing techniques, parts of an act or scene may be recorded over and over again if slight flaws are noted. Most "performances" heard on recordings, as a result, are synthetic: they never took place in any continuous sense. The person who knows opera primarily from recordings may at times be disappointed by a live performance. Without the doctoring of recording engineers voices are apt to sound fainter in relation to the orchestra. After such an experience one may wonder about the appropriateness of the term "high fidelity," though a recording engineer will reply that he has given you the best seat in the house, placing you in the acoustically most favorable position.

Before the appearance of high fidelity records opera had been carried into many American homes by way of broadcasts. The history of radio opera goes back to 1910, when a broadcast was made from the stage of the Met. (This was an experiment; there were as yet no home radios.) In 1927 a broadcast was undertaken by the Chicago Civic Opera, and on Christmas Day 1931 a complete opera, *Hansel and Gretel*, was heard over the air from the Metropolitan stage. From that period to the present day the Saturday matinee broadcasts from the Met have been a most important aspect of American operatic life. The early broadcasts brought strong public response of many kinds, including many requests for information about the operas heard. In 1935 the Metropolitan Opera Guild was formed, largely in answer to such requests, and its magazine *Opera News* began to appear the following year. According to some estimates certain Met broadcasts were listened to by as many as eleven million people, from all walks of life, many living in remote areas. Until television became widely available several other radio programs featured operatic concerts. Menotti's opera *The Old Maid and the Thief*, commissioned by the National Broadcasting Company in 1938, was written for radio and its special requirements, using sound effects and narration.

Broadcasting a live performance at which an audience also is present has many problems, chiefly that of achieving balance of sound. Microphones must be concealed; they are stationary while

the singers move around. Reverberation cannot be controlled, and extraneous noises from the audience cannot be eliminated. Rehearsals in which microphone placements and other technical problems can be considered are usually impossible. Because of experience gained, and improved equipment and techniques, opera broadcasts today are superior to those of the 1930's and '40's, but even today a live broadcast cannot achieve the musical fidelity and balance of a studio recording. For many in the radio audience an awareness that they are listening in on a live performance more than compensates for this.

What kind of musical drama is likely to be rewarding and exciting to the public of the 1970's—to the generation that has grown up with rock and psychedelic art and does not remember a time when there was no television?

A LOOK TO THE FUTURE

Traditional opera continues to attract a devoted public and is likely to live on, perhaps flourish, in a few establishments in larger cities. Experience has shown that the public which supports the Met wishes above all to see these classics—the standard repertory of proven masterpieces with which we have chiefly concerned ourselves in this book. To call the Met and similar institutions museums need not imply disparagement: museums fulfill a desirable and indeed necessary function.

Some knowledgeable people have predicted that opera will soon be dead. One well-known composer—conductor has even suggested that opera houses everywhere should be blown up, to accelerate the demise of this old-fashioned art form. Others are considerably less pessimistic about its future, pointing to the substantial number of operas written since World War II.

For a number of reasons discussed above, including financial ones, it is unlikely that traditional opera will ever reach a substantially larger segment of our population than it does now. A different kind of musical theater, growing out of dramatic and musical styles of our own immediate past, is more likely to achieve this. Menotti's *Consul* represents but one kind of musical drama that has this relevance; Gershwin's *Porgy and Bess* represents another. Some successful musicals of recent years also belong here, having both dramatic and musical substance and dealing with subjects, serious or light, that are topical today. The musical idiom frequently defies classification as "popular" or "serious"—but it is an idiom with which we are familiar from categories other than dramatic music.

There is much experimentation going on today. Combinations of music and drama utilize film, light projection, mime and dance, and electronic and other sound effects produced and reproduced in various ways. They often are performed in buildings other than traditional theaters. The result may be far removed from opera or even musical theater as we understood these in the past, but it may be dramatic, exciting, and meaningful to many people who have had little if any contact with opera.

The new music theater is not a single, unitary movement or form but a combination of ideas, styles, forms, contents, techniques and media. It is almost easier to define by what it is not than by what it is. It is not musical comedy, and it is not opera. It is indubitably Off-Off-Broadway and Off-Off-Lincoln Center. It is, by and large, a product of the electronic age and the most recent evolutions and revolutions in the arts. It is post-"modern," anti-specialist and anti-category. It has not yet any rules or set forms, but it is often full of vitality, anti-pure and highly evocative, inclusive rather than exclusive, concrete rather than abstract— the new *Gesamtkunstwerk* struggling to be born.[18]

Whatever combinations of music and theater the future may bring, they will succeed or fail to the extent that they do or do not

[18] Eric Salzman, "Something Else," *ON,* November 2, 1968. The author provides a good overview of today's experimental musical theater.

have a strong, immediate impact on an audience that experiences them without preconceived attitudes, with little if any preparation. Operas like *Figaro, Freischütz,* or *Carmen* made that impact on their audiences, though not necessarily at the first performance. There is every reason to believe that the fusion of music and drama of our own age can bring forth equally rewarding results.

GLOSSARY

NOTE: Terms defined in the text are not included here; see the index for page references. The definitions given here are minimal. For detailed explanations, consult a good music dictionary: the *Harvard Dictionary of Music* is recommended.

Aleatory music. Music, especially of recent times, in which a greater amount of freedom is given to the performer than is customary in traditional music, in which the composer fixes all or most elements (pitch, time, rhythm, dynamics, phrasing). In aleatory, or "chance," music, the performer may be given general instructions such as "improvise for two bars in the key of d minor."

Arioso. Aria-like. A vocal passage, not as speechlike as recitative but lacking important characteristics of an aria such as formal cohesion and rhythmic regularity. Its function in opera may be close to that of accompanied recitative: i.e., to convey stronger sentiment than would normally be expressed through secco recitative.

Basso continuo (Figured bass). In Baroque opera, a system of musical shorthand applied to the bass line of a composition. Numerals written below the bass line indicate, in a general way, the harmonies to be supplied by the harpsichord player. In Baroque and Classic opera, secco recitative is accompanied by the harpsichord only, though a melody instrument may reinforce the bass line. (See illustration, p. 70.)

Basso ostinato. See *Ostinato*.

Bel canto. Literally, "beautiful singing." A style of vocal music, and of singing, characterized by lightness, agility, and purity of tone. The term is applied particularly to opera from the late eighteenth and early nineteenth centuries in Italy. Rossini, Donizetti, and Bellini are among the outstanding composers of bel canto operas.

Cabaletta. In early nineteenth-century Italian opera, an aria in a light, somewhat popular style. In the later nineteenth century, the rapid, vigorous closing section of an aria that began in another mood. In that meaning it is closely related to the term "stretto" (or "stretta") close or finale.

Cadence, Cadential. A progression (melodic or harmonic) that gives an impression of greater or lesser finality, comparable to a period or comma in a sentence. In traditional harmony, a progression from a "five-chord" (dominant) to a "one-chord" (tonic) is the most frequent and definitive one, called a full or authentic cadence.

Cadenza. A portion of an aria during which the accompaniment rests while the singer performs a florid, elaborate, and usually difficult passage. Cadenzas originally were improvised by the singer, i.e., not written out by the composer.

Canon. A composition, or a portion of one, in which there is exact imitation between voices or instrumental parts. (A melody in one voice is imitated by one or more other, successively entering, voices.) A round (such as *Three Blind Mice*) is the most common form of canon, with each voice starting on the same note.

Cantus firmus. Literally, "fixed melody." A melody, already in existence, which a composer incorporates into a new, larger musical composition. Gregorian chant melodies, Protestant chorales, and folk songs have frequently been used in this way by composers from the Middle Ages to the present time.

Canzona. A fairly simple, lyrical song in Italian operas from the eighteenth and nineteenth centuries.

Cavatina. In late eighteenth- and early nineteenth-century opera, a fairly simple, direct, and short song, usually lyrical, often sentimental. A beautiful example is Agathe's song "Und ob die Wolke" in Weber's *Der Freischütz*.

Chromaticism, Chromatic. The use of many tones outside the basic key or scale (see *Diatonic*). Nineteenth-century music increasingly used chromaticism in melody and harmony, Wagner's late operas, for example, containing numerous examples of extremely chromatic harmony. A melodic progression C–C♯–D is chromatic.

Coloratura. Term applied to an aria containing much "coloring," i.e., many embellishments, rapid passage work, and high notes. Music of this type was written, principally for sopranos, during the late eighteenth and the nineteenth centuries, though important coloratura roles are also found in twentieth-century operas, e.g., those of Richard Strauss.

Continuo. See *Basso continuo.*

Counterpoint, Contrapuntal. See *Homophony.*

Diatonicism, Diatonic. The use of the normal tones of a key or scale, without added (chromatic) tones. In the key of D major the melodic progression D–E–F♯ is diatonic.

Dominant. The fifth scale step, e.g., E in the key of A major. Hence, in traditional harmony, the chord (triad or seventh-chord) based on the fifth scale step. The dominant seventh chord in A major is E–G♯–B–D.

Fermata. Literally, "stop." A sign ⌢ indicating that the note over which it appears is to be held longer than its normal time value. In Baroque and Classic music the sign may indicate the place where a cadenza is to be sung or played, or the end of the passage to be repeated in a da capo aria.

Figured bass. See *Basso continuo.*

Ground bass. See *Ostinato.*

Homophony, Homophonic music. Music that is essentially chordal in style, as opposed to counterpoint, in which several vocal or instrumental lines or melodies are sung or played simultaneously.

Imitation. The repetition (more or less exact) of a melody, motive, or figure in the various voices of a composition. Voices or instruments may enter successively, the entrances being similar or identical. See *Canon.*

Incidental music. Music written for a stage play, to be performed before it or between scenes, or to form part of a particular scene. Mendelssohn's incidental music for Shakespeare's *A Midsummer Night's Dream* is a famous example, including not only the beloved Wedding March but also some vocal music. Beethoven's contributions are less well known, including music for Goethe's *Egmont* and Kotzebue's *The Ruins of Athens.* As the term implies, incidental music does not form an essential part of the drama, which would be complete (and often is performed) without it.

Melodrama. The simultaneous use of spoken dialogue and orchestral background music, the latter heightening the intensity and dramatic impact of the former. It already appeared in Renaissance plays. Experiments to accompany entire plays in this manner occurred in the late eighteenth century but were not found satisfactory, and the technique normally is reserved for individual scenes or moments of a work. The grave-digging scene of Beethoven's *Fidelio* is the best-known example today.

Microtone music. Music employing smaller divisions of pitch than the half-tone, e.g., a tone falling between C and C♯. Such intervals are found in music of other civilizations (in Hindu and Arabian music, for example). Except for isolated experiments they have been introduced into Western music only in the twentieth century.

Modality, Mode. The terms have several musical meanings, including that of a scale pattern. The melodic and harmonic system of medieval and Renaissance music, based on the so-called church modes, is referred to as modality; it gradually gave way to the system, based on the major and minor scales, called tonality.

Modulation. Progression within a composition from one key or tonality to another.

"Musical." Perhaps the most significant outgrowth of nineteenth-century operetta, the American musical—the Broadway show—has, especially since World War II, achieved popularity all over the world. It is characterized by spoken dialogue and tuneful music (solo, ensemble, and choral), elaborate staging and costuming, quick pace, and general precision, especially in the choral and dance sequences. Subject matter varies greatly, but two kinds of subjects seem to be favored: those with a distinctly American flavor (*Oklahoma!*, 1943, *South Pacific*, 1949, with music by Richard Rodgers) and those that amount to a rewriting, in a contemporary idiom, of well-known stories or plays (Cole Porter's *Kiss Me, Kate*, 1948, based on Shakespeare's *The Taming of the Shrew;* Leonard Bernstein's *West Side Story*, 1957, based on *Romeo and Juliet*).

Obbligato. An important soloistic instrumental part, usually combined with (or pitted against) a solo vocal part. Literally, "obligatory," i.e., "must not be omitted," in reference to a particular instrument—as in *trumpet obbligato.*

Operetta. As the diminutive word ending implies, a light (though not necessarily short) variety of opera. It flourished, especially in Paris and Vienna, from about 1840 on. Of the composers who were successful in Paris, Jacques Offenbach is the one best known today; among Viennese composers, Franz von Suppé and Johann Strauss the younger; in England, Arthur Sullivan and his librettist, W. S. Gilbert; and in the United States, Victor Herbert and Sigmund Romberg. Subjects, though light, were not necessarily comic but often sentimental. Popular, too, were satirical treatments of the subject matter and conventions of serious opera. Offenbach's *Orpheus in the Underworld* and *The Beautiful Helena* are in this tradition. Open or veiled criticism and satire of contemporary persons and events are frequently found.

Ostinato. Literally, "obstinate." A melodic line or phrase that is repeated again and again, especially in the bass, where it is called *basso ostinato* or *ground bass*.

Parlando. Speechlike. A vocal line (or a manner of singing) that approaches normal speech. Usually rapid, with one note to each syllable.

Primary triad. See *Triad*.

Romanza, Romanze. A lyrical, often sentimental song. In late eighteenth- and in nineteenth-century opera, a Romanza may be an aria relating an adventurous, exciting tale.

Soubrette. The young, often flirtatious and flippant servant girl found in much eighteenth- and nineteenth-century light opera. The light and flexible voice quality required for such a role.

Stretta finale. See *Cabaletta*.

Strophic. Consisting of strophes, i.e., stanzas. An aria in strophic form consists of several verses of text set to the same music.

Sul ponticello. Bowing close to the bridge of the violin or other instruments of the string family, thus producing a hissing tone color different from the normal sound of the instrument.

Tessitura. Literally, "texture." The way a vocal part "lies" —i.e., its general highness or lowness. It differs from range in that the latter indicates the exact extent of the vocal part, from the lowest to the highest tone.

Tonic. The first scale step, e.g., the note A in the key of A major. Hence *tonic chord:* the triad based on that scale step— A–C♯–E in A major.

Tonality. See *Modality*.

Tremolo. Rapid repetitions of the same tone, on a string instrument, or of groups of tones, as on a piano. The intended effect often is of drama and suspense.

Triad, Primary triad. A chord consisting of two consecutive thirds (such as F–A–C or C–E–G); the most common type of chord in traditional harmony. Primary triads are based on the first, fourth, and fifth scale steps in any key.

Unison. Literally, "one sound." All voices (or instruments) singing (or playing) the same note or melodic line.

Vocal score. A condensed score of a work for voices and orchestra, containing all the voice parts but only a reduction (for piano, on two staves) of the orchestral parts. A full score contains all vocal and instrumental parts.

ILLUSTRATIONS

INDEX

A

Acting, 7, 23ff, 33f, 36, 75, 197, 214, 228, 328, 342, 346f, 359, 406, 409ff, 432f, 435
Académie Royale de Musique, 77
Adam, Adolphe, 165
Addison, Joseph, 85
Algarotti, Francesco, 93f
America, opera in:
  in 19th century, 258ff, 373f
  in 20th century, 374f, 417ff, 423ff
  in films, 406
Appia, Adolphe, 342, 344
Aoyama, Toshio, 349
Applause, 38f
Aria, dramatic function, 14, 66, 113, 359
Aria types:
  in Baroque, 68ff, 72, 78, 82f, 86

Aria types (*cont.*)
  Mozart, 113
  19th century, 136, 142, 145, 188, 366
  Stravinsky, 366
Arne, Thomas, 258
Atonality, 337
Auber, François, 165, 425
Auden, W. H., 5, 43, 354, 358f, 369f, 389, 428
Audiences:
  Baroque, 61ff, 72ff
  19th century, 127f, 180, 191, 194f
  20th century, 415, 427ff, 437ff

B

Bach, J. S., 402
Bacon, Ernst, 374
Balakirev, M. A., 231